OP

Philosophical Perspectives on Metaphor

Philosophical Perspectives on Metaphor

Mark Johnson, *editor*

Department of Philosophy
Southern Illinois University
Carbondale

University of Minnesota Press
Minneapolis

Copyright ©1981 by the University of Minnesota
All rights reserved.
Published by the University of Minnesota Press,
2037 University Avenue Southeast, Minneapolis, MN 55414
Printed in the United States of America

Library of Congress Cataloging in Publication Data

Main entry under title:

Philosophical perspectives on metaphor.

   Bibliography: p.
   Includes index.
   1. Metaphor—Addresses, essays, lectures. I. Johnson, Mark.
BH301.M4P48   415   81-872
ISBN 0-8166-1056-8   AACR2
ISBN 0-8166-1057-6 (pbk.)

For My Parents

Contributors

MONROE C. BEARDSLEY
Department of Philosophy, Temple University

TIMOTHY BINKLEY
Humanities Department, School of Visual Arts

MAX BLACK
Department of Philosophy and Program on Science,
Technology and Society, Cornell University

TED COHEN
Department of Philosophy, University of Chicago

DONALD DAVIDSON
Department of Philosophy, University of California, Berkeley

NELSON GOODMAN
Department of Philosophy, Harvard University

PAUL HENLE
Was Professor of Philosophy, University of Michigan

MARK JOHNSON
Department of Philosophy, Southern Illinois University, Carbondale

GEORGE LAKOFF
Department of Linguistics, University of California, Berkeley

INA LOEWENBERG
Iowa City, Iowa

I. A. RICHARDS
Was a Fellow of Magdalene College, Cambridge

PAUL RICOEUR
John Nuveen Professor, University of Chicago

JOHN R. SEARLE
Department of Philosophy, University of California, Berkeley

Preface

We are in the midst of a metaphormania. Only three decades ago the situation was just the opposite: poets created metaphors, everybody used them, and philosophers (linguists, psychologists, etc.) ignored them. Today we seem possessed by metaphor. As Wayne Booth has mused, judging from the jump in interest in metaphor between 1940 and the present, if we extrapolate to the year 2039, there will then be more students of metaphor than there are people.[1] And, like most cases of possession, this one has led to excesses, such as those of zealots for whom everything is metaphorical.

I am convinced that, once the frenzy subsides a bit and we can more modestly assess the impact of this remarkable movement, the philosophical importance of the study of metaphor will be firmly established. What I think will be revealed is that the examination of metaphor is one of the more fruitful ways of approaching fundamental logical, epistemological, and ontological issues central to any philosophical understanding of human experience. It is in this spirit that I offer these essays on metaphor to those in any discipline who wish to orient themselves in the field, as it has come to be delineated and explored by philosophers.

I have tried to bring together some of the most important philosophical perspectives that reveal the central issues and offer promising ways of dealing with them. In order to grasp the significance of each essay, it is essential to understand the context in which it occurs—what questions it addresses, what views it challenges, what tradition it continues, and what innovations it proposes.

Providing a context of this sort is the primary purpose of my introductory essay. Early on, I abandoned the notion that this could be done by collecting historical references, for these proved typically to be too thin and fragmentary to stand on their own. Instead, the first half of my introduction is a brief historical survey which summarizes views of important thinkers, identifies their epistemological and ontological presuppositions, and traces lines of influence that set the stage for later work. I have cited key passages and supplied references for those who want to pursue the views of a particular philosopher.

In the second half of my introduction I turn to a problem-oriented discussion of recent views, since the mass of literature becomes too unwieldy for a chronological survey. The point here is to place the collected essays in their proper context and to suggest their importance in setting out new perspectives.

Finally, I have prepared abstracts of a number of key sources, as a tool for those who wish to pursue some particular issue and want to determine quickly the relevance of a given essay or book.

I offer this volume, then, with the conviction that metaphor is not just an issue of passing interest; rather, the exploration of how we recognize, comprehend, and use metaphors is intimately tied up with a network of central epistemological and metaphysical concerns. Thus, the study of metaphor opens up new ways of exploring, and even reformulating, perennial issues of Western philosophy. As such, it also provides a theoretical focus for those in other disciplines who have been possessed by metaphor too.

Notes

1. Wayne C. Booth, "Metaphor as Rhetoric: The Problem of Evaluation," *Critical Inquiry* 5, no. 1 (1978):49-72.

Acknowledgments

This anthology is one manifestation of my strong conviction that exploring metaphor is one of the most promising and exciting ways of addressing, in a novel and productive manner, some of the traditional logical, epistemological, and ontological concerns of philosophy. I owe my initial enthusiasm for the subject to my teachers, Ted Cohen and Paul Ricoeur, who, from very different perspectives, convinced me of the philosophical importance of an adequate understanding of how we create, recognize, comprehend, and employ metaphors. And, although I suspect that neither man would be completely comfortable with my current views, I hope that each will recognize his positive influence on my thinking.

My general view, which emerges in the introductory essay, draws on the work of scores of philosophers and linguists, whose influence will be obvious even where I have not explicitly referred to their works. I am especially indebted to George Lakoff, whose collaboration on *Metaphors We Live By* was an important factor in shaping my present views. I have also benefited greatly and repeatedly from ongoing debate with a number of colleagues and friends, especially Stan Deetz, Glenn W. Erickson, Sandra McMorris Johnson, Robert McCawley, John R. Searle, and, in particular, George McClure, who provided constructive criticism and support throughout this project.

Finally, I want to thank the Office of Research Development and Administration, Southern Illinois University, for supporting the research assistantships of John Russell, who helped in locating and evaluating historical references, and Thomas Pearson, who assisted me in preparing the annotated bibliography. I am also grateful to Debbie Brockmeyer for her speedy and expert help in typing the manuscript.

Table of Contents

Philosophical Perspectives on Metaphor

Introduction: Metaphor in the Philosophical Tradition

Mark Johnson

In the last decade or so the study of metaphor has become, for an ever-increasing number of philosophers, a way of approaching some of the most fundamental traditional concerns of philosophy. Metaphor is no longer confined to the realm of aesthetics narrowly conceived—it is now coming to be recognized as central to any adequate account of language and has been seen by some to play a central role in epistemology and even metaphysics. This burgeoning of interest is a curious phenomenon. Why is it that as recently as twenty years ago (and for centuries before that) it was imprudent to say nice things about metaphor in respectable philosophical circles? And why is it now an embarrassment to be caught without an account of the nature, function, and proper role of metaphor?

In this essay I propose an interpretation of the movement of metaphor from the status of a subsidiary concern to the status of a central problem. This will involve, first, a brief account of the development of the traditional philosophical devaluation of metaphor from the Greeks through mid-twentieth century. Then, because the material explodes after 1960, I turn from a chronological survey to a problem-centered discussion of the most important contemporary debates. Here my concern is not so much with summarizing alternative viewpoints as with answering my central question—Why metaphor now?—through an assessment of the importance of these new developments

3

for philosophy generally. Metaphor, I shall suggest, is not an isolated problem of passing interest—just the reverse: it raises deep episte-mological and ontological issues and challenges many traditional assumptions, especially those of Anglo-American philosophy. In short, besides placing the essays in this volume in a philosophic con-text that reveals their insights, underscores their importance, and sets the stage for criticism, I also want to offer a personal perspective on the nature and significance of central developments in philosophical reflection on metaphor.

The Development of the Traditional View

One view of metaphor has, with a few brave exceptions, dominated philosophers' thinking on the subject. That view can be summarized as follows: A metaphor is an elliptical simile useful for stylistic, rhetorical, and didactic purposes, but which can be translated into a literal paraphrase without any loss of cognitive content. To under-stand the manifestations of this view in contemporary thought, it is helpful to examine some of the more important influences in this de-veloping tradition, with its characteristic suspicion of metaphor.

Greek Thought

Early on, metaphor flourished in myth and poetry. It was natural for the pre-Socratic philosophers to feel at home with the mythic modes of their predecessors and to utilize figurative language to ex-press their insights. Indeed, their philosophic fragments constitute one vast network of interrelated metaphors—and to make sense of their thought is, above all, to unpack these metaphors.

It is one of the ironies of history that Plato (428/27-348/47 B.C.), the master of metaphor, having left no explicit treatment of his pri-mary art, should have been taken as providing the basis for the traditional suspicion of metaphor. That alleged basis is his discussion of the "old quarrel between philosophy and poetry" (*Republic*, X, 607b). Plato defends the banishment of philosophically uneducated imitative poets on two grounds: (1) These poets have no genuine knowledge of that which they imitate—they produce imitations of imitations of the real and are thus "three removes from the king and the truth as are all other imitators" (*Republic*, X, 597e). (2) Poetry "feeds and waters the passions, instead of drying them up; she lets them rule instead of ruling them as they ought to be ruled, with a view to the happiness and virtue of mankind" (*Republic*, X, 606d).

Plato's expulsion of the imitative poets must not, of course, be read as a condemnation of figurative language per se. But it does show his awareness of the power of metaphor and myth to influence conviction, and it reveals his fear of their potential for misuse. This vulnerability to abuse seems to be the reason for his claim that the poet, "knowing nothing but how to imitate, lays on with words and phrases the colors of the several arts in such fashion that other equally ignorant men, who see things only through words, will deem his words most excellent . . ." (*Republic*, X, 601a). It is on similar grounds that he criticizes sophists who care nothing for truth and who "make trifles seem important and important points trifles by the force of their language" (*Phaedrus*, 267a-b).

Plato's attack is directed against the poet or sophist whose misuse of language leads others away from truth. The irony here, to repeat, is that his critique of imitative poetry has often been read as applying to metaphor generally, despite his supreme use of metaphor to convey his most important philosophical convictions.

It is Aristotle (384-322 B.C.) who provides the first extended philosophical treatment of metaphor. Aristotle describes metaphor, under the art of poetry, as a means by which the poet provides knowledge through artistic imitation (*mimesis*), and again, under the art of rhetoric, as having a philosophically significant role in the making of persuasive arguments. In both cases, metaphor is a powerful means of achieving insight.

Aristotle's seminal definition appears in the *Poetics* as part of his discussion of various types of noun available to the poet:

> Metaphor consists in giving the thing a name that belongs to something else; the transference being either from genus to species, or from species to genus, or from species to species, or on grounds of analogy (*Poetics*, 1457b).

It is with this famous definition that the troubled life of metaphor begins. First, the metaphoric transfer is located at the level of *words*, rather than sentences. As Paul Ricoeur (1977) argues, this analysis of metaphor, restricted to study of changed meanings of *words*, established a precedent broken only in the twentieth century, after the realization that the basic semantic unit is larger than the word.

Second, metaphor is understood as a *deviance* from literal usage, since it involves the transfer of a name to some object to which that name does not properly belong. "Diction becomes distinguished and non-prosaic by the use of unfamiliar terms, i.e., strange words, metaphors, lengthened forms, and everything that deviates from ordinary modes of speech" (*Poetics*, 148a). Metaphors can, it is true, render poetic diction both clear and interesting, when properly employed. So there is an appropriate place for deviance from ordinary usage. But the fatal separation—figurative *vs.* literal—has been made.

The third corner of this fateful triangle is that metaphor is said to be based on *similarities* between two things. Whether the transfer of the name is from genus to species, species to genus, species to species, or by analogy, there are always some underlying resemblances which make the transfer possible. It is because metaphors involve comparisons, that for the poet

> the greatest thing by far is to be a master of metaphor. It is the one thing that cannot be learnt from others; and it is also a sign of genius, since a good metaphor implies an intuitive perception of the *similarity* in dissimilars (*Poetics*, 1459a [my emphasis]).

Thus the future of metaphor is prefigured in terms of these three basic components: (i) focus on single words that are (ii) deviations from literal language, to produce a change of meaning that is (iii) based on similarities between things.

One corollary of this triad of half-truths is that there is a good and proper, as well as a bad, use of metaphor. As Aristotle argued the merits of poetic metaphor (in the *Poetics*), likewise, in the *Rhetoric* he stresses that metaphor is of great value in *prose, too, as long as it is properly employed.*

> Metaphor, moreover, gives style clearness, charm, and distinction as nothing else can: and it is not a thing whose use can be taught by one man to another. Metaphors, like epithets, must be fitting, which means they must fairly correspond to the thing signified: failing this, their inappropriateness will be conspicuous (*Rhetoric*, 1405a).

The potential for misuse of metaphor is stressed even more strongly in the *Topics*, where we are warned to beware of metaphors in framing definitions, "[f]or a metaphorical expression is always obscure" (*Topics*, 139b). The question raised here is how we are to determine when a metaphor is fitting and provides genuine insight, rather than being misleading or obscure. The answer, given in the *Rhetoric*, is that metaphors in prose must not be ridiculous (1406b), too grand and theatrical (1406b), or farfetched (1410b). More specifically, a good metaphor places things in a new light, so that we can see them in a way we have never seen them before. Thus, it ought to "set the scene before our eyes" (1410b) with a vividness that induces an alteration of perspective that lets us "get hold of new ideas" (1410b). The choice of metaphor will depend on which aspects of the thing described one wishes to highlight. Aristotle's lengthy discussion of why various metaphors are either fitting or farfetched hinges mainly on the appropriateness of the relevant similarities emphasized by the metaphor.

A striking metaphor, then, is remarkably like a riddle, the solution of which brings insight and delight (1405b). The trick is to stretch the imagination, but always within appropriate bounds, keeping in mind the underlying similarity at work. "Metaphors must be drawn, . . . , from things that are related to the original things, and yet not obviously so related—just as in philosophy also an acute mind will perceive resemblances even in things far apart" (1412a).

Finally, there is one further aspect of Aristotle's view that has had unhappy influences on the tradition, namely, his account of the relation of metaphor to simile:

> The Simile is also a metaphor; the difference is but slight. When the poet says of Achilles that he
>
> > Leapt on the foe as a lion,
>
> this is a simile; when he says of him 'the lion leapt,' it is a metaphor—here, since both are courageous, he has transferred to Achilles the name of 'lion'.
> . . . [Similes] are to be employed just as metaphors are employed, since they are really the same thing except for the difference mentioned (1406b).

This remark has been taken throughout history as supporting the ever-recurring view that metaphor is an elliptical simile. I shall discuss this time-honored (and, I believe, erroneous) view below. At this point it is important only to note that Aristotle's remarks do not necessarily imply that metaphors can always be reduced to literal statements of similarities between objects. Aristotle *may* have held such a view, but he need not have done so on the basis of his account of simile. Marsh McCall (1969) points out that, though similes are metaphors, it does not follow that all metaphors are similes. In fact,

Aristotle argues the superiority of metaphor over simile with respect to instructive power, since the latter is poetical and longer (see McCall, 1969, esp. pp. 32-41). Still, the basic idea that both function by virtue of shared properties sets the tradition for centuries to come.

After Aristotle there followed over twenty-three hundred years of elaboration on his remarks. From a philosophical point of view, at least, virtually every major treatment up to the twentieth century is prefigured in Aristotle's account. As we shall see, there are those who are more or less vociferous about the merits or dangers of figurative language in seeking after truth, but no radically new account of metaphor emerges until mid-twentieth century.

Classical and Medieval Rhetoric and Theology

For several centuries after Aristotle, metaphor is mentioned, first, by the rhetoricians and, later, by medieval theologians. Both groups show a certain Aristotelian respect for metaphor, but neither focuses any special attention on it. Cicero (106-43 B.C.), for example, treats metaphor as merely one of several forms of comparison which can play a role both in proof and in the embellishment of language. Like Aristotle, Cicero sees metaphor as a species of borrowing between *words*:

> A metaphor is a brief similitude contracted into a single word; which word being put in the place of another, as if it were in its own place, conveys, if the resemblance be acknowledged, delight; if there is no resemblance, it is condemned (*De Oratore*, 3.38.156-39.157).

Cicero departs from Aristotle in one important respect only—he takes metaphor to be a subordinate form of comparison, whereas Aristotle takes metaphor as the principal genus. Quintilian (c. 35-c. 100), too, sees metaphor as a "shorter form of simile, while there is this further difference, that in the latter we compare some object to the thing which we wish to describe, whereas in the former this object is actually substituted for the thing" (*Institutio Oratoria*, bk. VIII, vi. 8-9).

This reversal of dominance, placing simile over metaphor, helps to explain why Cicero, Quintilian, and other Latin rhetoricians give metaphor a less important place in persuasive speech than Aristotle did. If metaphor is only a brief form of comparison, it has no unique function in proof. It is valued chiefly as ornamentation that gives force, clarity, and charm to language. Cicero expresses the standard view: "there is no mode of embellishment more effective as regards single words, nor any that throws a greater lustre upon language" (*De Oratore*, 3.41).

The praise that Cicero and Quintilian give metaphor is even more damning when coupled with their equally strong warnings against its improper use. As in Aristotle, there are numerous ways in which a metaphor can either fail or mislead: it may be too lowly, exalted, or crude for the subject; it may be farfetched (where dissimilarity overcomes resemblances), or it may be overused. What we find in these early rhetorical theories, then, is a basically Aristotelian theory, altered by placing metaphor subordinate to simile; and this change further reduces metaphor's usefulness in philosophical argument, because it becomes a mere comparison with no distinctive cognitive function.

Medieval rhetoric continued this reduction of the philosophical importance of metaphor, and, in addition, mounted a new attack on the embellishment of language in general. Just as one must be suspicious of immoral pagan art, so, one must take care not to be led astray by pagan eloquence. Thus Bede (c. 673-735), in his *De schematibus et tropis*, takes pains to show that Holy Scripture surpasses, in its use of figures, the writings of the Greeks. "I have chosen," he writes, "to demonstrate by means of examples collected from Holy Writ that teachers of secular eloquence in any age have not been able to furnish us with any of these figures and tropes which did not first appear in Holy Writ" (*Concerning Figures and Tropes*, p. 97).

In Bede's treatise on figures we see the emergence of a pattern that will contribute to the decline of metaphor for many centuries to come: rhetoric is distinguished from logic and then reduced to a manual of style. Thus metaphor, treated traditionally under rhetoric, becomes a stylistic device divorced from serious philosophical argument. Bede contributes to this devaluation of rhetoric (and figuration) by considering only style, dropping any discussion of invention, disposition, and memory. There is, however, no attack on figurative language as such; instead, he attempts to show the superiority of the scriptural use of figurative language.

More overt and hostile criticisms of figurative language grew out of the monastic emphasis on the inward and spiritual over the outward and physical. Words are outward signs for expressing our inner truths.

But they can be misused, as by those who clothe falsehoods in pleasing language and style. In his *Flowers of Rhetoric*, a treatise on the art of letter writing, Alberic of Monte Cassino warns that since figures "are not of themselves necessary at all," but are often able to add a degree of nobility and good style to a work, one must be constantly on guard against metaphors which seem to have a "certain apparent dignity":

> For the method of speaking in metaphors has this characteristic: it turns one's attention from the particular qualities of the object (being described); somehow, by this distraction of attention, it makes the object seem something different; by making it seem different, it clothes it, so to speak, in a fresh new wedding garment; by so clothing it, it sells us on the idea that there is some new nobility bestowed. . . . If a meal were served up in this way, it would disgust us, would nauseate us, would be thrown out. . . . Take care that in your eagerness to please with some novel delight, you do not start serving "poppycock." Be careful, I say, that when you invite someone to enjoy himself you don't afflict him with boredom to the point of vomiting (*Flowers of Rhetoric*, pp. 146-147).

There is a second strain of medieval thought that stands in contrast to such warnings. It evolves from the desire to account for the profusion of metaphors in Holy Scripture, and it leads to a more favorable appraisal of figurative discourse. St. Thomas Aquinas (1224-1274) argues that sacred doctrine "makes use of metaphors as both necessary and useful" (*Summa Theologiae*, I, 1, 9ad.1). His principal point is that, since human beings grasp many intellectual truths through sensible likenesses, it is fitting that spiritual truths are sometimes known by means of comparisons with material things (*ST*, I, 1, 9). Although these passages suggest that there are some spiritual truths expressible only through metaphor, the suggestion is weakened by his claim that many important truths are taught metaphorically in one part of Scripture and "more openly" in another. Still, it is sometimes useful to "hide truths" in metaphors for the "exercise of thoughtful minds and as a defense against the ridicule of the unbelievers" (*ST*, I, 1, 9ad.2).

St. Thomas's claim that metaphorical expression is necessary seems to hold only for truths of sacred doctrine, because we cannot univocally predicate human attributes of God. His Aristotelian view of metaphor as the transference of a name to something that it does not properly signify, based on a proportional similarity between the two things, is clearly seen when he explains:

> So it is that all names applied metaphorically to God are applied to creatures primarily rather than to God, because when said of God they mean only similitudes to such creatures. For as *smiling* applied to a field means only that the field in the beauty of its flowering is like to the beauty of the human smile by proportionate likeness, so the name *lion* applied to God means only that God manifests strength in His works, as a lion in his (*ST,* I, 13, 6).[1]

So, the medieval view has two aspects. Metaphors are good when used in Scripture and bad when used (or misused) to mask untruths with seductive figures. The same underlying conception remains, however, in both cases: metaphor is a *deviant* use of a *word* to point up *similarities*.

Modern Philosophy

In the post-medieval development of empiricist and rationalist systems, it is mistrust, rather than appreciation, that dominates philosophical accounts of metaphor. During the rise of empiricist epistemologies in the sixteenth and seventeenth centuries, metaphors suffered one beating after another at the hands of "scientific-minded" philosophers. It is especially important to understand the typical empiricist stand on metaphor, for it is essentially the same view as that held today by the inheritors of the empiricist legacy.

Thomas Hobbes (1588-1679) provides the most complete and clear example of the epistemological basis for the empiricist attack on metaphor. Hobbes holds that speech consists of names that are connected by us so that we may record our thoughts, recall them in memory, and express them to others. One of the chief reasons for expressing our thoughts is to communicate our knowledge. This function is frustrated and impeded whenever we *"use words metaphorically; that is, in other sense than that they are ordained for; and thereby deceive others"* (*Leviathan*, pt. I, chap. 4 [my emphasis]).

Hobbes thought that "metaphors, and senseless and ambiguous words, are like *ignes fatui*; and reasoning upon them is wandering amongst innumerable absurdities; and their end, contention and sedition, or contempt" (*Leviathan*, pt. I, chap. 5). It is easy to see why. From his Aristotelian view of metaphor as the transference of a name from its proper object to some other object, it was natural to fear that such a transfer was likely to deceive those who had taken the word or name in question as signifying only the original object. This confusion over definitions and references can lead to incorrect "reckoning" (reasoning). Hobbes then attacks speech that undermines proper reasoning and leads to absurd conclusions. Included in his displeasure is

> the use of metaphors, tropes, and other rhetorical figures, instead of words proper. For though it be lawful to say, for example in common speech, *the way goeth, or leadeth hither or thither; the proverb says this or that*, whereas ways cannot go, nor proverbs speak; yet in reckoning, and seeking of truth, such speeches are not to be admitted (*Leviathan*, pt. I, chap. 5).

Here we have the essentials of an argument against metaphor that has flourished in, sometimes even dominated, philosophical thinking about figurative language since Hobbes. For comparison with contemporary views, it is useful to set aside the peculiarities of Hobbes's linguistic theory and to extract the core of his view, which I shall call the "literal-truth paradigm":

(1) The human conceptual system is essentially literal — literal language ("words proper") is the *only* adequate vehicle for (a) expressing one's meaning precisely, and (b) making truth claims, which together make possible correct reasoning by the philosopher.

(2) Metaphor is a deviant use of words in other than their proper senses, which accounts for its tendency to confuse and to deceive.

(3) The meaning and truth claims of a metaphor (if there are any) are just those of its literal paraphrase.

These three theses, or variants, have served as the philosophical commonplaces about metaphor throughout most of our history. They have been challenged only in the last few years, and then only within certain philosophical movements.

The literal-truth paradigm typically went hand-in-hand with a further empiricist theme — the association of metaphor with rhetoric. The alleged connection is simple: if truth can be formulated in literal terms, then figurative discourse can be, at best, an alternative form of expression, utilized merely for rhetorical purposes or stylistic embellishment. This stance assumes, of course, that rhetoric is nothing more than the art of persuasively communicating truths that are grasped originally in literal terms and then rephrased using alternative formulations. Such is the view of John Locke (1632-1704), whose vehement attack on tropes is typical of the animosity of philosophers toward rhetoric generally and figurative language in particular:

> But yet if we would speak of things as they are, we must allow that all the art of rhetoric, besides order and clearness; all the artificial and figurative application of words eloquence hath invented, are for nothing else but to insinuate wrong ideas, move the passions, and thereby mislead the judgment; and so indeed are perfect cheats: and therefore, however laudable or allowable oratory may render them in harangues and popular addresses, they are certainly, in all discourses that pretend to inform or instruct, wholly to be avoided; and where truth and knowledge are concerned, cannot but be thought a great fault, either of the language or the person that makes use of them (*Essay Concerning Human Understanding,* bk. III, chap. X, 34).

The received view during the period that set the foundations of modern thought is thus essentially a continuation and extension of the medieval view that, because metaphors are words used in other than their proper senses, they are liable to seduce and mislead us by their eloquent charms. The implications for philosophical rectitude seemed clear—as Bishop Berkeley concluded: "a philosopher should abstain from metaphor" ("Of Motion").

Toward the end of the eighteenth century, mention of metaphor in philosophical writing diminished considerably. Philosophers tended either to ignore the subject or to repeat the stock views and criticisms carried over from earlier thinkers and preserved in manuals of rhetoric such as Richard Whately's *Elements of Rhetoric* (1828) and George Campbell's *Philosophy of Rhetoric* (1841). Thus Hegel (1770-1831) defines metaphor as nothing more than an "abridged comparison" and argues that "metaphor cannot pretend to the value of an independent representation, but only to that of an accessory one. Even in its highest degree it can appear only as a simple ornament for a work of art . . . " (*The Philosophy of Fine Art*, pp. 40-41). John Stuart Mill (1806-1873) sees metaphors as analogies that may be used, not to prove propositions, but only to suggest proofs and to aid in the apprehension of them: "A metaphor, then, is not to be considered an argument, but as an assertion that an argument exists; that a parity subsists between the case from which the metaphor is drawn and that to which it is applied"(*A System of Logic*, bk. V, chap. V, § 7, p. 800).

Kant and Neitzsche are refreshing exceptions to this general lack of philosophical interest in figurative language. Although Kant (1724-1804) offers no sustained treatment of metaphor, his discussion of genius and imagination in the *Critique of Judgment* (1790) is illuminated by respectful reference to poetic metaphor. Kant's work here is important not only because he attempts to explain how imagination can be creative, rather than merely reproductive, but also because he suggests an explanation of originality in language. Kant argues that artistic genius is the ability to generate aesthetical ideas when there is no technique (i.e., no set of rules or concepts or algorithm, as we would say, to guide this creative activity). By "aesthetical idea" he means "that representation of the imagination which occasions much thought, without however any definite thought, i.e., any *concept*, being capable of being adequate to it . . . " (*Critique of Judgment*, §49, p. 157). In other words, the artist creates an *original* representation of something (in paint, tones, language, stone, etc.), but this activity is not a mere mechanical following of rules for producing a thing. Furthermore, the created object gives rise to a play of imagination and understanding in the perceiver that is *felt* as being adequate to the thing represented, although there is no conceptual way to demonstrate its adequacy. Kant cites as a supporting example of this imaginative process a poetic passage attributed to Frederick the Great, in which the serene close of a beautiful summer day is a metaphor for a calm disposition at the end of a long and fruitful life.

Kant's fresh insight here[2] is (i) that our metaphoric capacity is one expression of our general capacity for creativity and (ii) that such imaginative metaphoric representations generate more thought than can be reduced to our captured by any literal concept(s). However, Kant would probably have denied cognitive import to metaphor, on the grounds that, since comprehending a metaphor is not a wholly rule-governed activity, it does not produce knowledge (through determinate concepts).

It was Romantic artists and poets, rather than philosophers, who preserved and celebrated the notion of creative imagination. They tended to see metaphor as a fundamental creative activity or principle of language that transcends our everyday literal understanding. Worship of poetic genius was based on its alleged ability to transcend ordinary rational categories to achieve a profound intuitive insight into nature and life. Metaphor was thereby associated with art and religion and dissociated from "sterile" scientific understanding, the latter much despised by Romantics.

The essentials of this Romantic exaltation of poetic imagination generally, and figurative language specifically, are prefigured in Jean-Jacques Rousseau's (1712-1778) speculations on the origins of language. Rousseau argued that all language grows by a process of meaning transfer, i.e., by figuration. We transfer words because of our "passionate fascination" with new discoveries, and only afterward do we recognize our error, invent proper words for the new objects, and restrict the metaphorically transferred words back to their original domain. In short,

> As man's first motives for speaking were of the passions, his first expressions were tropes. Figurative language was the first to be born. Proper meaning was discovered last. One calls things by their true name only when one sees them in their true form. At first only poetry was spoken; there was no hint of reasoning until much later (*Essay on the Origin of Languages*, chap. 3).

Nietzsche (1844-1900) carries this Romantic affirmation of the figurative origins of language to even greater heights. He refuses to separate metaphor from "proper words" and sees metaphoric understanding as pervasive in human thought and speech, i.e., as essential to all knowledge. He describes the "creator of language" as one who designates the relations of things to men by the use of daring metaphors. Metaphor is not merely a linguistic entity, but rather a *process* by which we encounter our world: "A nerve stimulus, first transformed in a percept! First metaphor! The percept again copied into a sound! Second metaphor!" ("On Truth and Falsity in Their Ultramoral Sense").

Nietzsche denies that words are signs matching up to original and independent experiences, capturing some "essence" of the experienced thing; rather, words are forced to fit innumerable more or less similar cases (e.g., as when "leaf" fits many individual and highly different leaves). Thus, we experience reality metaphorically. What we know, we know metaphorically. And the "fixed truths" of our culture are nothing but metaphorical understandings that have become conventionalized to the point where their metaphoricity is forgotten. Nietzsche summarizes:

> What therefore is truth? A mobile army of metaphors, metonymies, anthropomorphisms: in short a sum of human relations which become poetically and rhetorically intensified, metamorphosed, adorned, and after long usage seem to a nation fixed, canonic and binding; truths are illusions of which one has forgotten that they *are* illusions; worn-out metaphors which have become powerless to affect the senses . . . (ibid., p. 180).

Philosophers generally ignored Nietzsche's radical equation of metaphor and thought,[3] though in many respects his boldest remarks only repeat those of earlier Romantic poets. These poets, more than anyone else, kept alive interest in figurative discourse. On the other hand, they may have actually delayed serious philosophical study by reinforcing the dissociation of metaphor from "rational" scientific discourse, on behalf of creativity and against philistinism. In short, the nineteenth century produced some high praise of poetic metaphor but very little serious philosophical examination of its nature and workings.

The Twentieth-Century Revival

Just as postmedieval empiricism proved unhealthy for metaphor, so *logical* empiricism has been bad for metaphor, too. Although positivism is officially dead, its influence is still very much with us and is one of the chief obstacles to an adequate understanding of metaphor. With a few important exceptions (discussed below) twentieth-century Anglo-American thinking about metaphor has been emasculated, narrowed, and inhibited by logical positivist views of language and is therefore either hostile or patronizing toward figurative expression. To show the breadth of this baleful influence, I want to describe the original positivist attack on metaphor, show how strongly positivism has influenced certain popular contemporary views of language, explain the chief challenges to this dominant tradition, and, finally, suggest that real progress in explaining metaphoric understanding requires the overthrow of certain entrenched positivist views about language. This overthrow will not merely liberate the study of metaphor, though that is my first objective, but will also benefit our understanding of language, thought, and action generally.

The first point to be appreciated, then, is that the positivist treatment of metaphor that prevailed during the first half of this century is actually a version of the traditional centuries-old empiricist critique of metaphor. This positivist criticism of metaphor rests on two foundations: (1) the distinction between the alleged "cognitive" and "emotive" functions of language, and (2) the attendant belief that scientific knowledge could be reduced to a system of literal and verifiable sentences. These two tenets are compatible with the earlier empiricist "literal-truth paradigm" in the following sense: they were typically conjoined with the view that metaphor is a deviance from literal (cognitive) discourse, such that, if the metaphor has any cognitive import at all, it is expressible by literal statements of comparison.

The cognitive/emotive distinction and its implications for metaphor are concisely stated as early as 1923 by Ogden and Richards in *The Meaning of Meaning*:

> The symbolic use of words is *statement*; the recording, the support, the organization and the communication of reference. The emotive use is a more simple matter, it is the use of words to express or incite feelings and attitudes. It is probably more primitive. If we say "The height of the Eiffel Tower is 900 feet" we are making a statement, we are using symbols in order to record or communicate a reference, and our symbol is true or false in a strict sense and is theoretically verifiable. But if we say "Hurrah!" or "Poetry is a Spirit" or "Man is a worm," we may not be making statements, not even false statements; we are most probably using words merely to evoke certain attitudes (Ogden and Richards, 1946, p. 149).

Thus described, metaphor can be ignored on the basis that it serves chiefly emotive functions and, therefore, has no serious philosophical use. This prejudice was reinforced by the belief that science (taken as *the* model of cognitive virtue) could be reconstructed into an ideal language consisting of literal statements separately capable of verification or falsification. According to this view, the philosopher's task in analyzing language is to give an account of meaning and truth conditions for literal cognitive utterances. Typically, such treatments either ignored metaphor as wholly emotive or insisted that the truth claims of any nonliteral expression could be captured by a literal paraphrase without loss of cognitive content.

By mid-twentieth century the twin bases of the positivist condemnation of metaphor had been officially demolished. The "verification theory of meaning" was dismantled by some of those very persons who had originally given it elegant expression.[4] The cognitive/emotive dichotomy had also been shown, by J.L. Austin and many others, to be a grotesque distortion and oversimplification of the nature and variety of uses of language. Nevertheless, in spite of these revelations, the positivist line on metaphor—that a metaphor is a comparison reducible without cognitive loss to a literal statement of similarities between the compared things or events—remained dominant. Though undermined, the positivist edifice still remained standing.

It is in contrast to this positivist background that the early challenges to the standard view raised by I. A. Richards and Max Black stand out in bold relief. Richards was not a philosopher by trade, but his work has proved so prophetic and philosophically significant that it cannot be omitted from any serious treatment of the subject. In *The Philosophy of Rhetoric* (1936) Richards made several claims that merit special attention, because of the challenge they posed to the dominant tradition.

(1) Metaphor is not a matter of language alone, nor is it a trope at the level of individual words. Instead, it is an omnipresent principle of thought: "Thought is metaphoric, and proceeds by comparison, and the metaphors of language derive therefrom" (p. 94). (2) Neither is metaphor only a deviation from "ordinary" speech—it permeates all discourse. In so far as our ordinary conceptual system is metaphorically structured, the pretense to do without metaphor "is never more than a bluff waiting to be called" (p. 92).

(3) Because philosophers, linguists, and rhetoricians have missed these two points, they have taken metaphor as a cosmetic rhetorical device or a stylistic ornament. On the contrary, any adequate treatment of metaphor raises deep metaphysical and epistemological issues. This becomes evident once we discover the way in which metaphoric thought influences our experience. Richards suggests that our world is a "projected world" and that "the processes of metaphor in language, the exchanges between the meanings of words which we study in explicit verbal metaphors, are superimposed upon a perceived world which is itself a product of earlier or unwitting metaphor" (pp. 108-109).

(4) Another of Richards's important contributions is his attempt to provide a more adequate way of talking about how metaphors work.

He describes the principle of metaphor as "two thoughts of different things active together and supported by a single word, or phrase, whose meaning is a resultant of their interaction" (p. 93). In "John is a rock," for example, the "thoughts" active together consist of the "tenor" or underlying idea (e.g., John's personality) and the "vehicle" or figure (e.g., the rock) by which we grasp this idea.

(5) Finally, Richards uses his account of how metaphors work in order to argue that they often do not involve images (p. 98), are frequently based just as much on dissimilarities between things as on similarities (p. 107), and cannot be reduced to literal paraphrases, since their meaning is a product of a special interaction of contexts (p. 100).

Philosophers paid little attention to Richards's work when it appeared. After all, in 1936 it was not prudent to insist that thought is essentially metaphoric, that metaphors are cognitively irreducible and indispensable, and that any adequate account of meaning and truth must give a central place to metaphor. Richards showed too much interest in idealistic tendencies recently discarded by philosophers, and he did not possess the appropriate credentials to command philosophers' respect. Logical positivist treatments of language seemed then to be having such success that it was thought to be only a matter of time until all questions of language would be solved or dissolved. It took another twenty years and many failures of the positivist program before a respected philosopher, Max Black, finally succeeded in getting a few adventuresome souls to take metaphor seriously.

Black's essay, "Metaphor," is perhaps *the* landmark by which we may orient ourselves in attempting to understand recent work on the subject. This is not to say that philosophers rushed to take up Black's call for intensive work on metaphor. On the contrary, even though his claims were more modest than those of Richards, he still posed an unpopular challenge to certain basic assumptions of mainstream Anglo-American philosophy. For instance, he insisted that the problem of metaphor was at least partly a *semantic* (not just a pragmatic) issue, and he argued that some metaphors are not reducible to cognitively equivalent literal expressions. He also made the provocative claim that, in some cases, metaphors may more nearly *create* similarities between things, rather than merely express preexisting ones.[5]

Had Black not possessed impeccable credentials as an analytic philosopher, such unorthodox claims might have been taken as proper grounds for dismissal of his position.

Black's essay (discussed in greater detail below) represented the start of a trickle of philosophical interest in metaphor that has now swelled to flood proportions. After Black, it is no longer practical to attempt a chronological survey of key works; instead, we must turn to a problem-oriented discussion which locates the chief positions in relation to the traditional view, as I have sketched and analyzed it.

The Philosophical Issues of Metaphor

The problems of metaphor that have been of interest to philosophers, linguists, and psychologists may be organized under three general questions: (1) What is it? This is the question of how we are able to identify metaphors and to separate them off from both literal and other nonliteral expressions. (2) How does it work? Under this heading fall questions concerning creativity in language, the distinctive "mechanism" of metaphor, how it is processed, and so on. (3) What is its cognitive status? This includes questions about the nature of metaphorical meaning, whether it is reducible to literal paraphrase, and what role it may play in various cognitive disciplines. In the end, these questions are all interdependent, but their artificial separation facilitates discussion. What follows is a discussion of the major contemporary answers to these questions, especially as these answers are exemplified by the essays collected in this volume.[6]

How Do We Identify Metaphor?

At the beginning of contemporary work on metaphor Black (1954-55) and Beardsley (1962) pointed out that any adequate theory must explain how we are able to recognize metaphors and distinguish them from other types of speech. This has seemed a reasonable starting point to almost everybody, since an answer to this question would both carve out a domain of discourse and identify essential components of metaphoric comprehension. But although native speakers can easily identify figurative utterances and understand them, explaining *how* this is possible has proved to be one of the more intractable problems of metaphor.

One standard strategy has been to search for some syntactic or semantic deviance within a sentence that clues one to the presence of metaphor. But syntactic deviance would seem to be neither a necessary nor a sufficient condition of metaphor—metaphorical utterances may take any mood (declarative, interrogative, imperative, etc.) and they may be as syntactically well formed as any other kind of utterance.

A much more promising approach has been to characterize metaphor "on the competence level in terms of a distinction between semantically deviant and non-deviant sentences" (Matthews, 1971, p. 424). On this account metaphor constitutes a violation of selectional restriction rules within a given context, and this is supposed to explain the semantic tension one experiences in comprehending a metaphor. For example, I am alerted to the nonliteral character of "Smith is a pig" by, among other things, the incompatibility of the [+ two-legged] marker attaching to 'Smith' and the [+ four-legged] marker for 'pig.' The idea that metaphors are recognized by virtue of their literal inappropriateness is, of course, a variation on old habits of Western thought that have carried over into recent work. Beardsley (1958), for example, argued that a metaphor is either "indirectly self-contradictory or obviously false in its context" (p. 142), but later (1962) revised this to the claim that the "metaphorical twist" occurs whenever there is a "logical opposition" of a special sort between the meanings of the terms in the metaphorical expression. Henle (1958) argued that our awareness and comprehension of metaphor involves a "clash of literal meanings" (p. 183), and Goodman (1968) suggested that "[a] pplication of a term is metaphorical only if to some extent contra-indicated" (p. 69).

The main problem with proposals of this sort is that they try to elevate a condition that frequently holds (namely, semantic deviance) into a *necessary* condition of metaphor. Semantic deviance (or violation of selectional restriction rules) cannot be a necessary condition of metaphor, because, as Loewenberg (1975) notes, "[a] ny sentence can be provided contexts . . . in which it can receive either literal or metaphorical interpretations" (p. 322). The allegedly deviant *She was a morsel for a monarch* (Shakespeare) might involve no anomaly, for example, in a situation where the unfortunate woman was, in fact, a culinary treat for some cannibal king. Loewenberg correctly concludes that, because there *may be* no syntactic or semantic deviance at the level of the sentence, an adequate account of metaphor can be given only at the level of the *utterance in its total context.* The upshot of this is that "[m]etaphorical utterances are identifiable only if some knowledge possessed by speakers which is decidedly not knowledge of relationships among linguistic symbols can be taken into account" (Loewenberg, 1975, p. 331).

Although Loewenberg is correct in stressing the importance of nonlinguistic and extrasentential context, her attempt to remedy previous deficiencies falls short, because it still assumes that metaphors are identifiable, at least in part, by their literal falsity (p. 333). Binkley (1974) and Cohen (1976) have attacked this assumption by showing that some metaphorical expressions are not literally false. The woman in Loewenberg's example may, indeed, have been a morsel for a voracious monarch, both metaphorically *and* literally. Instances of what Cohen has felicitously named "twice-true metaphors" are easy to construct, for example, *Idi Amin is an animal, she lives in a glass house,* and *my brother-in-law is a Marine* (as said with reference to his personality, although he does serve in the Marine Corps). George Yoos (1971) has also pointed out that our *apprehension* of metaphor almost never involves prior awareness of literal meanings. Only in conscious acts of *interpretation*, after the fact, do we focus on literal meanings of component terms and on the literal truth or falsity of the utterance.

The inability to find simple criteria for identifying metaphor has led many to adopt Loewenberg's view that it is only in its total context (and not merely at the level of the sentence) that an utterance can be comprehended as metaphorical. Black (1977) sums up the situation precisely:

> The decisive reason for the choice of interpretation may be, as it often is, the patent falsity or incoherence of the literal reading—but it might equally be the banality of that reading's truth, its pointlessness, or its lack of congruence with the surrounding text and nonverbal setting. . . . And just as there is no infallible test for resolving ambiguity, so there is none to be expected in discriminating the metaphorical from the literal (p. 450).

The last few years have thus compelled general acknowledgement that any adequate account of the identification and comprehension of a metaphor must explain the complex interaction of both extrasentential and extralinguistic knowledge. We apprehend an utterance as metaphorical, not because of its literal falsity (though that may be a clue), but, more generally, because of a tension between the literal reading and its context (of which literal falsity is one instance). If there was not some tension, some "contraindication," some "clash," there would be nothing to suggest the metaphorical reading.

Ted Cohen (1975) has taken beginning steps in trying to explain this tension by suggesting that we view metaphors as illocutionary analogues of figurative speech acts. His argument utilizes Austin's (1975) distinction between acts done *in* saying something (illocutions) and acts done *by* saying something (perlocutions). Uttering "I promise to pay you back," for instance, may involve the illocution of making a promise plus any of several possible perlocutions, e.g., your accepting my promise, my making you happy, my repairing our friendship, and so on. Cohen argues that certain speech acts cannot be performed unless the appropriate perlocution associated with each act is possible in the given context. I cannot, for example, perform the illocutionary act of promising, if the situation of my utterance is such that I cannot make the promise in question. I may utter the words "I promise to live past 1992," but since this is something I cannot promise, the normal illocution does not go through. Such utterings may be called figurative speech acts. Cohen suggests that an analogous process may be at work in cases of metaphor. Our identification of an utterance as metaphorical does seem to involve some strain between the normal sense of the utterance and the total speech situation in which it occurs. This "strain" is precisely what earlier views tried to define as "logical absurdity," "clash of meanings," "tension," and so on. Cohen summarizes:

> The semantic resources of the language yield novel meaning when they are made to collide, either with one another or with other parts of the speech situation. The utterance forces at our disposal yield novel acts when they are somehow askew. I have given some examples in which the force collides with meaning, but I have wished to concentrate more on collision between force and perlocutionary possibility (1975, p. 683).

The sketchiness of Cohen's view reminds us of just how far we have yet to go in explaining how we are able to recognize metaphor. Only ten years ago it was taken for granted by most philosophers that some fairly simple and obvious feature of utterances marked their metaphoricity. Once it is pointed out that some metaphors are neither syntactically nor semantically deviant, nor even literally false, one is surprised to see that this was overlooked for so long. At present we seem forced to start over, though now with greater understanding, and to focus special attention (as Cohen and Loewenberg suggest) upon the relation of an utterance to the total speech situation in which it occurs. This will take us beyond mere linguistic knowledge to an exploration of how both our apprehension and comprehension of metaphor involve our knowledge of speaker, speech situation, and world. Perhaps if we can understand better how features of context influence our interpretation of a metaphor, we can get clearer about how we identify the metaphor in the first place.

How Do Metaphors Work?

Although there has recently been an amazing eruption of literature on the subject of how we comprehend a metaphor, there have never been more than a couple of basic theories variously elaborated. Roughly, there are those which treat metaphor as an elliptical simile, attributing to it no significant cognitive function; and there are those which clearly distinguish simile from metaphor, arguing that the latter is not cognitively reducible to the former. Black (1954-55) set the stage for recent discussions of how we can understand metaphors by identifying three main theories (the first two of which are of the same kind).

(1) *Substitution view*: A metaphor of the "A is B" form (e.g., *Man is a wolf*) is nothing but an indirect way of presenting some intended literal meaning "A is C" (e.g., *Man is fierce*).

(2) *Comparison view*: A metaphor of the "A is B" form is a means of indirection by which we get at the speaker's intended literal meaning "A *is like* B, in the following respects: . . ." (e.g., *Man is like a wolf, in being* . . .). According to this view, the meaning of the metaphor is a literal set of relevant similarities picked out by the context of the utterance. In what follows, the substitution view will be considered as a special case of the more general comparison view.

The comparison theory has been the single most popular and widely held account of how metaphors work. As the previous historical survey indicates, there is a long, unbroken philosophical tradition that treats metaphor as a mere stylistic ornament that is reducible to literal statements without loss of cognitive content. We can discern some of the merits of the view by considering one of its more cogent and elegant formulations, that of Paul Henle (1958).

Henle's account of how metaphors work draws on Peirce's distinction between a *symbol*, i.e., a sign that signifies by convention, and an *icon*, which signifies by virtue of similarity with the thing signified. In metaphor there is an underlying analogy in which one component (the iconic) is used to present the other. Henle sums up the "double sort of semantic relationship" present in metaphor as follows:

> First, using symbols in Peirce's sense, directions are given for finding an object or situation. . . . Second, it is implied that any object or situation fitting the direction may serve as an icon of what one wishes to describe. The icon is never actually present; rather, through the rule, one understands what it must be and, through this understanding, what it signifies (Henle, 1958, p. 178).

The superiority of Henle's particular version over other comparison theories is evident at two points. First, as Ricoeur (1978) notes, the claim that the iconic element provides a rule for reflecting on some object or situation constitutes a preliminary account of how imaginative metaphoric insight is possible. Second, Henle argues that not only are metaphors based on similarities, but they may also induce similarities. Thus Henle offers a comparison theory that, he believes, need not lead to the view that metaphors are cognitively dispensable. Unfortunately, he gives very little argument for this controversial claim.

The long-lived and widespread popularity of the comparison theory is easy to explain. First, if the theory were correct, it would make the problem of metaphor fairly simple and readily solvable within the presuppositions of the dominant tradition. Second, there is often *some* basis in similarity for a number of metaphors, i.e., much of what many metaphors mean can be stated in terms of a list of similarities. Primarily for this second reason, the similarity theorist draws the (erroneous, I believe) conclusion that all metaphor is nothing more than assertion of similarities.

Hardly anyone denies that our comprehension of *some* metaphors partially involves awareness of similarities; but many have denied that this explains everything that happens in understanding a metaphor. Among the more cogent objections to the view that metaphors are abridged comparisons are the following:

(i) As Black (1954-55) noted long ago, the comparison theory "suffers from a vagueness that borders on vacuity" (p. 284). The theory simply does not tell us how we are to compute the meaning of any given metaphor. *Any* two objects are similar in *some* respects, and the comparison view does not explain how we are able to pick out the relevant similarities in each instance.

(ii) Richards (1936) and Khatchadourian (1968) have argued that, by overemphasizing the role of similarities, the theory ignores the sometimes crucial role of differences and disanalogies. The insight we gain is often less a product of perceived similarities highlighted by the metaphor and more a result of dissimilarities that force us imaginatively to restructure our way of comprehending things.

(iii) In one of the most cogent criticisms of the comparison view to date, John Searle (1979) has offered three further arguments, in addition to the first objection above. He first challenges those crude versions that assume that understanding a metaphor requires the existence of two objects that are compared. Searle points out that in many cases there simply are not two existing objects being compared, as in the case of *Sally is a dragon*.

(iv) The previous objection is preliminary to the more serious criticism that "the metaphorical assertion can remain true even though it turns out that the statement of similarity on which the inference to the metaphorical meaning is based is false" (Searle, 1979, p. 89). *Richard is a gorilla* may be true, for example, if it is taken to mean *Richard is fierce, nasty, prone to violence, and so forth.* According to the comparison theory this metaphor is based on the belief that Richard and gorillas are similar in being fierce, nasty, prone to violence, and so on. But it is, in fact, *false* that gorillas have these characteristics. So the metaphor is true but the relevant statement of similarity upon which it is based is false. The point here is similar to that of Beardsley (1962), who shows that metaphors need not depend on *actual* properties of existing objects, but rather on relations at the level of meanings or of beliefs about objects.

(v) The final objection is that for many metaphors there simply are no literal similarities between objects as required by the theory. Searle asserts that the burden rests on the comparison theorist to supply complete lists of literal similarities for any metaphor one cares to examine; and Searle offers very simple metaphors (e.g., "Sally is a block of ice") for which this does not seem feasible. Lakoff and I (1980b) have also argued that many metaphors, such as "orientational" metaphors, are grounded on correlations within experience rather than on similarities. The orientational metaphor MORE IS UP (as in "The number of crimes keeps going up," "His draft number is high," "Her income fell last year"), for example, seems to be based, not on any similarities, but on the correlation between adding more to a pile or substance and seeing the level rise.

The core of all these objections is expressed by Searle as follows: "though similarity often plays a role in the *comprehension* of metaphor, the metaphorical assertion is not necessarily an *assertion* of similarity" (p. 88). Comparison theorists make at least two mistakes: First, they assume that because similarity often plays a role in our comprehension of a metaphor, it is therefore the essence of the *meaning* of the metaphor; and, second, they take similarity as the sole basis for the act of comprehension.

Criticisms like these have been the basis for alternative theories that claim to capture aspects of metaphoric comprehension that go beyond mere recognition of resemblances. Chief among these is Black's third theory, the "interaction view." Black's account is basically a development of Richards's cryptic remark that the metaphorical generation of meaning results from the "interaction between co-present thoughts" (Richards, 1936, p. 93).

(3) *Interaction view*: In the metaphor "A is B" (e.g., *Man is a wolf*), the "system of associated commonplaces" of *A* interacts with that of *B* to produce emergent metaphorical meaning. The "associated commonplaces" are whatever properties and relations are commonly believed to be true of an object, person, event, etc., even if they do not actually apply. For instance, "is a mammal," "is a predator," "travels in packs," "is fierce," and so on, might be commonplaces of "wolf" involved in our comprehension of the metaphor, regardless of the fact that wolves may not actually be fierce in the way or to the extent that they are believed to be fierce. The point here is that

understanding a metaphor is not typically a matter of comparing actual properties of objects; rather, it is based upon what the terms of the metaphor call to mind for us.

Black's chief and distinguishing contribution was the notion of "interaction." Contrary to the standard comparison theory, comprehending a metaphor is *not* merely a matter of comparing objects to determine what discrete properties or relations applying to one also apply to the other in the same or in some similar sense. Instead, we use one entire *system* of commonplaces (e.g., that of *wolf*) to "filter" or organize our conception of some other *system* (e.g., that of *man*). The "interaction" is a screening of one system of commonplaces by another to generate a new conceptual organization of, a new perspective on, some object.

Black claims that this projection of one system onto another is a distinctive intellectual operation not reducible to any mere comparison of objects to mark their similarities. If this is true, it might be possible to justify claims about the indispensability of metaphor for cognitive insight (see following section for an account of Black's irreducibility thesis). However, in the two decades since Black's essay appeared, it has become clear that we need a more detailed account of the alleged "interaction" upon which metaphors are based. Black's latest work on this problem (Black, 1977) restates his case and supplies some long-awaited details, but it does not substantially alter his initial formulation.[7] Much of the recent literature on how metaphors work consists of attempts to go beyond Black's groundwork to explain more fully the "mechanism" by which a metaphor creates new meaning and generates insight.

One important earlier effort is Beardsley's (1962) critique of the "Object-comparison" theory, according to which metaphor is an implicit comparison in which the focus or vehicle term retains its standard designation but is used to highlight similarities between its referent and that of the principal subject. Against this, Beardsley argues that inherent tensions within the metaphor cause the metaphoric predicate to lose its ordinary extension and thereby to obtain a new intension, namely, its previous connotation. More specifically, a term will have a central meaning (its ordinary designation) and a marginal meaning (its connotation). The standard designation of "wolf," for example, might include "mammal," "four-legged," "canine," whereas the marginal meaning would include "fierce," "voracious," "clever," and so on. In metaphor there occurs a "logical opposition" between the ordinary designated properties of the two things juxtaposed by the metaphor—men are not four-legged nor are they members of the canine family. This failure of primary reference or designation forces us to call up the associated connotations of the modifying term *(wolf)*, which are then applied to the principal subject *(man)* in their new senses. Thus, I understand *Man is a wolf* as suppressing the conflicting designated properties and highlighting such potential connotations as "is fierce," "is clever," "is greedy," etc., which can be seen as applying to human beings.

According to this "Verbal-opposition theory," then, a metaphor induces insight by calling up or actualizing connotations that were previously potentially available but unnoticed. Beardsley goes beyond Black in claiming that metaphor does not simply call upon "associated commonplaces" but may actualize connotations not yet brought forward in our present conceptual system. But, as Paul Ricoeur (1977) has noted, Beardsley cannot fully explain metaphoric creativity, because he cannot explain where the "potential connotations" come from. Ricoeur's own position (1978) attempts to supply the missing explanation (see following section for a discussion of Ricoeur's view).

Another illuminating, although only partially developed, explanation of the peculiar power of metaphor for inducing insight has been inspired by Wittgenstein's (1953) notion of "seeing-as" or perspectival seeing. The ability to see a given visual array first as one thing, then as another (e.g., seeing the duck-rabbit figure first as a duck, then as a rabbit) involves an imaginative activity partially subject to the will and not identical with an act of mere perception. I *perceive* the formal configuration on the page, but I imaginatively notice one aspect (the duck) or another (the rabbit). Aldrich (1958) suggests that aesthetic perception is best understood as a type of perspectival seeing and that the artist has a special capacity to embody certain aspects in an artwork. The poet, for instance, in creating metaphors, exploits imagistic language to reveal aspects of objects previously unnoticed.

A more thorough treatment of seeing-as in relation to metaphor is Hester's (1966) explanation of the similarities and differences between

between visual and metaphorical aspect seeing. "Metaphorical seeing as is a seeing as between the metaphorical subject and the metaphorical predicate, either one or both of which must be image-exciting" (p. 207). In visual seeing-as there is an actual physical object or configuration which may be construed in alternative ways, whereas in metaphorical seeing-as the images are those called up by the meanings of the words in the metaphor. In some metaphors both terms are "image-laden," but in others one term will be more image-exciting and it will be used to understand the more abstract term. In *Death is a grim reaper,* for instance, the more abstract notion *(death)* is grasped in terms of the more imagistic notion *(grim reaper).*

Another crucial difference between visual and metaphorical seeing-as is that with the visual cases I am given one gestalt (the duck-rabbit configuration) and asked to see two or more aspects, whereas with metaphor I must perform the reverse imaginative leap of seeing how two apparently dissimilar things share a common ground or belong together in a fundamental way. Understanding "Man is a worm" for Hester requires an imaginative grasp of the common gestalt between men and worms, namely, the senses in which men are like worms.

One of the more serious problems with Hester's view is his over-emphasis on images. From the observation that some poetic metaphors involved images, we cannot conclude either that all poetic metaphors are necessarily imagistic or that the images are always necessary for one's comprehension. For example, just because I form an image of a wolf when I hear the remark "Man is a wolf," it is not clear that I must form such an image to understand the metaphor. At present, it is not even clear how one could demonstrate the necessity of images in metaphoric understanding.

The real value of Hester's view lies in its focus on the gestalt switch or flash of insight induced by a good metaphor. In this respect he echoes Black's claim that in understanding a metaphor we use one system of implications as a "filter" or "screen" through which we see some other system. This screening process highlights certain associated implications, suppresses others, and redefines still others.

Lakoff and I (1980b) have recently developed a more detailed account of the gestalt switch described by Hester and others. We argue that actions, events, and objects are understood by us in terms of "experiential gestalts," i.e., structured meaningful wholes within experience. Each gestalt consists of various recurring subpatterns of the whole structure and can be analyzed into these patterns, though to do so destroys the relationships that make the *whole* structure meaningful for us. The gestalt for "war," for example, involves the standard subpatterns or dimensions of structure for any action, but they are specified in a way peculiar to war: PARTICIPANTS (people/nations as adversaries), PARTS (two positions, planning strategy, attack, defense, counterattack, surrender, etc.), STAGES (one adversary attacks, both sides maneuver, one side retreats, etc.), LINEAR SEQUENCE (retreat after attack, counterattack after attack, etc.), CAUSATION (attack results in defeat, etc.), PURPOSE (victory). Although any activity or event can thus be broken into dimensions such as these, it is only the complex relationship of these aspects that constitutes the meaning of war for some individual. In short, meaning emerges at the level of experiential gestalts, which give coherence and structure to our experience. In metaphor we understand one kind of thing or experience in terms of another of a different kind. Consider, for example, the ARGUMENT IS WAR metaphor, which structures not only the way we *talk* about argument (as in "He *attacked* the weak points in my argument," "I *defended* my position and *destroyed* his," "His criticisms were *right on target*," "He *shot down* my best arguments") but also the very way we *conceive of* and *carry on* arguments in our culture. The metaphorical meaning is based upon the projection of one common gestalt structure (e.g., WAR) onto another (e.g., ARGUMENT). What emerges is a new gestalt that restructures aspects of our experience, thought, and language.

Some philosophers have seen such accounts of the cognitive activity involved in processing a metaphor as pointing to the basis of the true epistemological and ontological significance of metaphor, namely, that it serves as a device for reorganizing our perceptual and/or conceptual structures. There is a ground for this view in Black's claim that metaphor creates novel meaning by giving modified senses to various concepts. If Black is correct, metaphor is a principal device for altering or restructuring our concepts and categories. Drawing on Ryle's (1949) notion of a category mistake, Turbayne (1970) argues that metaphor is a form of "sort-crossing" in which objects ordinarily falling under one category are seen as falling under some new category.

Interpreting "Man is a worm" forces us to stretch or otherwise alter our normal categorizations. Expanding Turbayne's account, Peckham (1970) defines metaphor as the creation of a novel or emergent category: "We perceive a metaphor as metaphor, therefore, when we encounter words . . . which conventionally do not belong to the same category. A metaphor, then, is an assertion that they do" (p. 405).

Nelson Goodman (1968) also sees metaphor as a "calculated category mistake" in which "a term with an extension established by habit is applied elsewhere under the influence of that habit" (p. 71). Goodman's account stands out, not only for its witty and elegant simplicity, but especially because it offers a purely extensional account of how metaphors work: "A label along with others constituting a schema is in effect detached from the home realm of that schema and applied for the sorting and organizing of an alien realm" (p. 72). In recent years Goodman's account has appealed to many who are attracted by his preliminary attempts to explain nonliteral discourse within a nominalistic framework.

As one attempts to evaluate each of the major representative views outlined so far, it soon becomes clear that they all share a common shortcoming—while each account highlights some important aspect of metaphor comprehension, no one theory comes even close to telling the whole story. Nowhere do we find an appropriately detailed statement of the knowledge required for understanding any metaphor, nor is there an account of how the relevant knowledge is brought to bear in specific cases.

With precisely this problem in mind, John Searle (1979) has provided the groundwork for a more complete explanation of how relevant knowledge is brought to bear in understanding a metaphor. Searle begins by reformulating the question of how metaphors work in terms of the speech-act distinction between *word or sentence meaning* (i.e., what the word or sentence means literally) and *speaker's utterance meaning* (i.e., what the speaker means by uttering words or sentences with literal meanings). In terms of this distinction, the central problem of metaphor is to state the principles relating literal sentence meaning to metaphorical utterance meaning (p. 78). That is, how can a speaker utter a sentence of the form "S is P" (having a literal sentence meaning) and mean metaphorically "S is R"?

A similar project was suggested by Paul Grice (1975) in his treatment of "conversational implicatures," but he provided only the most general statement of the kinds of rules that might be relevant to metaphor (and other nonliteral speech acts). Searle goes beyond Grice by trying to provide *specific* principles for explaining the three basic steps in the understanding of a metaphor: (1) How does the hearer know to look for a metaphorical interpretation in the first place? (2) What strategies or principles allow the hearer to compute possible values of R (where "S is P" is uttered in order to mean "S is R")? (3) What principles guide the restriction of the range of possible Rs to get the precise meaning of the metaphor?

One of the chief merits of Searle's view is that he takes the risk of offering several principles that would on his view be typically relevant for the above three steps, for example, his third principle: "Things which are P are often said or believed to be R, even though both speaker and hearer may know that R is false of P . . ." (p. 108). Searle makes no claim to completeness for his proposed set of principles; rather, he hopes that his strategy will suggest the *kind* of principles necessary for determining appropriate values of R.

Searle has correctly assessed the superficiality of our present attempts to explain how metaphors work, and he has seen that we must move from general (and vague) claims about the wonders of metaphor to detailed explanations supported by examples. Thus he calls for *specific* principles relating sentence meaning (of "S is P") to metaphorical speaker's meaning ("S is R"). Lakoff and I (1980b), too, have stressed the importance of justifying general claims by reference to numerous and varied metaphors of common speech, and we offer detailed analyses of particular metaphors that structure our everyday language, thought, and action. We have also argued that any adequate theory must explain both how metaphors are grounded in common experience within a culture and how new metaphors can alter the conceptual system in terms of which we experience and talk about our world. Finally, it is becoming clear that linguistic and philosophical analyses of metaphor will have to be consistent with empirical psychological research on metaphor processing. The results of psychological research reported in Ortony (1979) and Hoffman and Honeck (1980) suggest that any adequate account of metaphor comprehension will have to take account of developments in this field. To sum up, the only consensus that seems to emerge from all of this argument about how metaphors work is not agreement on any one theory, but rather on the kind of work now called for.

Recently, however, this entire tradition of theorizing has received a radical challenge. In a highly controversial essay, Donald Davidson (1978) has argued that some of this apparent mudddle is due to an erroneous assumption underlying virtually all the standard theories of metaphor to date—namely, the assumption that there is some special "metaphorical meaning" in addition to the metaphor's literal meaning. Davidson denies this premise, stating, "metaphors mean what the words, in their most literal interpretation, mean, and nothing more" (p. 32).

But if literal meaning is the *only* kind of meaning there is, how are we to account for the particular power of metaphor to enlighten? Davidson's answer is simple—in metaphor we *use* an expression with its literal meaning in order to direct the hearer's attention, to get the hearer to see or grasp something, to suggest insights, and so on. The crux of this view is explained as follows:

> I depend on the distinction between what words mean and what they are used to do. I think metaphor belongs exclusively to the domain of use. It is something brought off by the imaginative employment of words and sentences and depends entirely on the ordinary meanings of those words and hence on the ordinary meanings of the sentences they comprise (p. 33).

This is not just another version of Searle's speech-act approach, for Davidson denies that there is such a thing as metaphorical speaker's meaning. Metaphor, for him, is not really a semantic issue, but a matter of pragmatics, broadly conceived. The question of metaphor becomes the question of how one can use sentences with literal meanings to "intimate" things, or to "lead us to notice what might not otherwise be noticed" (p. 41).

It is curious that, in denying that metaphor is a semantic issue, Davidson challenges the very claim with which Black (1954-55) started contemporary discussion twenty-five years ago. Does this mean that we are back where we started? The answer is "yes and no." It is "no" insofar as we have learned a great deal about how some metaphors work (as witnessed by the work just discussed). But the answer is "yes" in the sense that we are taken back to certain of

the *same issues* about meaning and truth. In some respects Davidson's insistence that there is no special metaphorical meaning and his
claim that "literal meaning and literal truth conditions can be assigned to words and sentences apart from particular contexts of use"
(p. 33) are reminiscent of views Black was challenging three decades
ago.

The importance of Davidson's essay thus lies in its resurrection of
fundamental questions about the nature of meaning and truth, as
they are brought into focus by the investigation of how we understand metaphors. There is much at stake here concerning important
semantic issues, and that is why Black (1979) and Goodman (1979)
have both replied to Davidson's challenge, albeit from very different
perspectives. Now that these issues have been raised again, it will be
necessary for any adequate theory of how metaphors work to deal
with these problems, such as whether there is such a thing as metaphorical meaning and whether metaphors are the kind of thing that
can be true or false. It is this latter question in particular that raises
the general question of the cognitive status of metaphor.

What Is the Cognitive Status of Metaphor?

The two central issues concerning the cognitive status of metaphor are whether a metaphorical utterance can be used to make truth
claims and, if so, whether those truth claims can be adequately expressed in literal language. The mainstream philosophical tradition,
dominated by the comparison view, has held that insofar as metaphors may be used to communicate knowledge, that knowledge can
be reduced to a set of cognitively equivalent literal utterances. Any
distinctive effects of metaphor will be limited to its stylistic, rhetorical, or didactic advantages (e.g., metaphors are more pleasing,
forceful, or striking than ordinary literal discourse).

As the previous historical survey of philosophers' views reveals,
there were notable exceptions to this general downgrading of the
epistemic importance of metaphor, but these alternative accounts
had little or no lasting effect. In fact, by the third decade of this
century the positivists had gone beyond the standard view that metaphors are cognitively reducible to literal language to the extreme
position that they can make no truth claims at all. Instead, it was
claimed, they function only emotively to express feelings, moods, or

attitudes. It is against this background that Black's (1954-55) interaction theory again stands out as a major challenge to the Anglo-
American tradition, and to the strong positivist emotivist position in
particular. Black's central claim in this area is that the use of one
complex system of implications to select, emphasize, and organize
relations in another field of implications is a "distinctive *intellectual*
operation" not reducible to any mere comparison between elements
within the two fields (p. 293). No literal paraphrase or statement of
similarities will capture the cognitive insight provided by the metaphor. Furthermore, contrary to the comparison view, many metaphors are not merely assertions of preexistent likenesses between two
objects: "It would be more illuminating in some of these cases to say
that the metaphor *creates* the similarity than to say that it formulates some similarity antecedently existing" (p. 285).

Black might have gotten by with the claim that no literal paraphrase provides the *insight* of the metaphor, for "insight" might have
been spelled out in psychological terms. But he raised an outcry with
his remark about "creating" similarities. Supporters of his interaction
account tried to downplay or ignore this remark, preferring to focus
on the notion of cognitive insight. Martin Warner (1973), for example,
defines the "cognitive content" of an utterance as its truth conditions, and he then argues that there could be no *in principle* argument
that the truth claims of a metaphor cannot be stated literally. This
leads him to the view that the irreducible *insight* of a metaphor is not
its cognitive content (= truth claims). Warner argues that metaphors
are not principally in the business of stating truths or of conveying
information through assertions. Rather, metaphor has a unique "hortatory" or "suggestive" illocutionary force, by virtue of which it can
be used to help the hearer see one thing in terms of another.

Loewenberg (1975), too, denies the claim that metaphors can be
used to make truth claims. Instead, the metaphorical speech act has
a special illocutionary force, for which Loewenberg coins the term
"*proposal*$_m$." She argues that one interprets an utterance as metaphorical when one "judges that the speaker was not making a truth claim a-
bout the referents in the words of the sentence he uttered but rather a
proposal about a way to view, understand, etc., those referents" (p.335).

The idea that metaphors do not have truth values has appealed
to some who are convinced that metaphors are indispensable for

obtaining certain insights, but who are unable to accept the existence of truth claims that are not literally expressible. If metaphors only "suggest" ways of viewing things, they need not compete with *real* assertions. In other words, metaphorical "seeing-as" is not the same as "seeing that" something is the case.

In approaching the question of whether metaphors can have truth values, many writings have turned the tables and challenged the commonplace (enshrined in the "literal-truth paradigm") that literal assertions are somehow better or more obvious bearers of truth than metaphors are. One need not claim that the truth conditons of metaphors are obvious, straightforward, or unproblematic, but only that those of literal assertions are not either. As Goodman (1968) notes, "[t]he question why predicates apply as they do metaphorically is much the same as the question why they apply as they do literally" (p. 78)—and there are no ready answers to either question.

Binkley (1974) and Cohen (1976) have also stressed similarities between literal and metaphorical truth claims. They argue that we typically assess the truth or falsity of metaphors in a manner essentially the same as that for literal expressions. Cohen notes that there are polemical reasons for arguing that "The chairman ploughed through the committee" has truth conditions just as "Snow is white" does:

> I do not care to begin the argument by asserting that truth is truth, literal or figurative, and that metaphors are "cognitive," "verifiable," and true just as any statements are; but I do want to assert this as a reply to the dogma that only such statements are good or serious or scientific and that metaphors are not like that (Cohen, 1976, p. 255).

The point is not to put metaphors on a par with literal statements but to explode the myth that they are radically different and that metaphor is cognitively inferior. Binkley constructs a hypothetical argument over the truth of "Richard is a fox" in order to show that a metaphorical claim can be made "which is amenable to argument, which has more or less determinate criteria of evaluation, which can be supported and weakened with evidence, and so on" (1974, p. 174). Binkley then proceeds to identify several identities between the procedures for evaluating literal and metaphorical truth claims.

In a further move, Lakoff and I (1980b) have provided detailed analyses of what it would take to make certain metaphors true or false, thus probing some of the complexities involved in the truth of any assertion. Our claims about the similarities between literal and metaphorical assertions are based on an explanation of the way in which our ordinary human conceptual system is metaphorically structured. Even our most "literal" expressions may involve unnoticed "conventional" metaphors, e.g., "orientational" metaphors based on common spatial orientations like UP/DOWN, IN/OUT, NEAR/FAR, ON/OFF, and so on. We conceptualize a broad range of our everyday experiences by means of metaphors based on such orientations. Thus we find many domains of experience structured by UP/DOWN metaphors, for instance, "I'm feeling up today," "He's at the peak of health," "I'm on top of the situation," "She has high standards," "Things are at an all-time low," and so on. The myth that literal assertion (untainted by figuration) is somehow the pristine model of perspicuous communication hides the pervasiveness of such "conventional" metaphors in the way we think, experience, talk, and act in our everyday world. Once we see that unquestionably "cognitive" and "true" statements involve many conventional metaphors, we lose our prejudice against metaphors as bearers of truth values, because the dichotomy it presupposes has broken down.

But even if metaphors can have truth values, we are still faced with the original problem of whether metaphors can be reduced to literal paraphrases without loss of cognitive content. The focus of debate on this issue has turned out to be Black's enigmatic remarks about cognitive insight and the creation of similarities. Too much of the discussion of these issues consists of vague claims about "irreducible" acts of understanding.

One typical proposal is James Manns's (1975) attempt to defend Black against Warner's (1973) criticism. Manns argues that "cognitive content" involves far more than simple truth claims, namely: (1) directing attention toward features of our environment; (2) aiding us to cultivate a skill ("knowing how"); and (3) altering our categorization of the world (p. 361). Manns then emphasizes those aspects of metaphorical insight that go beyond verifiable or falsifiable literally expressible truth claims. Unfortunately, no explanation is offered as to why these three achievements should be unique to metaphor, nor is any account given as to how these cognitive insights are achieved by metaphor.

A somewhat more detailed argument for irreducibility is provided by Felicity Haynes (1975), who identifies a comparative and an interactive level in the comprehension of metaphor.

> On the comparative level we are transferring characteristics of Y to X in order to say something about X. On the interactive level, placing known characteristics of Y against those of X may provide *new* insights, either about X or about a new third, Z, an irreducible synthesis by juxtaposition which it is difficult to reduce to simile or to literal language (p. 273).

At the comparison level we comprehend similarities between objects (X and Y) in a *rule-governed, systematic way*. This is what the comparison theory has understood. But the comparison view cannot explain the gestalt switch, the "intuitive grasping of a whole which is not reducible to any system" (p. 276), that occurs at the interactive level. Unfortunately, Haynes does not explain how the alleged gestalt switch is possible or why the insight it provides cannot be literally expressed.

I (1980) have tried to remedy these defects by offering models of metaphoric comprehension for Haynes's two levels. The basis for these models is Kant's account of reflective judgment, in which the imagination freely plays with (reflects on) a series of representations in search of a unifying principle. I suggest that the comparative (or what I call the "canonical" or "rule-governed") level functions analogously to Kant's teleological reflective judgment, where we imaginatively reflect on forms of nature to find concepts that unify those varied forms. The interactive (or "noncanonical") level involves a play of the imagination analogous to Kant's aesthetical reflective judgment. In such "judgments of taste" the imaginative act of reflection is *felt* as adequate to the representations it organizes, even though there are no concepts (or rules) governing that reflective activity.

Using this model, we can begin to explain the elusive irreducibility of metaphorical insight by arguing that the imaginative leap occurring in the metaphor is not rule-governed, and therefore not reducible to a set of rules, or a systematic procedure of understanding. Furthermore, if our comprehension of metaphor involves something like a free reflective judgment, then making metaphors would constitute a free (not wholly rule-governed) act of originality, which Kant calls an act of "genius." Genius is the creative capacity to produce "aesthetical ideas," where an aesthetical idea is an imaginative representation that "occasions much thought, without however any definite thought, i.e., any *concept*, being capable of being adequate to it; it consequently cannot be completely compassed and made intelligible by language" (Kant, 1790, § 49, p. 157). In other words, metaphors are like miniature works of art that produce imaginative insights not exhaustively expressible by statements of simple literal similarities.

My proposed models of metaphoric comprehension presuppose a theory of imagination outlined only sketchily by Kant. Ricoeur (1978) offers a more fully developed account of the role of imagination in metaphoric insight. He claims that an adequate semantic theory of metaphor, i.e., "an inquiry into the capacity of metaphor to provide untranslatable information" (p. 143), requires a psychological theory of imagination that is not merely psychological but also semantic. Specifically, what is required for explaining how metaphors work is an account of the "mode of functioning of similarity and accordingly of imagination which is immanent—that is, non-extrinsic—to the predicative process itself" (p. 147).

There are three steps in this account. In the first, imagination is described in what Kant called its *productive* mode, in which it schematizes (or provides a procedure for) a synthetic operation of understanding. In metaphor this synthesis is the imaginative leap in which we see how two previously unassociated systems of implications fit together to reveal an underlying unity (even while retaining the surface incompatibility). The second step is the pictorial dimension in which metaphor provides images that fill out the sense or meaning of the metaphor. Ricoeur emphasizes that images are not, or need not necessarily be, mental pictures; rather, they are ways of presenting relations in a depicting mode. Finally, imagination in metaphor involves a "negative" step in which primary reference to the everyday world is suspended, in order to make possible a new creative reference, a "remaking" of reality. Ricoeur sums up this threefold movement of imagination as follows:

> Imagination does not merely *schematize* the predicative assimilation between terms by its synthetic insight into similarities nor does it merely *picture* the sense thanks to the display of images aroused and

controlled by the cognitive process. Rather, it contributes concretely to the *epoche* of ordinary reference and to the *projection* of new possibilities of redescribing the world (p. 154).

I am convinced that work like Ricoeur's on the theory of imagination as a *semantic*, and not merely a psychological, inquiry will open the way for new progress on how metaphors work. This strategy holds promise especially for those who would claim that metaphor is cognitively irreducible. For it is in the movement of the imagination in what Ricoeur calls the schematizing process of predicative assimilation that new meaning and new insight is born.

A second aspect of Ricoeur's work suggests new strategies for dealing with the cognitivity issue, namely, his view that, as Goodman says, reality can be remade. In discussions concerning whether a metaphor can be replaced by literal paraphrase without loss of cognitive content, the discussants seem, at last, to be reaching agreement about what is really at issue here. The underlying issue is whether "reality" is objectively given, so that, as knowers, we can only stand apart and comment on it, or whether we have a "world" only by virtue of having a language and system of value-laden concepts that make experience possible for us. This, as Ricoeur and many others note, is not a question limited to metaphor—it is a fundamental ontological and epistemological issue.

In saying that a consensus is beginning to emerge about the nature of the cognitivity issue, I mean that it is becoming more evident what irreducibility theorists (like Black, Loewenberg, Ricoeur, Lakoff, and myself) will have to assert in order to make a case for the metaphoric creation of similarities. In general, they must hold that we encounter our world, not passively, but by means of projective acts influenced by our interests, purposes, values, beliefs, and language. Because our world is an imaginative, value-laden construction, metaphors that alter our conceptual structures (themselves carried by older metaphors) will also alter the way we experience things. In his latest work on this issue, Black (1977) expresses the essence of this position:

> If some metaphors are what might be called "cognitive instruments," indispensable for perceiving connections that, once perceived, are *then* truly present, the case for the thesis would be made out . . .
>
> For such reasons as this, I wish to contend that some metaphors enable us to see aspects of reality that the metaphor's production helps

to constitute. But that is no longer surprising if one believes that the world is necessarily a world *under a certain description*—or a world seen from a certain perspective. Some metaphors can create such a perspective (p. 454).

New Directions

The preceding analysis of the major contemporary views reveals, I believe, that we are currently in the midst of an important battle over the place metaphor holds in a philosophical account of human understanding. Roughly, in the last couple of decades metaphor has been moving slowly from the periphery of philosophical interest toward a more prominent position. This movement, which I have tried to trace, is basically a turning away from certain positivist or narrow empiricist presuppositions that have dominated philosophical reflection on language and cognition for several decades, or, in some cases, for several centuries. We now seem to be slowly distancing ourselves from what I have called the "literal-truth paradigm," though its influence lingers in many corners.

In particular, the destruction of simplistic dichotomies concerning the functions of language and the classification of speech acts has made it easier to free ourselves from the illusion that literal discourse constitutes the ideal medium for the communication of meaning and truth. This, in turn, has led most philosophers to acknowledge that metaphors are cognitively meaningful. One of the strongest supports here has been the growing body of literature on the pervasiveness and indispensability of metaphor in science (see, for example, Hesse (1966), Barbour (1974), MacCormac (1976), Boyd (1979), and Kuhn (1979)). Many have become convinced that there can no longer be facile dismissal of the cognitive importance of metaphor. The question of just *how* important and indispensable metaphor is remains the subject of much heated debate, but it is clear that metaphor cannot be ignored when so eminent an empiricist as W. V. O. Quine admits that metaphor "flourishes in playful prose and high poetic art, but it is vital also at the growing edges of science and philosophy"(1978, p. 161).

The recognition that science cannot do without metaphor—that all theories are elaborations of basic metaphors or systems of metaphors—is only one part of a larger emerging awareness of the pervasiveness of metaphor in *all* language. Many philosophers are now willing to grant Goodman's (1968) claim that metaphor "permeates all discourse, ordinary and special" (p. 80). This acknowledgement has, in turn, set the stage for what promises to be an even more important and vigorous debate, namely, the question of whether metaphor is not merely a *linguistic* phenomenon but *also* a fundamental principle of *thought* and *action*. Urging just such a view, Lakoff and I have argued that "no account of meaning and truth can be adequate unless it recognizes and deals with the way in which conventional metaphors structure our conceptual system"(Lakoff and Johnson, 1980a, p. 486).

Whether one thinks, as I do, that the metaphoric process is an omnipresent principle of *cognition* (e.g., that all experience has an "as" structure) or only that metaphor pervades all *language*, the very existence of this debate attests to the widespread recognition that metaphor cannot be ignored. More and more, metaphor is coming to be regarded as a test case for theories of meaning, such that any adequate theory must account satisfactorily for the way we comprehend metaphor and for its unique cognitive role. This alone is quite a revolution.

Finally, this problem of the cognitive status of metaphor raises basic epistemological and ontological challenges to our theories of how experience is possible for us. If metaphors actually *create* similarities, any ontological description of the way things stand forth or reveal themselves to us as meaningful will itself be inextricably linked to metaphor. And even if metaphors do no more than *reveal* similarities, we will still need a detailed epistemological explanation of how it is possible for us to conceptualize experience metaphorically. Either way, we can expect considerable continued interest in the nature, function, and role of metaphor in language, thought, and action.

It appears, then, that metaphor has finally come of age in the eyes of philosophers. By examining certain classical and contemporary views, I have tried to show how the study of metaphor leads directly to basic epistemological and ontological issues—fundamental questions about language, meaning, truth, and human understanding. The essays in this volume reveal where we have been and where we are at present in our search for an adequate set of metaphors for talking about metaphor and language generally. The more innovative of these essays propose new metaphors for conceptualizing human understanding in its metaphoric aspect. Now, as always, the general problem of metaphor is to do justice to its role in the way we meaningfully understand, conceptualize, and talk about our experience.

NOTES

1. For a detailed explanation of St. Thomas's view of the nature of metaphor as distinguished from proportional analogy, see Ralph M. McInerny, *The Logic of Analogy* (The Hague: Martinus Nijhoff, 1961), pp. 144-152.

2. In "A Philosophical Perspective on The Problems of Metaphor," in *Cognition and Figurative Language*, ed. R. Hoffman and R. Honeck (Hillsdale, N.J.: Lawrence Erlbaum, 1980), I have argued that the importance of Kant's account of genius and reflective judgment for an adequate model of metaphoric comprehension has not been appreciated.

3. The idea that the human conceptual system is essentially metaphoric has never been popular in Western thought. Only recently has this claim found any widespread support, especially in Continental hermeneutics. Richards (1936) and Lakoff and Johnson (1980a and 1980b) also argue for this view.

4. See Carl Hempel, "Empiricist Criteria of Cognitive Significance: Problems and Changes," in his *Aspects of Scientific Explanation* (New York: Free Press, 1965), for a survey of the course of discussion on this issue.

5. These claims are discussed in more detail in the following sections.

6. Selected portions of the following three sections have appeared previously in my "A Philosophical Perspective on The Problems of Metaphor," in *Cognition and Figurative Language*, ed. R. Hoffman and R. Honeck (Hillsdale, N.J.: Lawrence Erlbaum, 1980).

7. The most helpful amplification of Black's account of the interaction of systems occurs in the section "Thinking in Metaphors," where he describes the nature of the gestalt switch that occurs when we *see* one thing *as* another.

REFERENCES

Alberic of Monte Cassino. *Flowers of Rhetoric*. Translated by Joseph Miller. In *Readings in Medieval Rhetoric*, edited by Joseph Miller, Michael Prosser, and Thomas Benson. Bloomington, Indiana: Indiana University Press, 1973.

Aldrich, Virgil. "Pictorial Meaning, Picture-thinking, and Wittgenstein's Theory of Aspects." *Mind* 62 (1958):70-79.

Aristotle. *Poetics*. Translated by Ingram Bywater. In *Introduction to Aristotle*, edited by Richard McKeon. New York: Random House, 1941.

Aquinas, Thomas. *Summa Theologica*. Translated by Anton Pegis. In *Introduction to St. Thomas Aquinas*, edited by Anton Pegis. New York: Modern Library, 1945.

Austin, J. L. *How to do Things with Words.* 2nd ed. Cambridge, Mass.: Harvard University Press, 1975.

Barbour, Ian. *Myths, Models, and Paradigms.* New York: Harper and Row, 1974.

Beardsley, Monroe C. *Aesthetics: Problems in the Philosophy of Criticism.* New York: Harcourt, Brace, and World, 1958.

———. "The Metaphorical Twist." *Philosophy and Phenomenological Research* 22, no. 3 (1962):293-307.

Bede. *Concerning Figures and Tropes.* Translated by Gussie Hecht Tannenhaus. In *Readings in Medieval Rhetoric,* edited by Joseph Miller, Michael Prosser, and Thomas Benson. Bloomington, Indiana: Indiana University Press, 1973.

Berkeley, George. "Of Motion." Translated by A. A. Luce. In *The Works of George Berkeley Bishop of Cloyne,* edited by A. A. Luce and T. E. Jessop. London: Thomas Nelson and Sons, 1951.

Binkley, Timothy. "On the Truth and Probity of Metaphor." *Journal of Aesthetics and Art Criticism* 33, no. 2 (1974):171-180.

Black, Max. "How Metaphors Work: A Reply to Donald Davidson." In *On Metaphor,* edited by Sheldon Sacks, pp. 181-192. Chicago: University of Chicago Press, 1979.

———. "Metaphor." *Proceedings of the Aristotelian Society.* N. S. 55 (1954-55):273-294.

———. "More about Metaphor." *Dialectica* 31, nos. 3-4 (1977):431-457.

Boyd, Richard. "Metaphor and Theory Change: What is 'Metaphor' a Metaphor for?" In *Metaphor and Thought,* edited by A. Ortony, pp. 356-408. Cambridge: Cambridge University Press, 1979.

Cicero. "On the Character of the Orator." In *Cicero on Oratory and Orators,* translated and edited by J. S. Watson. Carbondale, Ill.: Southern Illinois University Press, 1970.

Cohen, Ted. "Figurative Speech and Figurative Acts." *Journal of Philosophy* 72, no. 19 (1975):669-684.

———. "Notes on Metaphor." *Journal of Aesthetics and Art Criticism* 34, no. 3 (1976): 249-259.

Davidson, Donald. "What Metaphors Mean." *Critical Inquiry* 5, no. 1 (1978):31-47.

Goodman, Nelson. *Languages of Art.* Indianapolis: Bobbs-Merrill, 1968.

———. "Metaphor as Moonlighting." In *On Metaphor,* edited by Sheldon Sacks, pp. 175-180. Chicago: University of Chicago, 1979.

Grice, H. P. "Logic and Conversation." In *Syntax and Semantics* (Vol 3: *Speech Acts*), edited by P. Cole and J. Morgan, pp. 41-58. New York: Academic Press, 1975.

Haynes, Felicity. "Metaphor as Interactive." *Educational Theory* 25, no. 3 (1975):272-277.

Hegel, George Wilhelm Friedrich. *The Philosophy of Fine Art* (2nd part of Hegel's *Aesthetik*). Translated by Wm. M. Bryant. New York: Appelton, 1879.

Henle, Paul. "Metaphor." In *Language, Thought, and Culture,* edited by P. Henle, pp. 173-195. Ann Arbor: University of Michigan, 1958.

Hesse, Mary B. *Models and Analogies in Science.* Notre Dame: University of Notre Dame Press, 1966.

Hester, Marcus B. "Metaphor and Aspect Seeing." *Journal of Aesthetics and Art Criticism* 25 (1966):205-212.

Hobbes, Thomas. *The Leviathan. The English Works of Thomas Hobbes of Malmesbury.* Edited by Sir William Molesworth. London: John Bohn, 1834.

Hoffman, Robert, and Honeck, Richard. *Cognition and Figurative Language.* Hillsdale, N.J.: Lawrence Erlbaum, 1980.

Johnson, Mark. "A Philosophical Perspective on the Problems of Metaphor." In *Cognition and Figurative Language,* edited by Robert Hoffman and Richard Honeck, pp. 47-67. Hillsdale, N.J.: Lawrence Erlbaum, 1980.

Kant, Immanuel. *Critique of Judgment* (1790). Translated by J. H. Bernard. New York: Hafner Press, 1951.

Khatchadourian, Haig. "Metaphor." *British Journal of Aesthetics* 8, no. 3 (1968):227-243.

Kuhn, Thomas. "Metaphor in Science." In *Metaphor and Thought*, edited by A. Ortony, pp. 409-419. Cambridge: Cambridge University Press, 1979.

Lakoff, George, and Johnson, Mark (1980a). "Conceptual Metaphor in Everyday Language." *Journal of Philosophy* 77, no. 8 (1980):453-486.

———— (1980b). *Metaphors We Live By.* Chicago: University of Chicago Press, 1980.

Locke, John. *Essay Concerning Human Understanding.* Edited by A. C. Fraser. New York: Dover, 1959.

Loewenberg, Ina. "Identifying Metaphors." *Foundations of Language* 12 (1975):315-338.

McCall, Marsh. *Ancient Rhetorical Theories of Simile and Comparison.* Cambridge, Mass.: Harvard Unversity Press, 1969.

MacCormac, Earl. *Metaphor and Myth in Science and Religion.* Durham, N.C.: Duke University Press, 1976.

Manns, James. "Metaphor and Paraphrase." *British Journal of Aesthetics* 15, no. 4 (1975): 358-366.

Matthews, Robert J. "Concerning a 'Linguistic Theory' of Metaphor." *Foundations of Language* 7 (1971):413-425.

Mill, John Stuart. *A System of Logic Ratiocinative and Inductive.* Edited by J. M. Robson. Toronto: University of Toronto Press, 1974.

Nietzsche, Frederick. "On Truth and Falsity in their Ultramoral Sense" (1873). In *The Complete Works of Frederick Nietzsche,* edited by Oscar Levy, translated by Maximilian A. Magge. New York: Gordon Press, 1974.

Ogden, C. K., and Richards, I. A. *The Meaning of Meaning.* 8th ed. New York: Harcourt, Brace, and Co., 1946.

Ortony, Andrew, ed. *Metaphor and Thought.* Cambridge: Cambridge University Press, 1979.

Peckham, Morse. "Metaphor: A Little Plain Speaking on a Weary Subject." In *The Triumph of Romanticism,* pp. 401-420. Columbia, S.C.: University of South Carolina Press, 1970.

Plato. *Phaedrus.* Translated by R. Hackforth. In *The Collected Dialogues of Plato,* edited by Edith Hamilton and Huntington Cairns. Princeton: Princeton University Press, 1961.

————. *Republic.* Translated by Paul Shorey. In *The Collected Dialogues of Plato,* edited by Edith Hamilton and Huntington Cairns. Princeton: Princeton University Press, 1961.

Quine, W. V. O. "A Postscript on Metaphor." *Critical Inquiry* 5, no. 1 (1978):161-162.

Quintilian. *Institutio Oratoria.* Translated by H. E. Butler. In *The Institutio Oratoria of Quintilian.* Cambridge, Mass.: Harvard University Press, 1953.

Richards, I. A. *The Philosophy of Rhetoric.* Oxford: Oxford University Press, 1936.

Ricoeur, Paul. "The Metaphorical Process as Cognition, Imagination, and Feeling." *Critical Inquiry* 5, no. 1 (1978): 143-159.

————. *The Rule of Metaphor.* Translated by Robert Czerny with Kathleen Mchaughlin and John Costello. Toronto: University of Toronto Press, 1977.

Rousseau, Jean-Jacques. *Essay on the Origin of Languages.* Translated by John H. Moran. In *On the Origin of Language,* translated by John H. Moran and Alexander Code. New York: Frederick Ungar, 1966.

Ryle, Gilbert. *The Concept of Mind.* London: Hutchinson's University Library, 1949.

Searle, John R. "Metaphor." In *Expression and Meaning,* pp. 76-116. Cambridge: Cambridge University Press, 1979.

Turbayne, Colin. *The Myth of Metaphor.* Columbia, S.C.: University of South Carolina Press, 1970.

Warner, Martin. "Black's Metaphors." *British Journal of Aesthetics* 13, no. 4 (1973):367-372.

Wittgenstein, Ludwig. *Philosophical Investigations.* Translated by G. E. M. Anscombe. Oxford, 1953.

Yoos, George. "A Phenomenological Look at Metaphor." *Philosophy and Phenomenological Research* 32, no. 1 (1971):78-88.

The Philosophy of Rhetoric

I. A. Richards

Lecture V
Metaphor

It was Aristotle, no lesser man, who said, in *The Poetics,* "The greatest thing by far is to have a command of metaphor." But he went on to say, "This alone cannot be imparted to another: it is the mark of genius, for to make good metaphors implies an eye for resemblances." I do not know how much influence this remark has had: or whether it is at all responsible for our feeling that what it says is commonsense. But question it for a moment and we can discover in it, if we will to be malicious, here at the very beginning of the subject, the evil presence of three of the assumptions which have ever since prevented the study of this 'greatest thing by far' from taking the place it deserves among our studies and from advancing, as theory and practice, in the ways open to it.

One assumption is that 'an eye for resemblances' is a gift that some men have but others have not. But we all live, and speak, only through our eye for resemblances. Without it we should perish early. Though some may have better eyes than others, the differences between them are in degree only and may be remedied, certainly in some measure, as other differences are, by the right kinds of teaching and study. The second assumption denies this and holds that, though everything else may be taught, "This alone cannot be imparted to another." I cannot guess how seriously Aristotle meant this or what other subjects of teaching he had in mind as he spoke. But, if we consider how we all of us attain what limited measure of a command of metaphor we possess, we shall see that no such contrast is valid. As individuals we gain our command of metaphor just as we learn whatever else makes us distinctively human. It is all imparted to us from others, with and through the language we learn, language which is utterly unable to aid us except through the command of metaphor which it gives. And that brings up the third and worst assumption—that metaphor is something special and exceptional in the use of language, a deviation from its normal mode of working, instead of the omnipresent principle of all its free action.

Throughout the history of Rhetoric, metaphor has been treated as a sort of happy extra trick with words, an opportunity to exploit the accidents of their versatility, something in place occasionally but requiring unusual skill and caution. In brief, a grace or ornament or *added* power of language, not its constitutive form. Sometimes, it is true, a writer will venture on speculations that go deeper. I have just been echoing Shelley's observation that "Language is vitally metaphorical. That is, it marks the before unapprehended relations of things and perpetuates their apprehension, until words, which represent them, become, through time, signs for portions or classes of thought instead of pictures of integral thoughts: and then, if no new poets should arise to create afresh the associations which have been thus disorganised, language will be dead to all the nobler purposes of human intercourse." But that is an exceptional utterance and its implications have not yet been taken account of by rhetoricians. Nor have philosophers, as a body, done much better, though historians of language have long taught that we can find no word or description for any of the intellectual operations which, if its history is known, is not seen to have been taken, by metaphor, from a description of some physical happening. Only Jeremy Bentham, as successor to Bacon and Hobbes, insisted—with his technique of archetypation and phraseoplerosis—upon one inference that might be drawn; namely, that the mind and all its doings are fictions. He left it to Coleridge,

F. H. Bradley and Vaihinger to point to the further inference; namely, that matter and its adventures, and all the derivative objects of contemplation, are fictions too, of varied rank because of varied service.

I have glanced for a moment at these deep waters into which a serious study of metaphor may plunge us, because possibly fear of them may be one cause why the study has so often not been enterprising and why Rhetoric traditionally has limited its inquiry to relatively superficial problems. But we shall not advance in even these surface problems unless we are ready to explore, as best we can, the depths of verbal interaction which give rise to them.

That metaphor is the omnipresent principle of language can be shown by mere observation. We cannot get through three sentences of ordinary fluid discourse without it, as you will be noticing throughout this lecture. Even in the rigid language of the settled sciences we do not eliminate or prevent it without great difficulty. In the semi-technicalised subjects, in aesthetics, politics, sociology, ethics, psychology, theory of language and so on, our constant chief difficulty is to discover how we are using it and how our supposedly fixed words are shifting their senses. In philosophy, above all, we can take no step safely without an unrelaxing awareness of the metaphors we, and our audience, may be employing; and though we may pretend to eschew them, we can attempt to do so only by detecting them. And this is the more true, the more severe and abstract the philosophy is. As it grows more abstract we think increasingly by means of metaphors that we profess *not* to be relying on. The metaphors we are avoiding steer our thought as much as those we accept. So it must be with any utterance for which it is less easy to know what we are saying than what we are not saying. And in philosophy, of which this is almost a definition, I would hold with Bradley that our pretence to do without metaphor is never more than a bluff waiting to be called. But if that is a truth, it is easier to utter than to accept with its consequences or to remember.

The view that metaphor is omnipresent in speech can be recommended theoretically. If you recall what I tried to say in my Second Lecture about the context theorem of meaning; about meaning as the delegated efficacy of signs by which they bring together into new unities the abstracts, or aspects, which are the missing parts of their various contexts, you will recollect some insistence that a word is normally a substitute for (or means) not one discrete past impression but a combination of general aspects. Now that is itself a summary account of the principle of metaphor. In the simplest formulation, when we use a metaphor we have two thoughts of different things active together and supported by a single word, or phrase, whose meaning is a resultant of their interaction.

"As to metaphorical expression," said Dr. Johnson, "that is a great excellence in style, when it is used with propriety, for it gives you two ideas for one." He is keeping, you see, to the limited traditional view of metaphor. As to the excellence of a style that gives you two ideas for one, that depends on what the two ideas do to one another, or conjointly do for us. We find, of course, when we look closer that there is an immense variety in these modes of interaction between co-present thoughts, as I will call them, or, in terms of the context theorem, between different missing parts or aspects of the different contexts of a word's meaning. In practice, we distinguish with marvelous skill between these modes of interaction, though our skill varies. The Elizabethans, for example, were far more widely skilled in the use of metaphor—both in utterance and in interpretation—than we are. A fact which made Shakespeare possible. The 18th Century narrowed its skill down, defensively, to certain modes only. The early 19th Century revolted against this and specialized in other modes. The later 19th Century and my generation have been recovering from these two specializations. That, I suggest, is a way of reformulating the Classic-Romantic antithesis which it would be interesting to try out.

But it could not be tried out without a better developed theory of metaphor than is yet available. The traditional theory noticed only a few of the modes of metaphor; and limited its application of the term *metaphor* to a few of them only. And thereby it made metaphor seem to be a verbal matter, a shifting and displacement of words, whereas fundamentally it is a borrowing between and intercourse of *thoughts,* a transaction between contexts. *Thought* is metaphoric, and proceeds by comparison, and the metaphors of language derive therefrom. To improve the theory of metaphor we must remember this. And the method is to take more note of the skill in thought which we possess and are intermittently aware of already. We must translate more of our skill into discussable science. Reflect better upon what we do already so cleverly. Raise our implicit recognitions into explicit distinctions.

As we do so we find that all the questions that matter in literary history and criticism take on a new interest and a wider relevance to human needs. In asking how language works we ask about how thought and feeling and all the other modes of the mind's activity proceed, about how we are to learn to live and how that "greatest thing of all," a command of metaphor—which is great only because it is a command of life—may best, in spite of Aristotle, "be imparted to another." But to profit we must remember, with Hobbes, that "the scope of all speculation is the performance of some action or thing to be done" and, with Kant, that—"We can by no means require of the pure practical reason to be subordinated to the speculative, and thus to reverse the order, since every interest is at least practical, and even that of the speculative reason is but conditional, and is complete only in its practical use." Our theory, as it has its roots in practice, must also have its fruit in improved skill. "I am the child," says the Sufi mystic, "whose father is his son, and the wine whose vine is its jar," summing up so the whole process of that meditation which does not forget what it is really about.

This much has been an introduction or preparation to put the theory of metaphor in a more important place than it has enjoyed in traditional Rhetoric. It is time to come down from these high speculations to consider some simple steps in analysis which may make the translation of our skill with metaphor into explicit science easier. A first step is to introduce two technical terms to assist us in distinguishing from one another what Dr. Johnson called the two ideas that any metaphor, at its simplest, gives us. Let me call them the tenor and the vehicle. One of the oddest of the many odd things about the whole topic is that we have no agreed distinguishing terms for these two halves of a metaphor—in spite of the immense convenience, almost the necessity, of such terms if we are to make any analyses without confusion. For the whole task is to compare the different relations which, in different cases, these two members of a metaphor hold to one another, and we are confused at the start if we do not know which of the two we are talking about. At present we have only some clumsy descriptive phrases with which to separate them. 'The original idea' and 'the borrowed one'; 'what is really being said or thought of' and 'what it is compared to'; 'the underlying idea' and 'the imagined nature'; 'the principal subject' and 'what it resembles' or, still more confusing, simply 'the meaning' and 'the metaphor' or 'the idea' and 'its image.'

How confusing these must be is easily seen, and experience with the analysis of metaphors fully confirms the worst expectations. We need the word 'metaphor' for the whole double unit, and to use it sometimes for one of the two components in separation from the other is as injudicious as that other trick by which we use 'the meaning' here sometimes for the work that the whole double unit does and sometimes for the other component—the tenor, as I am calling it—the underlying idea or principal subject which the vehicle or figure means. It is not surprising that the detailed analysis of metaphors, if we attempt it with such slippery terms as these, sometimes feels like extracting cube-roots in the head. Or, to make a more exact comparison, what would the most elementary arithmetic feel like, if we used the word *twelve* (12) sometimes for the number one (1), sometimes for the number two (2) and sometimes for the number twenty-one (21) as well, and had somehow to remember, or see, unassisted by our notation, which uses we were making of it at different places in our calculations? All these words, *meaning, expression, metaphor, comparison, subject, figure, image*, behave so, and when we recognize this we need look no further for a part, at least, of the explanation of the backward state of the study. Why rhetoricians have not long ago remedied this defect of language for their purpose, would perhaps be a profitable matter for reflection. I do not know a satisfactory answer. As the best teacher I ever knew, G. E. Moore, once remarked, "Why we should use the same form of verbal expression to convey such different meanings is more than I can say. It seems to me very curious that language should have grown up as if it were expressly designed to mislead philosophers; and I do not know why it should have."

The words 'figure' and 'image' are especially and additionally misleading here. They both sometimes stand for the whole double unit and sometimes for one member of it, the vehicle, as opposed to the other. But in addition they bring in a confusion with the sense in which an image is a copy or revival of a sense-perception of some sort, and so have made rhetoricians think that a figure of speech, an image, or imaginative comparison, must have something to do with the presence of images, in this other sense, in the mind's eye or the mind's ear. But, of course, it need not. No images of this sort need come in at any point. We had one instance of the vicious influence of this red-herring in my first lecture—Lord Kames' antic with the mental picture he supposed we must form of Shakespeare's peacock-feather. Whole schools of rhetoric and criticism have gone astray after it. Lessing's discussion of the relations of the arts, for example, is grievously spoilt by it. We cannot too firmly recognize that how a figure of speech works has nothing necessarily to do with how any images, as copies or duplicates of sense perceptions, may, for reader or writer, be backing up his words. In special cases for certain readers they may come in—then is a long chapter of individual psychology which is relevent here. But the words can do almost anything without them, and we must put no assumption about their necessary presence into our general theory.

I can illustrate both the convenience of such technical terms as *tenor* and *vehicle* and the evil influence of the imagery assumption, with another citation from Lord Kames, from Chapter 20, paragraph 6, of his *Elements of Criticism.* You will see from the very difficulty of making out just what he is saying, how much we need rigid technicalities here. His point is, I think, evidently mistaken; but before we can be satisfied that it is mistaken, we have to be certain what it is; and what I want first to direct your attention upon is the clumsy and distracting language in which he has to state it. He is preparing to set up a rule to be observed by writers in 'constructing a metaphor.' He says, "In the fourth place, the comparison . . . being in a metaphor sunk by imagining the principal subject to be that very thing which it only resembles; an opportunity is furnished to describe it (i.e., the principal subject) in terms taken strictly or literally with respect to its imagined nature."

To use my proposed terms—we can describe or qualify the tenor by describing the vehicle. He goes on, "This suggests another rule: That in constructing a metaphor, the writer ought to make use of such words only as are applicable literally to the imagined nature of his subject." That is, he must not use any further metaphor in describing the vehicle. "Figurative words," he says "ought carefully to be avoided; for such complicated figures, instead of setting the principal subject in a strong light, involve it in a cloud; and it is well if the reader, without rejecting by the lump, endeavour patiently to gather the plain meaning, regardless of the figures.''

Let me invite you to consider what is being done here very carefully, for it illustrates, I believe, most of the things which have made the traditional studies of metaphor not very profitable. And notice first how it shows the 18th Century assumptions that figures are a mere embellishment or added beauty and that the plain meaning, the tenor, is what alone really matters and is something that, 'regardless of the figures,' might be gathered by the patient reader.

A modern theory would object, first, that in many of the most important uses of metaphor, the co-presence of the vehicle and tenor results in a meaning (to be clearly distinguished from the tenor) which is not attainable without their interaction. That the vehicle is not normally a mere embellishment of a tenor which is otherwise unchanged by it but that vehicle and tenor in co-operation give a meaning of more varied powers than can be ascribed to either. And a modern theory would go on to point out that with different metaphors the relative importance of the contributions of vehicle and tenor to this resultant meaning varies immensely. At one extreme the vehicle may become almost a mere decoration or coloring of the tenor, at the other extreme, the tenor may become almost a mere excuse for the introduction of the vehicle, and so no longer be 'the principal subject.' And the degree to which the tenor is imagined "to be that very thing which it only resembles" also varies immensely.

These are differences I return to next week. Let us study Lord Kames a little longer first: How about this suggested rule that we should carefully avoid mounting metaphor upon metaphor? What would be the effect of taking it seriously? It would, if we accepted and observed it, make havoc of most writing and speech. It is disregarding—under cover of the convenient excuse that they are dead—the most regular sustaining metaphors of all speech. It would make, I think, Shakespeare the faultiest writer who ever held a pen; and it turns an obstinately blind eye upon one of the most obvious features of current practice in every minute of our speech. Look, for example, at Lord Kames' own sentence. "Such complicated figures, instead of setting the principal subject in a strong light, involve it in a cloud." What about that 'strong' light? The light is a vehicle and is described—with-

out anyone experiencing the least difficulty—by a secondary metaphor, a figurative word. But you may say, "No! *Strong* is no longer
a figurative word as applied to light. It is as literally descriptive of light
as it is of a man or a horse. It carries not two ideas but one only. It
has become 'adequated,' or is dead, and is no longer a metaphor." But
however stone dead such metaphors seem, we can easily wake them up,
and, if Kames were right, to wake them up would be to risk involving
the tenor in a cloud, and nothing of the sort happens. This favourite
old distinction between dead and living metaphors (itself a two-fold
metaphor) is, indeed, a device which is very often a hindrance to the
play of sagacity and discernment throughout the subject. For serious
purposes it needs a drastic re-examination.

We are in fact immeasurably more adroit in handling complicated
metaphors than Kames will allow us to be. He gives an example of a
breach of his rule which is worth examining if only to show how
easily a theory can paralyse normal aptitude in such things. He takes
these two lines

> A stubborn and unconquerable flame
> Creeps in his veins and drinks the streams of life.

"Let us analyse this expression," he says. "That a fever may be
imagined a flame, I admit; though more than one step is necessary to
come at the resemblance." I, for my part, would have supposed, on
the contrary, that we could hardly find a simpler transference, since
both a fever and a flame are instances of a rise in temperature! But
he goes on to detail these steps. "A fever by heating the body, resembles fire; and it is no stretch to imagine a fever to be a fire. Again,
by a figure of speech, flame may be put for fire, because they are
commonly conjoined; and therefore a fever may be termed a flame.
But now, admitting a fever to be a flame, its effects ought to be explained in words that agree literally to a flame. This rule is not observed here; for a flame drinks figuratively only, not properly."

Well and good! But who, for all that, has any difficulty in understanding the lines? The interactions of tenor and vehicle are not in
the least hampered by the secondary vehicle.

I have taken this instance of vain pedantry chiefly to accustom
you to my use of these technical terms, but partly too to support the
contention that the best part of the traditional discussion of meta-

phor is hardly more than a set of cautionary hints to over-enthusiastic schoolboys, hints masquerading as fundamental theory of language. Lord Kames is not exceptionally limited in his treatment or abnormally obtuse. You will find similar things in Johnson when he discusses Cowley and Donne for example, in Monboddoe, and Harris and Withers, and Campbell, in all the chief 18th Century Rhetoricians.

Not until Coleridge do we get any adequate setting of these chief problems of language. But Coleridge's thought has not even yet come into its own. And, after Coleridge, in spite of the possibilities which he opened, there was a regrettable slackening of interest in the questions. The 18th Century was mistaken in the way it put them and in the technique it attempted to use, but it at least knew that they were important questions and that there is unlimited work to be done upon them. And so Lord Kames' *Elements of Criticism,* though I may seem to have been making fun of it in places, and though it is so full of similar things as to be most absorbing reading, is still a very valuable and instructive book offering a model not only of misconceptions to be avoided but of problems to be taken up, reframed and carried forward. Turning his pages you will again and again find points raised, which, if his treatment of them is unsatisfactory, are none the less points that no serious study of language should neglect. One such will serve me as a peg for a pair of warnings or morals of which any ambitious attempt to analyse metaphors is constantly in need.

Kames quotes from *Othello* the single line

> Steep'd me in poverty to the very lips

and comments, "The resemblance is too faint to be agreeable—Poverty must here be conceived to be a fluid which it resembles not in any manner." Let us look at Othello's whole speech. We shall find that it is not an easy matter to explain or justify that "steep'd.' It comes, you will recall, when Othello first openly charged Desdemona with unfaithfulness,

> Had it pleas'd heaven
> To try me with affliction, had he rain'd
> All kinds of sores, and shames, on my bare head,
> Steep'd me in poverty to the very lips,
> Given to captivity me and my utmost hopes,

I should have found in some part of my soul
A drop of patience; but alas! to make me
The fixed figure for the time of scorn
To point his slow and moving finger at;
Yet could I bear that too; well, very well.
But there, where I have garner'd up my heart,
Where either I must live or bear no life,
The fountain from the which my current runs,
Or else dries up; to be discarded thence!
Or keep it as a cistern for foul toads
To knot and gender in!

What are we to say of that word *steep*, how answer Kames? He is indeed too mild, in saying "the resemblance is too faint to be agreeable." It's not a case of lack of resemblance but of too much diversity, too much sheer oppositeness. For Poverty, the tenor, is a state of deprivation, of desiccation; but the vehicle—the sea or vat in which Othello is to be steeped—gives an instance of superfluity. In poverty all is outgoing, without income; were we "steeped to the very lips" it would be the incomings that we would have to fight against.[1] You will have noticed that the whole speech returns again and again to these liquid images: "had they rained," "a drop of patience," "The fountain from the which my current runs, Or else dries up." None of these helps *steep* out, and one of them "a drop of patience" makes the confused, disordered effect of *steep* seem much worse. I do not myself find any defence of the word except this, which seems indeed quite sufficient—as dramatic necessities commonly are—that Othello is himself horribly disordered, that the utterance is part of "the storm of horrour and outrage" with which he is assailing Desdemona and that a momentarily deranged mind speaks so and *is* obsessed with images regardless of their fittingness. Othello, we might say, is drowning in this storm, (Cf. Act II, i, 212-21) and knows it.

The morals I would point with this instances are: First, that not to see how a word *can* work is never by itself sufficient proof that it will not work. Second, conversely, that to see how it ought to work will not prove that it does. Any detailed examination of metaphor brings us into such risk of pedantry and self-persuasion, that these morals seem worth stress. Yet a critical examination of metaphor, with these morals in mind, is just now what literary criticism chiefly needs.

To come back to Kames, his objection that "the resemblance is too faint to be agreeable" (notice the amusing assumption that a writer must of course always aim to be agreeable!)—assumed that tenor and vehicle must be linked by their resemblance and that their interaction comes about through their resemblance one to another. And yet Kames himself elsewhere takes some pride, and justifiably, in pointing out a type of figure which does not depend upon resemblance but upon other relations between tenor and vehicle. He says that it has been overlooked by former writers, and that it must be distinguished from other figures as depending on a different principle.

"Giddy brink, jovial wine, daring wound are examples of this figure. Here are adjectives that cannot be made to signify any quality of the substantives to which they are joined: a *brink*, for example, cannot be termed *giddy* in a sense, either proper or figurative, that can signify any of its qualities or attributes. When we examine attentively the expression, we discover that a *brink* is termed *giddy* from producing that effect in those who stand on it. . . . How," he asks, "are we to account for this figure, which we see lies in the thought (I am not sure what *lies* means here. I think he means 'has its ground or explanation in the thought' not 'utters falsehood.') and to what principle shall we refer it? Have the poets a privilege to alter the nature of things, and at pleasure to bestow attributes upon a subject to which they do not belong?" Most moderns would say "Of course, they have!" But Kames does not take that way out. He appeals instead to a principle of contiguous association. "We have had often occasion to inculcate, that the mind passeth easily and sweetly along a train of connected objects, and, when the objects are intimately connected, that it is disposed to carry along the good or bad properties of one to another, especially when it is in any degree inflamed with these properties." He then lists eight varieties of these contiguous inflammations—without, I think, at all clearly realizing what an immense extension of the theory of possibilities of metaphoric interaction he has made with this new principle. Once we begin 'to examine attentively' interactions which do not work through *resemblances* between tenor and vehicle, but depend upon other relations

between them including *disparities,* some of our most prevalent, over-simple, ruling assumptions about metaphors as comparisons are soon exposed.

But let us take one more glance at this *giddy brink* first. Is Kames right in saying that a *brink* cannot be termed *giddy* in a sense that can signify any of its qualities or attributes? Is he right in turning *giddy* into *giddy-making*—a brink is termed giddy from producing that effect in those who stand on it"? Is it not the case that at the moment of giddiness the brink itself is perceived as swimming? As the man totters in vertigo, the world spins too and the brink becomes not merely giddy-making but actually vertiginous, seems itself to stagger with a dizziness and to whirl with a bewildering rapidity. The eyes nystagmically rolling give away their motion to the world—including the brink. Thus the brink as perceived, which is the brink that the poet is speaking of, actually itself acquires a giddiness. If so, we may doubt for a moment whether there is a metaphor here at all—until we notice how this whirling that infects the world as we grow giddy comes to it by a process which is itself radically metaphoric. Our eyes twitch, but it is the world which seems to spin. So it is with a large part, perhaps, in the final account, with *all* our perceptions. Our world is a projected world, shot through with characters lent to it from our own life. "We receive but what we give." The processes of metaphor in language, the exchanges between the meanings of words which we study in explicit verbal metaphors, are super-imposed upon a perceived world which is itself a product of earlier or unwitting metaphor, and we shall not deal with them justly if we forget that this is so. That is why, if we are to take the theory of metaphor further than the 18th Century took it, we must have some general theorem of meaning. And since it was Coleridge who saw most deeply and clearly into this necessity, and, with his theory of the imagination, has done most to supply it, I may fittingly close this Lecture with a passage from Appendix C of *The Statesman's Manual,* in which Coleridge is stating that theory symbolically.

A symbol, for him, is a translucent instance, which "while it enunciates the whole, abides itself as a living part of that unity of which it is the representative." So here he takes the vegetable kingdom, or any plant, as an object of meditation through and in which to see the universal mode of imagination—of those metaphoric exchanges by which the individual life and its world grow together. If we can follow the meditation we are led, I believe, to Coleridge's conception of imaginative growth more easily and safely than by any other road. For, as the plant here is a symbol, in his sense, of all growth, so the passage too is itself a symbol, a translucent instance of imagination.

He has been speaking of the book of Nature that "has been the music of gentle and pious minds in all ages, it is the poetry of all human nature, to read it likewise in a figurative sense, and to find therein correspondences and symbols of the spiritual world.

"I have at this moment before me, in the flowery meadow, on which my eye is now reposing, one of its most soothing chapters, in which there is no lamenting word, no one character of guilt or anguish. For never can I look and meditate on the vegetable creation, without a feeling similar to that with which we gaze at a beautiful infant that has fed itself asleep at its mother's bosom, and smiles in its strange dream of obscure yet happy sensations. The same tender and genial pleasure takes possession of me, and this pleasure is checked and drawn inward by the like aching melancholy, by the same whispered remonstrance, and made restless by a similar impulse of aspiration. It seems as if the soul said to herself: From this state hast *thou* fallen! Such shouldst thou still become, thy Self all permeable to a holier power! thy self at once hidden and glorified by its own transparency, as the accidental and dividuous in this quiet and harmonious object is subjected to the life and light of nature which shines in it, even as the transmitted power, love and wisdom, of God over all, fills and shines through nature! But what the plant is, by an act not its own and unconsciously—that must thou make thyself to become! must by prayer and by a watchful and unresisting spirit, join at least with the preventive and assisting grace to make thyself, in that light of conscience which inflameth not, and with that knowledge which puffeth not up!

"But further . . . I seem to myself to behold in the quiet objects on which I am gazing, more than an arbitrary illustration, more than a mere simile, the work of my own fancy. I feel an awe, as if there were before my eyes the same power as that of the reason—the same power in a lower dignity, and therefore a symbol established in the truth of things. I feel it alike, whether I contemplate a single tree or flower, or meditate on vegetation throughout the world, as one of the great organs of the life of nature. Lo!—with the rising sun it commences its outward life and enters into open communion with all the elements at once assimilating them to itself and to each other. At the same moment it strikes its roots and unfolds its leaves, absorbs and respires, steams forth its cooling vapour and finer fragrance, and breathes a repairing spirit, at once the food and tone of the atmosphere, into the atmosphere that feeds *it*. Lo!—at the touch of light how it returns an air akin to light, and yet with the same pulse effectuates its own secret growth, still contracting to fix what expanding it had refined. Lo!—how upholding the ceaseless plastic motion of the parts in the profoundest rest of the whole, it becomes the visible *organismus* of the whole silent or elementary life of nature and therefore, in incorporating the one extreme becomes the symbol of the other; the natural symbol of that higher life of reason."

What Coleridge has here said of this "open communion" is true also of the word—in the free metaphoric discursive sentence. "Are not words," he had asked nineteen years before, "Are not words parts and germinations of the plant?"

NOTES

1. In the partly parallel 'And steep my senses in forgetfulness' (*Henry IV*, P. II, III, i) Lethe, by complicating the metaphor, removes the difficulty.

Metaphor

Max Black

> "Metaphors are no arguments, my pretty maiden."
> (*The Fortunes of Nigel,* Book 2, Ch. 2.)

To draw attention to a philosopher's metaphors is to belittle him —like praising a logician for his beautiful handwriting. Addiction to metaphor is held to be illicit, on the principle that whereof one can speak only metaphorically, thereof one ought not to speak at all. Yet the nature of the offence is unclear. I should like to do something to dispel the mystery that invests the topic; but since philosophers (for all their notorious interest in language) have so neglected the subject, I must get what help I can from the literary critics. They, at least, do not accept the commandment, "Thou shalt not commit metaphor", or assume that metaphor is incompatible with serious thought.

I

The questions I should like to see answered concern the "logical grammar" of "metaphor" and words having related meanings. It would be satisfactory to have convincing answers to the questions:

Reprinted from *Proceedings of the Aristotelian Society*, N.S. 55 (1954-55): 273-294 by courtesy of the author and the Editor of The Aristotelian Society. © 1955 The Aristotelian Society.

"How do we recognize a case of metaphor?", "Are there any criteria for the detection of metaphors?", "Can metaphors be translated into literal expressions?", "Is metaphor properly regarded as a decoration upon 'plain sense'?", "What are the relations between metaphor and simile?", "In what sense, if any, is a metaphor 'creative'?", "What is the point of using a metaphor?". (Or, more briefly, "What do we *mean* by 'metaphor'?." The questions express attempts to become clearer about some uses of the word "metaphor"—or, if one prefers the material mode, to analyze the notion of metaphor.)

The list is not a tidy one, and several of the questions overlap in fairly obvious ways. But I hope they will sufficiently illustrate the type of inquiry that is intended.

It would be helpful to be able to start from some agreed list of "clear cases" of metaphor. Since the word "metaphor" has some intelligible uses, however vague or vacillating, it must be possible to construct such a list. Presumably, it should be easier to agree whether any given item should be included than to agree about any proposed analysis of the notion of metaphor.

Perhaps the following list of examples, chosen not altogether at random, might serve:—

   (i) "The chairman ploughed through the discussion."
   (ii) "A smoke-screen of witnesses."
   (iii) "An argumentative melody."
   (iv) "Blotting-paper voices" (Henry James).
   (v) "The poor are the negroes of Europe" (Baudelaire).
   (vi) "Light is but the shadow of God" (Sir Thomas Browne).
   (vii) "Oh dear white children, casual as birds.
        Playing amid the ruined languages" (Auden).

I hope all these will be accepted as unmistakeable *instances* of metaphor, whatever judgements may ultimately be made about the meaning of "metaphor". The examples are offered as clear cases of metaphor, but, with the possible exception of the first, they would be unsuitable as "paradigms". If we wanted to teach the meaning of "metaphor" to a child, we should need simpler examples, like "The clouds are crying" or "The branches are fighting with one another". (Is it significant that one hits upon examples of personification?) But I have tried to include some reminders of the possible complexities that even relatively straightforward metaphors may generate.

Consider the first example—"The chairman ploughed through the discussion". An obvious point to begin with is the contrast between the word "ploughed" and the remaining words by which it is accompanied. This would be commonly expressed by saying that "ploughed" has here a metaphorical sense, while the other words have literal senses. Though we point to the whole sentence as an instance (a "clear case") of metaphor, our attention quickly narrows to a single word, whose presence is the proximate reason for the attribution. And similar remarks can be made about the next four examples in the list, the crucial words being, respectively, "smoke-screen", "argumentative", "blotting paper", and "negroes".

(But the situation is more complicated in the last two examples of the list. In the quotation from Sir Thomas Browne, "Light" must be supposed to have a symbolic sense, and certainly to mean far more than it would in the context of a text-book on optics. Here, the metaphorical sense of the expression, "the shadow of God" imposes a meaning richer than usual upon the subject of the sentence. Similar effects can be noticed in the passage from Auden (consider for instance the meaning of "white" in the first line). I shall have to neglect such complexities in this paper.)

In general, when we speak of a relatively simple metaphor, we are referring to a sentence or another expression, in which *some* words are used metaphorically, while the remainder are used non-metaphorically. An attempt to construct an entire sentence of words that are used metaphorically results in a proverb, an allegory, or a riddle. No preliminary analysis of metaphor will satisfactorily cover even such trite examples as "In the night all cows are black". And cases of symbolism (in the sense in which Kafka's castle is a "symbol") also need separate treatment.

II

"The chairman ploughed through the discussion." In calling this sentence a case of metaphor, we are implying that at least one word (here, the word "ploughed") is being used metaphorically in the sentence, and that at least one of the remaining words is being used literally. Let us call the word "ploughed" the *focus* of the metaphor, and the remainder of the sentence in which that word occurs the *frame*. (Are *we* now using metaphors—and mixed ones at that? Does it matter?) One notion that needs to be clarified is that of the "metaphorical use" of the focus of a metaphor. Among other things, it would be good to understand how the presence of one frame can result in metaphorical use of the complementary word, while the presence of a different frame for the same word fails to result in metaphor.

If the sentence about the chairman's behaviour is translated word for word into any foreign language for which this is possible, we shall of course want to say that the translated sentence is a case of the *very same* metaphor. So, to call a sentence an instance of metaphor is to say something about its *meaning*, not about is orthography, its phonetic pattern, or its grammatical form.[1] (To use a well-known distinction, "metaphor" must be classified as a term belonging to "semantics" and not to "syntax"—or to any *physical* inquiry about language.)

Suppose somebody says, "I like to plough my memories regularly". Shall we say he is using the same metaphor as in the case already discussed, or not? Our answer will depend upon the degree of similarity we are prepared to affirm on comparing the two "frames" (for we have the same "focus" each time). Differences in the two frames will produce *some* differences in the interplay[2] between focus and frame in the two cases. Whether we regard the differences as sufficiently striking to warrant calling the sentences *two* metaphors is a matter for arbitrary decision. "Metaphor" is a loose word, at best, and we must beware of attributing to it stricter rules of usage than are actually found in practice.

So far, I have been treating "metaphor" as a predicate properly applicable to certain expressions, without attention to any such occasions on which the expressions are used, or to the thoughts, acts, feelings, and intentions of speakers upon such occasions. And this is surely correct for *some* expressions. We recognize that to call a man a "cesspool" is to use a metaphor, without needing to know who uses the expression, or on what occasions, or with what intention. The rules of our language determine that some expressions must count as metaphors; and a speaker can no more change this than he can legislate that "cow" shall mean the same as "sheep". But we must also recognize that the established rules of language leave wide latitude for individual variation, initiative, and creation. There are indefinitely many contexts (including nearly all the interesting ones) where the meaning of a metaphorical expression has to be reconstructed from the speaker's intentions (and other clues) because the broad rules of standard usage are too general to supply the information needed. When Churchill, in a famous phrase, called Mussolini "that *utensil*", the tone of voice, the verbal setting, the historical background, helped to make clear *what* metaphor was being used. (Yet, even here, it is hard to see how the phrase "that utensil" could ever be applied to a man except as an insult. Here, as elsewhere, the general rules of usage function as limitations upon the speaker's freedom to mean whatever he pleases.) This is an example, though still a simple one, of how recognition and interpretation of a metaphor may require attention to the *particular circumstances* of its utterance.

It is especially noteworthy that there are, in general, no standard rules for the degree of *weight* or *emphasis* to be attached to a particular use of an expression. To know what the user of a metaphor means, we need to know how "seriously" he treats the metaphorical focus. (Would he be just as content to have some rough synonym, or would only *that* word serve? Are we to take the word lightly, attending only to its most obvious implications—or should we dwell upon its less immediate associations?) In speech we can use emphasis and phrasing as clues. But in written or printed discourse, even these rudimentary aids are absent. Yet this somewhat elusive "weight" of a (suspected or detected[3]) metaphor is of great practical importance in exegesis.

To take a philosophical example. Whether the expression "logical form" should be treated in a particular frame as having a metaphorical sense will depend upon the extent to which its user is taken to be conscious of some supposed analogy between arguments and other things (vases, clouds, battles, jokes) that are also said to have "form". Still more will it depend upon whether the writer wishes the analogy to be active in the minds of his readers; and how much his own thought depends upon and is nourished by the supposed analogy. We must not expect the "rules of language" to be of much help in such inquiries. (There is accordingly a sense of "metaphor" that belongs to "pragmatics", rather than to "semantics"—and this sense may be the one most deserving of attention.)

III

Let us try the simplest possible account that can be given of the meaning of "The chairman ploughed through the discussion", to see how far it will take us. A plausible commentary (for those presumably too literal-minded to understand the original) might run somewhat as follows: —

"A speaker who uses the sentence in question is taken to want to say *something* about a chairman and his behaviour in some meeting. Instead of saying, plainly or *directly*, that the chairman dealt summarily with objections, or ruthlessly suppressed irrelevance, or something of the sort, the speaker chose to use a word ('ploughed') which, strictly speaking, means something else. But an intelligent hearer can easily guess what the speaker had in mind."[4]

This account treats the metaphorical expression (let us call it " M ") as a substitute for some other literal expression (" L ", say) which would have expressed the same meaning, had it been used instead. On this view, the meaning of M, in its metaphorical occurrence, is just the *literal* meaning of L. The metaphorical use of an expression consists, on this view, of the use of that expression in other than its proper or normal sense, in some context that allows the improper or abnormal sense to be detected and appropriately transformed. (The reasons adduced for so remarkable a performance will be discussed later.)

Any view which holds that a metaphorical expression is used in place of some equivalent *literal* expression, I shall call a *substitution view of metaphor*. (I should like this label to cover also any analysis which views the entire sentence that is the locus of the metaphor as replacing some set of literal sentences.) Until recently, one or another form of a substitution view has been accepted by most writers (usually literary critics or writers of books on rhetoric) who have had anything to say about metaphor.

To take a few examples. Whately defines a metaphor as "a word substituted for another on account of the Resemblance or Analogy between their significations."[5] Nor is the entry in the Oxford Dictionary (to jump to modern times) much different from this: "Metaphor: The figure of speech in which a name or descriptive term is transferred to some object different from, but analogous to, that to which it is properly applicable; an instance of this, a metaphorical expression."[6] So strongly entrenched is the view expressed by these definitions that a recent writer who is explicitly arguing for a different and more sophisticated view of metaphor, nevertheless slips into the old fashion by defining metaphor as "saying one thing and meaning another."[7]

According to a substitution view, the focus of a metaphor, the word or expression having a distinctively metaphorical use within a literal frame, is used to communicate a meaning that might have been expressed literally. The author substitutes M for L; it is the reader's task to invert the substitution, by using the literal meaning of M as a clue to the intended literal meaning of L. Understanding a metaphor is like deciphering a code or unravelling a riddle.

If we now ask why, on this view, the writer should set his reader the task of solving a puzzle, we shall be offered two types of answer. The first is that there may, in fact be no literal equivalent, L, available in the language in question. Mathematicians spoke of the "leg" of an angle because there was no brief literal expression for a bounding line; we say "cherry lips", because there is no form of words half as convenient for saying quickly what the lips are like. Metaphor plugs the gaps in the literal vocabulary (or, at least, supplies the want of convenient abbreviations). So viewed, metaphor is a species of *catachresis*, which I shall define as the use of a word in some new sense in order to remedy a gap in the vocabulary. Catachresis is the putting of new senses into old words.[8] But if a catachresis serves a genuine need, the new sense introduced will quickly become part of the *literal* sense. "Orange" may originally have been applied to the colour by catachresis; but the word is now applied to the colour just as "properly" (and unmetaphorically) as to the fruit. "Osculating" curves don't kiss for long, and quickly revert to a more prosaic mathematical contact. And similarly for other cases. It is the fate of catachresis to disppear when it is successful.

There are, however, many metaphors where the virtues ascribed to catachresis cannot apply, because there is, or there is supposed to be, some readily available and equally compendious literal equivalent. Thus in the somewhat unfortunate example,[9] "Richard is a lion", which modern writers have discussed with boring insistence, the literal meaning is taken to be the same as that of the sentence, "Richard is brave".[10] Here, the metaphor is not supposed to enrich the vocabulary.

When catachresis cannot be invoked, the reasons for substituting an indirect, metaphorical, expression are taken to be stylistic. We are told that the metaphorical expression may (in its literal use) refer to a more concrete object than would its literal equivalent; and this is supposed to give pleasure to the reader (the pleasure of having one's thoughts diverted from Richard to the irrelevant lion). Again, the reader is taken to enjoy problem-solving—or to delight in the author's skill at half-concealing, half-revealing his meaning. Or metaphors provide a shock of "agreeable surprise"—and so on. The principle behind these "explanations" seems to be: When in doubt about some pecularity of language, attribute its existence to the pleasure it gives a reader. A principle that has the merit of working well in default of any evidence.[11]

Whatever the merits of such speculations about the reader's response, they agree in making metaphor a *decoration*. Except in cases where a metaphor is a catachresis that remedies some temporary imperfection of literal language, the purpose of metaphor is to entertain and divert. Its use, on this view, always constitutes a deviation from the "plain and strictly appropriate style" (Whately).[12] So, if philosophers have something more important to do than give pleasure to their readers, metaphor can have no serious place in philosophical discussion.

IV

The view that a metaphorical expression has a meaning that is some transform of its normal literal meaning is a special case of a more general view about "figurative" language. This holds that any figure of speech involving semantic change (and not merely syntactic change, like inversion of normal word order) consists in some transformation of a *literal* meaning. The author provides, not his intended meaning, m, but some function thereof, $f(m)$; the readers task is to apply the inverse function, f^{-1}, and so to obtain $f^{-1}(f(m))$, i.e., m, the original meaning. When different functions are used, different tropes result. Thus, in irony, the author says the *opposite* of what he means; in hyperbole, he *exaggerates* his meaning; and so on.

What, then, is the characteristic transforming function involved in metaphor? To this the answer has been made: either *analogy* or *similarity*. *M* is either similar or analogous in meaning to its literal equivalent *L*. Once the reader has detected the ground of the intended analogy or simile (with the help of the frame, or clues drawn from the wider context) he can retrace the author's path and so reach the original literal meaning (the meaning of *L*).

If a writer holds that a metaphor consists in the *presentation* of the underlying analogy or similarity, he will be taking what I shall call a *comparison view* of metaphor. When Schopenhauer called a geometrical proof a mousetrap, he was, according to such a view, *saying* (though not explicitly): "A geometrical proof is *like* a mousetrap, since both offer a delusive reward, entice their victims by degrees, lead to disagreeable surprise, etc." This is a view of metaphor as a condensed or elliptical *simile*. It will be noticed that a "comparison view" is a special case of a "substitution view." For it holds that the metaphorical statement might be replaced by an equivalent literal *comparison*.

Whately says: "The Simile or Comparison may be considered as differing in form only from a Metaphor; the resemblance being in that case *stated*, which in the Metaphor is implied".[13] Bain says that "The metaphor is a comparison implied in the mere use of a term" and adds, "It is in the circumstance of being confined to a word, or at most to a phrase, that we are to look for the pecularities of the metaphor—its advantages on the one hand, and its dangers and abuses on the other".[14] This view of the metaphor, as condensed simile or comparison, has been very popular.

The chief difference between a substitution view (of the sort previously considered) and the special form of it that I have called a comparison view may be illustrated by the stock example of "Richard is a lion". On the first view, the sentence means approximately the same as "Richard is brave"; on the second, approximately the same as "Richard is *like* a lion (in being brave)", the added words in brackets being understood but not explicitly stated. In the second translation, as in the first, the metaphorical statement is taken to be standing in place of some *literal* equivalent. But the comparison view provides a more elaborate paraphrase, inasmuch as the original statement is interpreted as being about lions as well as about Richard.[15]

The main objection against a comparison view is that it suffers from a vagueness that borders upon vacuity. We are supposed to be puzzled as to how some expression (*M*), used metaphorically, can function in place of some literal expression (*L*) that is held to be an approximate synonym; and the answer offered is that what *M* stands for (in its literal use) is *similar* to what *L* stands for. But how informative is this? There is some temptation to think of similarities as "objectively given", so that a question of the form, "Is *A* like *B* in respect of *P*?" has a definite and predetermined answer. If this were so, similes might be governed by rules as strict as those controlling the statements of physics. But likeness always admits of degrees, so that a truly "objective" question would need to take some such form as "Is *A* more like *B* than like *C* in respect of *P*?"—or, perhaps, "Is *A* closer to *B* than to *C* on such and such a scale of degrees of *P*?" Yet, in proportion as we approach such forms, metaphorical statements lose their effectiveness and their point. We need the metaphors in just the cases when there can be no question as yet of the precision of scientific statement. Metaphorical statement is not a substitute for a formal comparison or any other kind of literal statement, but has its own *distinctive* capacities and achievements. Often we say, "*X* is *M*", evoking some imputed connexion between *M* and an imputed *L* (or, rather, to an indefinite system, L_1, L_2, L_3, . . .) in cases where, prior to the construction of the metaphor, we would have been hard put to it to find any *literal* resemblance between *M* and *L*. It would be more illuminating in some of these cases to say that the metaphor *creates* the similarity than to say that it formulates some similarity antecedently existing.[16]

V

I turn now to consider a type of analysis which I shall call an *interaction view* of metaphor. This seems to me to be free from the main defects of substitution and comparison views and to offer some important insight into the uses and limitations of metaphor.[17]

Let us begin with the following statement: "In the simplest formulation, when we use a metaphor we have two thoughts of different things active together and supported by a single word, or phrase, whose meaning is a resultant of their interaction."[18]

We may discover what is here intended by applying Richard's remark to our earlier example, "The poor are the negroes of Europe".

The substitution view, at its crudest, tells us that something is being *indirectly* said about the poor of Europe. (But what? That they are an oppressed class, a standing reproach to the community's official ideals, that poverty is inherited and indelible?) The comparison view claims that the epigram *presents* some comparison between the poor and the negroes. In opposition to both, Richards says that our "thoughts" about European poor and (American) negroes are "active together" and "interact" to produce a meaning that is a resultant of that interaction.

I think that this must mean that in the given context the focal word "negroes" obtains a *new* meaning, which is *not* quite its meaning in literal uses, nor quite the meaning which any literal substitute would have. The new context (the "frame" of the metaphor, in my terminology) imposes *extension* of meaning upon the focal word. And I take Richards to be saying that for the metaphor to work the reader must remain aware of the extension of meaning—must attend to both the old and the new meanings together.[19]

But how is this extension or change of meaning brought about? At one point, Richards speaks of the "common characteristics" of the two terms (the poor and negroes) as "the ground of the metaphor" (*op. cit.*, p. 117), so that in its metaphorical use a word or expression must connote only a *selection* from the characteristics connoted in its literal uses. This, however, seems a rare lapse into the older and less sophisticated analyses he is trying to supersede.[20] He is on firmer ground when he says that the reader is forced to "connect" the two ideas (p. 125). In this "connexion" resides the secret and the mystery of metaphor. To speak of the "interaction" of two thoughts "active together" (or, again, of their "interillumination" or "co-operation") is to *use* a metaphor emphasizing the dynamic aspects of a good reader's response to a non-trivial metaphor. I have no quarrel with the use of metaphors (if they are good ones) in talking about metaphor. But it may be as well to use several, lest we are misled by the adventitious charms of our favourites.

Let us try, for instance, to think of a metaphor as a *filter*. Consider the statement, "Man is a wolf". Here, we may say, are *two* subjects —the *principal subject*, Man (or: men) and the *subsidiary subject*, Wolf (or: wolves). Now the metaphorical sentence in question will not convey its intended meaning to a reader sufficiently ignorant about wolves. What is needed is not so much that the reader shall know the standard dictionary meaning of "wolf"—or be able to use that word in literal senses—as that he shall know what I will call the *system of associated commonplaces*. Imagine some layman required to say, without taking special thought, those things he held to be true about wolves; the set of statements resulting would approximate to what I am here calling the system of commonplaces associated with the word "wolf". I am assuming that in any given culture the responses made by different persons to the test suggested would agree rather closely, and that even the occasional expert, who might have unusual knowledge of the subject, would still know "what the man in the street thinks about the matter". From the expert's standpoint, the system of commonplaces may include half-truths or downright mistakes (as when a whale is classified as a fish); but the important thing for the metaphor's effectiveness is not that the commonplaces shall be true, but that they should be readily and freely evoked. (Because this is so, a metaphor that works in one society may seem preposterous in another. Men who take wolves to be reincarnations of dead humans will give the statement "Man is a wolf" an interpretation different from the one I have been assuming.)

To put the matter in another way: Literal uses of the word "wolf" are governed by syntactical and semantical rules, violation of which produces nonsense or self-contradiction. In addition, I am suggesting, literal uses of the word normally commit the speaker to acceptance of a set of standard beliefs about wolves (current platitudes) that are the common possession of the members of some speech community. To deny any such piece of accepted commonplace (*e.g.*, by saying that wolves are vegetarians—or easily domesticated) is to produce an effect of paradox and provoke a demand for justification. A speaker who says "wolf" is normally taken to be implying in some sense of that word that he is referring to something fierce, carnivorous, treacherous, and so on. The idea of a wolf is part of a system of ideas, not sharply delineated, and yet sufficiently definite to admit of detailed enumeration.

The effect, then, of (metaphorically) calling a man a "wolf" is to evoke the wolf-system of related commonplaces. If the man is a wolf, he preys upon other animals, is fierce, hungry, engaged in constant struggle, a scavenger, and so on. Each of these implied assertions has now to be made to fit the principal subject (the man) either in normal or in abnormal senses. If the metaphor is at all appropriate, this can be done—up to a point at least. A suitable hearer will be led by the wolf-system of implications to construct a corresponding system of implications about the principal subject. But these implications will *not* be those comprised in the commonplaces *normally* implied by literal uses of "man". The new implications must be determined by the pattern of implications associated with literal uses of the word "wolf". Any human traits that can without undue strain be talked about in "wolf-language" will be rendered prominent, and any that cannot will be pushed into the background. The wolf-metaphor suppresses some details, emphasises others—in short, *organizes* our view of man.

Suppose I look at the night sky through a piece of heavily smoked glass on which certain lines have been left clear. Then I shall see only the stars that can be made to lie on the lines previously prepared upon the screen, and the stars I do see will be seen as organised by the screen's structure. We can think of a metaphor as such a screen, and the system of "associated commonplaces" of the focal word as the network of lines upon the screen. We can say that the principal subject is "seen through" the metaphorical expression—or, if we prefer, that the principal subject is "projected upon" the field of the subsidiary subject. (In the latter analogy, the implication-system of the focal expression must be taken to determine the "law of projection".)

Or take another example. Suppose I am set the task of describing a battle in words drawn as largely as possible from the vocabulary of chess. These latter terms determine a system of implications which will proceed to control my description of the battle. The enforced choice of the chess vocabulary will lead some aspects of the battle to be emphasized, others to be neglected, and all to be organized in a way that would cause much more strain in other modes of description. The chess vocabulary filters and transforms: it not only selects, it brings forward aspects of the battle that might not be seen at all through another medium. (Stars that cannot be seen at all, except through telescopes.)

Nor must we neglect the shifts in attitude that regularly result from the use of metaphorical language. A wolf is (conventionally) a hateful and alarming object; so, to call a man a wolf is to imply that he too is hateful and alarming (and thus to support and reinforce dislogistic attitudes). Again, the vocabulary of chess has its primary uses in a highly artificial setting, where all expression of feeling is formally excluded: to describe a battle as if it were a game of chess is accordingly to exclude, by the choice of language, all the more emotionally disturbing aspects of warfare. (Similar bye-products are not rare in philosophical uses of metaphor.)

A fairly obvious objection to the foregoing sketch of the "inter-action view" is that it has to hold that some of the "associated commonplaces" themselves suffer metaphorical change of meaning in the process of transfer from the subsidiary to the principal subject. And *these* changes, if they occur, can hardly be explained by the account given. The primary metaphor, it might be said, has been analyzed into a set of subordinate metaphors, so the account given is either circular or leads to an infinite regress.

This might be met by denying that *all* changes of meaning in the "associated commonplaces" must be counted as metaphorical shifts. Many of them are best described as *extensions* of meaning, because they do not involve apprehended connexions between two systems of concepts. I have not undertaken to explain how such extensions or shifts occur in general, and I do not think any simple account will fit all cases. (It is easy enough to mutter "analogy", but closer examination soon shows all kinds of "grounds" for shifts of meaning with context—and even no ground at all, sometimes.)

Secondly, I would not deny that a metaphor may involve a number of subordinate metaphors among its implications. But these subordinate metaphors are, I think, usually intended to be taken less "emphatically", *i.e.*, with less stress upon *their* implications. (The implications of a metaphor are like the overtones of a musical chord; to attach too much "weight" to them is like trying to make the overtones sound as loud as the main notes—and just as pointless.) In any case, primary and subordinate metaphors will normally belong to the same field of discourse, so that they mutually reinforce one and the same system of implications. Conversely, where substantially new metaphors appear as the primary metaphor is unravelled, there is serious risk of confusion of thought (*cf.* the customary prohibition against "mixed metaphors").

But the preceeding account of metaphor needs correction, if it is to be reasonably adequate. Reference to "associated commonplaces" will fit the commonest cases where the author simply plays upon the stock of common knowledge (and common misinformation) presumably shared by the reader and himself. But in a poem, or a piece of sustained prose, the writer can establish a novel pattern of implications for the literal uses of the key expressions, prior to using them as vehicles for his metaphors. (An author can do much to suppress unwanted implications of the word "contract", by explicit discussion of its intended meaning, before he proceeds to develop a contract theory of sovereignty. Or a naturalist who really knows wolves may tell us so much about them that *his* description of man as a wolf diverges quite markedly from the stock uses of that figure.) Metaphors can be supported by specially constructed systems of implications, as well as by accepted commonplaces; they can be made to measure and need not be reach-me-downs.

It was a simplification, again, to speak as if the implication-system of the metaphorical expression remains unaltered by the metaphorical statement. The nature of the intended application helps to determine the character of the system to be applied (as though the stars could partly determine the character of the observation-screen by which we looked at them). If to call a man a wolf is to put him in a special light, we must not forget that the metaphor makes the wolf seem more human than he otherwise would.

I hope such complications as these can be accommodated within the outline of an "interaction view" that I have tried to present.

VI

Since I have been making so much use of example and illustration, it may be as well to state explicitly (and by way of summary) some of the chief respects in which the "interaction" view recommended differs from a "substitution" or a "comparison" view.

In the form in which I have been expounding it, the "interaction view" is committed to the following seven claims: —

(1) A metaphorical statement has *two* distinct subjects—a "principal" subject and a "subsidiary" one.[21]

(2) These subjects are often best regarded as *"systems* of things" rather than "things".

(3) The metaphor works by applying to the principal subject a system of "associated implications" characteristic of the subsidiary subject.

(4) These implications usually consist of "commonplaces" about the subsidiary subject, but may, in suitable cases, consist of deviant implications established *ad hoc* by the writer.

(5) The metaphor selects, emphasizes, suppresses, and organizes features of the principal subject by *implying* statements about it that normally apply to the subsidiary subject.

(6) This involves shifts in meaning of words belonging to the same family or system as the metaphorical expression; and some of these shifts, though not all, may be metaphorical transfers. (The subordinate metaphors are, however, to be read less "emphatically".)

(7) There is, in general, no simple "ground" for the necessary shifts of meaning—no blanket reason why some metaphors work and others fail.

It will be found, upon consideration, that point (1) is incompatible with the simplest forms of a "substitution view", point (7) is formally incompatible with a "comparison view"; while the remaining points elaborate reasons for regarding "comparison views" as inadequate.

But it is easy to overstate the conflicts between these three views. If we were to insist that only examples satisfying all seven of the claims listed above should be allowed to count as "genuine" metaphors, we should restrict the correct uses of the word "metaphor" to a very small number of cases. This would be to advocate a persuasive definition of "metaphor" that would tend to make all metaphors interestingly complex.[22] And such a deviation from current uses of the word "metaphor" would leave us without a convenient label for the more trivial cases. Now it is in just such trivial cases that "substitution" and "comparison" views sometimes seem nearer the mark than "interaction" views. The point might be met by *classifying* metaphors as instances of substitution, comparison, or interaction. Only the last kind are of importance in philosophy.

For substitution-metaphors and comparison-metaphors can be replaced by literal translations (with possible exception for the case of catachresis)—by sacrificing some of the charm, vivacity, or wit of the original, but with no loss of *cognitive* content. But "interaction-metaphors" are not expendable. Their mode of operation requires the reader to use a system of implications (a system of "common-places"—or a special system established for the purpose in hand) as a means for selecting, emphasizing, and organizing relations in a different field. This use of a "subsidiary subject" to foster insight into a "principal subject" is a distinctive *intellectual* operation (though one familiar enough through our experiences of learning anything whatever), demanding simultaneous awareness of both subjects but not reducible to any *comparison* between the two.

Suppose we try to state the cognitive content of an interaction-metaphor in "plain language". Up to a point, we may succeed in stating a number of the relevant relations between the two subjects (though in view of the extension of meaning accompanying the shift in the subsidiary subject's implication system, too much must not be expected of the literal paraphrase). But the set of literal statements so obtained will not have the same power to inform and enlighten as the original. For one thing, the implications, previously left for a suitable reader to educe for himself, with a nice feeling for their relative priorities and degrees of importance, are now presented explicitly as though having equal weight. The literal paraphrase inevitably says too much—and with the wrong emphasis. One of the points I most wish to stress is that the loss in such cases is a loss in *cognitive* content; the relevant weakness of the literal paraphrase is not that it may be tiresomely prolix or boringly explicit—or deficient in qualities of style; it fails to be a translation because it fails to give the *insight* that the metaphor did.

But "explication", or elaboration of the metaphor's grounds, if not regarded as an adequate cognitive substitute for the original, may be extremely valuable. A powerful metaphor will no more be harmed by such probing than a musical masterpiece by analysis of its harmonic and melodic structure. No doubt metaphors are dangerous—and perhaps especially so in philosophy. But a prohibition against their use would be a wilful and harmful restriction upon our powers of inquiry.[23]

NOTES

1. *Any* part of speech can be used metaphorically (though the results are meagre and uninteresting in the case of conjunctions); any form of verbal expression may contain a metaphorical focus.

2. Here I am using language appropriate to the "interaction view" of metaphor that is discussed later in this paper.

3. Here, I wish these words to be read with as little "weight" as possible!

4. Notice how this type of paraphrase naturally conveys some implication of *fault* on the part of the metaphor's author. There is a strong suggestion that he ought to have made up his mind as to what he really wanted to say — the metaphor is depicted as a way of glossing over unclarity and vagueness.

5. Richard Whately, *Elements of Rhetoric* (7th revised ed., London, 1846), p. 280.

6. Under "Figure" we find: "Any of the various 'forms' of expression, deviating from the normal arrangement or use of words, which are adopted in order to give beauty, variety, or force to a composition; *e.g.,* Aposiopesis, Hyperbole, Metaphor, etc." If we took this strictly we might be led to say that a transfer of a word not adopted for the sake of introducing "beauty, variety, or force" must necessarily fail to be a case of metaphor. Or will "variety" automatically cover *every* transfer? It will be noticed that the O.E.D.'s definition is no improvement upon Whately's. Where he speaks of a "word" being substituted, the O.E.D. prefers "name or descriptive term." If this is meant to restrict metaphors to nouns (and adjectives?) it is demonstrably mistaken. But, if not, what *is* "descriptive term" supposed to mean? And why has Whately's reference to "Resemblance or Analogy" been trimmed into a reference to analogy alone?

7. Owen Barfield, "Poetic Diction and Legal Fiction," in *Essays Presented to Charles Williams* (Oxford, 1947), pp. 106-127. The definition of metaphor occurs on p. 111, where metaphor is treated as a special case of what Barfield calls "tarning". The whole essay deserves to be read.

8. The O.E.D. defines catachresis as: "Improper use of words; application of a term to a thing which it does not properly denote; abuse or perversion of a trope or metaphor." I wish to exclude the pejorative suggestions. There is nothing perverse or abusive in stretching old words to fit new situations. Catachresis is merely a striking case of the transformation of meaning that is constantly occurring in any living language.

9. Can we imagine anybody saying this nowadays and seriously meaning anything? I find it hard to do so. But in default of an authentic context of use, any analysis is liable to be thin, obvious and unprofitable.

10. A full discussion of this example, complete with diagrams, will be found in Gustaf Stern's *Meaning and Change of Meaning* (Göteborgs Högskolas Arsskrift, vol. 38, 1932, part I), pp. 300 ff. Stern's account tries to show how the reader is led by the context to *select* from the connotation of "lion" the attribute (bravery) that will fit Richard the man. I take him to be defending a form of the substitution view.

11. Aristotle ascribes the use of metaphor to delight in learning; Cicero traces delight in metaphor to the enjoyment of the author's ingenuity in overpassing the immediate, or in the vivid presentation of the principal subject. For references to these and other traditional views, see E. M. Cope, *An Introduction to Aristotle's Rhetoric* (London; 1867), "Appendix B to Book III, ch. II: *On Metaphor*".

12. Thus Stern *(op. cit.)* says of all figures of speech that "they are intended to serve the expressive and purposive functions of speech better than the 'plain statement'" (p. 296). A metaphor produces an "enhancement" *(Steigerung)* of the subject, but the factors leading to its use "involve the expressive and effective (purposive) functions of speech, not the symbolic and communicative functions" (p. 290). That is to say, metaphors may evince feelings or predispose others to act and feel in various ways—but they don't typically *say* anything.

13. Whately, *loc. cit.* He proceeds to draw a distinction between "Resemblance, strictly so called, *i.e. direct* resemblance between the objects themselves in question, (as when we speak of *'table*-land', or compare great waves to *mountains)*" and "Analogy, which is the resemblance of Ratios—a similarity of the relations they bear to certain other objects; as when we speak of the *'light* of reason', or of 'revelation'; or compare a wounded and captive warrior to a stranded ship".

14. Alexander Bain, *English Composition and Rhetoric* (Enlarged edition, London, 1887), p. 159.

15. Comparison views probably derive from Aristotle's brief statement in the *Poetics:* "Metaphor consists in giving the thing a name that belongs to something else; the transference being either from genus to species, or from species to genus, or from species to species, or on grounds of analogy" (1457*b*). I have no space to give Aristotle's discussion the detailed examination it deserves. An able defense of a view based on Aristotle will be found in S. J. Brown's *The World of Imagery* (London, 1927, especially pp. 67 ff).

16. Much more would need to be said in a thorough examination of the comparison view. It would be revealing, for instance, to consider the contrasting types of case in which a formal comparison is preferred to a metaphor. A comparison is often a prelude to an explicit statement of the grounds of resemblance; whereas we do not expect a metaphor to explain itself. (Cf. the difference between *comparing* a man's face with a wolf mask, by looking for points of resemblance—and seeing the human face *as* vulpine). But no doubt the line between *some* metaphors and *some* similies is not a sharp one.

17. The best sources are the writings of I. A. Richards, especially Chapter 5 ("Metaphor") and Chapter 6 ("Command of Metaphor") of his *The Philosophy of Rhetoric* (Oxford, 1936). Chapters 7 and 8 of his *Interpretation in Teaching* (London, 1938) cover much the same ground. W. Bedell Stanford's *Greek Metaphor* (Oxford, 1936) defends what he calls an "integration theory" (see especially pp. 101 ff) with much learning and skill. Unfortunately, both writers have great trouble in making clear the nature of the positions they are defending. Chapter 18 of W. Empson's *The Structure of Complex Words* (London, 1951) is a useful discussion of Richards' views on metaphor.

18. *The Philosophy of Rhetoric,* p. 93. Richards also says that metaphor is "fundamentally a borrowing between and intercourse of *thoughts,* a transaction between contexts" (p. 94). Metaphor, he says, requires two ideas "which co-operate in an inclusive meaning" (p. 119).

19. It is this, perhaps, that leads Richards to say that "talk about the identification or fusion that a metaphor effects is nearly always misleading and pernicious" *(op. cit.,* p. 127).

20. Usually, Richards tries to show that similarity between the two terms is at best *part* of the basis for the interaction of meanings in a metaphor.

21. This point has often been made. *E.g.:* — "As to metaphorical expression, that is a great excellence in style, when it is used with propriety, for it gives you two ideas for one." (Samuel Johnson, quoted by Richards, *op. cit.,* p. 93)

The choice of labels for the "subjects" is troublesome. See the "Note on terminology" appended to this paper.

22. I can sympathise with Empson's contention that "The term ['metaphor'] had better

correspond to what the speakers themselves feel to be a rich or suggestive or persuasive use of a word, rather than include uses like the *leg* of a table" (*The Structure of Complex Words*, p. 333). But there is the opposite danger, also, of making metaphors too important by definition, and so narrowing our view of the subject excessively.

23. *(A note on terminology)*: For metaphors that fit a substitution or comparison view, the factors needing to be distinguished are: — (i) some word or expression E; (ii) occurring in some verbal "frame" F; so that (iii) $F(E)$ is the metaphorical statement in question; (iv) the meaning $m'(E)$ which E has in $F(E)$; (v) which is the same as the literal meaning, $m(X)$, of some literal synomyn, X. A sufficient technical vocabulary would be: "metaphorical expression" (for E), "metaphorical statement" (for $F(E)$), "metaphorical meaning" for m') and "literal meaning" (for m).

Where the interaction view is appropriate, the situation is more complicated. We may also need to refer (vi) to the principal subject of $F(E)$, say P (roughly, what the statement is "really" about), (vii) the subsidiary subject, S (what $F(E)$ would be about if read literally); (viii) the relevant system of implications, I, connected with S; and (ix) the resulting system of attributions, A, asserted of P. We must accept at least so much complexity if we agree that the meaning of E in its setting F depends upon the transformation of I into A by using language, normally applied to S, to apply to P instead.

Richards has suggested using the words "tenor" and "vehicle" for the two *"thoughts"* which, in his view, are "active together" (for "the two *ideas* that metaphor, at its simplest, gives us", *Op. cit.*, p. 96, my italics) and urges that we reserve "the word 'metaphor' for the whole double unit" (Ib.). But this picture of two *ideas* working upon each other is an inconvenient fiction. And it is significant that Richards himself soon lapses into speaking of "tenor" and "vehicle" as "things" (*e.g.* on p. 118). Richards' "vehicle" vacillates in reference between the metaphorical expression *(E)*, the subsidiary subject *(S)* and the connected implication system *(I)*. It is less clear what his "tenor" means: sometimes, it stands for the principal subject *(P)*, sometimes for the implications connected with that subject (which I have not symbolized above), sometimes, in spite of Richards' own intentions, for the *resultant* meaning (or as we might say the "full import") of E in its context, $F(E)$.

There is probably no hope of getting an accepted terminology so long as writers upon the subject are still so much at variance with one another.

Metaphor

Paul Henle

I

There is little new to be said on the subject of metaphor. It has been discussed from ancient times to the present and on the whole there has been a rough agreement. The excuse for the present chapter is not that it sets forth new truths concerning metaphor, but that it attempts to fit the old ones into a more general theory of symbolism by characterizing metaphor semantically and by showing its semantic functions. Two such functions shall engage us principally, the use to extend language to meet new situations and the poetic use to give language color and nuance.

Because of the continuity in the discussions of metaphor, we may develop a chracterization of it by beginning with and modifying Aristotle's explanation. He says: "Metaphor consists in giving the thing a name that belongs to something else; the transference being either from genus to species, or from species to genus, or from species to species, or on grounds of analogy."[1]

With reservations to be indicate shortly, we may follow this account which emphasizes two aspects of metaphor: a shift of nomenclature—from 'something else' to what is being named, and a

Reprinted from *Language, Thought, and Culture* by Paul Henle (ed.), The University of Michigan Press, 1958, pp. 173-195, by permission of The University of Michigan Press.

specification of the property in virtue of which the transfer takes place. Each of these may be considered briefly.

It is apparent that the terms 'thing' and 'name' in Aristotle's account must be construed very broadly — 'thing' referring not merely to physical objects but also to any topic of thought. Similarly, 'name' must be used not in the restricted sense of proper or common names but must be taken as any sign whatever. Thus, what we are left with is the notion that some object of thought is referred to by means of the sign for some other such object. This will do well enough, but it is a little more convenient to say essentially the same thing from the side of the sign rather than from the object signified. Thus we may say that in a metaphor a sign having a conventional sense is used in a different sense. Though too broad in some respects and incomplete in others this may serve as the basis for an account. Thus when Milton says of Belial:

> through his tongue
> Dropt Manna, and could make the worse appear
> The better reason . . .[2]

clearly he does not intend us to conclude that Belial exuded food; rather, 'tongue,' 'dropt' and 'manna' are used in an unusual sense to suggest that he spoke soothingly and persuasively. Each of these words appears in a double role — first in its conventional sense such as it might have in other contexts and second in a sense characteristic of this metaphor. This is what is central in Aristotle's statement.

This duality of sense is characteristic of metaphor and some terminology will make reference to it easier. By the *literal sense* of a word we may mean the sense which a word has in other contexts and apart from such metaphoric uses. By *figurative sense* we may mean that special sense on which the metaphor hinges. Thus, in Milton's figure quoted above, the literal sense of 'manna' is a food which appeared miraculously to the Israelites in the desert: its figurative sense is, approximately, delightful language. This duality of sense is referred to by other writers on the subject. Thus our two senses correspond generally, but not always, to I. A. Richards' use of 'vehicle' and 'tenor.'[3] Our literal sense also corresponds closely to what Empson[4] calls the "head meaning" of a word. In any case, the literal sense most often would be the meaning of a term given by a dictionary or, if there is more than one dictionary meaning, the meaning which is appropriate in context. There may be cases, however, in which an author gives terms a special sense, either implicitly or by explicit convention, and this may serve as the literal sense.

It may happen that the figurative sense of a term in a metaphor is identical with the literal sense of some other term. If this does not occur, there would at least always be a literal sense which is as close to the figurative sense as any literal sense can come. This literal sense we shall call the *paraphrase* of the metaphor. By introduction of this term we do not wish to prejudge the issue as to whether metaphors have equivalent literal senses, we have merely provided the terminology for discussing it. The question may now be phrased in what respects may the paraphrase of a metaphor be adequate; this is a question which we shall take up later.

One other bit of terminology will be required. 'Literal sense' and 'figurative sense' both refer to meanings of terms. We shall want some way of referring to the relationship between a word and its various meanings. This may be accomplished by saying that a word is an *immediate sign* of its literal sense and a *mediate sign* of its figurative sense. These terms are appropriate since is it only through the literal sense that one arrives at the figurative.

In the definition quoted, Aristotle speaks of the basis of the transference of names or—in our terminology—of the bases for the shift from literal to figurative sense. He enumerates a number of these—substitution of genus for species, of species for genus, of one species for another, or shifts by analogy. A later tradition used the generic term 'trope' to cover all of these and some others, and restricted the term 'metaphor' to cases where analogy was the ground of the shift in sense. While the most recent tendency is to use 'metaphor' in Aristotle's generic sense, there are important differences between metaphor and the other tropes, so we shall observe the finer distinction.

Traditionally, the transitions from literal to figurative sense by way of substitution of genus for species or species for genus, as well as similar substitutions of whole for part and part for whole, go by name of *synecdoche*. In the figure quoted from Milton, the use of 'tongue' to mean organs of speech would be a case in point. Again looser connections by way of some relation felt to be important, as when one speaks of reading an author instead of his works, go by name of *metonymy*. In *irony* the connection between literal and figurative sense is by way of negation. These together with metaphor complete the standard catalogue of tropes. Whether metonymy is elastic enough to include deliberate and transparant overstatement is not clear; if not, this is a separate trope.

We may take from Aristotle then a general definition of trope of which metaphor is one species. In all tropes at least one term signifies mediately, thus acquiring a figurative meaning. Every figurative meaning has a literal paraphrase—though how adequate remains to be seen. To get at what is typical of metaphor, however, we must consider analogy which characterizes it as the means of transition from literal to figurative sense.

It must be noticed at the beginning that there is no one sort of analogy or parallel which is characteristic of all metaphors. In some two distinct situations are indicated and the one understood in terms of the other; in other metaphors however there is a mere qualitative similarity between two characteristics of the same thing. Still others are intermediate. We may begin with a few examples. When, in one of his early verses, Keats writes:

> When by my solitary hearth I sit,
> And hateful thoughts enwrap my soul in gloom[5]

there are two distinct situations evoked by the second line, the one of someone or something enveloping a person in something. It may be a cloak or a blanket or something of the sort. It may be a net in which the person is caught or it may even be a monstrous web, but, at any rate, it is something concrete.[6] The other situation is that of hateful thoughts making one gloomy. The second is presented in terms of the first and this metaphor is developed in terms of quite distinct situations. On the other extreme, we have such a metaphor as is involved in calling a sly person an old fox. Here the parallel does not involve sets of things in relation but is limited to the common characteristic of the two. Intermediate between these examples is such a metaphor as the following: "An obliging thrush hopped across the lawn; a coil of pinkish rubber twisted in its beak."[7] Here the contorted worm is described in terms of another situation, but the bird which holds it is not. Thus the extent of the parallelism may vary, but, in some degree, it is always present.

II

In terms of this parallelism, it is possible to explain metaphor as a type of symbolism and to assimilate it to a more general theory of symbolism. This is most easily done by recourse to the distinctions made by C. S. Peirce between symbolic and iconic modes of significa-tion.[8] A sign is a *symbol* insofar as it signifies according to an arbi-trary rule, insofar as it is a conventional sign. A sign is an *icon* to the extent that it signifies in virtue of similarity. Thus, ordinary words are symbols, but onomatapoeic words contain an iconic element as well. Such a sign as a map is primarily iconic although, in such details as having special designations for county seats, there is also a conven-tional, and so symbolic, element.

Given this distinction, there is clearly an iconic element in meta-phor. We have just seen that a metaphor, as distinguished from other tropes, depends on analogy, and in this analogy one side is used to present the other. Thus, envelopment in a cloak is used to present the notion of gloom; the character of a man is presented through its likeness to a fox, and the appearance of a worm through its likeness to a bit of rubber. In each case we are led to think of something by a consideration of something like it, and this is what constitutes the iconic mode of signifying.

But if there is an iconic element in metaphor, it is equally clear that the icon is not presented, but is merely described. In the sen-tence from Virginia Woolf, we are not given a coil of rubber—a piece of rubber could not be part of a sentence—rather we are given a description of such a coil. It is as if information concerning a country were given not by showing its map, but by describing the map, by saying, as for example one might of Chile, that it looks long and skinny on the map. This situation regarding the icon may be stated in a number of ways. We may say that we are given not the icon, but a description of what would be an icon. Alternatively, one might say that not the icon, but its essence is brought before the reader. Again, to say approximately the same thing more safely, one may claim that what is presented is a formula for the construction of icons. Thus Virginia Woolf may be understood as saying something like: "Take any coil of pinkish rubber of a size to be carried by a thrush and you have an icon of what I mean."

Metaphor, then, is analyzable into a double sort of semantic relationship. First, using symbols in Peirce's sense, directions are given for finding an object or situation. Thus, use of language is quite ordinary. Second, it is implied that any object or situation fitting the direction may serve as an icon of what one wishes to describe. The icon is never actually present; rather, through the rule, one understands what it must be and, through this understanding, what it signifies.

There is, of course, an advantage in not having the icon actually present. Confronted with a thrush carrying a coil of rubber, one would most likely mistake it for a worm and so lose the comparison. The rubbery aspect of the worm would escape attention completely. Or, to take a case where such confusion is impossible, if a person wrapped in a cloak were exhibited as indicating the character of gloom, so many other aspects of the person's appearance and demeanor would be prominent that the intended relationship might never be noticed. Thus, the double symbolism of metaphor allows calling attention to aspects of an icon which might not be prominent in the presentation of the icon itself.

Given the general role of icons in metaphor, we may notice their various types a little more closely. Peirce shows two ways, *prima facie* different, in which icons may signify, and both are relevant to metaphor. In the one, there is a direct qualitative similarity between sign and thing signified, as when a colored square on a chart represents a given shade of color. It exemplifies the color and so is directly similar. A more involved type of icon occurs when sign and thing signified have little or no direct similarity, but rather the two have a similar structure. In this sense a map of Michigan is an icon of Michigan even though the map is small, smooth, and easily folded, while Michigan itself is large, relatively rough, and comparatively resistant to folding. The structure of the two is the same, however, and, for example, the angle between two roads in Michigan is the same as the angle between their representation on the map. In this type of sign-relationship, not merely does one complex structure represent another, but elements of one structure represent elements of the other in virtue of holding analogous positions. Thus, one dot on the map of Michigan represents Ann Arbor not because the two look alike—Ann Arbor does not look round—nor because they have the same structure—Ann Arbor is not homogeneous—but because they occupy corresponding places in similar structures.

Although the alternatives of qualitative and structural similarity leave open a vast number of possibilities, it must not be thought that anything may be an icon of any other thing. While it may be that any two things are similar in some respect, this, by itself, is not sufficient to make one an icon of the other unless someone is led to consider one by its similarity to the other. The similarity must be noticed and used as a means of signifying. This would require at the very least that the similarity between an icon and what it signifies should not be shared by a great many other things as well. Thus, while the number seventeen is similar to an elephant in that they share the characteristics of being different from the moon, this is an insufficient basis for iconicity. Some special or striking similarity is required. We have just seen that, by describing an icon rather than presenting it, a metaphor may call attention to similarities which might otherwise pass unnoticed; but even here there are limits to similarities which may be used without simply leaving the reader blank or making him think that the similarity is trivial.

Icons involving both qualitative and structural similarities enter into metaphor. In the metaphor of the fox there is the same sort of relationship between the fox and the characteristic of being sly that there is between the color card and the shade it embodies. In the metaphor in which thoughts enwrap the soul the relationship between the two situations set up is closer to that involving the map. It is not precisely the same as the relation of the map to the territory mapped, however, because this relationship can be expressed entirely in formal, mathematical terms. In the metaphor, it is not merely that there are parallel situations—the same elements in the same arrangement, but also that there is a felt similarity between corresponding components. Thus, gloom in some way or other is thought as something amorphous and enveloping, capable of surrounding in the same way a cloak or blanket does. A cloak or blanket is preferable to a coat because there are no analogues of sleeves in gloom. For similar reasons it would not have done to speak of hateful thoughts entrapping the soul in gloom although it would have left the metre unchanged. However multifarious the forms of traps they are all sharp, with definite edges, and this spoils the correspondence with gloom.

If one asks why only certain objects are felt appropriate to represent gloom the reply would be in terms of the characteristics of gloom itself. Gloom is a pervasive affair in that it influences one's entire mental outlook. It need not have consciously felt causes or itself be the object of direct awareness but rather it tinges all other mental activities. In these respects it is like a wrapping which covers the whole of an object and which allows its form to show through, though modified by the covering. Thus the aptness of metaphor depends on the capability of elaborating it—of extending the parallel structure. In this respect the parallelism is like that of the map and what is mapped, though to a lesser degree and without the rigid similarity.

It is this capability of extension which justifies the differentiation of metaphor from the other tropes. In a figure where the species stands for the genus, one apprehends the relationship, one gains a flavor of concreteness, one perhaps attributes to the entire genus something of the feeling toward the species, and that is all. No further development of the synecdoche is possible. Metaphor, on the other hand, can be spun out, following a line of analogy or even several lines at once, carrying it quite far. For poetry, this is of primary importance; hence the separation of metaphor from the other tropes.

So far metaphor has been described in semantic terms but not yet defined. The characterization given is too broad and includes other things besides metaphor. Thus, we have paraphrased Virginia Woolf's figure as by the phrase "Take any coil of pinkish rubber of a size to be carried by a thrush and you have an icon of what I mean." This phrase itself symbolizes an icon but it is not a metaphor. For some purposes its differences from metaphor are unimportant, and we may use the terms 'metaphoric statement' and 'metaphoric thought' in any case in which there is a reference to anything or any situation by symbolizing its icon. Metaphor then becomes a particular kind of metaphoric statement whose differentia is the following: In a metaphor some terms symbolize the icon and others symbolize what is iconized. This may be said, though less succinctly, in other terms. We have noticed that a metaphor is developed by suggesting parallel situations. In a metaphor some terms refer literally to one situation and figuratively to the second while other terms refer literally only and refer to the second situation only. Thus, in Keats's line 'enwrap' refers literally to the situation of a person with a cloak and figuratively to that of the melancholy person. 'Soul' however has no figurative use and refers only to the melancholy person.

Since we have a semantic characterization of metaphor, this is a convenient point to distinguish it from two related forms—simile and allegory. Simile is differentiated in that it contains no terms with figurative senses. It is true that a simile makes a comparison, often elaborate, which provides a situation parallel to one under discussion, but both sides of the comparison are overtly stated instead of one being symbolized through the other. The similarity between two situations is explicitly mentioned rather than being used symbolically. Everything is on the surface instead of having different semantic levels. Nevertheless, because of the parallel, one side could be used as an icon of the other so a simile may be an invitation to metaphoric thought. Perhaps this is what J. Middleton Murry has in mind in claiming that metaphor is compressed simile.[9] That it is compressed no one will doubt, but, more than this, it is the materials of a simile used to create a new symbolism.

If none of the terms of a simile signify mediately, all those of an allegory do—or at least all the important terms. Thus, an allegory may be considered merely on its literal level and presents a complete account, but there is a deeper meaning, never presented but to be inferred by its parallel to the more superficial meaning. In contrast to this, a metaphor contains some terms which have both literal and figurative meaning (e.g., 'enwrap' in Keats's line) and others which have a literal sense only (e.g., 'soul' and 'gloom' in the same line). Or, to put the point in other words, we have said that there are parallel situations contemplated in a metaphor. Some of the words, taken in their literal sense, refer to one of the situations and some to the other. It is this mixture of literal references to different situations which at once differentiates metaphor from allegory and gives it the impact which psychologically is its distinctive feature.

III

Besides being discussed from the point of view of the symbolism involved, metaphor may be considered from the point of view of the listener. Here its outstanding characteristic is the sort of shock which it produces. Ordinarily one takes words in their literal sense and this is impossible in a metaphor. This impossibility in fact is what drives one on to seek a figurative sense. When Homer makes the shade of Agamemnon lament:

> Upon my son Clytemnestra gave me no time to feed my eyes,[10]

it is absurd to think of eyes literally being fed, so one looks for a figurative sense. Occasionally, a metaphor occurs in which the literal sense is not absurd but merely conveys the wrong meaning. Thus Shakespeare begins his description of Cleopatra's meeting with Anthony as follows:

> The barge she sat in, like a burnish'd throne
> Burn'd on the water[11]

Here 'Burn'd' would make literal sense in the description of a conflagration, but since the context clearly rules this out, a further meaning must be sought. Whether taking all terms in their literal sense produces an absurdity or merely something incongruous the clash of literal meanings must be felt. If it is not, one of two situations must obtain—either the passage is taken literally without encountering any difficulty and no suspicion of a metaphor arises, or else the figurative meaning is so usual that the reader goes to it immediately. In this case one has an idiom or a "dead metaphor" which, properly, is no metaphor at all.

Where the clash of literal senses is felt, however, the problem is to discover which terms cannot be taken in a literal sense and what figurative sense may be attributed to them. That a well-constructed metaphor provides clues for deciding these problems may be seen from a consideration of the metaphor in the following lines:

> Romira stay
> And run not thus like a young Roe away
> No enemie
> Pursues thee (foolish girle) tis only I

I'll keep off harms
If thou'l be pleased to garrison mine arms;[12]

the metaphor in question is that in the last line quoted. Here there is a sort of pun on 'arms' in the sense of upper limbs and also in the sense of weapons. The latter gives an air of paradox with 'garrison' since arms might be used in garrisoning but would not themselves be garrisoned. Since, however, it is the other sense which is intended, this aspect of the line may be neglected, though it unquestionably adds to the effect.

Coming directly to the analysis of the figure, the phrase 'garrison mine arms' contains a clash and cannot be an immediate sign of an attribute of Romira—or of anyone else for that matter. Taken in their literal sense these terms are either meaningless or at best apply to nothing. On the general principle that people try to talk sense and to make statements which are at least possibly true, the passage must be construed as containing a figurative sense. The next question is, what is literal and what is figurative? This question may be answered by noticing that the phrase is applied to Romira, so 'garrison' must be used in a figurative sense. It would be unusual to speak of one person garrisoning anything and, if one did, it must be a redoubtable hero, not a fleeing maiden. Granted this, 'arms' must be taken in a literal sense, for the clash can be resolved only by taking one term of the phrase literally and the other figuratively; and it must be 'arms' in the sense of appendages, not weapons, for there is presumably nothing which Romira could do with a sword or pistol which would make it worthwhile chasing her. Thus far we know that Romira is being instructed to do something mediately signified by 'garrison' to his arms. What she is to do may be discovered by following out the literal sense of 'garrison.' Ordinarily, the only people who garrison anything are soldiers and what they garrison is a fort or citadel or something of the sort. Thus, Romira is to have the same relation to his arms that soldiers have to a fort in garrisoning it. Soldiers defend forts and this may contribute an overtone but it cannot be the basis for a parallel between the situations. The arms are in no need of defense; they seem, rather, bent on aggression. Soldiers also occupy forts and this gives something like the desired sense.

It would be silly to suggest that the term 'occupy' exhausts the meaning of the metaphor; it is merely a first approximation to it.

Nor need one suggest that, in reading the lines, one goes through the explicit process set forth above. The intent was not to paraphrase the metaphor or to describe the conscious stages in the apprehension of it, but to show that there were enough clews in the passage to account for the metaphor's being understood. It might happen, moreover, in difficult metaphors that there was some such conscious process.

In simpler metaphors in which there is merely an attribute used in a figurative sense, analysis of this sort is more difficult since there are no articulated parallel structures on which to work back and forth. If one calls a man an old bear there is no relational network in which one can work out the parallel situations; 'bear' has a figurative sense —but there is no structure to delimit it. One must choose therefore some prominent characteristic of the animal as the point of similarity. Where, as in this case, the animal has a number of distinctive characteristics it is a matter of convention which is selected. Thus, the roughness and clumsiness of the bear have been chosen as the basis of the metaphor and this has become entirely standardized. Under other circumstances or in another civilization the fact that the bear is omniverous might have been more impressive and a person of catholic tastes described as a bear. Campbell in his *Philosophy of Rhetoric* remarked:

> . . . let it be observed that the noun *sail* in our tongue is frequently used, and by the same trope the noun *puppis* in Latin, to denote a ship. Let these synecdoches of a part of the whole, which are so very similar, be translated and transposed, and you will immediately perceive that a man would not be said to speak Latin, who in that language should call a ship *velum*; nor would you think that he spoke better English, who in our language should call it a *poop*.

What he says of synecdoche applies equally to metaphor, and he continues:

> . . . of two words even in the same language, which are synonymous or nearly so, one will be used figuratively to denote an object, which it would be insufferable to employ the other to denote, though naturally as fit for suggesting it. It hath been said, that "an excellent *vein* of satire runs through the whole of Gulliver's travels:" substitute here *artery* in the room of vein, and you will render the sentence absolutely ridiculous.[13]

Campbell's point may be stated in another way. There is a narrow sense of understanding a language in which one may be said to understand a language when he knows the grammar, the literal meanings of all the terms, and even the meaning of idioms. Such knowledge does not suffice for the understanding of the metaphors of the language. In addition one must know something of linguistic conventions—such as that governing the choice of 'vein' and 'artery' and even of minor facets of the general culture, such as what characteristics of bears are uppermost in people's minds. This aspect is especially prominent in metaphors where an evaluation is the basis of the parallel. A popular song of some years ago praised a young lady by saying to her "You're the cream in my coffee." Entirely the wrong impression would be obtained in a community which drank its coffee black. This sociological aspect of metaphors has been employed by Whorf and his students in using language as a means of of analyzing culture,[14] comparing widely differing cultures, though its value with more closely related societies remains to be seen. For this purpose commonplace and more or less standard metaphors are, of course, of greater value than the more original creations of poets.

Thus far we have seen something of the semantic structure of metaphor and something of the psychological elements leading to its apprehension—the consciousness of clash of literal senses from which its starts and the clues and conventions by which it is apprehended. This is not to claim, of course, that everyone can understand every metaphor. Often, of course, metaphors are not understood; they rest on a similarity which is unfamiliar to the reader or on a convention which he does not know. Often also a metaphor is only partly understood. One develops a feeling for the kind of parallel required without quite seeing what it is.

IV

The function of metaphor in general is to extend language, to say what cannot be said in terms of literal meanings alone. Such extension may be in either of two directions, by way of increasing the scope or breadth of language or alternatively by increasing the finesse or depth of language. Metaphor is the same in either case, it is the sort of thing we have been describing, but the use to which it is put is different and the qualifications for successful use vary accordingly. It will be advantageous, therefore, to discuss these two uses separately.

Metaphor may be used whenever something new is invented requiring a name or whenever it seems desirable to call attention to an undesignated aspect of something already known. In such a case there are a number of possibilities open—the obvious one is to create an entirely new word, but this has the disadvantage of being completely unintelligible when first heard. A common alternative is to construct a compound word whose sense is derivative from that of its components: 'microscope' and the German *'fernsprecher'* are cases in point. Alternatively a metaphor may be used. In many cases this has the advantage of enabling the person hearing the metaphor to identify the object even though he has never seen it before and never heard the word in its figurative sense. Thus, the lower shell of a turtle is called its plastron, which originally meant a breastplate, as in a suit of armor. When applied to a turtle this must originally have been a metaphor, yet knowing only what then was the literal meaning of the term and seeing a turtle there would be no doubt as to what was its plastron. Again, when automobiles became common, a terminology became necessary to their various parts. The name given to the part over the motor was assigned by what was originally a metaphor, i.e., it was what stood in the same relation to a car that a hood did to a person. It is interesting to notice, in this connection, that the metaphor 'hood of a car' could have been designated either of two parts —the hood or the top which is called 'hood' in England. Here the metaphor does not uniquely select the intended object but, by limiting the possibilities, still serves a useful purpose.

Metaphors of this type tend to vanish, not in the sense that they are no longer used, but in the sense that they become literal, so that today no one would think of saying that 'plastron of a turtle' or 'hood of a car' were metaphors. What seems to be involved in the shift away from metaphors seems to be approximately as follows: One way of coming to understand a term is to know how to apply it. It has been argued that this is the only way, but this controversy need not detain us here since, certainly, it is a way. Thus, hearing the metaphor 'hood of a car,' when this was a metaphor, one was enabled to discover the required part by looking for something in proper relationship to the car. Having found it, however, one could notice its shape, its position on the car and its relation to other parts and so recognize it. Independent of the metaphor, one would have memories of how hoods had looked and expectations of how they should look. Then any meaning for 'hood' except these memories and expectations became unimportant and the metaphorical element dropped out. We have seen that a metaphor requires a clash of terms. When the phrase was first heard there would be such a clash — a wondering what a head-covering would do on an automobile. Once the required part was recognized, however, the clash may be forgotten and the phrase might be considered a single unit, designating something whose appearance is known. Thus the metaphor would disappear and a new literal sense would be born. As we shall notice subsequently, there is considerable discussion among literary critics as to whether metaphors may be paraphrased adequately and so reduced to literal meanings. Metaphors of the type here discussed have obviously been forgotten in such controversies since, clearly, they become literal meanings.

There are other metaphors which become literal and extend language, although not in the simple fashion noticed above. Eric Havelock has traced the development of some of the Greek philosophic concepts from the stage at the time of Homer.[15] They were not expressible in Homeric Greek, and metaphor is one of the principal means whereby they were developed. So for example, Havelock suggests that the term 'cosmos' originally referred to a pleasing sort of array such as a woman's headdress or the trappings of a horse's harness. Later, by a metaphorical extension it was applied to the ranks of an army and then, by a further extension of the same sort, to the order of the universe as a whole. Here again the term did not remain metaphorical, but engendered a literal meaning. The process used to explain the earlier examples will not serve here, however, since there can be no recognition or identification of a cosmos in the same sense that a hood of a car can be recognized. We know of no satisfactory theory as to how such terms become literal and presumably it must wait on the working out of a general theory of meaning. In the cases of this sort, however, metaphor is even more important for extended language than in those considered before. After all, the undershell of a turtle is simply there and can be pointed at if necessary to call attention to it. A world order may equally be there, but it certainly cannot be pointed at in the same way. The only means of thinking about it may be the metaphor. Perhaps the new idea is inconceivable apart from the metaphor.

There can be no doubt then that both in the development of concrete and abstract terms metaphor plays an important role, but how important has not been sufficiently worked out.

Cohen[16] gives some hint of it when he says: "Indeed whenever we speak of the mind doing anything, collecting its data, perceiving the external world, and the like, we are using the metaphor of reification, just as we use the metaphor of personification whenever we speak of bodies attracting and repelling each other." Regardless of whether or not one wishes to agree that all these terms are metaphors, at least this is how they all must have originated. While a tremendous number of etymologies attest to the scope of metaphor in linguistic change, there seem to have been no general studies of the topic. Cohen has mentioned two pervasive metaphors; are there others equally prevalent? Can they be classified in any way? Are the same general types of metaphors common to all languages? These are similar questions; all remain unanswered. The importance of metaphor in the development of abstract concepts similarly can only be guessed at and any more accurate determination must await further studies.

V

The use of metaphor discussed in the preceding section is creative in that it adds to the range of a language, enabling it to deal with new situations. The literary or poetic use of metaphor is also creative, but in a different way, bringing out a new aspect, or showing a new way of feeling, concerning something already describable in the language. Because metaphor symbolizes one situation by means of another, there is the opportunity of infusing the symbolized situation with the feeling belonging to the one which functions as symbol. That this transfer of feeling occurs may be seen from a consideration of inverse metaphors, whose existence was already pointed out by Aristotle. He says: "As old age (D) is to life (C), so is evening (B) to the day (A). One will accordingly describe evening (B) as the 'old age *of the day*' (D+A)—or by the Empodoclean equivalent; and old age (D) as the 'evening' or 'sunset of life' (B+C)."[17]

That such inversion is possible is of course a consequence of the iconic character of metaphor. It would be possible in every metaphor but, and this is the point, the feeling tone is different in the two cases. Both Aristotle's metaphors are hackneyed by now and have lost their bite, but even so there is a pleasant and cheerful feeling in talking of the sunset of life—because the sunset itself is this sort of event—and there is something cold about the old age of the day. In a society which placed a premium on old age this might be different, but these examples indicate at least that the feeling which goes with the literal sense carries over to the figurative one.

To make the same point with less trite examples, we may recall Hall's metaphor inviting Romira to garrison his arms. It not merely suggests occupying or coming within as was claimed above but suggests a certain way of doing it—the way in which soldiers might occupy a fort. They take possession—a self-assertive act. They show, or prepare to show, courage in the forthcoming defense. Thus the suggestion is not merely that Romira come to him, but that she comes confidently, as if this were her proper place, and bravely instead of ignominiously running away. This, of course, is no more than a suggestion of the feeling indicated, but let us look at those in the converse metaphor. In the given case Romira was asked to come into his arms through being asked to garrison them. Conversely —changing grammatical subject and object—that a fort is garrisoned might be expressed by saying that the fort embraced the troops. But here the suggestion is different. Instead of merely receiving them, we now have the notion that the fort welcomed them, that there was joy in their reception. Here again in either the metaphor or its converse there is a carryover from the feeling of the literal sense to that of the figurative.

Thus there are two similarities which may enter into a metaphor —an antecedent similarity, the aspect which makes it possible for one situation to represent another iconically which was discussed in Section II. In addition there may be an induced similarity, such as the similarity of feeling which, as we have just noticed, is transferred from symbolizing situation to situation symbolized. 'Transferred,' however, is too strong a word here—the feeling is not simply carried across from one situation to the other, rather an aura of the feeling in the one case pervades the other. We do not feel toward Romira's coming as we would to soldiers entering a fort, but the comparison has created just the suggestion of a proud or triumphal entry. This nuance of feeling may well be the reason for the employment of the figure, for in many cases there does not seem any other way of conveying just the same impression.

In the preceding chapter, various aspects of meaning, cognitive and noncognitive, were pointed out, and it was maintained that a term in a metaphor must have a double primary cognitive content —that involved in its literal sense and that involved in its figurative sense. What we are now suggesting is that there is similarly a double feeling expressed in the metaphor but that the two are not unrelated and that the feeling accompanying the figurative sense is modified by and in fact caused by the feeling accompanying the literal sense. This modification of the way of thinking of what the metaphor symbolizes indirectly may be called the *induced content* of the metaphor. The matter may be put in this way: a metaphor we have noticed has to do with two situations—that symbolized literally and that symbolized figuratively. There must be an initial similarity between them to make the metaphor possible. We are now arguing that supervening on this initial similarity there may be an additional similarity suggested or caused by the use of the metaphor. This is the induced content.

In the above discussion the only sort of induced content considered was feeling. On the other hand the definition was framed so as to avoid any such limitation. This at once raises the question as to whether there may not be induced conceptual content as well. Such contents, if they exist, are of relatively minor importance in poetic use of metaphor and so have not been discussed here. They may however be of importance in connection with the use of metaphor to extended language in cases where the metaphor vanishes. In some cases, we noticed that the metaphor acquired a literal meaning by the development of the ability to recognize what it designated; in other cases this explanation could not be given. Many philosophical terms are of this latter sort and it is difficult if not impossible to develop means of recognition for such terms as 'substance' or 'ego.' It may be in such cases that part of the meaning is given by an induced content. There must in the case of 'substance,' for example, have been a primary similarity between the characteristic of an object and the foundation of a house. In terms of this, one could metaphorically refer to something standing under the qualities, but additional properties of substance such as its permanence would seem to be induced content.

To return to the literary use of metaphor, something similar to the view suggested here has been quite differently but admirably expressed by Kenneth Burke, who writes: "Metaphor is a device for seeing something *in terms* of something else. . . . A metaphor tells us something about one character considered from the point of view of another character. And to consider A from the point of view of B is, of course, to use B as a *perspective* upon A."[18]

The use of 'perspective' here is of course itself metaphorical but it is hard to see what it would mean except that one situation is seen in terms of the feelings of another. Perhaps this also is in Murry's mind when he suggests that metaphor is "the means by which the less familiar is assimilated to the more familiar, the unknown to the known."[19] In general, the conceptual subject matter of poetry is familiar enough, but it is the way of feeling which needs explanation.

It is this aspect of metaphor which renders the question of paraphrases of metaphors difficult. In the language-building function, we have seen, a metaphor becomes its own paraphrase, but in the cases where subtlety of way of seeing and feeling are desired this is not the case and there is doubt whether a paraphrase can express anything like the exact import of the original. There are all sorts of opinion to be found on the point. Thus Herschberger has argued:

> . . . that metaphor, the distinctive feature of poetry, *is* fundamentally an expository, and—in its way—economic prose usage; that in principle, through scientific study of the aesthetic experience, a metaphor is reducible to a multiplicity of integrated prose arguments; that science is admittedly inadequate at the present time, for this analysis; and that pseudo-scientific analysis has discredited such an approach by failing to be conducted by aesthetically sensitive persons.[20]

While on the other hand Cleanth Brooks in discussing the view that poetry makes an assertion says:

> Let the reader try to formulate a proposition that will say what the poem "says." As his proposition approaches adequacy, he will find, not only that it has increased greatly in length, but that it has begun to fill itself up with reservations and qualifications—and most significant of all—the formulator will find that he has himself begun to fall back upon metaphors of his own in his attempt to indicate what the poem "says."

In sum his proposition, as it approaches adequacy ceases to be a proposition.[21]

Clearly, for Brooks, metaphors can never give way to their paraphrases. Cohen expresses a similar view.[22]

Without going into the arguments in either side, it may be well to follow a suggestion of I. A. Richards in discussing what one wants when he attempts to express a metaphor in other terms. He says: "We can put varying sorts of limitations on 'express'; they give us different kinds of meaning—mere sense, sense and implications, feelings, the speaker's attitudes to whatever it is, to his audience, the speaker's confidence, and other things."[23] Richards then goes on to argue that while perhaps any of these senses may be paraphrased, all of them cannot be in a single paraphrase.

In one respect at least Richards is unquestionably right. There is a sense of shock about a metaphor which we have noticed before and which results from the clash of juxtaposed literal sense. It has almost an epigrammatic quality and this must be lost in any paraphrase. Unquestionably it is part of the effect of the metaphor and, if all effects be counted as part of the meaning, then no paraphrase can be adequate. Even given this limitation it seems quite probable as Richards suggests, that further sacrifices must be made in paraphrase.

For one thing, many poetic metaphors are multiple iconic—there being not merely one basic similarity on which the metaphor is based but several. Each of these may be capable of indefinite expansion, and there may be interactions between the similarities. Where one leaves open a range of possibilities, another may narrow them. Perhaps this interaction might be paraphrased if one were willing to take the similarity successively instead of almost simultaneously, but clearly there would be a tremendous loss of effect. If one is willing to sacrifice this aspect as well then there is no absurdity in holding that there should be a literal sense with the same cognitive content and emotional expression as is contained in a metaphor. Two points must be remembered however; first, that a paraphrase of this sort would not be equivalent to a metaphor in effect. It would be very long and cumbersome and would lose the interaction of the similarities. Second, while such a paraphrase is a theoretical possibility its construction would, to say the least, be very difficult and, practically speaking, impossible. Thus, as a matter of fact though not of logical necessity one must agree with Brooks' remark. This is not to say, however, that Herschberger is right in claiming the possibility of an ideal paraphrase into scientific statements. To make this claim is either to maintain that scientific statements may be more than cognitive or to claim that noncognitive aspects of meaning are reducible to cognitive. Since this problem is discussed in Chapter 5 we need here only indicate our disbelief in either alternative. There is one more aspect to the problem. We have seen that where metaphor is used to extend language, the disappearance of the primary clash of senses produces a literal sense of the term. In metaphors of the more poetic type, something of the same sort may go on, resulting in a well-established figurative sense of a term and a trite metaphor. Thus one may call a man an old goat or a poor fish with hardly any consideration of either animal, something may be nipped in the bud without much thought of flowers, and one may claim something is liquidated while hardly considering fluids. Such metaphors have been used in so wide a variety of circumstances and so often that there is a tendency to consider merely a sort of standard figurative meaning without paying attention to the literal one. Wherever this happens, a metaphor may be more easily paraphrased.

We may conclude that apart from the impact of a metaphor in presenting a conflict in so small a compass, there is no obstacle in principle to the adequate paraphrase of a metaphor though the difficulties may be very great in practice. They are least when the metaphor has become trite. Metaphors, like chemical elements, display unusual powers in a nascent state.

NOTES

1. *Poetics* Chap. 21, 1457b, trans. by Bywater.

2. *Paradise Lost*, II, 112.

3. Thus in 'The Oxford Movement may be a spent wave' Richards says that the vehicle is the spent wave—which agrees with our use of literal sense—but the tenor is the Oxford Movement whereas we would say that the figurative sense, approximately, is no longer having influence. Cf. *Interpretation in Teaching* (London, 1938), p. 121.

4. *The Structure of Complex Words* (London: Chatto & Windus, 1951), p. 38.

5. "To Hope," in *Poems*, 1817.

6. It makes some difference to the imagery which is chosen. A person huddled in a blanket suggests someone cold and forlorn, but not the active malevolence of the other possibilities. This affects what will be called the induced content of the metaphor later in this chapter.

7. Virginia Woolf, *Between the Acts* (New York, 1941), p. 9.

8. Cf. *Collected Papers* (Cambridge, Mass., 1932), II, Bk. II, Chap. 3. It is not always clear whether Peirce treats icon and symbol as distinct kinds of signs or as distinct ways of symbolizing, both of which might be embodied in the same sign. We have taken the latter view. Peirce also distinguishes a third mode of signifying, the indexical, but this is irrelevant to the present discussion.

9. *Countries of the Mind*, 2d series (Oxford, 1931), p. 3.

10. *Odyssey XI*, trans. by T.E. Shaw.

11. *Anthony and Cleopatra*, II, 2.

12. Opening line from John Hall's "The Call."

13. New York, 1859. Pp. 304-5.

14. See Chap. 1.

15. In discussions, unfortunately unpublished, presented to this group studying language and symbolism.

16. *A Preface to Logic* (London, 1946), p. 83.

17. *Poetics* Chap. 21, 1457b.

18. *A Grammar of Motives*, by Kenneth Burke, (c) 1945, by Prentice-Hall, Inc., published by Prentice-Hall, Inc., Englewood Cliffs, New Jersey, pp. 503-4.

19. Murry, *op. cit.*, p. 2.

20. R. Herschberger, "The Structure of Metaphor," *Kenyon Review*, 5 (1943): p. 433.

21. *The Well-wrought Urn* (New York, 1947), p. 181.

22. *Op. cit.*, p. 84.

23. *Interpretation in Teaching*, p. 135.

The Metaphorical Twist

Monroe C. Beardsley

Of all the questions about metaphor that interest the literary theorist or philosophic aesthetician, the foremost—that is, first and funda-mental—one is, of course: what is it? To give an adequate account of metaphor as linguistic phenomenon, on which to base our account of it as poetic phenomenon, is to say what is peculiar to metaphorical expressions, how they differ from literal ones, how we recognize them and know what they mean.

It is not easy to say exactly what are the issues over this problem. There are several ways of describing metaphor, some of them going back to ancient times, that are so familiar and so confidently echoed from one writer to another that they all have the air of being roughly equivalent. But there is, I believe, an important distinction among them, and part of my purpose here is to drive a wedge—to separate things out more sharply than has been done. I want to distinguish what might be called a thing-approach and a word-approach to the problem of analyzing metaphor.

According to one of these views, taken broadly, the modifier (as I call it) in the metaphor—for example, the word "spiteful" in "the

Reprinted from *Philosophy and Phenomenological Research* 22, no. 3 (1962): 293-307 by permission of the author and *Philosophy and Phenomenological Research*.

spiteful sun"—retains its standard designative role when it enters into the metaphor and therefore continues in that context to denote the same objects it denotes in literal contexts. Thus the metaphor is an implicit comparison, an elliptical simile, and says in effect that the sun is like a spiteful person. The spiteful person is referred to, in this context, just as is the sun—there are two objects. The metaphor, as Johnson said, "gives you two ideas instead of one." Mr. John Crowe Ransom has classified metaphors as "Importers" that introduce "foreign objects" into the "situation"[1]—I guess he was thinking of those fancy importers of exotic foodstuffs, like truffles and candied bees. The metaphor, in his view, drags an alien and uncalled-for object into the context (delighting us, the Eighteenth Century theorist might say, by its charm and novelty), and thereby adds to that "local texture of irrelevance" that Ransom considers so essential to poetry.

Let us call this the Object-comparison Theory of metaphor. According to its rival, the Verbal-opposition Theory, no such importation or comparison occurs at all, but instead a special feat of language, or verbal play, involving two levels of meaning in the modifier itself. When a predicate is metaphorically adjoined to a subject, the predicate loses its ordinary extension, because it acquires a new intension—perhaps one that it has in no other context. And this twist of meaning is forced by inherent tensions, or oppositions, within the metaphor itself.

I propose to give reasons for rejecting the Object-comparison Theory, both in its general form and in a special form that has recently been offered. Then I shall explain more fully the Verbal-opposition Theory, and defend it against some possible objections.

I

Now up to a point, I admit, it does not matter whether you talk of metaphors in the object-fashion or in the semantical fashion. But only up to a point. Thus suppose the word "briar" is introduced metaphorically into a certain context, as, say, in "East Coker"—the reference to

frigid purgatorial fires
Of which the flame is roses, and the smoke is briars.[2]

You can start your explication either in object-language (talking about the characteristics of briars) or in metalanguage (talking about the connotations of the *word* "briars"). You can say, "Briars have the capacity to scratch people, to retard their progress, to be made into pipes," and so on. Or you can say, "The word 'briars' connotes such properties as being scratchy, retarding progress, being made into pipes," and so on. But though these two ways of speaking overlap, since in part the connotations of the *word* derive from what is generally true of the *objects*, they do not coincide completely.

For the connotations are controlled not only by the properties the object actually has but by those it is widely *believed* to have —even if the belief is false. This is my first argument against the Object-comparison Theory, then—that a consistent adherence to that theory would produce incorrect or incomplete explications of metaphors in cases where the modifier has connotations, applicable in that context, that are not common accidental features of the objects denoted. For example, some of the important marginal meaning of "briars" in the Eliot poem comes, of course, from the way the crown of thorns figures in the Christian story. And quite apart from its historical truth, the existence of that religion is sufficient to give the word that meaning. If in explicating this line we limit ourselves to what we know about briars, we would not fully understand it.

My second argument against the Object-comparison Theory is that once we commit ourselves to finding, or supplying, an object to be compared with the subject of the metaphor (that is, in I. A. Richards' terms, a "vehicle" to make it go) we open the way for that flow of idiosyncratic imagery that is one of the serious barriers between a reader and a poem. Consider an example also discussed by Mr. Ransom, the lines about Brutus's sword in Antony's speech:

> Mark how the blood of Caesar follow'd it,
> As rushing out of doors, to be resolv'd
> If Brutus so unkindly knock'd or no

(III, ii, 178). Ransom speaks of the "shift" from the tenor (the blood) to a "page" opening the door, the page being the vehicle.[3] Now there is obviously no page in these lines, any more than there is a rudely-awakened householder or soon-to-be-embattled farmer alarmed by

Paul Revere. Where does the page come from? The tenor-vehicle terminology, with its underlying assumption that the metaphor must be a comparison, tempts the explicator to invent, where he cannot discover, a vehicle; and so we get the page. But "rushing out of doors" is not exactly synonymous with "page rushing out of doors," as applied to Caesar's blood. And it is the first meaning that the explicator is to keep his eye on, not the further meaning imported — a good description — by his own fancy. Quoting a characteristic metaphor of Samuel Johnson's, "Time is, of all modes of existence, most obsequious to the imagination," William K. Wimsatt, Jr., remarks, "We need not imagine Time as a butler bowing to his master the Imagination."[4]

My third argument against the Object-comparison Theory is that is tends to lead to the unfortunate doctrine of "appropriateness." If a metaphor is a comparison, it is possible to ask whether the comparison is "apt" or "farfetched." We see this in Aristotle's fourth type of bad taste, his objection to the phrase of Gorgias, "events that are fresh and full of blood."[5] If we take Macbeth's words, (II, iii),

their daggers

Unmannerly breech'd with gore

to be comparing bloody daggers and breeched legs, and if we inquire into its appropriateness, we are likely to say, like the Nineteenth Century critic quoted by Cleanth Brooks,[6] that Shakespeare "disgusts us with the attempted comparison." But the correct question is what is *meant* by the words — what properties are attributed to the daggers via the marginal meanings of the metaphorical attribute. It is of no moment whether bloody daggers in general are best so described; the question is what we learn from this description about *these* daggers, and their role in the whole story — or about the speaker who describes them this way.

To put the point more generally: Suppose the poet remarks, "My sweetheart is my Schopenhauer." On the Comparison Theory we are to ask what his sweetheart and Schopenhauer have in common. But we don't *know* his sweetheart, so how can we answer this question until he tells us, by the metaphor itself, what she is like? The correct question is what possible meanings of "Schopenhauer" can apply to the sweetheart, and are not ruled out by the context.

II

My general objections to the Object-comparison Theory apply, I believe, with like force to the very interesting form of this theory that has been advanced by Paul Henle: the Iconic Signification Theory.[7] Mr. Henle actually seems to hold both of the theories that I have named. His version of the Verbal-opposition Theory, however, is described in terms of the reader's response—his "shock" at the "clash of meanings."[8] I prefer to state the theory as a theory, not about the effect of metaphor, but about the linguistic structure that causes the effect—about the "clash of meanings" itself. Mr. Henle says little about this, and he does not explain its relation to his other, and main, theory—indeed, he does not say why there should be any shock, or any clash, if the other is correct.

Mr. Henle holds that "there is an iconic element in metaphor," and he proposes to analyze metaphorical attributions in terms of the concept of iconic signs. In his example from Keats, "hateful thoughts enwrap my soul in gloom," he says there are two relationships: first, the word "enwrap" designates a certain action—"envelopment in a cloak." Second, this action is made an iconic sign of gloom.[9] "In a metaphor, some terms symbolize the icon and others symbolize what is iconized."[10]

We might begin by asking how the cloak gets into this explication. The Iconic Theory seems to import an alien object of some sort—like Mr. Ransom's page—and it is subject to the difficulties in the theory of importation. Mr. Henle has even yielded to the "appropriateness" doctrine, which, as I suggested, the Comparison Theory at least makes tempting. Thus he says that "it would not have done to speak of hateful thoughts *entrapping* the soul in gloom," because traps "are all sharp, with definite edges, and this spoils the correspondence with gloom."[11] Perhaps I should not put so much stress on this remark, but I must say that it would generalize into a most astonishing critical principle. For my part, I think the question whether wraps or traps are better iconic signs of gloom is a wholly unanswerable question, and fortunately it does not need to be asked. If the speaker in the poem had been trapped in gloom, rather than wrapped in it, that would simply have said something different about him, and about how he felt, and came to feel that way—which might have made a worse poem, or a better one, depending on several other things.

Mr. Henle cites one of Aristotle's examples of the way in which "proportional analogies" can be inverted: another is that we can say either that the shield is the bowl of Ares or the bowl is the shield of Dionysus.[12] "That such inversion is possible is of course a consequence of the iconic character of metaphor," says Mr. Henle.[13] And maybe it does follow from any Object-comparison Theory, for if A can be compared to B, why not B to A? And a statement of likeness is equivalent to its own converse. But if it follows, that is a fatal objection to the theory. Now Mr. Henle realizes that there is a difficulty, and so he says that though metaphors are always reversible, sometimes the "feeling tone is different." I don't believe this will do: the difference between "this man is a lion" and "that lion is a man"[14] is in what the different metaphorical modifiers attribute to the two subjects. In the Verbal-opposition Theory, it does not follow that because A's are metaphorically B's, therefore B's are metaphorically A's. That is just the difference between a metaphor and Aristotle's proportional analogy, or relational simile—even if Aristotle himself thought the difference was not great. And surely the Verbal-opposition Theory is correct in this consequence, while the Iconic Theory, if it entails that in calling men lions and lions men we are in both cases attributing the same properties, is clearly false.

One other objection can, I think, be fairly made against the Iconic Signification Theory. It should be counted as a merit in a theory of metaphor that it can analyze metaphor in the same terms that will do for oxymoron. This makes for economy of theory, and it fits in with the evidently deep affinities between these two types of expression. Now the Iconic Theory is somewhat handicapped here, for it does not seem to work well for oxymoron. In "mute cry" (if that may be taken as an example), we should have to say that a mute person was being made an iconic sign of something that is not mute: soundlessness becomes a sign of sound. This is not very convincing. The truth seems rather to be that in oxymoron we have the archetype, the most apparent and intense form, of verbal opposition.

III

If we turn from the objects referred to in the metaphor, and consider the significations of the words themselves, we must look for the

metaphoricalness of the metaphor, so to speak, in some sort of conflict that is absent from literal expressions. One direction in which
this conflict has been searched for may, I think, be quickly marked
off as a dead end. This approach contrasts the meaning of the expression itself and the idea in the speaker's (or writer's) mind. To call A a
B metaphorically, in this view, is to say that A is a B without meaning it—metaphor is a form of irony.[15] The implicit appeal here is to
intention, and the theory suffers from all the ills associated with that
notion. We do not decide that a word in a poem is used metaphorically because we know what the poet was thinking; rather we know
what he was thinking because we see that the word is used metaphorically. The clues to this fact must somehow be in the poem itself, or
we should seldom be able to read poetry.

There is a hint of a similar view in the excellent account of metaphor in Isabel Hungerland's recent book.[16] In the metaphor, she says,
"There must be some ascertainable point in the deviation from or
violation of ordinary usage—another way of putting it is that the violation must be deliberate." Mrs. Hungerland has since said that the
second clause here was inadvertent; I mention it only to emphasize
that the two clauses are surely far from equivalent, because accidental or unintended metaphors are perfectly possible.[17]

The opposition that renders an expression metaphorical is, then,
within the meaning-structure itself. The central features of such a
Verbal-opposition Theory I have already expounded elsewhere,[18] but
I should like to recapitulate them briefly here. In that version, I said
that the possibility of the metaphorical performance—the opportuni-
ties that a living language presents for fooling around with meanings
in this particular way—depend upon a felt difference between two
sets of properties in the intension, or signification, of a general term:
first, those properties that (at least in a given sort of context) are
taken to be necessary conditions for applying the term correctly in a
particular sense (these are the defining, or designated, properties, or
the central meaning of the term in that sort of context); second,
those properties that belong to the marginal meaning of the term, or
(in the literary critic's sense of the word) its connotation—properties
that a speaker can, in appropriate contexts, show that he attributes
to an object by using that term without claiming to follow a rule that
he would not apply the term to that kind of object if it did not have

that property. I said that when a term is combined with others in such a way that there would be a logical opposition between its central meaning and that of the other terms, there occurs that shift from central to marginal meaning which shows us the word is to be taken in a metaphorical way. It is the only way it can be taken without absurdity. The term "logical opposition" here includes both direct incompatibility of designated properties and a more indirect incompatibility between the presuppositions of the terms—as when our concept of the sun rules out the possibility of voluntary behavior that is presupposed by the term "spiteful." The logical opposition is what gives the modifier its metaphorical twist.

A metaphorical attribution, then, involves two ingredients: a semantical distinction between two levels of meaning, and a logical opposition at one level. Thus there is no question of "spiteful," in a metaphorical context, denoting spiteful people and injecting them for the purpose of comparison; the price it pays for admission to this context is that it functions there to signify only its connoted characteristics.

Such is the Simple Verbal-opposition Theory as I have defended it, and it seems to me to be right up to a point. That is, I believe that the phenomenon it describes, the shift from designation to connotation, actually occurs. But I am afraid it is not enough. Something else that is very important also happens in at least some metaphors, I now think.[19] And to explain it, we must make (or make more explicit than was done in the earlier version) two distinctions.

The connotations of a word standing for objects of a certain kind, it will be agreed, are drawn from the total set of accidental properties either found in or attributed to such objects. Let us call this set of accidental properties the *potential range of connotation* of that word. At a given time in the history of the word, however, not all of these properties will perhaps have been made use of. Thus, think of a number of properties characteristic of trees, though not necessarily present in all: leafiness, shadiness, branchiness, tallness, slimness, having bark, suppleness in the wind, strength, and so on. Some of these, such as leafiness, shadiness, tallness, clearly belong among the recognized connotations of "tree," readily called into play in familiar metaphors. They may be called *staple connotations*. Other properties, such as perhaps slimness and having bark, do not seem to be staple connotations, though they may be sufficiently characteristic of trees to be available in the potential range of connotation. They may wait, so to speak, lurking in the nature of things, for actualization—wait to be captured by the word "tree" as part of its meaning in some future context.

My first distinction, then, is between two sets of accidental properties—not a sharp distinction, not one that can always be cut with confidence, but still objectively determinable. My second distinction is between two kinds of metaphor—and it is subject to similar qualifications.

Suppose we begin by trying to divide metaphors into two classes. Let us try putting into Class I metaphors like "smiling sun" and "the moon peeping from behind a cloud." Note that these are not dead metaphors—that is not the problem involved here. They are live, but somehow they are different from those we might put into Class II: "the spiteful sun," "unruly sun," "faithful sun," "inconstant moon." We recognize, it seems safe to say, that those in Class II are more interesting than those in Class I—which is not, of course, to say that they are better in every poetic context. But what is the difference?

Now, in terms of the Simple Verbal-opposition Theory, something can be said by way of explanation. The Class II metaphors are more complex than the Class I metaphors. They seem to say more about the object. They are thus more precise, more discriminating, as descriptions. To speak of the sun as "smiling" is to imply a broad contrast with a sun that does not succeed in smiling, perhaps, or that is angry and beats down on the desert. But to speak of the sun as "unruly" is to imply a sharper distinction between this quality and other qualities conceived with comparable specificity: obedience, punctuality, deference to one's wishes. Now the Verbal-opposition Theory, even in its simple form, allows degrees of complexity, and so perhaps it can at least partly explain the difference between the two classes. Yet there seems to be more to the matter even than this.

It is at this point that we encounter a very tricky question indeed. For one suggestion that seems obvious enough is this: the Class I metaphors are trite and banal; the Class II metaphors are fresh and novel. If there is truth in this description, it can only be won and kept by skillful maneuvering around some deceptive shoals. In the first place, we must not, I think, suppose that it is a matter of mere repetition. Perhaps "smiling sun" has been said more often than "inconstant moon," but even if we were to repeat the phrase from *Romeo and Juliet* over and over until we were tired of it, and therefore were in no position to attend to its meaning, that would not alone make it trite. In any case, if triteness is a frequency-notion, then it is not what makes the difference here. Yet in the second place, the nature of a particular metaphor cannot be entirely independent of its date in the history of English literature. For what it does mean, or can mean, at a given time must depend to some extent on what other contexts the words have appeared in, and what analogous or parallel expressions exist in the language.

IV

Let us suppose that when the metaphor "th'inconstant moon" is first constructed in English, it is the first time that "inconstant" has been used metaphorically—or at least the first time it has been applied to an inanimate object. (This, of course, does not preclude the possibility that it may originally have applied *only* to inanimate objects, say, to their rotational motion; if at some time it came to have the psychological or behavioral meaning as its primary one, then we can speak of the first metaphorical use after this time). At this moment the word "inconstant" *has* no connotations. When, therefore, we find "inconstant moon," we sieze upon the verbal opposition, all right, but when we look for relevant connotations we are balked. How, then, can we explicate it? Given the surrounding syntax and the prevailing tone, it claims to make sense; therefore we must try to make it make sense. And so we look about among the accidental or contingent properties of inconstant people in general, and attribute these properties, or as many of them as we can, to the moon. And these properties would, for the moment at least, become part of the meaning of "inconstant," though previously they were only properties of those people. Then we might say that the metaphor transforms a *property* (actual or attributed) into a *sense*. And if, taking their lead from this license, other poets were to find other metaphorical applications for "inconstant," which employed the same properties and created similar, or overlapping, senses, then those senses might become closely enough connected with the word so that they would be relatively fixed as connotations of that word. In this way the metaphors would not only actualize a potential connotation, but establish it as a staple one.

Here is where the Object-comparison Theory makes its contribution after all. For it is correct in saying that sometimes in explicating metaphors we must consider the properties of the objects denoted by the modifier. But those objects are not referred to for comparison: they are referred to so that some of their relevant properties can be given a new status as elements of verbal meaning.

Let us suppose that at a given time in the history of the English language we have already in existence such metaphors as "smiling sky," "smiling sea," and "smiling garden." The modifier cannot, of course, mean exactly the same thing in all these contexts, but there will be some meaning in common. And let us suppose this common meaning is already established as the connotation of "smiling." When a poet for the first time speaks of a "smiling sun," what will happen? The logical opposition is plain, so we turn first to the staple connotations of "smiling" and apply them to the sun (as the simple Verbal-opposition Theory says). But we go no further. Perhaps we cannot go further; perhaps we are just not forced to. In any case, we see that it is a metaphor, and we can read it correctly, but we do not take it as *creating* meaning in the same way as Class II metaphors. It is merely borrowing its sense, relying on what is already established and available.

The Revised Theory can be well illustrated by a very interesting metaphor that I have borrowed from Paul Henle. In one of his devotional works, Jeremy Taylor says that "Chaste marriages are honourable and pleasing to God," that widowhood can be "amiable and comely when it is adorned with gravity and purity," but that "virginity is a life of angels, the enamel of the soul . . . "[20] This was not the earliest metaphorical use of "enamel;" we learn from the NED that Donne, in 1631, had already used the phrase "enameled with that beautiful Doctrine of good Workes," and that Evelyn, in 1670, had used the phrase "enamel their characters." Moreover, Taylor himself, in the dedication to his *Sermons*, spoke of "those truths which are the enamel and beauty of our churches." Perhaps such usages had already established some of the properties of enamel as staple connotations of the word; perhaps not. We would have to know this in order to know exactly how definitely in Class II was the metaphor "the enamel of the soul" in the context of Taylor's *Of Holy Living*. But of our own time we can make a surer judgment. Enamel is hard, resistant to shock and scrape, applied with labor and skill, and decorative. I should think some of these are not fully established as recognized connotations of the word. Yet to speak of virginity as the enamel of the soul is surely to say (as Mr. Henle points out) that it is a protection for the soul, and that it is the final touch of adornment on what is already well-made. Thus this metaphor does not merely thrust latent connotations into the foreground of meaning, but brings into play some properties that were not previously meant by it.

It seems to me that we probably have to distinguish at least three stages in this metamorphosis of verbal meaning, even though the points of transitition are not clearly marked. In the first stage we have a word and properties that are definitely not part of the intension of that word. Some of those properties are eligible to become part of the intension, to join the range of connotation. In order to be eligible, they have to be fairly common (actual or imputed) properties, typical properties—not just in the statistical sense, but normally or characteristically present in the objects denoted by the word. Thus, for example, suppose someone said that whiteness could become a connotation of "enamel." This could happen, I should think, if most or all enamel were white, or if enamel were usually white except when affected by external conditions, or if the best enamel were white, or if the whitest white things were enamelled things.

When the word comes to be used metaphorically in a certain sort of context, then what was previously only a property is made, at least temporarily, into a meaning. And widespread familiarity with that metaphor, or similar ones, can fix the property as an established part of the meaning. It is still, in this second stage, not a necessary condition for applying the word. Even if "tree" connotes tallness, there is no contradiction in speaking of a short or stunted tree. Still, if someone said that his tree was a tree "in the fullest sense" (compare "He is in every sense a man,") we should, I think, be justified in taking him to be saying, among other things, that it had reached a good height, at least for its species.

When a connotation becomes so standardized for certain types of context, it may be shifted to a new status, where it becomes a necessary condition for applying the word in that context. It then constitutes a new standard sense. This third stage is illustrated by the dead metaphor: "tail," used in connection with automobile lights, now owes nothing to animal tails, and its meaning can be learned by someone who never heard that animals had tails. Not all connotations, of course, pass into this third stage, but some are always doing so.

Perhaps some portion of this history can be traced in words like "warm" and "hard" that are taken over from the sensory realm and applied to human personality—as apparently happens in many languages.[21] I should think that the first application of "warm" to a person had to change some accidental properties of warm things into part of a new meaning of the word, though now we easily think of these properties as connotations of "warm"—for example, approachable, pleasurable-in-acquaintance, inviting. These qualities were part of the potential range of connotation of "warm" even before they were noted in warm things, which may not have been until they were noted in people and until someone, casting about for a word that would metaphorically describe those people, hit upon the word "warm." But before those qualities could come to belong to the staple connotation of "warm," it had to be discovered that they could be *meant* by the word when used in an appropriate metaphor. Finally, although it has not happened yet, "warm person" may come to lose its metaphorical character, with the present connotations of "warm" changing into a new designation. It would then be a dead metaphor.

If the Revised Verbal-opposition Theory is correct, it would account for a good deal. It does better than the simple theory at explaining the remarkable extent to which metaphor can expand our verbal repertoire beyond the resources of literal language.[22] It allows for novelty, for change of meaning, even for radical change. It admits the unpredictability of metaphor, the surprising ideas that may emerge even from chance juxtapositions of words. It shows that a metaphor can be objectively explicated, for the properties of things and the connotations of words are publicly discoverable, and disputes about them are in principle resolvable. And it explains the comparative obscurity, or momentary puzzlingness, of the Class II metaphor, which may take time to understand completely.

V

It seems that, in its revised form, the Verbal-opposition Theory may go a long way toward providing a satisfactory account of metaphor —if it can be defended against two possible lines of objection that are suggested by recent developments.

The first objection might be raised by those who are committed to an extensionalist theory of meaning, as opposed to an intensionalist one. The Verbal-opposition Theory cannot be formulated without speaking of properties (that is, qualities and relations) that are incompatible with each other; but the extensionalist does not believe that there are such things as properties. Could we not, he might ask, get along without the concept of incompatibility, and treat metaphors as simply a special case of materially *false* statements? Of course there is a difference between saying that someone is bald when he isn't and saying that he is a lion when he isn't. But perhaps the difference is merely that the latter is more surprising, more obviously and certainly known to be untrue. We see how the speaker might make a mistake about baldness, but we don't see how he could confuse a man with a lion, and so it is the sheer improbability of the latter remark (in the light of common knowledge) that makes us reject it literally and take it metaphorically—rather than any internal opposition of meaning.

We could make out a case for this Improbability Theory of metaphor, and we can even support it by examples of certain degenerate cases of metaphor that may be analyzable in this way. For example, the joker says, "I was in Philadelphia once, but it was closed."[23] Is this really self-contradictory? True, the word "closed" is ordinarily, and most appropriately, applied to individual enterprises, like stores and museums, which have doors that can be locked and bolted. But perhaps without stretching the term very much, a whole city could be literally closed, too. Let us suppose so. In that case, the peculiar metaphorical effect—the denigration of the vitality of Philadelphia night life—must depend on our rejecting the statement as false out of hand, because it is so absurdly unlikely. Yet granting that this verbal maneuver occurs, it does not cover all the cases. At the opposite extreme is oxymoron. A reviewer in the *Reporter* a while back described the literary figures of the Beat Movement as "writers who don't write who write." That is not merely improbable. And it seems to me that metaphors, for the most part, have something of this built-in self-controversion, quite distinguishable from the Philadelphia crack. Borderline cases there of course must be, where there is a not-too-remote possibility of taking the modifier in a way that will literally apply to the subject: for example, the phrase "bak'd with frost," in Shakespeare's *Tempest* (I, ii, 256), where "bak'd" could mean "thickened," and so the whole expression could have been literal in Shakespeare's time.[24]

The second objection to the Verbal-opposition Theory might be put this way: even if there are properties to be opposed, they are not, in ordinary language, so fixed in the designation of general terms that sharp and clear contradiction can occur. It is conceded that "brother" and "male sibling" may be practically perfect synonyms, as far as their central meanings are concerned (ignoring their connotations), and so "female brother" is internally contradictory —though not much of a metaphor, of course. But the thesis is that for most of the interesting words, the rules are not so definite, and so when these words are used metaphorically it cannot be because we detect an incompatibility of meaning on the level of designation.

Professor Michael Scriven[25] has argued that the word "lemon" has, in fact, no defining properties in the traditional sense—that is, properties that *must* be present if the word is to be correctly applied to an object. He quotes Webster's definition, "The acid fruit of a tree (*citrus limonia*), related to the orange," and this does not seem to give necessary conditions of lemonness, since it would not be a contradiction to say that a lemon grew on a banana tree, or no tree at all. Scriven, however, goes further, and claims that there is no single property of lemons that is individually necessary, if many others are present. And he holds that the same is true of most general terms in common use. They designate what he calls "cluster concepts," and have "criteria" of application, but not necessary conditions.

This important idea, if it can be sustained, would require some reformulation in the Verbal-opposition Theory as I have stated it above. It would not destroy the theory by implying that if the theory is true then the word "lemon" cannot be used metaphorically—as it evidently can. Scriven himself speaks of literal meaning as having "a shifting boundary beyond which only misuse and metaphor lie.''[26] If "lemon" has no necessary conditions, then it cannot be placed in a verbal context where some necessary condition is logically excluded, but it may be placed in a context where so many of its criteria are excluded that it cannot be literally applied —as when a second-hand car turns out to be a lemon.

I am not convinced that "lemon" and other ordinary words have *no* necessary conditions, and Mr. Scriven now holds his former view only in a modified form. I should think, for example, that having a certain organic texture—instead of being made of wood or wax —would be a necessary condition of lemonness. Surely being a material object is a necessary condition—a "spiritual lemon" would either be not literally a lemon or not literally spiritual. The questions involved here are subtle, too subtle for this occasion. For example, if I were to suddenly to come upon an object otherwise exactly like a lemon, but six feet in diameter, I suppose I could be persuaded to call it a giant "lemon"—I really haven't made up my mind. Does this show that I now use the property of being small-sized only as a "criterion," but not as a defining property, of lemons? Perhaps so— yet if someone says an object is a lemon *without* adding any remarks about its unusual size, I am justified, I think, in deducing that it is small. Perhaps we could follow a suggestion of the late Arthur Pap [27] and others who have discussed the "open texture"[28] of empirical terms, and weight the criteria as more or less required: distinguishing "degrees of meaning." Then we might identify a metaphorical modifier as one placed in a context where one of its more stringently required conditions is excluded. Even if small size is not an indispensable property of lemons, it might be a fairly central one, in which case a context that opposed this property would be enough to throw the word into a metaphorical posture.

This question I leave open here, satisfied for the present if I have shown that the Verbal-opposition Theory not only explains quite well a number of acknowledged features of metaphor, but makes no assumptions that a sound philosophy of language would be unwilling to grant.

NOTES

1. "William Wordsworth: Notes Toward an Understanding of Poetry," *Kenyon Review*, XII (Summer 1950): pp. 498-519.

2. T. S. Eliot, *Four Quartets*, New York: Harcourt, Brace, 1953, p. 16.

3. "Poetry: I. The Formal Analysis; II. The Final Cause," *Kenyon Review*, IX (Summer 1947): 436-56, (Autumn 1947): pp. 640-58.

4. *The Prose Style of Samuel Johnson*, New Haven: Yale University Press, 1941 (Yale Studies in English, Vol. 94), p. 66.

5. Lane Cooper, trans., *The Rhetoric of Aristotle*, New York: Appleton, 1932, p. 192.

6. *The Well Wrought Urn*, New York: Reynal and Hitchcock, 1947, p. 29. The New Variorum Edition, ed. H.H. Furness, 5th ed., Philadelphia: Lippincott, 1915, pp. 160-61, shows amusingly what a nagging puzzle this metaphor has been to Shakespearean explicators.

7. In his chapter on metaphor in Paul Henle, ed., *Language, Thought, and Culture*, Ann Arbor: University of Michigan Press, 1958, ch. 7, a development, and also a modification, of the view earlier set forth briefly in his Presidential Address to the Western Division of the American Philosophical Association, "The Problem of Meaning," in *Proceedings and Addresses of the American Philosophical Association*, 1953-54, Vol. XXVIII, Yellow Springs: Antioch Press, 1954.

8. *Language, Thought, and Culture*, pp. 182-83.

9. *Ibid.*, pp. 177-79.

10. *Ibid.*, p. 181.

11. *Ibid.*, p. 180.

12. Lane Cooper, trans., *op. cit.*, p. 193.

13. Henle, *op. cit.*, p. 190.

14. I take his example, but not his explanation, from R. P. Blackmur, "Notes on Four Categories in Criticism," *Sewanee Review*, LIV (October 1946): pp. 576-89. It would be, by the way, interesting to hear a defense of the reversibility of Ezra Pound's "Your mind and you are our Sargasso sea."

15. Anthony Nemetz, in a recent article, "Metaphor: The Daedalus of Discourse," *Thought*, XXXIII (Autumn 1958): pp. 417-42, bases his argument on the formula that "a metaphor consists of two parts: 1. What is said; 2. What is meant" (419); the question is, then, what is the relation between them? But this formulation gets the inquiry off on the wrong track. A metaphor is a "saying," just as a literal expression is: we can say things either literally or metaphorically, and in either case we can only be understood to mean what we can say. In a sarcastic remark, what is suggested is opposed to what is stated, but if we do not let the word "say" cover both, we are sure to think that interpreting the remark is a process of getting *around* it to a hidden intention behind.

16. *Poetic Discourse*, Berkeley and Los Angeles: University of California Press, 1958 (University of California Publications in Philosophy, No. 33), pp. 108-110.

17. See Walker Percy, "Metaphor as Mistake," *Sewanee Review*, LXVI (Winter 1958): pp. 79-99. Percy shows interestingly how there can be "mistakes which. . . have resulted in an authentic poetic experience" (80). Yet he too seems to weaken at the end, when he speaks of "that essential element of the meaning situation, the authority and intention of the Namer" (93).

18. See *Aesthetics: Problems in the Philosophy of Criticism*, New York: Harcourt, Brace, 1958, Ch. III.

19. The part that is new (to me) in my present account of metaphor did not occur to me until after, and in the light of, the papers by Mr. Henle and Mrs. Hungerland, who were my fellow-symposiasts when the present paper, in a different form, was read before the 17th annual meeting of the American Society for Aesthetics, Cincinnati, Ohio, Oct. 29-31, 1959. Mr. Henle's criticism of the Verbal-opposition Theory as incapable of explaining the element of novelty in metaphorical meaning, and the discussion that followed the papers, led me to the present line of thought.

20. *Of Holy Living*, ch. II, sec. 3, in *Works*, ed. C.P. Eden, Vol. III, London 1847, p. 56. Mr. Henle used this example in his symposium paper.

21. These personality metaphors have been interestingly investigated by Solomon E. Asch, "On the Use of Metaphor in the Description of Persons," in H. Werner, ed., *On Expressive Language*, Worcester: Clark University Press, 1955, and "The Metaphor: A Psychological Inquiry," in R. Tagiuri and L. Petrullo, eds., *Person Perception and Interpersonal Behavior*, Stanford: Stanford University Press, 1958. See also Roger Brown, *Words and Things*, Glencoe, Ill.: Free Press, 1958, pp. 145-54.

22. This is the way I interpret Wallace Stevens' poem, "The Motive for Metaphor" (*Collected Poems*, New York: Knopf, 1955, p. 286): metaphor enables us to describe, to fix and preserve, the subtleties of experience and change ("the half colors of quarter-things" in springtime), while words in their standard dictionary designations can only cope with

> The weight of primary noon,
> The A B C of being,
> The ruddy temper, the hammer
> Of red and blue . . .

It seems to me quite correct to say that new metaphors enlarge our linguistic resources, even if they do not "expand meaning" in the narrow sense objected to by J. Srzednicki, "On Metaphor," *The Philosophical Quarterly*, X (July 1960): pp. 228-37.

23. Another example has been given by Kenneth Burke, "Semantic and Poetic Meaning," in *The Philosophy of Literary Form*, Baton Rouge: Louisiana University Press, 1941, p. 144 — "New York City is in Iowa" can mean that the influence of New York stretches out, like its railway tracks, into the West.

24. See the interesting papers by Allan Gilbert, "Shakespeare's Amazing Words," *Kenyon Review*, XI (Summer 1949): 484-88, and Andrew Schiller, "Shakespeare's Amazing Words," *Kenyon Review*, XI (Winter 1949): pp. 43-49.

25. "Definitions, Explanations, and Theories," in Herbert Feigl, Michael Scriven, and Grover Maxwell, eds., *Minnesota Studies in the Philosophy of Science*, Vol. II: *Concepts, Theories, and the Mind-Body Problem*, Minneapolis: University of Minnesota Press, 1958, pp. 105-7.

26. *Ibid.*, p. 119.

27. *Semantics and Necessary Truth*, New Haven: Yale University Press, 1958, p. 327.

28. Friedrich Waismann, "Verifiability," *Proceedings of the Aristotelian Society*, Supplementary Vol. XIX, London, 1945, pp. 119-50. Cf. Georg Henrik von Wright, *A Treatise on Induction and Probability*, London: Routledge and Kegan Paul, 1951, ch. 6, §2, and Pap, *op. cit.*, chs. 5, 11.

Languages of Art

Nelson Goodman

The Sound of Pictures

V. Facts and Figures

The picture is literally gray but only metaphorically sad. But is it literally or metaphorically cold in color? Am I saying metaphorically that it (or its color) is cold to the touch? Or am I using "cold" as I use "gray", to assign the picture to a certain class of colored objects? Isn't "cold" about as straightforward a way of indicating a range of color as is "gray" or "brownish" or "pure" or "bright"? If "cold" here is metaphorical, is speaking of colors as tones also metaphorical? And in speaking of a high note am I using a metaphor or only indicating relative position in the scale of pitch?

The usual (and metaphorical) answer is that a term like "cold color" or "high note" is a frozen metaphor—though it differs from a fresh one in age rather than temperature. A frozen metaphor has lost the vigor of youth, but remains a metaphor. Strangely, though, with progressive loss of its virility as a figure of speech, a metaphor becomes not less but more like literal truth. What vanishes is not its veracity but its vivacity. Metaphors, like new styles of representation, become more literal as their novelty wanes.

Reprinted from Nelson Goodman: *Languages of Art*, (2nd ed., 1976) Hackett Publishing Co., Inc., Indianapolis, Indiana, pp. 68-85, by permission of the author and publisher.

Is a metaphor, then, simply a juvenile fact, and a fact simply a senile metaphor? That needs some modification but does argue against excluding the metaphorical from the actual. Metaphorical possession is indeed not *literal* possession; but possession is actual whether metaphorical or literal. The metaphorical and the literal have to be distinguished within the actual. Calling a picture sad and calling it gray are simply different ways of classifying it. That is, although a predicate that applies to an object metaphorically does not apply literally, it nevertheless applies. Whether the application is metaphorical or literal depends upon some such feature as its novelty.

Mere novelty, however, does not quite make the difference. Every application of a predicate to a new event or a new-found object is new; but such routine projection[1] does not constitute metaphor. And even the earliest applications of a coined term need not be in the least metaphorical. Metaphor, it seems, is a matter of teaching an old word new tricks—of applying an old label in a new way. But what is the difference between merely applying a familiar label to new things and applying it in a novel way? Briefly, a metaphor is an affair between a predicate with a past and an object that yields while protesting. In routine projection, habit applies a label to a case not already decided. Arbitrary application of a newly coined term is equally unobstructed by prior decision. But metaphorical application of a label to an object defies an explicit or tacit prior denial of that label to that object. Where there is metaphor, there is conflict: the picture is sad rather than gay even though it is insentient and hence neither sad nor gay. Application of a term is metaphorical only if to some extent contra-indicated.

This, however, does not distinguish metaphorical truth from simple falsehood. Metaphor requires attraction as well as resistance —indeed, an attraction that overcomes resistance. To say that our picture is yellow is not metaphorical but merely false. To say that it is gay is false both literally and metaphorically. But to say that it is sad is metaphorically true even though literally false. Just as the picture clearly belongs under the label "gray" rather than under the label "yellow", it also clearly belongs under "sad" rather than under "gay". Conflict arises because the picture's being insentient implies that it is neither sad nor gay. Nothing can be both sad and not sad unless "sad" has two different ranges of application. If the picture is (literally) not sad and yet is (metaphorically) sad,[2] "sad" is used first as a label for certain sentient things or events, and then for certain insentient ones. To ascribe the predicate to something within either range is to make a statement that is true either literaly or metaphorically. To ascribe the predicate to something in neither range (I leave other ranges of metaphorical application out of account for the moment) is to make a statement that is false both literally and metaphorically. Whereas falsity depends upon misassignment of a label, metaphorical truth depends upon reassignment.

Still, metaphor is not sheer ambiguity. Applying the term "cape" to a body of land on one occasion and to an article of clothing on another is using it with different and indeed mutually exclusive ranges but is not in either case metaphorical. How, then, do metaphor and ambiguity differ? Chiefly, I think, in that the several uses of a merely ambiguous term are coeval and independent; none either springs from or is guided by another. In metaphor, on the other hand, a term with an extension established by habit is applied elsewhere under the influence of that habit; there is both departure from and deference to precedent. When one use of a term precedes and informs another, the second is the metaphorical one. As time goes on, the history may fade and the two uses tend to achieve equality and independence; the metaphor freezes, or rather evaporates, and the residue is a pair of literal uses—mere ambiguity instead of metaphor.[3]

VI. Schemata

An understanding of metaphor further requires the recognition that a label functions not in isolation but as belonging to a family. We categorize by sets of alternatives. Even constancy of literal application is usually relative to a set of labels: what counts as red, for example, will vary somewhat depending upon whether objects are being classified as red or nonred, or as red or orange or yellow or green or blue or violet. What the admitted alternatives are is of course less often determined by declaration than by custom and context. Talk of schemata, categories, and systems of concepts comes down in the end, I think, to talk of such sets of labels.

The aggregate of the ranges of extension of the labels in a schema may be called a *realm*. It consists of the objects sorted by the schema

—that is, of the objects denoted by at least one of the alternative labels. Thus the range of "red" comprises all red things while the realm in question may comprise all colored things. But since the realm depends upon the schema within which a label is functioning, and since a label may belong to any number of such schemata, even a label with a unique range seldom operates in a unique realm.

Now metaphor typically involves a change not merely of range but also of realm. A label along with others constituting a schema is in effect detached from the home realm of that schema and applied for the sorting and organizing of an alien realm. Partly by thus carrying with it a reorientation of a whole network of labels does a metaphor gives clues for its own development and elaboration. The native and foreign realms may be sense-realms; or may be wider, as when a poem is said to be touching, or an instrument to be sensitive; or narrower, as when different patterns of black and white are said to be of different hues, or have nothing to do with sense-realms.

The shifts in range that occur in metaphor, then, usually amount to no mere distribution of family goods but to an expedition abroad. A whole set of alternative labels,[4] a whole apparatus of organization, takes over new territory. What occurs is a transfer of a schema, a migration of concepts, an alienation of categories. Indeed, a metaphor might be regarded as a calculated category-mistake[5]—or rather as a happy and revitalizing, even if bigamous, second marriage.

The alternatives of a schema need not be mutually exclusive; for instance, a set of color-terms with some of their ranges overlapping and some included in others will serve. Again, a schema is normally a linear or more complex array of labels; and the ordering —whether traditional as in the alphabet, syntactic as in a dictionary, or semantic as with color-names—and other relationships may be transferred. Moreover, the labels may themselves be predicates with two or more places; and such relative terms are no less amenable than categorical ones to metaphorical use. Just as "heavy" may apply metaphorically to a sound, so "heavier than" may apply metaphorically between one sound and another. A schema for sorting pairs of, and ordering, material objects is here applied for sorting pairs of, and ordering, sounds.

In all this, the aptness of an emphasis upon labels, of a nominalistic but not necessarily verbalistic orientation, becomes acutely apparent once more. Whatever reverence may be felt for classes or attributes, surely classes are not moved from realm to realm, nor are attributes somehow extracted from some objects and injected into others. Rather a set of terms, of alternative labels, is transported; and the organization they effect in the alien realm is guided by their habitual use in the home realm.

VII. Transfer

A schema may be transported almost anywhere. The choice of territory for invasion is arbitrary; but the operation within that territory is almost never completely so. We may at will apply temperature-predicates to sounds or hues or personalities or to degrees of nearness to a correct answer; but *which* elements in the chosen realm are warm, or are warmer than others, is then very largely determinate. Even where a schema is imposed upon a most unlikely and uncongenial realm, antecedent practice channels the application of the labels. When a label has not only literal but prior metaphorical uses, these two may serve as part of the precedent for a later metaphorical application; perhaps, for instance, the way we apply "high" to sounds was guided by the earlier metaphorical application to numbers (via number of vibrations per second) rather than directly by the literal application according to altitude.[6]

Operant precedent does not, however, always consist solely of the way a label has been applied. What the label *exemplifies* may also be a powerful factor. This is most striking in the much discussed dichotomy of a miscellany under such a pair of nonsense syllables as "ping" and "pong".[7] The application of these words looks back not to how they have been used to classify anything but to how they have themselves been classified—not to what they antecedently denote but to what they antecedently exemplify. We apply "ping" to quick, light, sharp things, and "pong" to slow, heavy, dull things because "ping" and "pong" exemplify these properties. In our discussion of self-denoting terms, we have already noticed this phenomenon of samples taking over the denotation of terms they exemplify. Often a simple sample replaces a complex mixture of predicates, some literally and some metaphorically exemplified. Where the new labels had no prior denotation,[8] such supplantation does not constitute metaphor under the definition given; for rather than a label changing its extension, an extension here changes its label, and with respect to that extension the new label will be only as metaphorical as the old. But when a label already has its own denotation and in replacing what it exemplifies usurps another, the new application is metaphorical.

The mechanism of transfer is often much less transparent. Why does "sad" apply to certain pictures and "gay" to others? What is meant by saying that a metaphorical application is 'guided by' or 'patterned after' the literal one? Sometimes we can contrive a plausible history: warm colors are those of fire, cold colors those of ice. In other cases, we have only fanciful alternative legends. Did numbers come to be higher and lower because piles grow higher as more stones are put on (despite the fact that holes go lower as more shovelfuls are taken out)? Or were numerals inscribed on tree trunks from the ground upward? Whatever the answer, these are all isolated questions of etymology. Presumably, we are being asked, rather, for some general account of how metaphorical use of a label reflects its literal use. On this there has been some suggestive speculation. Current literal use of many a term has been specialized from an initial, much broader application. The infant at first applies "mama" to almost anyone, learning only gradually to make important distinctions and restrict the range of the term. What seems a new use of a term may then consist of reapplying it over a region earlier vacated; and the way a term or schema applies there may depend upon half-conscious recollection of its earlier incarnation.[9] Personification may thus echo aboriginal animism. The reapplication is nevertheless metaphorical; for what is literal is set by present practice rather than by ancient history. The home realm of a schema is the country of naturalization rather than of birth; and the returning expatriate is an alien despite his quickening memories. Explanation of metaphors along these lines has been provocatively set forth by Cassirer and others.[10] But however illuminating it may be, and however true for some cases, it obviously does not explain the metaphorical applications of all or even most terms. Only rarely can the adult adventures of a label be thus traced back to childhood deprivations.

The general question remains: what does a metaphor say and what makes it true? Is saying that a picture is sad saying elliptically that it is like a sad person? Metaphor has often been so construed as elliptical simile, and metaphorical truth as simply the literal truth of the expanded statement. But the simile cannot amount merely to saying that the picture is like the person in some respect or other; any-thing is like anything else to that extent. What the simile says in effect is that person and picture are alike in being sad, the one literally and the other metaphorically. Instead of metaphor re-ducing to simile, simile reduces to metaphor; or rather, the differ-ence between simile and metaphor is negligible.[11] Whether the lo-cution be "is like" or "is", the figure *likens* picture to person by picking out a certain common feature: that the predicate "sad" applies to both, albeit to the person initially and to the picture derivatively.

If we are pressed to say what sort of similarity must obtain between what a predicate applies to literally and what it applies to metaphori-cally, we might ask in return what sort of similarity must obtain among the things a predicate applies to literally. How must past and future things be alike for a given predicate, say "green", to apply literally to them all? Having some property or other in common is not enough; they must have a *certain* property in common. But what property? Obviously the property named by the predicate in ques-tion; that is, the predicate must apply to all the things it must apply to. The question why predicates apply as they do metaphorically is much the same as the question why they apply as they do literally. And if we have no good answer in either case, perhaps that is because there is no real question. At any rate, the general explanation why things have the properties, literal and metaphorical, that they do have—why things are as they are—is a task I am content to leave to the cosmologist.

Standards of truth are much the same whether the schema used is transferred or not. In either case, application of a term is fallible and thus subject to correction. We may make mistakes in applying either "red" or "sad" to colored objects; and we may bring tests of all sorts to bear upon our initial judgments: we may look again, compare, examine attendant circumstances, watch for corroborating and for conflicting judgments. Neither the status of initial credibility nor the process of verification by maximizing total credibility over all our judgments[12] is different in the two cases. Of course, a metaphorical sorting under a given schema is, since more novel, often less sharp and stable than the correlated literal sorting; but this is only a differ-ence of degree. The literal as well as the metaphorical may be afflicted by vagueness and vacillation of all kinds; and literal applications of some schemata are, because of the delicacy or the unclarity of the distinctions called for, much less crisp and constant than some metaphorical applications of others. Difficulties in determining truth are by no means peculiar to metaphor.

Truth of a metaphor does not, indeed, guarantee its effectiveness. As there are irrelevant, tepid, and trivial literal truths, there are farfetched, feeble, and moribund metaphors. Metaphorical force requires a combination of novelty with fitness, of the odd with the obvious. The good metaphor satisfies while it startles. Metaphor is most potent when the transferred schema effects a new and notable organization rather than a mere relabeling of an old one. Where the organization by an immigrant schema coincides with an organization already otherwise effected in the new realm, the sole interest of the metaphor lies in how this organization is thus related to the application of the schema in its home realm, and sometimes to what the labels of the schema exemplify. But where an unaccustomed organization results, new associations and discriminations are also made within the realm of transfer; and the metaphor is the more telling as these are the more intriguing and significant. Since metaphor depends upon such transient factors as novelty and interest, its mortality is understandable. With repetition, a transferred application of a schema becomes routine, and no longer requires or makes any allusion to its base application. What was novel becomes commonplace, its past is forgotten, and metaphor fades to mere truth.

Metaphor permeates all discourse, ordinary and special, and we should have a hard time finding a purely literal paragraph anywhere. In that last prosaic enough sentence, I count five sure or possible—even if tired—metaphors. This incessant use of metaphor springs not merely from love of literary color but also from urgent need of economy. If we could not readily transfer schemata to make new sortings and orderings, we should have to burden ourselves with unmanageably many different schemata, either by adoption of a vast vocabulary of elementary terms or by prodigious elaboration of composite ones.

VIII. Modes of Metaphor

Metaphor comes in many varieties, most of them listed in the prodigious if chaotic standard catalogue of figures of speech. Some of these figures, of course, do not qualify as metaphors. Alliteration and apostrophe are purely syntactic, involving no transfer; and onomatopoeia consists merely of using a self-denoting label of a certain kind. Whether a euphemism is a metaphor or not depends upon whether it applies labels for proper things to improper things or only substitutes proper for improper labels.

Among metaphors some involve transfer of a schema between disjoint realms. In personification, labels are transferred from persons to things; in synecdoche, between a realm of wholes or classes and a realm of their proper parts of subclasses[13]; in antonomasia between things and their properties or labels.

But not for all metaphors are the two realms disjoint; sometimes one realm intersects or is an expansion or a contraction of the other. (See Figure 2) In hyperbole, for instance, an ordered schema is in effect displaced downward. The large olive becomes supercolossal and the small one large; labels at the lower end of the schema (e.g., "small") are unused, and things at the upper end of the realm (the exceptionally large olive) are unlabeled in this application of the schema—unless the schema is extended, say by iteration of the prefix "super". In litotes, or understatement, exactly the opposite occurs. A superb performance becomes pretty fair and a good one passable; the top labels go unused and the bottom of the realm is undescribed. Hyperbole or understatement may be, so to speak, double-ended, with the entire schema squeezed into a central part of the original realm (leaving no labels for the extremes), or with a central part of the schema stretched out to cover the whole original realm (leaving nothing for the end labels to denote).

Although metaphor always involves transfer in the sense that some labels of the schema are given new extensions, the realm itself may remain constant under the transfer. In irony, for example, a schema is simply turned end for end and applied to its own realm in the opposite direction. What results is not a re-sorting but a reorientation. A misfortune becomes 'a fine thing' and a windfall 'tough luck'. In other cases a schema may return to its home realm by a longer route. Consider, for example, the metaphorical application of "blue" to pictures. Since "blue" also has a literal application to pictures, the metaphorical and literal applications are to the same territory. What has happened here is transfer from realm to realm and back again. A schema of color-predicates is carried first over to feel-

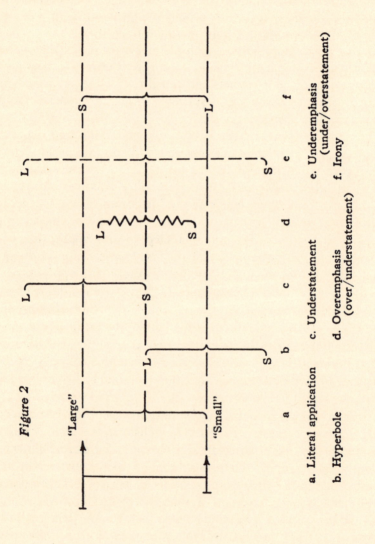

Figure 2

ings and then back to colored objects. Its travels result in some displacement on its return (otherwise we shouldn't even know it had been away); but the displacement is far from total: a metaphorically blue picture is more likely to be literally blue than literally red. Sometimes a schema may take a longer round trip, with more stopovers, and be more drastically displaced on its return.

Two or more types of transfer are sometimes combined, as when an unreliable machine is called a true friend. Other metaphors are curbed or modified. Calling a picture brutal in coloring is not calling it brutal; the way is left open for calling the picture gentle in other respects, say in drawing, or even as a whole. "Brutal in coloring", since it has no different prior denotation, applies literally rather than metaphorically to the picture. It is a coloring-description in that although it may denote objects that differ in specific coloring it does not distinguish among objects of the same specific coloring. Yet clearly a metaphor is involved. In effect, the term "brutal" is metaphorically applied to the picture with respect to the coloring alone. In such a modified metaphor, a schema is, so to speak, transferred under explicit or tacit restrictions; its sorting of a realm must not cut across certain groupings already made there. Given free rein, the "brutal"-"gentle" schema sorts objects in one way; transferred under orders to effect a sorting based on coloring or based on pattern, the same schema sorts objects in other ways. Traveling under various instructions or along various routes, a given schema may have several different metaphorical applications in one realm.

Nonverbal as well as verbal labels may, of course, be applied metaphorically, say in a cartoon of a politician as a parrot, or of a despot as a dragon. And a blue painting of a trombone player involves complex, if unsubtle, transfer.

So much for metaphorical denotation. Metaphorical possession and exemplification are likewise parallel to their literal counterparts; and what was said earlier (section 3) about predicates and properties applies here as well. A picture is metaphorically sad if some label—verbal or not—that is coextensive with (i.e., has the same literal denotation as) "sad" metaphorically denotes the picture. The picture metaphorically exemplifies "sad" if "sad" is referred to by and metaphorically denotes the picture. And the picture metaphorically exemplifies sadness if some label coextensive with "sad" is referred to by and metaphorically denotes the picture. Since, as we have seen, the features that distinguish the metaphorical from the literal are transient, I shall often use "possession" and "exemplification" to cover both literal and metaphorical cases.

NOTES

1. On projection and projectibility, see *FFF*, esp. pp. 57-58, 81-83, 84-99. [Editor's note: *FFF* refers to Nelson Goodman's *Fact, Fiction, and Forecast*, 2nd ed., Indianapolis and New York: Bobbs-Merrill, 1965.]

2. Of course, where "sad" applies metaphorically, "metaphorically sad" applies literally; but this tells little about what constitutes being metaphorically sad.

3. The treatment of metaphor in the following pages agrees in many matters with the excellent article by Max Black, "Metaphor", *Proceedings of the Aristotelian Society*, vol. 55 (1954), pp. 273-294, reprinted in his *Models and Metaphors* (Ithaca, N.Y., Cornell University Press, 1962), pp. 25-47. See also the well-known treatments by I. A. Richards, *The Philosophy of Rhetoric* (London, Oxford University Press, 1936), pp. 89-183, and by C. M. Turbayne, *The Myth of Metaphor* (New Haven, Yale University Press, 1962), pp. 11-27.

4. The implicit set of alternatives—the schema—may consist of two or many labels, and varies widely with context. To say that an idea is green is to contrast it not with ideas having other colors but with ideas having greater ripeness; and to say that an employee is green is simply to contrast him with others who are not green.

5. On the notion of a category-mistake, see Gilbert Ryle, *The Concept of Mind* (London, Hutchinson's University Library, and New York, Barnes and Noble, Inc., 1949), pp. 16ff.

6. Or perhaps the metaphorical application to sounds preceded and guided later metaphorical application to numbers. My point does not depend upon the correctness of my etymology.

7. See Gombrich, *Art and Illusion* (cited in I, note 5), p. 370.

8. Having an established null denotation is quite a different matter from not having any established denotation. The extension of such terms as "centaur" and "Don Quixote" is null; and these terms, like terms with non-empty extensions, become metaphorical upon transfer.

9. The idea invites elaboration: the metaphorical application might with much use become literal also, with ambiguity thus resulting; and the two literal ranges might ultimately be reunited into the original one.

10. See Ernst Cassirer, *The Philosophy of Symbolic Forms* (original German edition, 1925), trans. Ralph Manheim (New Haven, Yale University Press, 1955), vol. II, pp. 36-43; Cassirer's *Language and Myth*, trans. S. K. Langer (New York and London, Harper Brothers, 1946), pp. 12, 23-39; and Owen Barfield, *Poetic Diction* (London, Faber and Faber, 1928), pp. 80-81.

11. Max Black makes this point clearly and forcefully in his article on metaphor; see his

Models and Metaphors, p. 37: "It would be more illuminating in some of these cases to say that the metaphor creates the similarity than to say that it formulates some similarity antecedently existing."

12. Concerning this general matter, see my "Sense and Certainty", *Philosophical Review*, vol. 61 (1952), pp. 160-167.

13. A realm of wholes is of course disjoint from a realm of their proper parts, and a realm of classes from a realm of their proper subclasses.

On the Truth
and Probity of Metaphor

Timothy Binkley

Metaphor is not often granted a voice among truth-tellers until after doing penance for her perversion of language. Her usual atonement is to submit to the exaction of paraphrase. She can be the bearer of truth, but only mediately, only after being translated into a literal expression which is straightforwardly true or false. The most common device employed for this purpose is the simile: "He's a clown" means "He's like a clown, he's funny." Her only other option is to forswear all pretence to stating facts and accept the role of an entertaining bard: she can "ring true" but not deliver truth.

This view of metaphor makes the common assumption that a metaphor taken at face value is either false or meaningless. Furthermore, it is supposed that metaphorical expressions are abnormal or nonstandard uses of language and that their falsity is a consequence of this fact. The linguistic norm is literal; metaphor departs from the norm and pays the price. Expressions of discontent with metaphorical language are many and varied. William Alston says ". . . when one is speaking metaphorically, it is generally more difficult to be sure of exactly what he is saying than when he is speaking literally."[1] Paul Henle explains this as follows: "Ordinarily one takes words in

Reprinted from *The Journal of Aesthetics and Art Criticism* 33, no. 2 (1974): 171-180 by permission of the author and *The Journal of Aesthetics and Art Criticism*.

their literal sense and this is impossible in a metaphor."[2] The reason is that, "Whether taking all terms in their literal sense produces an absurdity or merely something incongruous the clash of literal meanings must be felt."[3] Nelson Goodman seems to agree that metaphors put a strain on language: "Application of a term is metaphorical only if to some extent contra-indicated."[4] Consequently, metaphorical uses of language are not quite proper and that is why they purvey false and absurd ideas.

Yet rightly understood, metaphor proves itself capable of as simple and straightforward a truth as literal language. More specifically, we shall discover (a) that metaphors need not involve false or nonsensical uses of language, (b) that metaphors can be true, i.e., they can be used to state true propositions, and (c) that the truth-value of a metaphorical claim can be discerned in fundamentally the same way we discern the truth-value of a literal one.[5] Metaphorical and literal language alike do not require, although they might both benefit from, explications of meaning prior to a determination of truth-value.

I

Consider the hackneyed textbook example of metaphor:

(1) Richard is a fox.

What would lead someone to suggest that such a statement is false?[6] Perhaps the fact that

(2) Richard is not a fox, he's a man.

And this makes the matter appear to be a very simple one. Yet consider another pair of sentences:

(3) Your pipes need cleaning.
(4) Your pipes do not need cleaning.

Assuming these sentences are not graffiti which materialize before us, we shall reserve judgment about whether they are contradictories until we find out in each case whether plumbing or smoking is being discussed. Groups of words which *can* be used as contradictories *will* be contradictory only if they are used with the same sense (but for the negation) and in the same context. By the same token, we have to know whether (1) and (2) occur in discourse about the Black Forest or the Asphalt Jungle before we can decide whether they are contradictories. (2) is the negation of (1) only where they are employed with the same sense and in the same general context.[7] But if (2) is literal, as it must be to support the claim that metaphors are false (or nonsensical), while (1) is metaphorical, they possess different (though related) meanings. Discounting the negation, they still express very different propositions. Thus if someone uttered (1) as a metaphor, while someone else countered with (2) as a literal statement, they would be at odds no more than a plumber telling a man his pipes are clean and a smoker telling him his pipes are dirty. The person who asserts (2) might be misunderstanding, but not gainsaying, the person who states (1). This is because (2) would involve a use of the word "fox" in which something could not be said to be both a fox and a man, while in (1) the relevant use of "fox" does not imply the incompatibility. (1) leads me to believe that Richard is cunning but not that he has a red coat, whereas the literal reading of (1) would suggest just the opposite. If Richard is a real forest fox he probably has a red coat, but I shall not be surprised if he is rather a dullard.

The belief that (2) contradicts (1) probably results from confusing (1) with

(5)   Richard is a fox. (used literally).

Yet (1) and (5) are entirely different statements, even though made with the same sentence. The fact that Richard is a man falsifies (5), but not (1). Admitting the truth of (2) forces the speaker of (5) to retract or modify what he has said, but the speaker of (1) is not so constrained. If the two statements were rendered pictorially, (1) would be a caricature and (5) would be a photograph, as would (2). So to contradict (1) we shall have to say something more on the order of "Richard is a sheep."

It should not be concluced that (1) and (2) involve simple equivocation the way (3) and (4) might. Yet neither are they univocal opposites. Although the uses of "fox" in the first pair are related, the meanings and uses of the statements as a whole have radically divergent orientations. The *words* composing (1) can be used to contradict (2) since they can be given a reading (namely the literal one presented in (5)) on which they are used to assert a false proposition. But if (1) is used as a metaphor, the literal proposition (5) is not asserted, even though it may in some sense be "present" as a prerequisite for understanding the metaphor. A person using (1) as a metaphor is not propounding, or even entertaining, a false proposition. He does not *mean* the literal sense (5), although he could not mean what he does without it.

II

Then what could it mean to say (1) is false? It might mean something such as this:

(6)   Richard is not literally a fox.

Although (6) would have a point primarily in those situations where the hearer has misunderstood the speaker by taking him literally, it would not be false to assert (6) if Richard is a man. But how does the falsity of (1) follow from (6)? More specifically, what is the import of the word "literally?" Perhaps we could say that (1) construed literally is false—i.e., that (5) is false. This would be unobjectionable but it would not get us very far. No one has ever suggested that a sentence such as (1) will turn out to be true when construed literally, just as no one would want to hold that (3) will be true or false independently of whether it refers to plumbing or smoking. In both (1) and (5) misinterpretation is possible, calling for the assertion of either (6) or

(7)   Richard is not metaphorically a fox.

The latter corrects a misunderstanding of (5), the former corrects a misunderstanding of (1). But (6) proves the falsity of (1) no more than (7) proves the falsity of (5). (6) might be taken as support for a general thesis to the effect that when we give a metaphorical expression a literal reading, a false proposition will result. But then (6) implies only that there is a proposition derivable and different from (1) which is false, namely (5), not that (1) itself is false.

Moreover, there are serious problems which beset the general thesis (6) is taken to support. One of the most widespread myths about metaphors is the idea that at the literal level they harbor an impropriety of language. This notion is part of the foundation of most theories of metaphor. Both Henle and Goodman affirm such a view in the passages quoted above: there is said to be a "clash of meanings" or "contraindication." Monroe Beardsley captures this feature of metaphor with the "Controversion Theory," which states that "a metaphor is a significant attribution that is either indirectly self-contradictory or obviously false in its context, and in which the modifier connotes characteristics that can be attributed, truly or falsely, to the subject."[8] The notion that the literal reading of a metaphor is false or nonsensical is too familiar to need thorough documentation. Yet there appear to be simple counter-examples to this almost universally held belief. Consider the trite "He lives in a glass house." This statement may, but need not, involve a strain in language, even at the literal level. A man who "throws stones" might literally live in a house constructed primarily with glass, and this fact could afford us an added dimension of humor when we say metaphorically "He lives in a glass house." We know that the statement is metaphorical not because we know the person in question lives in a brick house (we may have no information about where he lives), but because the conversation has been about his behavior and not about his residence.[9] Similar examples abound. "He's a clown," mentioned earlier, could be used in such a way that it is true both literally and metaphorically. So could "That man is an animal," "He was caught with his pants down," "They took the shirt right off his back." Adjectival metaphors can also be literally true. "Anchorage is a cold city" could express two true propositions if, for example, both the climate is cold and the people are unfriendly.

It is simply not true that metaphorical uses of language must involve an impropriety. Although an obviously false or nonsensical literal interpretation may make the metaphoricalness conspicuous, such a clue is neither a necessary ingredient in the making nor an essential aid in the understanding of a metaphor. Even when the literal reading of a metaphor is false, there is no genuine impropriety of language so long as the two different claims are kept distinct.

We find, then, that (6) might give rise to a general thesis about metaphor which is mistaken. But there is an alternative way of explicating the force of (6). It might be claimed that truth must be literal, that a metaphorical sentence cannot itself express a true proposition, either because it cannot be used to make a statement or because if it makes a claim it does so only through the mediation of a literal sentence which explicitly makes the same claim. I shall now turn to this suggestion.

III

There is a statement which does appear to contradict (1) and which can be expressed with the same words as (2):

(8)   Richard is not a fox. (used metaphorically).

However, statements such as (8) are not always true and hence do nothing toward showing that metaphors are false—they are metaphors themselves. If we examine more fully the relationship between (1) and (8) I believe we will discover how metaphorical statements can be true, and true as directly as literal statements.

Consider the following exchange between two persons discussing, say, a lawyer:

A: That Richard is a fox, isn't he? Did you notice how he slyly equivocated on the defendant's statement?

B: Oh, I don't think he's a fox. It was probably just a lucky blunder. You should have seen him last week and you'd find it hard to believe he's a fox too.

Fatuous though the example, the point is clear. B is here contradicting A by sticking with the original (metaphorical) sense of the statement (1) and asserting its negation (8). We could say that A and B are arguing over whether Richard is a fox, and that in this exchange the dispute centers on whether a particular act is sly and whether it fits into a pattern. It is either true or false that Richard is a fox. The disagreement over whether he is a fox is in this respect not fundamentally different from a disagreement over whether he is a politician, a buffoon, a good husband, or an evil man. In all these cases, a claim can be made which is amenable to argument, which has more or less determinate criteria of evaluation, which can be supported and weakened with evidence, and so on. Although the boundaries are not sharp, we all know pretty much what it means to call a person a fox and how one would go about determining whether that assertion is true or false. The claim is no more vague and ill-defined, no less connected with definite criteria, than "Richard is a good husband" or "Richard is a scoundrel." What indeterminateness there is in the claim is not something peculiar to or endemic to metaphors. It appears then that there is nothing to be gained by insisting that metaphors cannot be used to make claims which are either true or false. Richard is not a fox in the sense in which Reddy the fox is, but it can still be true that Richard is a fox. Metaphors can embody assertions of propositions as well as assertions or proclamations of feelings and attitudes. Furthermore, whether a metaphor can be true does not depend upon its age. A dead metaphor will act almost as though it were literal, and will consequently raise no special problems about truth. But a fresh metaphor is no less capable of stating truths if its author wants to make claims with it.

IV

However, it is sometimes contended that metaphorical claims are not true as directly as literal claims; they are said to achieve the status of propositions only by virtue of their connections with literal language. Metaphorical statements must be understood as embellished literal statements, dressed up for a special occasion, but still, underneath the facade, they are the same old literal propositions. Accordingly, the truth of the claim expressed by (1) is nothing other than the truth of some such claim as "Richard is sly," since if the former is a genuine claim, it must be so only as proxy for the latter or something like it. Metaphors can be true, but only indirectly.

The single most influential factor which has bolstered this subordination of metaphorical language is the familiar doctrine that metaphors are "parasitic upon" literal usage.[10] Yet due to some carelessness in the way the doctrine is usually stated, it has been too easy for its proponents to fall prey to a confusion between two different kinds of priority. A metaphor cannot be understood as a metaphor unless one can understand the literal meanings of the words used to make the metaphor. The meaning of the metaphor rests upon awareness of literal meaning: to this extent metaphors are parasitic upon literal language. However, it is a big step from this truism to the claim that metaphorical language is *tout court* parasitic upon literal language, that the true meaning of a metaphor is its translation into some literal expression. We have to distinguish between a literal reading of the words in a metaphor and a literal translation of the sense of the metaphor. The literal meaning of the words in (1) is that Richard is one of those animals we see in the zoo. The literal translation of the metaphor expressed by (1), however, is something more like "Richard is cunning." The fact that we have to know the former to understand the metaphor does not make the latter its true meaning. The two are totally different and only a failure to see this can lead to a form of the parasitology doctrine which would lend support to the notion that metaphorical meaning is fancy literal meaning. The fact that water is one of the materials people are made of does not mean that people are glorified water.

The way a metaphor gets its meaning may be less direct than the way a literal statement gets its meaning, since we need to grasp first the literal meanings of words used in metaphors. But once metaphorical meaning is secured, the words and the meaning are not mediated by a third term, the literal translation of the metaphor. Although there is a sense in which metaphorical meaning is less direct than literal meaning, this has nothing to do with truth or falsehood. Meaning and understanding metaphors may be a more complex procedure than meaning and understanding literal utterances, but this does not make metaphorical meaning nothing but a way of not quite saying something literal.

In the dispute characterized above, the two participants seem capable of carrying on their argument without recourse to literal paraphrase. There are only some kinds of circumstance in which an expression stands in need of translation into another, more perspicuous one. If someone makes an error in his use of language, he is corrected with an expression saying what he really intended to say. The error might be factual ("You mean John, not Peter, broke the plate") or it might be linguistic ("You mean 'relative,' not 'relevant'"). Translation of this sort seems proper where there is a need to specify the meaning of an as yet unclear expression. A man who yells "Brick!" may not be making himself clear as to whether he wants a brick brought to him or whether he is calling someone's attention to a lost brick. But if a bricklayer calls out "Brick!" and is perfectly well understood by his assistant to mean what is also meant by "Bring me a brick," it seems rather otiose and quite misleading to insist that what he *really* means is "Bring me a brick"—as though he is not saying what he really means to begin with.[11] Although the latter is certainly a genuine *explication* of the meaning of the former, it is not an *excavation* of its meaning, it does not dig up the true meaning which was hidden in the first expression. The latter expression is only more explicit, hence more useful in explications. In some cases the shorter expression may be an accepted abbreviation of the longer, more explicit one. If this is so, the meaning of the abbreviation will be dependent upon what it is an abbreviation of. However, the relationship between two expressions, one of which makes more explicit what is said in the other, is not usually simple abbreviation; and when it is not we need not view the shorter expression as an imperfect, imprecise, or indirect embodiment of meaning. In short, it appears as though an expression requires replacement or translation only where language is faulty or needs redirection for special purposes. In other cases, alternative expressions will not supply "the real meaning."

A similar point could be made about metaphors in general and about metaphorical claims in particular. If someone says "Richard is a fox," there is no reason why that cannot be really and precisely what he means (although, to be sure, it cannot be literally what he means).[12] If there is some reason for an explication—if, for example he is misunderstood—there may be a need to advert to something such as "Richard is sly." And if he is inaccurate or inexpressive—if he really means to be saying something more like "Richard is a lion"—an excavation of meaning is in order. But if he is ingenuous and communication is successful, the sentence can stand as what he really means. Sentences which can be clarifications in particular cases do not always supersede what they explicate.

Furthermore, neither explications nor excavations of meaning are always maps from non-literal to literal language. A metaphorical (or other non-literal) expression could be clarified or corrected with either a literal or a non-literal one; and similarly, there is nothing odd about clarifying or correcting the meaning of a literal expression with a metaphor. The literal can sometimes be just as unruly as the metaphorical. An argument over whether Richard is sly or cunning might be reported or explained as an argument over whether

Richard is a fox; neither has an *a priori* claim on real meaning. Assessing the truth of a statement such as (1) does not require attention to any literal translation of the metaphor.

V

If we examine the picture of language underlying the view that metaphorical claims are only disguised literal claims, we will find that it embodies a quite peculiar and unacceptable way of understanding language. According to this conception of the relationships among linguistic expressions and meanings, there are certain sentences we can really mean, and then there is that large class of sentences we do not really mean but which gallivant around wildly in even the most ordinary discourse as incognitos for the sentences which do express "real" or "pure" meaning.[13] We are presented with a picture of a realm where quintessential meanings subsist as demigods who can be directly approached only by the high priests of literal language: words represent meanings, only some words are on better terms with their meanings than others.

It is difficult to know how to react to this picture of language. The idea that literal language is correct language may arise from thinking that literal language is a more precise expression of meaning than metaphorical language. For many purposes, the literal is indeed a useful tool in clarifying meaning; however this is no reason to presume that it is any more precise in expressing meaning or any closer to "true" meaning than the metaphorical. To defend such a belief, one must imagine that meanings can be isolated and compared with particular expressions of them. There would have to be some criteria for telling how close to a meaning a given type of expression of it comes. But no such criteria are forthcoming since our usual access to meanings expressible in language is just the language in which they are expressed. It may be that literal language is less often misunderstood; however, this does not give the literal any logical priority in a hierarchy of meaning. It provides the literal, at best, only with a practical priority in communication. The literal does not "state," though it may explicate, meaning more precisely. Sometimes we mean *precisely* something which is inexact, ambiguous, or non-literal. The literal is a more precise language only with reference to particular types of linguistic endeavor, such as clarifying, explaining, or elaborating meaning. But this does not make the literal a more exact *expression* of meaning. Saying exactly what one means is not the same thing as saying what one means exactly, i.e., translating it into a type of language which conforms to one or another standard of precision. Failure to express what one means is very different from failure to explain (precisely or literally) what one means. The two concepts of precision (precise expression and precise explanation) come from radically different activities, and only when we confuse the two do we understand literal language to be a more correct or precise way of expressing meaning. Translating the metaphorical into the literal may be an aid to understanding, but it is not the formula for saying more accurately what one wants to say, what one means.

Another reason the above picture of language seems plausible comes from a consideration of category mistakes and other transgressions of logic (logical grammar). To talk of green ideas is to violate "the rules of logic" because ideas are not the sort of thing which can be colored. Similarly, it is sometimes argued that metaphors violate the rules of logic by associating properties suitable for things in one category with something in another category. This idea is supported by the belief that all metaphors are contra-indicated or contain a clash of literal meanings. As we have seen, this belief is false. But in any event, a genuine category mistake does not occur unless the words in the sentence in question are used in certain senses. Thus, some classic category mistakes can be given meaningful metaphorical interpretations. "Green ideas" might be read as a metaphor for ideas at an early stage of development. Read as a metaphor, the "mistake" recedes into the background since the words are no longer used to mean something absurd. A metaphor is not a category mistake since only a literal reading can (though it won't always) produce nonsense. For example, (1) could be construed as a category mistake only if we mistake it for (5). Moreover, category mistakes and similar errors might occur with improper uses of metaphors as well as of literal language. After talking about Richard as a fox, it would be improper to begin calling a coin a fox in the same sense, and this is because coins cannot be foxes in the sense in which Richard can. This shows that improprieties in language are not always abuses of the literal.

VI

So far we have considered the idea that literal language is a more precise expression of meaning than metaphorical language. There is another way in which the precision of the literal is conceived. Instead of holding that the literal expresses meaning more precisely, it might be argued that literal language is a more exact way of describing reality, so that "Richard is cunning" gives a more accurate picture of the way things are than "Richard is a fox." This approach to the precision of the literal may draw support from the assumption that there is a determinate set of criteria for using a word such as "fox" which supply strict rules directing what we can literally say, though no such rules are available for metaphors.

In response to this alternative account of precision, it might first be pointed out that even if metaphors give a rougher picture of reality, that does not make them any less capable of being true or false. Descriptive power may be affected by the precision of an expression, but truth-value is not. Even literal expressions can be very imprecise but nonetheless true (or false).

Perhaps it is thought that (1) is false because Richard is not covered with red fur, does not have a bushy tail or black feet, etc. All these are criteria for the literal use of "fox." However, metaphors are no less furnished with similar criteria of their own, as already pointed out. We know what verifies and falsifies (1) just as we know what verifies and falsifies "Reddy is a fox." Neither statement has a corner on reality, though their ways of reaching it differ. In neither case do the criteria supply the true meaning of "fox." They simply delimit different senses of the word. It is difficult to see why the literal should fit reality any more directly than the metaphorical. Metaphorical meaning is a more complex achievement, but once the meaning is fixed, a metaphorical statement can be true or false without the help of a literal synonym which has a direct line to the real. Even the dictionary can unabashedly list as one of the meanings of "fox," "A crafty, sly, or clever person."[14]

There may be a sense in which literal language is a more "exact" way of describing reality. But if so, its exactness will be measured against certain limited, albeit very important, functions of language, such as explaining the meaning of an expression to a foreigner or stating facts with scientific accuracy. Its exactness will be only one type of exactness suited to one class of purposes. For other purposes, a metaphor might be a more exact way of describing reality. A poet could come up with a metaphorical description of a feeling, for example, whose precision is unparalleled by any literal expression. And sometimes even scientific theory rests upon metaphors which are difficult to replace with literal expressions.

VII

Unacceptable as the picture of metaphor as fancy literal meaning is, it is not hard to see why philosophers might find themselves tempted to adopt it. When someone wants to put forth an example of a use of language he exhibits an expression out of context. Sometimes he will specify at least part of the context in which we are to imagine the expression occurring, but even in these cases the expression is still out of its context of use. Further, since the example is an example of language, the particulars in the situation of actual use are eclipsed even more by our attention being focused on the words.

Because of the nature of linguistic example-giving, it will appear as though those expressions whose meanings are (on the average) less context-dependent or less in need of explication will be the most perspicuous conveyors of meaning. The examples of language which are most readily exhibited and most easily understood *in the context of example-giving* will be those which are least context-dependent for their meanings. Accordingly, those expressions which will appear to embody their meanings most limpidly when they are exhibited in philosophical discourse will be explicit literal sentences whose meanings are not highly sensitive to changes in context and do not rest heavily upon circumstances of their use. The troublesome picture then arises in the subtle, but dangerous, shift from the situation of example-giving to the situation of actual use; it is supposed that a sentence which conveys its meaning more clearly and directly (with less ancillary stage-setting) as an example will also convey meaning more clearly and more directly in actual use. But this is far from true. The meaning of an expression in use can be quite clear regardless of whether it would be clear out of context. In fact, sometimes the opposite is true. We could imagine the bricklayer's assistant baffled when all of a sudden he is given the command "Bring me a brick!" instead of the usual "Brick!" He might wonder whether the bricklayer is angry or whether it is a joke of some kind. Imagine also how strange it would be to have a conversation with a close friend in which he was careful to avoid all metaphors and other tropes. Once again, we would be more likely to read his words as expressions of coldness or anger than as expressions of the literal meanings they avow.

Ordinary language is fraught with nonliteral expressions of all types which do not seem in actual use any less direct bearers of meaning than literal expressions. We can be sensitive to this fact only if we put in proper perspective the activities of explicating and excavating meaning and of philosophical example-giving. Although metaphors are not "literally true," there is no reason to suppose that truth has to be literal. "Richard is a fox" may require explication more often than "Richard is a husband," but neither stands proxy for a more fundamental expression.

VIII

So why is it someone should want to assert that metaphors are false or nonsensical? Consider an example given by Monroe Beardsley: "That building is a dump."[15] Beardsley points out that the falsity of the sentence is a clue to its being a metaphor. Yet how might it be false? Perhaps we would think of a story such as this. A friend from Germany comes to stay in this country for awhile and I take her for a drive to show her the city. We drive past an unpleasant building and I unthinkingly say "That's a dump." Having heard about the immense opulence of the United States, she is not particularly incredulous to find even the city dumps housed in expensive structures. Next day she shows up with her garbage. Now, what has gone awry?; has she taken a false statement for true? What we will say is that she misunderstood. She thought I intended the sentence literally instead of metaphorically. She did indeed take a false statement for true, but the mistake lay in the way the sentence was taken in the first place, not in the assessment of the truth-value of an already determinate claim. The fact that the sentence yields a false statement when interpreted literally indicates that it should not be taken literally unless we have reason to believe the speaker wants to make a false claim. But we need to be specific about which statement is false. It is not the metaphorical claim I made, but another, completely different one. Thus it can be misleading to say just that the statement is false. What is false is not a claim asserted, but a claim merely used, as it might be used on the stage. Moreover, not only falsity, but many other defects will act as guards against various misunderstandings of words.

IX

There are three distinctions we might note which, if fittingly deployed, elucidate how metaphors can be true or false, while indicating also the confusions which tempt us to the view that they are never true or only vicariously true.

a) First, it is necessary to keep separate the two different activities of establishing the truth and establishing the meaning of an expression. Although literal and metaphorical sentences have different types of meaning, when they are used to make claims those claims can be true or false in roughly the same way, i.e., without the mediation of an additional expression of their meanings. It is usually (though not always) somewhat more involved to explain to someone the meaning of a metaphor or other trope than of a literal expression. But once the meaning is clear, the truth of the claim can be established without the assistance of translations into literal meanings. The ability of a sentence to refer and state is independent of whether it is metaphorical, although metaphorical sentences may refer, state, and mean in ways literal sentences usually do not.

b) Second, it would be useful to distinguish metaphor as a resource of language from the various uses to which it is put. Metaphorical expressions, like literal expressions, elegant expressions, crude expressions, euphemisms, ellipses, hyperboles, etc., can all be put to use questioning, stating, commanding, reporting, storytelling, and so on. Metaphor, so we are told, is typically a poetic device. But it is not exclusively so. It is hardly less common in everyday speech than in poetry these days, though the metaphors in poetry are usually more interesting. We may consider metaphors especially fit for non-propositional language, but they can, and very often are, used to state facts. Whether some sentence can be true or false is determined only by whether it is a statement, not by the style of language used in making the statement. In short, metaphor is not a speech act; it is rather a linguistic device which can be put to use making speech acts. Consequently, the terms "literal" and "metaphorical" in (6) and in (7) refer to the way the sentences mean, and not to the kind of claim being made. A "literal claim" is nothing other than a claim made with literal language. Literal truth is not a kind of truth, but a truth expressed in literal language.

c) Finally, and most importantly, we should avoid confusing the meaning of a metaphor (or any other expression) with an explication of its meaning.[16] There is a sense in which literal language supports and makes possible metaphorical language; but there may also be a sense in which the converse holds. One wonders where literal language would be left without metaphors to express new ideas and give added dimensions to our discourse—something without which there would be no place for the literal to stand *qua* literal. In any event, the fact that having metaphorical language requires having literal language does not entail that the real meaning of any particular metaphor awaits its analysis into literal paraphrase. Explication of metaphors is often useful, but explication is not always excavation.

So there is no reason why truth must be literal—why it should have to be expressed in literal terms. This is not to deny the existence of an important relationship between the literal and the metaphorical, but only to deny that one must subserve the other when matters of meaning and truth arise. Of course, it still remains to specify the salient features of the intriguing and difficult relationship between the two.[17]

NOTES

1. William P. Alston, *Philosophy of Language* (Englewood Cliffs, N.J. 1964), p. 103.

2. Paul Henle, "Metaphor," in *Language, Thought, and Culture,* edited by Paul Henle (University of Michigan Press, 1958), p. 182.

3. *Ibid.*, p. 183.

4. Nelson Goodman, *Languages of Art* (Indianapolis, 1968), p. 69.

5. Although the second point is sometimes granted, the first and third rarely are. See, for example, Paul J. Olscamp, "How Some Metaphors May Be True Or False," *The Journal*

of Aesthetics and Art Criticism, XXIX, 1, 77-86. Olscamp holds that metaphors can have truth-value, but he insists that they must be translated into statements of similarity in order for the truth-value to be determined.

6. I am dealing only with the claim that (1) is false since this would probably be held more often than that it is meaningless. However, the basic arguments would remain unchanged if instead meaninglessness were at issue.

7. A change of context can make a literal statement metaphorical, and vice versa. Cf. Max Black, "Metaphor," in *Models and Metaphors* (Cornell University Press, 1962), p. 29. See also Ina Loewenberg, "Truth and Consequences of Metaphors," *Philosophy and Rhetoric*, VI, 1, 38.

8. *Aesthetics: Problems in the Philosophy of Criticism* (New York, 1958), p. 142. For a further development of the theory, see Beardsley's "The Metaphorical Twist," *Philosophy and Phenomenological Research* XXII, 8, 293-307. Beardsley devolves the assessment of the truth-value of metaphors upon characteristics connoted by the term used metaphorically. Thus, the truth-value of "Richard is a fox" is determined by first noting that slyness is a feature connoted by the word "fox" and then seeing whether slyness can be attributed to Richard. But Beardsley maintains that it is false or nonsensical to say that Richard is a fox.

9. Monroe Beardsley has suggested to me that the glass house example only isolates a new type of impropriety different from the two types he discusses in *Aesthetics*. In addition to self-contradiction and falsity, we can now add lack of compatibility with the linguistic context. I believe that the latter, like the former two, can be a clue to non-literal usage. However, even the third type of impropriety does not appear to be essential to metaphor. Consider, for example, a case where the conversation has included comments about both Richard's character and his dwelling. "He lives in a glass house" could then be used as a double entendre, and its literal sense would not clash with the context. I think the glass house example shows that in order for a metaphor to work it is more important that it be "pulled," or drawn out, by a suitable context than that it be "pushed" by an impropriety at the literal level. Many accounts of metaphor explain non-literal uses of language as instances where we seek an alternate meaning in the absence of a meaningful literal meaning.

10. See Alston, op. cit., p. 96, for an example of this common metaphor of parasitology.

11. Cf. Ludwig Wittgenstein's discussion of these two sentences in *Philosophical Investigations* (Oxford, 1953, 3rd ed. 1958), especially paragraphs 19 and 20.

12. Philip Wheelwright has a relevant if brief discussion of precision in his book, *Metaphor and Reality* (Indiana University Press, 1962), pp. 42-43. He points out that metaphors are sometimes more precise than literal language. However, he is relying more upon descriptive precision than precision in expression. I will say something about the former later on.

13. See, for example, John Searle, *Speech Acts: An Essay in the Philosophy of Language* (Cambridge University Press, 1969), especially pp. 19-20, where he talks about non-literal language as language in which the speaker does not say exactly what he means.

14. *The American Heritage Dictionary of the English Language* (Boston, 1970), p. 520.

15. "Metaphor," in *Encyclopedia of Philosophy*, ed. Paul Edwards, Volume V (New York, 1967), 284-289.

16. George E. Yoos makes a similar point in his article "A Phenomenological Look at Metaphor," *Philosophy and Phenomenological Research* XXXII, 1, 78-88. Still, Yoos thinks metaphors can be "descriptive" only metaphorically. I see no reason why a description, in

the literal sense of that term, could not be metaphorical. One should be careful not to confuse "a literal description" and "literally a description." A metaphor can literally be a
description, though certainly not a literal description, since it is not a literal use of
language.

17. I am indebted to Monroe Beardsley and Ann Clark for offering helpful comments
on earlier drafts of this paper.

Identifying Metaphors*

Ina Loewenberg

I. Introduction

There is considerable agreement within linguistics that metaphors are not identifiable by form. I will examine the basis for this claim and then suggest that by revising certain assumptions about the scope of linguistics a different conclusion is possible, at least for the most interesting class of metaphors.

Let me initially assume that our unreconstructed intuition as speakers of English permits us to recognize clear cases of metaphors. I will consider only those cases where metaphorical expressions, consisting of two or more lexical items, occur in sentences. My examples of clear cases are taken from Brooke-Rose's study of metaphor, which in turn takes them from a selection of poems in English.[1]

(1) I was a *morsel* for a monarch.
(2) Those are *pearls* that were his eyes.
(3) *Crazed through much child-bearing,* the moon is *staggering* in the sky.

It is an obvious fact that sentences in which metaphorical expressions occur are not distinguishable by syntactic form.[2] The word or words which are the 'focus' of the metaphor can belong to any

Reprinted from *Foundations of Language* 12 (1975): 315-338 by permission of the author.

syntactic category.[3] They can occur in sentences of any form, mood, tense, etc.

> Was she a morsel for a monarch?
> Let those eyes of his be pearls.
> The moon staggered in the sky.

The unpopularity of the study of metaphors in linguistics undoubtedly has something to do with their syntactic unwieldness as well as with their ubiquitousness. Yet it is an equally obvious fact that speakers of a language use and understand not only 'dead' but also novel metaphors with ease.[4] Despite syntactic diversity, there appears to be an underlying unity to all metaphors. They seem to exemplify a single principle of semantic change.

Formulating this principle adequately is another matter, and attempts have not been notably successful. 'Using one word and meaning another' will not do, nor will 'calling something by a different name'. I have argued in another paper that the traditional notion of metaphor as based on the comparison of similar properties is mistaken.[5] Brooke-Rose's definition is clearly too broad: "any identification of one thing with another, any replacement of the more usual word or phrase by another, is a metaphor."[6]

Any satisfactory formulation of the principle of metaphor requires the identifiability of metaphors since they cannot be understood or produced unless recognized as such.[7] Because the syntactic form of the sentences in which metaphorical expressions occur does not serve to identify metaphors, one must look elsewhere. Metaphors all appear to involve semantic change and therefore semantic theory is the likeliest source of a formula for identifying them. Can all metaphors, and only metaphors, be singled out by their semantic form? I will consider what linguistics has taken semantics to be and how the Katz-Fodor semantic theory and other theories critical of it answer this question. The negative results of this investigation lead me to some fundamental criticisms of linguistic theory from which a suggestion for identifying metaphors emerges.

II. Linguistic Semantics: Katz-Fodor's 'Anomaly'

Philosophers and linguists have cultivated different fields as 'semantics', although they go their different ways from a common starting point. There is initial agreement that a semantic theory must reflect *that* and *how* the meaning of a sentence is a function of the meanings of the words which compose it. Thus the philosopher Donald Davidson writes that

> a satisfactory theory of meaning must give an account of how the meanings of sentences depend upon the meanings of words.[8]

The linguist Uriel Weinreich describes the task of a semantic theory in almost identical words.[9] Another linguist, Manfred Bierwisch, states the first assumption of semantic analysis:

> The meaning of a given sentence can be accounted for on the basis of the words or, more precisely, the dictionary entries of which it consists, and the syntactic relations connecting these items.[10]

However, while Davidson then proceeds to develop a 'holistic' theory which concentrates on the truth-conditions for sentences and "leaves the whole matter of what individual words mean exactly where it was,"[11] Bierwisch offers, as the second assumption in semantics:

> The meanings of dictionary entries are not unanalyzable wholes, but can be decomposed into elementary semantic components.[12]

J. J. Katz blends Bierwisch's two assumptions from the start in characterizing the semantic component as a compositional function which "determines the semantic representations of a *constituent (including a sentence)* from the semantic representations of its subconstituents."[13] Katz's is a more general formulation: both words and sentences are constituents of sentences since a sentence is a part, although not a proper part (in logical terms), of itself. All constituents have subconstituents, semantic markers for words and words for sentences. Philosophers have not merely overlooked this aspect of semantics which deals with the components into which words can be analyzed; they deny that it is semantics at all. David Lewis writes,

> Semantic markers are *symbols*: items in the vocabulary of an artificial language we may call Semantic Markerese. . . . But we can know the Markerese translation of an English sentence without knowing the first thing about the meaning of the English sentence; namely, the conditions under which it would be true. Semantics with no treatment of truth conditions is not semantics.[14]

Linguistic semantics, however, has ignored truth conditions and concentrated exclusively on constituents of sentences and their subconstituents. Katz's formalism has dominated the field, even among his critics like Weinreich and Bierwisch.[15] The belief that "dictionary entries . . . can be decomposed into elementary semantic components" unites even interpretative and generative semanticists. It is, therefore, this linguistic conception of semantics with which I will first be concerned.

A composite schema of semantic representation in the formalist framework looks as follows:

(1) The *sense of a lexical item* is composed (not solely by conjunction) of 'markers' or 'features' which are its conceptual parts. Interrelationships among these parts are indicated by ordering or by the expression of entailments among them. Restrictions on the co-occurrence of parts are indicated.

(2) The *reading for a well-formed sentence* is a function of the senses of the lexical items of which it is composed.

According to the Katz-Fodor theory, a sentence receives more than one reading if it is ambiguous due to a lexical item in it having more than one sense. (E.g., 'he drove to the bank'.) if the co-occurrence restrictions for one of the lexical items in a sentence prevent its occurrence with *any* sense of the other lexical items in the sentence, the sentence receives *no* readings and is called 'anomalous'. (E.g., 'The square is foolish'.)[16]

This is as close as we can get, following the Katz-Fodor theory, to identifying sentences which contain at least one metaphorical expression. All such sentences will fail to receive any readings. In the sentence, 'Those are pearls that were his eyes', the metaphorical focus 'pearls' and the major frame-word 'eyes', which are referentially identified by the sentence, have mutually exclusive co-occurrence restrictions indicated in their senses. Labelling a sentence as anomalous is the end of concern for that sentence because anomalous sentences cannot be interpreted. Receiving zero readings is equivalent to not being interpretable, presumably also to 'having no meaning'.

It is curious that Katz comes to this conclusion about anomalous sentences since (1) as speakers, we know that some such sentences *are* interpretable in the context of utterance, and (2) Katz claims that "the readings that a speaker gives a sentence in setting are a selection from those the sentence has in isolation."[17] This claim is given to justify his position that "a theory of semantic interpretation [which is context-free] is logically prior to a theory of the selective effect of setting."[18] However, as Katz characterizes anomalous sentences, they have *no* readings from which a speaker can, 'in setting', select the contextually correct one. A selection from zero readings remains zero. Either Katz's general position is weakened by the existence of anomalous sentences which are interpretable metaphors in context or we must deny the testimony of our experience that there are such cases.

III. Linguistic Semantics: Interpretable Deviance

Some linguists who remain well within the framework of semantic representation shared with Katz have been dissatisfied with this as the only account given of metaphor by semantic theory. Weinreich, for example, inquired how Katz could explain that some deviant sentences were understood, and suggested that Katz's theory was "completely powerless to deal with intentional deviance as a communicative device."[19] He wrote, with obvious feeling,

> the theory is too weak to account for figurative usage (except the most hackneyed figures). . . . Whether there is any point to semantic theories which are accountable only for special cases of speech — namely, humorless, prosaic, banal prose — is highly doubtful.

> A semantic theory is of marginal interest if it is incapable of dealing with poetic uses of language, and more generally, with interpretable deviance.[20]

The revisions of Katzian theory with respect to metaphor tend to focus on reconciling the deviance of some sentences with their interpretability. I call them 'revisions', rather than different theories, because they all share some assumptions with Katz's theory which, as I will show later, play an important role in the problem of identifying metaphors.

These assumptions include the acceptance of two distinctions, and a conclusion drawn from them about the scope of linguistic theory. Two related distinctions were established as axiomatic 'in the beginning' by Chomsky. The first is the "fundamental distinction between *competence* (the speaker-hearer's knowledge of his language) and *performance* (the actual use of language in concrete situations).[21] The second distinction, presupposed by the first, is that between linguistic and extralinguistic or nonlinguistic knowledge, between knowledge of one's language and knowledge of the world. In consequence, linguistic theory is properly concerned only with competence, defined as linguistic knowledge.

Weinreich is important to a student of metaphor for his insistence that 'interpretable deviance' is a central phenomenon of language. However, despite the well-publicized differences between them, Weinreich does not move far from Katz's semantics. His is a theory of linguistic competence, concerned with the 'designational system' of a language and not with reference or context.[22] He attempts to give the *linguistic* grounds for how speakers give an interpretation to deviant sentences.

In Weinreich's account, sentences are identified as deviant by the operation of a rule of the 'Semantic Calculator' (which represents the semantic process the speaker goes through). The Transfer Rule performs the operation indicated by whatever 'transfer features' are part of the senses of the constituent lexical items of the sentence.[23] Transfer features attached to a lexical item impose selection restrictions on other lexical items with which the given lexical item can occur.[24] When such a restriction is transferred to the representation of another lexical item in the sentence, it may duplicate a feature already appearing (e.g., '*sail* a boat'); it may be consistent with other features but add information (e.g., '*sail* a vessel'); or it may conflict with another feature (e.g., '*sail* a car'). The Transfer Rule marks this redundancy or inconsistency when necessary. In the latter case, this amounts to identifying a sentence as deviant. For purposes of interpretation, other rules of the Semantic Calculator deal with redundancy and inconsistency by some form of elimination.[25]

Other writers have invoked the competence/performance distinction and have developed some sort of 'separation of powers' theory of metaphor. Robert Matthews' recent article is a lucid example of this approach, shaped by his insistence that "it is particularly important in [the analysis of metaphor] to conserve the distinction between language (competence) and the use of language (performance)."[26] He holds that the distinction between metaphors and non-metaphors is a "performance distinction . . . correctly characterized on the competence level in terms of a distinction between semantically deviant and non-deviant sentences."[27] Such deviance is identified by the "presence of a selectional restriction violation."[28] Matthews draws on Chomsky's discussion of selectional and subcategorization rules and their violations in *Aspects of the Theory of Syntax.*[29] He settles Chomsky's indecision about whether these rules should be part of the syntactic or semantic component by assuming that they are semantic.[30] His account has the virtue of recognizing that "given the proper context (linguistic and extralinguistic) almost *ANY* deviant sentence can be interpreted as metaphorical" and that "the distinction between metaphor and simple deviance involves the intention . . . to be metaphorical."[31]

A three-sided discussion of e. e. cummings' line 'he sang his didn't he danced his did' revolves around the respective roles of competence and performance in recognizing the deviance of the sentence and nevertheless coming to an interpretation of it.[32] Treating the line as an example of syntactic deviance,[33] Fowler holds that judgments of grammaticalness belong to competence while the "interpretative capability for all ungrammatical strings" is a "performance skill" "independent of linguistic competence."[34] Butters denies that such interpretation is exclusively a 'performance skill'. He distinguishes two senses of interpretation, one 'competence-related' and involving the semantic component of the theory and the other 'performance-related' and involving actual utterances.[35] About his attempt to rest at least some of the burden of interpretation on the semantic component and speakers' competence, he concludes:

> Admittedly, this is asking a great deal of a semantic component—but then, to leave the solution entirely up to performance is merely to shift the question from an area about which we know a little to an area about which we know almost nothing.[36]

IV. Sentences and Utterances: Criticisms of Anomaly/Deviance

These accounts of metaphor all use the concept of deviance which, in itself, can hardly be distinguished from Katz's 'anomaly'. The difference lies only in what follows the identification of a sentence as deviant or as anomalous: whether it can or cannot receive an interpretation. An interesting criticism of semantic anomaly has recently been given which applies with equal force to semantic deviance, namely that it is otiose and therefore unlikely to correspond to any part of a speaker's knowledge.

Robert Sanders writes that "it is likely that any so-called semantically anomalous sentence which is syntactically well-formed can be provided a context in which it is interpretable."[37] Sanders has in mind contexts in which such a sentence can be given a *literal* (i.e., standard) interpretation, but the consequences of what he writes are broader than that. Any sentence can be provided contexts (in which it is, therefore, an utterance) in which it can receive either literal or metaphorical interpretations. As Sanders notes, apparently deviant sentences can be 'literalized' by odd, but actual, states of affairs. Thus, to use our Shakespearean example, 'I was a morsel for a monarch' can be literally interpreted if the monarch referred to is a cannibal.[38] However, its original context in *Antony and Cleopatra,* in which Cleopatra refers to Caesar's dalliance with her, marks it as a metaphor. It is also the case that apparently nondeviant sentences can be uttered in contexts in which only a metaphorical interpretation can be given, as well as, of course, in standard contexts.[39] For example, 'John is a bear' receives a standard interpretation in the context in which 'John' refers to a pet bear or a bear at the zoo and a metaphorical one when the name refers to someone's friend or relative.

If the interpretation of a sentence thus depends on its context of utterance, and nothing depends on its 'anomaly' or 'deviance', what function do these concepts serve? Sanders writes that "such a state of affairs is contrary to a fundamental tenet of linguistic description: that the grammar must reflect all of the linguistic information which in principle is available to the speaker-hearer" [and only that information].[40] Characterizing sentences as anomalous or deviant is neither necessary nor sufficient for understanding them. Katz is consistent—but wrong—since, for him, identifying a sentence as anomalous has a function: it marks the sentence as *un*interpretable. Proponents of 'interpretable deviance' have simply introduced a useless step in the interpretation of sentences.

Sanders himself is committed, as firmly as Katz is, to the linguistic/nonlinguistic distinction and therefore does not carry his criticisms and his own proposals as far from the Katzian framework as he might. Despite his recognition of the importance of context of utterance, his own theory is a formalist one. He posits 'redefining conditions' which, when satisfied, make the application of optional 'redefining rules' possible.[41] Although he provides for two kinds of conditions and two kinds of rules for copula and non-copula sentences respectively, this strikes me as unnecessary luxury in the theory. In the notation of predicate logic, which Sanders uses, 'is- —' is an unbreakable predicate. 'It is blue' is not formally different from 'It floats'. Quine has shown that even when the blank is filled by a singular term (e.g., 'It is Massachusetts') 'is- —' can be construed in the same way.[42] Therefore, copula sentences do not have to be treated separately. Non-copula sentences, which can cover all predicative sentences, satisfy redefining conditions when, if x and y are arguments in a 2-place relationship $[J]$ and the 'lexical implication' ($[J]\,xy \rightarrow [K]\,x$) exists, x is *not* K.[43] In the more general terms we have been using, redefining conditions are met when there is a conflict between features (including entailed features) of different lexical items in a sentence.

Although Sanders notes that to give up semantic anomaly is to give up Katz's semantic component with its selection restrictions, since their function to 'delete deviant readings' is superfluous,[44] he remarks, in the exposition of his own theory, that "redefining conditions for non-copula sentences are based on the same kinds of implications expressed by selection restrictions and transfer features."[45] (No wonder Katz keeps answering his critics by calling their theories "terminological [or "notational"] variants" of his own!)[46]

Sanders' recognition of the importance of the context of utterance makes another approach to sentences possible. We can treat sentences as *ambiguous* with respect to whether they will be literal or metaphorical as utterances and we can consider any metaphorical utterance as ambiguous with respect to which term is the 'focus'.[47] Although there are no formal grounds for determining the focus of a metaphor, Sanders suspects that there are psycholinguistic constraints on speakers to 'resist' ambiguity of focus, and he tests this hypothesis empirically.[48]

If the marking of sentences as deviant has turned out to be a superfluous move in our attempt to identify metaphors, does the marking of sentences as ambiguous advance our cause? Hardly. If we treat *all* sentences as ambiguous because any sentence can be given contexts in which some literal and some metaphorical interpretations are appropriate, taking a very broad view of 'possible worlds', then we have succeeded in 'isolating' the totality of sentences of the language! If we only treat those sentences as ambiguous which do *not* meet redefining conditions, we continue to rely on discredited 'deviance' (by whatever name) and find ourselves with an enormous set of ambiguous sentences,[49] all of which may (or may not) be metaphors as utterances, and with another set of 'deviant' sentences, not all of which definitely will be metaphors as utterances.

It appears that linguistic theory cannot tell us anything very interesting or helpful about identifying *sentences* as metaphors. This should not come as a great surprise, and I propose that we henceforth concern ourselves with utterances rather than with sentences. That this has not been done, or that it has only been contemplated in a spirit of defeat and despair, is related to the fact that sentences are formal linguistic objects while utterances are occurrences in the world. The strong preference exhibited in linguistics for dealing with the former brings us back once more to the basic assumptions shared by so many. Since the use of sentences which may or may not be metaphorical inexorably involves speakers in referring to things in the world, perhaps these assumptions which effectively insulate language from the world should be critically examined.

V. Assumptions of Linguistic Theory

(1) The knowledge of language is fundamentally distinguishable from the use of language. (Competence/performance)
(2) Linguistic knowledge is distinguishable from nonlinguistic knowledge.
(3) Linguistic theory should account for linguistic competence.

Chomsky originally drew the competence/performance distinction in order to correct an excess in descriptive linguistics, namely the strong emphasis on compiling and analyzing actual instances of speech.

Although this work rested on assumptions about the typicalness of the informants as speakers of the language and extrapolated from the data to generalizations about the language, it failed, in Chomsky's view, to do justice to the extraordinary 'creativity' of a speaker of any language. Any speaker's creativity consists in his ability—from a tender age—to produce and understand sentences of his language which are completely novel. Since novel sentences will never appear in any corpus of utterances, however painstakingly gathered, because, by definition, they are the ones as yet unuttered, linguists should concentrate on the abilities of speakers rather than on what they actually say. A linguistic theory should represent the knowledge, more particularly, the linguistic knowledge of a fluent speaker of a language; it should be a competence theory.[50]

As we have seen, many linguists expend considerable worry to keep competence and performance from contaminating one another. But competence and performance, although certainly distinguishable, are not 'fundamentally distinct'. Correcting an excess in one approach not infrequently produces an equal and opposite excess in the replacing approach.

We are all aware that nervousness, fatigue, or other factors sometimes causes us to make mistakes in speech or to misspeak; we often recognize what we are doing as we hear ourselves. A professional pianist who hears himself hitting a wrong note during a concert is keenly aware of the distinction between competence and performance, as is a member of the audience who will not attribute the performer's mistake to his (lack of) competence unless it becomes a habit! However, regular patterns in my speech *do* reflect my competence, and regular patterns discernible in the speech of speakers of a language determine what counts as competence in that language. Competence and performance are distinguishable, but not independent. Their relationship is, in fact, one of interdependence.

This interdependence manifests itself, as Stemmer shows, at every stage in the development of a theory of language.[51] Performance data suggest the form and content of a theory of competence; the predictions of the competence theory concern performance data which, in that way, test the theory's adequacy.[52] The idealizations introduced as theoretical terms in competence theory, such as the 'ideal speaker', must be related by correspondence rules to observable speech events if they are to be of any empirical interest.[53] Since competence and performance are not 'fundamentally distinct', in Chomsky's extreme sense, Stemmer concludes that it is wrong to insist that it is necessary—or possible—to develop competence and performance theories independent of each other.[54]

A speaker's regular ability to identify utterances as metaphorical is surely an aspect of his competence or else he could not, in fact, do it. That something *is* the case entails that it is *possible* for it to be the case. (The converse is, of course, not true.) It is true that the speaker exercises his competence here in the context of actual spoken (or written) utterances and not on sentences since they are not determinable as metaphors. Why should this matter? It matters to linguists who press the distinction between competence and performance because of that other distinction, between linguistic knowledge and nonlinguistic knowledge. On the assumption that these two kinds of knowledge can be distinguished, it is held that linguists should steer clear of the latter in order to avoid the morass of the completely unmanageable.

Taking a speaker's nonlinguistic knowledge into account is unmanageable, according to Katz, because it is an impossible task. If a theory purports to "account for the manner in which settings determine how an utterance is understood," and "settings" denotes not linguistic contexts but "aspects of the socio-physical world," then the theory must be "able to represent all the nonlinguistic information required by speakers to understand sentences."[55] No item of knowledge about the world is irrelevant to the understanding of some sentence. Therefore, such a theory must "represent *all* the knowledge speakers have about the world," item by item, and this is clearly impossible because the list of items is without limit.[56]

Another 'conclusion' of requiring a theory to account for the contribution of context is that the theory then "cannot in principle distinguish between the speaker's knowledge of his language and his knowledge of the world."[57] I prefer to call this 'conclusion' the denial of the basic assumption on which Katz's conception of the scope of a semantic theory rests, which he does not want to give up. If the assumption is false or even highly questionable, as I believe it is, then fixing the 'upper bound'[58] of a semantic theory where Katz does might become the 'impossible' move.

Can we distinguish, in every sentence of the form 'I know that p', where p is a sentence, whether p is an item of my linguistic or of my nonlinguistic knowledge? In most such sentences? In any? It is only surprising that there is so little cross-fertilization between disciplines that this distinction is blandly assumed by many in linguistics[59] while it has been hotly contested in philosophy for over twenty years. W. V. Quine, who initiated the argument, holds that there are *no* analytic truths, that is, statements which are true by virtue of linguistic facts exclusively, truths *about* language. He has maintained that no definition of 'analytic' has been given which meets the conditions of being (1) noncircular, (2) explanatory, (3) empirically justifiable, (4) given in terms of meanings alone, (5) applicable dichotomously to all statements, and (6) interlinguistically valid. While many philosophers have rejected Quine's view and have held that some sense can be given to 'analytic', there is considerable agreement that *not all* truths about the world can be distinguished from truths about language.[60]

This distinction is often referred to by its adherents, in a short-cut way, as the difference between a dictionary and an encyclopedia. Some distinguished dictionary editors see that difference as "a fluctuating and dubious one."[61] A real dictionary (as opposed to 'ideal'— but see above, p. 165) " is concerned with giving information about the things for which [the] words and phrases stand *only so far* as correct use of the words depends on knowledge of the things."[62] How far is 'only so far'? It differs for different words; no general rule can be given.

Let us look at some examples, trying to distinguish our knowledge about these sentences as linguistic or nonlinguistic.

I was a morsel for a monarch.

Presumably most speakers would judge that something is wrong with this sentence (under certain assumptions about its likely context) and would locate the problem in a conflict between 'I' and 'morsel'. Following are some statements I claim to know relevant to this conflict:

(1) 'I' denotes the speaker.
(2) Speakers are human.
(3) A 'morsel' is a small, usually delicious, bit or bite of food.

(4) In the above sentence, 'I' is referentially identified with 'morsel'.

(5) Therefore, the speaker is identified with a small, usually delicious, bit or bite of food.

(6) Therefore, something human is identified with a small, usually delicious, bit or bite of food.

(7) Humans are (in most places at the present time) not used as food.

However the reader classifies statements (1)–(6), it seems clear to me that the crucial claim relevant to the conflict is (7) and that (7) cannot be classified as linguistic knowledge. This example shows only that to understand the conflict between the meanings of words in a very simple sentence we need 'mixed' knowledge. The next example shows that understanding a sentence may depend on knowledge that we hardly know how to classify in terms of 'linguistic' or 'nonlinguistic'.

> Crazed through much child-bearing, the moon is staggering in the sky.

(1)   Only animate beings stagger.

(2) (a) Only animate beings are crazed (unless it is the sense of 'crazed' in which china is crazed).

(b) Only humans bear children.

(c) 'Through' expresses a causal relationship.

(d) Therefore, only humans are crazed through much child-bearing.

(3) (a) The moon is not animate.

(b) Since if x is human, x is animate, then if x is not animate, x is not human.

(c) Therefore, the moon is not human.

(4)   Crazed behavior is sometimes associated with staggering.

(5)   The moon is, in some myths, associated with madness.

(6)   The moon is, in some myths, identified with a female.

(7)   The word denoting the moon belongs to the female gender in many languages.

(8)   A salient attribute of the moon is its change in size.

(9)   A salient attribute of a child-bearer is her change in size.

(10)   The moon goes through repeated cycles of change in size.

(11)   (10) is analogous to 'much child-bearing' with respect to size.

(12)   (10) can be used to measure and mark the passage of time.

Although these do not, of course, exhaust the knowledge I need to understand this sentence fully, I invite the reader to try classifying them.

Notice that if (1) were worded differently:

(1a)   'Stagger' takes an animate subject

it would appear to be an item of knowledge about language instead of, as given in (1), a generalization from experience about staggering things. Which is correct? They both are. Which comes first? Does the question make sense? If rocks sometimes moved in the way we characterize as 'staggering', both formulations would be false. If the shape or sound 'stagger' meant what it now does with the addition 'or remain in place', both formulations would be false. They are instead both true because of what the shape/sound 'stagger' means and because of the way things move.

Semantic formalists ignore the fact that (1) and (1a) are equivalent and, further, try to express all knowledge necessary for understanding sentences in the latter form. Their claim is that there is a finite set of semantic categories (features, markers), independent of particular languages and adequate to account for the conceptual components of every word in any language. They hold, in addition, that the meanings of sentences can be adequately accounted for by the conceptual components of their constituent words (in the relationships determined by syntax). Thus, we know 'The moon is not animate' is true because we know that the feature [−Animate] appears in the dictionary entry of 'moon'. Presumably, we must know 'Humans are not used as food' is true by similar means since we require this knowledge to understand the conflict between 'I' and 'morsel' in the first example. I am skeptical that this can be convincingly shown but the problems of semantic formalism go beyond problems with isolated cases.

First, the basic formalist claim is not yet substantiated. Despite impressive work, no one is anywhere near the formulation of an 'alphabet'[63] of semantic categories which meets the abovementioned conditions of universality and adequacy. We have only been issued a very large promissory note.[64] Second, the criteria have not been given to distinguish 'conceptual' components from contingent associations of a word. It will not do, on pain of circularity, to assert that categories which represent conceptual components are those which are parts of meanings and not parts of facts.

The third problem concerns the proportion of clear cases of true statements due to linguistic knowledge to all true statements. In any classification, there will be borderline cases. The existence of borderline cases does not, therefore, invalidate a principle of classification. However, in the case of the classification of statements into those which are true by virtue of meanings and those which are true by virtue of matters of fact, philosophers and linguists have significantly different purposes. It is enough for a philosopher defending the distinction against Quine's "more thorough pragmatism"[65] to show that there are *some clear cases* of analytic truths picked out by his proposed criteria, even if they are few and philosophically trivial.[66] A linguist who proposes that his field restrict itself to systematizing only the linguistic knowledge of speakers requires a distinction as close as possible to a dichotomy and a situation in which *most* cases are decidable. If he takes what philosophers like Putnam offer him in the way of analytically true statements as the basis for conceptual components, these will not suffice to determine the meanings of all words. If, on the other hand, he surreptitiously includes clear cases of nonlinguistic truths and unclear cases, the system will suffice but it will not, as claimed, be based on purely linguistic knowledge.

Katz is of course correct to insist that a linguistic theory cannot include an itemized list of all knowledge and beliefs possessed by all speakers. If all this information is relevant, then one cannot have it available in that form. But it is that conclusion, and not Katz's, which is justified by his argument. It is arbitrary to exclude clear cases of knowledge about the world since these are often essential to using language to talk about things in the world. It is equally arbitrary to overlook the undecidable cases because they represent *most* of our knowledge. In no way have the formalists, from Katz onward, demonstrated that they *can* do what they propose in semantic analysis beyond scattered examples. Therefore, let us take the linguistic/nonlinguistic distinction to be a blurred one at best and let us not view the competence of speakers as something existing apart from the world in which they speak.

VI. Identifying Metaphorical Utterances

Metaphors are identifiable only if we can identify some utterances as metaphors. I have shown that since some deviant sentences are *not* metaphors in the context of utterance and some *nondeviant* sentences are, in context, metaphors, we cannot hope to identify metaphors by singling out any kind of *sentence*. Giving up an excessively rigid notion of 'competence' permits us to consider utterances.

Metaphorical utterances are identifiable only if some knowledge possessed by speakers which is decidedly not knowledge of relationships among linguistic symbols can be taken into account. I shall argue that knowledge of—more accurately, beliefs about—the truth or falsity of statements and the intentions of the speaker are essentially involved in the identification of utterances as metaphorical. Giving up the assumption that we should—or even can—limit ourselves to 'linguistic' knowledge permits us to consider truth and intentions.

Searle writes

> It is not, as has generally been supposed, the symbol or word or sentence, or even the token of the symbol or word or sentence, which is the unit of linguistic communication, but rather it is the *production* of the token in the performance of the speech act that constitutes the basic unit of linguistic communication. To put this point more precisely, the production of the sentence token under certain conditions is the illocutionary act, and the illocutionary act is the minimal unit of linguistic communication.[67]

It may seem strange to invoke Searle since metaphors do not fit into the existing typology of speech-acts. The syntactic variety of sentences that can be used to make metaphorical utterances, which I have referred to so often, suggests that metaphorical expressions can occur in sentences performing all kinds of speech-acts. This is, in fact, the case. Questions, commands, promises, etc. can all be performed by the utterance of sentences that contain metaphorical expressions.

Am I a morsel for a monarch?
Go be a morsel for a monarch!

Even assertions can be made by the utterance of sentences containing suitably embedded metaphorical expressions.

She told me she was a morsel for a monarch.

However, this diversity is merely superficial. The following generalizations about metaphorical utterances seem to me to support a unified speech-act analysis for the identification of metaphors.

(1) No one correctly understands a metaphorical utterance unless he understands it *as* a metaphorical utterance.

(2) No one produces a metaphorical utterance (rather than a mistake) unless he utters a sentence *as* a metaphor.[68]

(3) Some unifying principle appears to underlie all metaphors.

All of these intuitions or commonplaces about metaphors seem to me to involve "the production of [a] sentence token under certain conditions." But what conditions? and what speech-act are we dealing with?

Those metaphors have been of philosophical interest which, in some queer way, appear to assert but are false as assertions; which nevertheless 'say something'. If they were merely false statements, they would not be particularly interesting. Recognizing that an utterance is this kind of metaphor is seeing that, if it were an assertion, it would be false, but it is not an assertion and must be taken differently. Beardsley says it better:

> the reader can see that you are not asserting the statement you make (to assert is to evince and to invite belief), but since the statement is made, and something is presumably being asserted, he looks about for a second level of meaning on which something *is* being said.[69]

I do not want to hold, as Beardsley does, that "something is presumably being asserted," but only that "something is being said." I think it is a mistake to use 'asserting' and 'saying something' interchangeably. An assertion makes a truth claim. 'Saying something' is much looser: it may even indicate nothing more than making a significant (i.e., meaningful) utterance. All metaphorical utterances 'say something' in that sense because they can all be given some interpretation and because they are all (see (2) above) purposeful utterances. I shall claim rather more for metaphorical 'saying something' that this but I reject the claim that metaphorical utterances are used to make truth claims.

We may indeed consider some of our metaphorical utterances more worth saying than any others. Truth claims may seem trivial next to claims made by one imagination on another. But however inspired the metaphor and however committed to it its author, I do not think that he will, on reflection, claim truth for it if he preserves a precise meaning for 'truth' and does not equivocate between truth and a-kind-of-truth.[70] Such equivocation smacks of the subsistence/ existence solution to a different philosophical problem. Bertrand Russell said, in that connection, "There is only one world, the 'real' world."[71] My analogous claim is that there is only one kind of truth. Therefore, those metaphorical statements which look like assertions are false if taken as assertions because they are literally false. But metaphors are never meant to be taken literally any more than they are meant to be taken as assertions.

The analysis that follows will deal only with this kind of metaphor and therefore only with utterances of indicative sentences. Indicative sentences in which the metaphorical expression is embedded in a relative clause or in a clause which is the object of a verb of saying, believing, promising, asking, etc., can be accommodated by treating those clauses as I treat the kernel sentences. I do not now know how to handle questions and imperatives.

The process of identifying utterances as metaphorical involves at least two stages, the first of which is the recognition that, if the utterance is an assertion, it is false. Why doesn't metaphorical utterance always *fail,* with the reader or hearer taking the utterance as a false assertion and attributing confusion, stupidity or misinformation to the speaker? From the hearer's point of view, a general principle of communication operates to avoid this:

> It is important to stress that a hearer will try to interpret or at least to account for a speaker's utterances. He will often accept and make sense even out of sentences that initially appear odd or contradictory when presented to him on semantic tests or in actual discourse. . . .[72]

David Lewis's 'convention of truthfulness' concerns the same phenomenon from the speaker's point of view:

Members of *P* [the population] will exchange utterances of sentences of
L, and they will almost always try to avoid uttering sentences not true in
L. (Sometimes they will lie; but we can tolerate exceptions to a conventional regularity. Sometimes they will be mistaken; but the regularity I
have in mind is that of *trying* to be truthful in *L*. . . .)[73]

Speakers and hearers are, after all, the same individuals on different
occasions of utterances. We try to make sense out of even peculiar
utterances, we try to avoid attributing false beliefs to our inter-
locutors, because we ourselves try and usually succeed in producing
utterances that can be made sense of, in making statements which
are more often true than false.

Having grasped that the utterance is false as an assertion, the
hearer assesses whether the utterance is indeed to be taken as an
assertion. According to Searle, these are the conditions which must
be met for the speech-act of assertion to be performed:

the preparatory conditions include the fact that the hearer must have some
basis for supposing the asserted proposition is true, the sincerity condition
is that he must believe it to be true, and the essential condition has to do
with the fact that the utterance is an attempt to inform the hearer and
convince him of its truth.[74]

The hearer takes into account the context (linguistic and situational)
in which the utterance was made as well as his judgment of the
beliefs and intentions of the speaker.[75] He then concludes either that
the speaker intends the utterance to be taken literally, in which case
he has performed the speech-act of assertion and made a false assertion, or that the speaker's intention is not reflected in a literal interpretation of the utterance, in which case the utterance *fails as an
assertion.* It is a necessary, but not sufficient, condition for an utterance to be a metaphor that, if taken as an assertion and interpreted
literally, it is false. If the hearer concludes that the utterance *fails
as an assertion,* what, if any, positive conclusion is he entitled to?
What speech-act is being performed if not that of assertion? What
does 'saying something' actually mean here?

Before suggesting answers to these questions, I would like to compare this conversational situation (which can just as well be an inter-
change between a reader and a text) with a feature of the speech-act
of requesting noted by Gordon and Lakoff. An utterance in the form

of a question, 'Can you —?' is either a request (to the person addressed) to — or a 'real question', a request for information about the
ability (of the person addressed) to—. (E.g., 'Can you take out the
garbage?')[76] The "conversational implied meaning [i.e., the request]
can be conveyed only if the literal meaning [i.e., the 'real question']
is not intended to be conveyed and if the hearer assumes that it
isn't."[77]

I believe that we have a similar situation here. A metaphorical
utterance is ambiguous because it can be taken as a false assertion
or as a metaphor. In concluding that such an utterance fails as an
assertion, the hearer identifies it as metaphorical. He judges that the
speaker was not making a truth claim about the referents of the
words in the sentence he uttered but rather a *proposal* about a way
to view, understand, etc. those referents. 'Saying something' by
means of metaphor is combining words in a semantically non-
standard way such that an interpretation of the sentence involves a
new, or at least non-standard, view of the things the sentence is
about. The speaker does not assert this view because he knows that
it does not represent what—actually and literally—is the case and he
expects his hearers to know this. However, his utterance is not
merely an expression, a blurting out, of his feelings, nor is he indif-
ferent to his effect on hearers. The speaker is implicitly proposing
that his hearer adopt the view expressed by the sentence he uttered.

Metaphorical utterances occur in such a variety of circumstances
that any common characterization of them must necessarily be
highly general. Sometimes a metaphor is a flash of insight, forgotten
almost as soon as it is uttered. Sometimes a metaphor is frivolously
uttered to amuse or to shock. At other times, it is the result of serious
searching for the most perspicuous, vivid or intelligible way to express
one's thoughts. The speaker's commitment to his proposal may be
fleeting or, where the metaphor is central to his perception of the
universe or to his life's work, it may be profound. In this case, he may
even be explicitly aware that he is proposing a certain view of things
in using the metaphor. In all of these cases, despite their range and
variety, I believe that the speaker can be said to be making a proposal,
in the above sense, by his metaphorical utterance. Furthermore, I
believe that 'making a proposal' distinguishes metaphorical utterances
from others more effectively than merely 'saying something' does.

If the speaker had made an assertion, his utterance would have had truth-value and would have been either true or false. Instead, in making a *proposal* that certain things be viewed or understood in a certain way, his utterance has heuristic value, positive or negative. By this I mean that the speaker considers his utterance suggestive, revealing or insightful, while, for his hearer, it is either that or misleading, confusing, distorting.[78] These terms are admittedly vague but I am afraid we have no others more precise.

The notion of heuristic value is familiar from discussions of the usefulness of models and, indeed, to attribute heuristic value to metaphors is to make explicit the continuity in function between the members of the family—metaphor—analogy—model—theory.[79] Continuity in function is, of course, not identity of function. A single metaphorical utterance, no matter how dazzling, cannot possibly influence our view of the world as profoundly as a model can. Suggestiveness, misleadingness and the rest can be explicated for models with much more rigor than for metaphors, but this is hardly surprising. The purposes for which models are employed are far more systematic than the purposes for which metaphors are uttered. I attribute heuristic value to metaphorical utterances to acknowledge that, although such utterances are not true or false, there are grounds for accepting or rejecting them.

According to the available typology of speech-acts, we can only say that a metaphorical utterance fails as an assertion; we cannot say that it succeeds as anything. But it is beyond dispute that the successful communication of metaphorical utterances is a common occurrence. Therefore, although I respect the principle of Ockham's razor, I suggest the introduction of a new speech-act which we can call *proposal*$_m$ (for metaphorical proposal).

The conditions to be met for the performance of the speech-act of *proposal*$_m$ are

(1) the speaker, in uttering p, believes that p, as an assertion, is false;

(2) he believes that his hearer also believes that p, as an assertion, is false;

(3) the hearer does believe that p, as an assertion, is false;

(4) the hearer believes that the speaker believes that p, as an assertion, is false;

(5) the speaker believes that to consider the referents of the constituent terms of p according to p has heuristic value;

(6) he believes that his hearer does not already consider the referents of the constituent terms of p according to p;

(7) the speaker intends his hearer to take his utterance of p as a proposal to consider the referents of the constituent terms of p according to p, and to know that he intends him to do so;

(8) the hearer takes the utterance of p to be such a proposal because he believes the speaker intends him to.

(1) through (4) stipulate the necessity of the speaker and hearer agreeing that p, uttered as an assertion, is false and believing that this agreement exists between them. On the other hand, (5) and (6) concern only the speaker's intention to enlighten his hearer. It would be too strong a requirement to demand that the hearer actually be enlightened. He can accept the utterance as a metaphor, a proposal (8) without accepting the particular metaphor-proposal. It may not enlighten him because he considers it a poor metaphor (he rejects the speaker's belief in (5)) or because it is not new to him (the speaker's belief in (6) is false).

It may also not enlighten him because he does not understand by p what the speaker understands by p. The speaker's beliefs and intentions determine that his utterance of p is to be taken as a metaphor but do not determine the meaning of p.[80] P, uttered as an assertion and interpreted literally, means what its constituent words mean; it is false because things are not the way p indicates. For most literal p_s, there is liable to be wide agreement among speakers about what p means. When p is a metaphorical utterance, its meaning is still, in some way, related to its constituent words, although much less determinately.[81] This lack of determinacy, however, does not entail that the metaphor p means what its author intends it to mean.

Thus I conclude that some utterances of indicative sentences can be identified as metaphors. The necessary and sufficient conditions for an utterance to be metaphorical are jointly

(1) The utterance is of a well-formed indicative sentence;

(2) the utterance is an assertion if and only if it is false;

(3) the utterance is not an assertion.

Where the variable u ranges over utterances,

$$(u) \; [(I_u \; \& \; (A_u{\equiv}F_u) \; \& \; {-}A_u){\equiv}M_u]$$

I: is a well-formed indicative sentence

A: is an assertion

F: is false

M: is metaphorical

Metaphors, as I have analzyed them, are statements without truth-value. Truth-value is centrally relevant to their identification since any metaphorical utterance is ambiguous and could be instead a false assertion. However, once identified as a metaphor, the statement is neither true nor false. As a philosopher, I would rather not be left with truth-value 'gaps', in Russell's term,[82] but I resist still more stretching truth to cover metaphorical proposals, particularly since, as truth-functional statements, they are false. In the last paragraph of his paper, Davidson grants that his theory leaves many kinds of sentences out of account, including those "that seem not to have truth values at all," and marks this as unfinished business in the achievement of a "comprehensive theory of meaning for a natural language."[83]

I doubt very much that this paper will be the last word on the problem of identifying metaphors. I do hope to have shown that the problem is not obviously without solution unless the investigator is arbitrarily handicapped by questionable assumptions. In philosophy, we often must try to persuade students that it is possible to talk about the world by (also) talking about language. I would like to persuade linguists that it is possible to talk about language by (also) talking about the world. In fact, in both cases, I believe it is necessary to do this.

NOTES

*I would like to thank Max Black of Cornell University and Larry W. Martin of the University of Iowa for their helpful comments on this paper. I would also like to acknowledge the good editorial judgment and encouragement I received from my husband Gerhard Loewenberg.

1. Christine Brooke-Rose, *A Grammar of Metaphor*, Secker & Warburg, London, 1958. Sources of examples: (1) Shakespeare, *Antony and Cleopatra*, I/v/30; (2) Eliot, *The Waste Land*, 48 (quoting Shakespeare); (3) Yeats, *The Crazed Moon*. It is better for the student of metaphor not to make up his own examples to illustrate or test his theories. Brooke-Rose emphasizes the variety of grammatical patterns of metaphors which makes her book a particularly good source of examples. I have marked the 'focus' of each metaphor. For the focus-frame terminology, see Max Black, 'Metaphor', in *Models and Metaphors*, Cornell University Press, Ithaca, 1962, p. 28.

2. It is not an obvious fact to those who accept Chomsky's suggestion that selectional and subcategorization rules may be included in the syntactic component (e.g., J. C. Nyiri, 'No Place for Semantics', *Foundations of Language* 7 (1971)). For them, metaphorical sentences will come out syntactically deviant. I believe that this treatment is particularly inappropriate for metaphors. That they are, in a narrower sense of syntax, typically syntactically well-formed while deviant in some other way is at least a start to distinguishing them from other sentences.

3. Establishing this, and examining metaphors grouped in this way, is the purpose of Brooke-Rose's study.

4. See my 'Truth and Consequences of Metaphors', *Philosophy & Rhetoric* 6 (1973), 31, 44. 'Dead' metaphors are best understood as literal expressions. However, the distinction is not a dichotomy but a continuum, constantly shifting for times and speakers.

5. *Ibid.*

6. *A Grammar of Metaphor*, p. 17.

7. It is Monroe Beardsley's insight that an essential part of any account of understanding metaphors must be an account of how they are identified. See his *Aesthetics*, Harcourt, Brace & World, New York, 1958, pp. 138-44, 159-62.

8. 'Truth and Meaning', *Synthese* 17 (1967), 304.

9. *Explorations in Semantic Theory*, Janua Linguarum, series minor 89, The Hague, 1972, p. 44.

10. 'On Classifying Semantic Features', in M. Bierwisch and K. E. Heidolph (eds.), *Progress in Linguistics*, Mouton, The Hague, 1970, p. 27.

11. 'Truth and Meaning', p. 318.

12. 'On Classifying Semantic Features', p. 27.

13. 'Interpretative Semantics vs. Generative Semantics', *Foundations of Language* 6 (1970), 225. Emphasis supplied.

14. 'General Semantics', *Synthese* 22 (1970/71), 18. See also Gilbert Harman, 'Three Levels of Meaning', *The Journal of Philosophy* 65 (1968), 600; J. C. Nyiri, 'No Place for Semantics', p. 67.

15. His paper, written with Jerry Fodor, 'The Structure of a Semantic Theory', was the first entry in semantics on the part of transformational grammar, and he has continued, through numerous publications, to be a spokesman for the field even when he has also been a target of criticism.

16. J. J. Katz and Jerry A. Fodor, 'The Structure of a Semantic Theory', in Fodor and Katz (eds.), *The Structure of Language,* Prentice-Hall, Englewood Cliffs, 1964, pp.497-8, 503.

17. *Ibid.,* p. 488. "It is clear that, *in general,* a sentence cannot have readings in a setting which it does not have in isolation. [There are some such cases] . But these cases are essentially idiomatic in the sense that meaning is determined either by special stipulation . . . or by special rules . . . or by special information about the intentions of the speaker." What does 'special' mean here? I deny that metaphors, interpretable in context, are like codes or even like idioms (see footnote 81).

18. *Ibid.*

19. *Explorations in Semantic Theory*, pp. 42-3.

20. *Ibid.,* pp. 18, 117.

21. Noam Chomsky, *Aspects of the Theory of Syntax*, MIT Press, Cambridge, 1965, p. 4.

22. 'On the Semantic Structure of Language', in Jos. Greenberg (ed.), *Universals of Language*, MIT Press, Cambridge, 1963, p. 152; *Explorations in Semantic Theory*, p. 44, fn. 1.

23. *Explorations in Semantic Theory*, p. 101.

24. *Ibid.,* p. 62.

25. *Ibid.,* pp. 103-6.

26. 'Concerning a 'Linguistic Theory' of Metaphor', *Foundations of Language* 7 (1971), 425.

27. *Ibid.,* p. 424.

28. *Ibid.*

29. See pp. 148-60. Matthews' 'selectional rules' include both Chomsky's selectional and subcategorization rules, as he admits, p. 418.

30. See pp. 418, 424, 425 f.n. 7.

31. *Ibid.,* pp. 416, 417. See pp. 8, 20ff.

32. Jan Aarts, 'A Note on the Interpretation of 'he danced his did'', *Journal of Linguistics* 7 (1971); Ronald R. Butters, 'On the Interpretation of 'deviant utterances'', *Journal of Linguistics* 6 (1969); Roger Fowler, 'On the Interpretation of 'nonsense strings'', *Journal of Linguistics* 5 (1969).

33. If one draws the distinction traditionally, this is surely a mixed case. 'sang' and 'danced' are used metaphorically — are semantically deviant — while 'didn't' and 'did' are syntactically deviant. This is typical of cummings.

34. 'On the Interpretation of 'nonsense strings'', pp. 82, 76.

35. 'On the Interpretation of 'deviant utterances'', p. 105.

36. *Ibid.,* p. 108.

37. 'Aspects of Figurative Language', *Linguistics*, No. 96 (1973), 60. For a dissenting view, see Angus McIntosh, 'Patterns and Ranges', *Language* 37 (1961).

McIntosh believes that there are some sentences for which "we cannot easily . . . conceive of any situation . . . where they might be appropriate," p. 327.

38. There is no problem about the speaker speaking from the grave: it was only a morsel, not a complete meal. See *Candide.*

39. Sanders recognizes this, albeit parenthetically, p. 80.

40. *Ibid.,* p. 61.

41. *Ibid.,* pp. 76-85. For his excellent defense of why redefining rules must not be obligatory, see p. 85.

42. W. V. Quine, *Word and Object*, MIT Press, Cambridge, 1960, pp. 178-9.

43. Sanders, 'Aspects of Figurative Language', p. 80.

44. *Ibid.*, p.61.

45. *Ibid.*, p. 79.

46. 'Recent Issues in Semantic Theory', *Foundations of Language* 3 (1967), 180; 'Interpretative Semantics vs. Generative Semantics', p. 240.

47. Cf. Sanders, 'Aspects of Figurative Language', pp. 80, 84-5. See also L. J. Cohen and Avishai Margalit, 'The Role of Inductive Reasoning in the Interpretation of Metaphors', *Synthese* 21 (1970), 483.

48. Sanders, *ibid.*, pp. 85-97.

49. See Cohen and Margalit: "almost every sentence is potentially ambiguous" (p. 483).

50. Chomsky defends his approach from the charge of ignoring the study of performance by claiming that "the only studies of performance, outside of phonetics . . . are those carried out as a by-product of work in generative grammar." Furthermore, "it is the descriptivist limitation-in-principle to classification and organization of data, to 'extracting patterns' from a corpus of observed speech, to describing 'speech habits' or 'habit structures', insofar as these may exist, etc., that precludes the development of a theory of actual performance." *Aspects of the Theory of Syntax*, p. 15.

51. Nathan Stemmer, 'A Note on Competence and Performance', *Linguistics*, No. 65 (1971).

52. *Ibid.*, pp. 86-87.

53. *Ibid.*, pp. 84, 88.

54. *Ibid.*, p. 83.

55. 'The Structure of a Semantic Theory', pp. 486, 488.

56. *Ibid.*, pp. 488-9.

57. *Ibid.*, p. 489.

58. *Ibid.*, p. 486.

59. There are exceptions. See, for example, Adrienne Lehrer, 'Indeterminacy in Semantic Description', *Glossa* 4 (1970), 87.

60. There is a vast literature on the subject. See W. V. Quine, 'Two Dogmas of Empiricism', in *From a Logical Point of View*, Harper & Row, New York, 1961; for a few responses, see Bruce Aune, 'On an Analytic-Synthetic Distinction', *American Philosophical Quarterly* 9 (1972); H. P. Grice and P. F. Strawson, 'In Defense of a Dogma', *Philosophical Review* 65 (1956); Benson Mates, 'Analytic Sentences', *Philosophical Review* 60 (1951); Hilary Putnam, 'The Analytic and the Synthetic', in H. Feigl and G. Maxwell (eds.), *Minnesota Studies in the Philosophy of Science III*, University of Minnesota Press, Minneapolis, 1966.

61. H. W. Fowler and F. G. Fowler (eds.), *The Concise Oxford Dictionary of Current English*, based on *The Oxford Dictionary*, 5th ed. (1964), p. vi.

62. *Ibid.* Emphasis supplied.

63. See J. Lyons' skeptical comment in his review of Katz and Postal's 'Integrated Theory of Linguistic Descriptions' in *Journal of Linguistics* 2 (1966), 124.

64. See Bierwisch's ambitious requirements in 'On Certain Problems of Semantic Representations', *Foundations of Language* 5 (1969), 181; also Charles J. Fillmore's in 'Types of Lexical Information', in D. Steinberg and L. Jakobovits (eds.), *Semantics: An Interdisciplinary Reader*, Cambridge University Press, 1971, p. 372; see R. M. W. Dixon's doubts in 'A Method of Semantic Description' in Steinberg and Jakobovits (eds.), p. 440.

65. 'Two Dogmas of Empiricism', p. 46.

66. Aune, 'On an Analytic-Synthetic Distinction', p. 242; Grice and Strawson, 'In Defense of a Dogma', p. 158; Putnam, 'The Analytic and the Synthetic', pp. 361-2, 366, 391-end.

67. J. R. Searle, 'What Is a Speech Act?', in Max Black (ed.), *Philosophy in America*, Allen & Unwin, London, 1965, pp. 221-2.

68. I overlook here, as I have implicitly throughout, completely 'dead' metaphors. They can of course be produced without awareness that they are metaphors. They present neither the problems of analysis nor the creative possibilities of more or less 'novel' metaphors. See footnote 4. Some think this ability to produce metaphors as metaphors is not developed in children until they are about twelve. See John Helmer, 'Metaphor', *Linguistics*, No. 88 (1972), 9-11.

69. *Aesthetics*, p. 138.

70. Larry W. Martin has noted that this position receives syntactic support from the 'oddity' of the following:

A: The moon staggered in the sky.
B: *No it didn't.
   *The moon staggered in the sky, didn't it?

Denials and tag-questions are perfectly normal with assertions.

71. This is the problem that Russell solved by the theory of definite descriptions. What should we do about sentences whose subjects refer to non-existent objects like golden mountains and the present King of France? Do some objects, i.e., physical objects, exist while others, i.e., nonexistent ones, 'subsist' in a nonspatial realm? See Bertrand Russell, *Introduction to Mathematical Philosophy*, Macmillan, New York & London, 1919, Ch. 16.

72. Edward H. Bendix, 'The Data of Semantic Description', in Steinberg and Jakobovits (eds.), p. 406.

73. *Convention*, Harvard University Press, Cambridge, 1969, pp. 178-9.

74. 'What Is a Speech Act?', p. 239. I find it hard to accept the 'he' of the sincerity condition as a reference to the hearer.

75. We make judgments of this kind all the time. See James D. McCawley, 'The Role of Semantics in a Grammar', in Emmon Bach and Robert Harms (eds.), *Universals in Linguistic Theory*, Holt, Rinehart & Winston, New York, 1968, pp. 129-30.

76. David Gordon and George Lakoff, 'Conversational Postulates', *Papers from the 7th Regional Meeting*, Chicago Linguistic Society (1971), p. 65.

77. *Ibid*.

78. Although at times we seem to part company on the issue of whether metaphors are ever true, Monroe Beardsley and Max Black frequently speak of metaphors in these terms and others like them.

79. See Douglas Berggren, 'The Use and Abuse of Metaphor', *The Review of Metaphysics* 16 (1962/63); Max Black, 'Models and Archetypes', in *Models and Metaphors*; my 'Truth and Consequences of Metaphors', pp. 43-5.

80. See Max Black, 'Meaning and Intention: An Examination of Grice's Views', *New Literary History* 4 (1972-73) for a criticism of intentionalist theories of meaning.

81. What this 'some way' is is an interesting and unsolved problem. I am convinced though that there is *not* 'unlimited distance' between literal and metaphorical senses as Weinreich maintains there can easily be between literal and idiomatic senses. See his 'Problems in the Analysis of Idioms', in J. Puhvel (ed.), *Substance and Structure of Language*, University of California Press, Berkeley and Los Angeles, 1969, p. 75.

82. Bertrand Russell, 'On Denoting', *Mind* 14 (1905), 482.

83. 'Truth and Meaning', p. 321.

Figurative Speech
and Figurative Acts

Ted Cohen

Metaphor, or what would be called figurative speech in general by those who use 'metaphor' for only certain kinds of tropes, is incompletely understood at least partly because it is characteristically studied as an isolated phenomenon. As a kind of Austinian, I am inclined to look to the speech acts in which they are animated whenever I have trouble understanding sentences. As an unorthodox Austinian, I am inclined to take Austin's suggestions into areas he explicitly put outside his proper interest. In this case the area is figurative language. The aim of this essay is to begin to relate metaphors, considered as kinds of sentences, to other elements that constitute whole speech acts.

I

My work on metaphor[1] has led me to two very general observations. First, metaphors are unpredictable, in this sense: if we were in possession of all the literal sentences of English (that is, if we had a "grammar" of English and that grammar were complete), we would still be unable to say which other sentences in English are acceptable.

Reprinted from *The Journal of Philosophy* 71, no. 19 (1975): 669-684 by permission of the author and *The Journal of Philosophy*.

There would be no consistent procedure for generating metaphors, and hence no mechanical way of acknowledging them as they came along. It is not merely that any procedure will miss some true (or apt) metaphors but that it will miss some metaphors—true or false—altogether. If one thinks that the grammatical strings of English are those generated by some set of rules, then I am saying that that set of rules, however augmented, will not also grind out all metaphors —unless, of course, it grinds out everything.

Metaphors are unpredictable in another sense which is, I suspect, related. Given a sentence that is known to be a metaphor, along with the literal meaning of the sentence and its components, I think there is no canonical way of arriving at its metaphorical meaning. The metaphorical meaning is somehow constructed out of literal meaning, but not according to any function. In this respect metaphor differs from other figures. Irony, for instance typically incorporates a function that leads from a given meaning to its reverse or opposite. It is not like this with metaphor. Whatever it is that a metaphor means, it is not in general true that this meaning can be calculated functionally from the literal meaning of the metaphorical sentence. It may be that this characteristic of metaphorical meaning—that though it arises from literal meaning, it sometimes seems to do so spontaneously, and not according to any recognized rule—underlies the fact that metaphors cannot be generated mechanically along with the literal sentences of the language.

If this observation about the unpredictability of metaphor is correct, then there is a special question concerning the relation of metaphors to what has come to be thought of as the grammar of a language. There are two options: to count metaphors as grammatical, and to take them as ungrammatical. The first option leads directly to the conclusion that the grammar is incomplete. I believe that most linguists take the second option and, in fact, think it an essential feature of metaphor that in its generation a metaphor transgresses the rules of the grammar. This option is a bit at odds with my assumption that it is characteristic of the capacity to use language that one have the ability to make and to understand metaphors. If a grammar is a formal reconstruction of a native speaker's competence, then why can't it handle metaphors? I suppose this needn't trouble a linguist. He might accept all my assumptions and simply stipulate that

that a grammar is to be a theory only of literal linguistic capacity, and indeed he might credit this stipulation with the ability to make a rigorous distinction between literal and nonliteral sentences (something I doubt native speakers can do).

The gist of my first observation is that metaphor is an intrinsic element in the use of language, whether or not it is accounted for in grammar, and that the production and comprehension of metaphors are not accomplished in terms of statable rules. Thus I think of metaphor as the language's intrinsic capacity to surpass its own (putative) limits. It is the abiding device for saying something truly new—but something curiously new, for it is made out of already existent meaning.[2]

My second point concerns the extent of the context to which one must look to find the mechanics of metaphor. What I have noted is that metaphor is not entirely a matter of sentential aberration. It has been commonly thought that a metaphorical sentence must exhibit some peculiarity when taken as a literal sentence. But this is not true. A metaphorical sentence can, when regarded literally, be altogether normal in its surface syntax and semantics, and it can even be true. (Possible examples are 'No man is an island', 'Jesus was a carpenter', 'Moscow is a cold city'; and others are easy to come by.) In such cases the forging of a new meaning from old elements, the execution of what Monroe Beardsley has nicely called "the metaphorical twist," is not accomplished within the sentence itself. Furthermore, because the bare sentence does not contain the elements that first clash and then jointly somehow generate the metaphorical meaning, the sentence itself cannot signal that it is a metaphor. To respond to this signal, to find the oddly juxtaposed elements, one must take note of the sentence along with its situation—that is, one must regard the "total speech act" in which the sentence is embedded. There one may find that, despite its pedestrian grammar, it is remarkable of the sentence to occur in these circumstances.

Many metaphors, including nearly all those which appear as examples in essays and books on the theory of metaphor, do exhibit oddities when considered as isolated sentences, and it once seemed to me that the others (the grammatically normal ones) were simply curious deviations from the normal form. Another possibility has

appeared: to try to see standard, textbook metaphors as themselves a special case of a more general phenomenon—namely, successful aberration within a speech act. This leads to wondering
whether there can be something like a metaphorical illocution.
That is the question of this experimental essay.

II

John Austin's "theory of speech acts" is familiar in outline, I think,
and that is all I need here.[3] Austin's sketch of a theory has been
widely criticized, but none of that discussion is relevant here except
for an emendation I have made.[4]

Total speech acts, as Austin conceives them, consist of three kinds
of acts—three ways of doing things with words. In an abbreviated
formula—which he qualifies extensively—he identifies them as

Acts of saying something: locutions (L)
Acts done in saying something: illocutions (I)
Acts done by saying something: perlocutions (P)

An example used by Austin for illustration is this:

(L) : He said to me 'Shoot her!'
(I) : He urged me to shoot her.
(P) : He persuaded me to shoot her.

This much, I hope, recalls Austin's framework, and it remains only
to introduce my refinement. A critical part of Austin's idea is the
way in which the relations of L, I, and P to one another are conceived.
In various senses of 'lead to', Austin thinks that they lead to one another, and it is with respect to this that I criticize him, once for being
careless and once for being wrong.

Austin thinks that illocutions are related to locutions by convention (whatever exactly that may mean) and that perlocutions are not
connected in this way. The commission of a locution leads to the occurrence of an illocution, but it does so automatically by means of
the rules of language. A perlocution, on the other hand, is supposed
to come about causally. Thus Austin's (mistaken) claim that from a
locution an illocution could be inferred, but not a perlocution. However successful this conception may be, Austin is careless in failing to

note what the perlocution is attached to. Every locution is accompanied by an illocution, according to Austin, and so it may seem adequate to regard a perlocution as an effect arising from the complex, L plus I. But it is not. If we think of the whole speech act like this:

$$(L \text{ plus } I) \rightarrow P$$

there will still be the question of whether I is instrumental in the production of P. I typically is an essential antecedent of P in the examples Austin gives, but it need not be. In speaking to me you may warn or threaten me, and thereby alert or intimidate me. Typically, these perlocutionary acts of alerting and intimidating occur because of the illocutionary acts of warning and threatening. Your locutionary acts lead to these perlocutions, but only because they first lead to illocutions. They might lead immediately to the perlocutions without the intermediate efficacy of the illocutions. For instance, the sounds and meanings of your words might alert me or intimidate me altogether independently of the illocutionary acts you were performing in uttering them. I have called such perlocutions *oblique*, and I call the standard, regular kind, those with illocutionary antecedents, *direct* perlocutions.

Austin's failure to note the difference between direct and oblique perlocutions, supplying instead only a characterization that applies indiscriminately to both kinds, may have been only an omission, but I think it prefigures his mistaken assessment of perlocutions. The mistake was to regard perlocutions uniformly as less integral parts of total speech acts, as essentially nonlinguistic results which are the causal by-products of the real internal speech-act machinery. There is a kind of perlocution that should not be thought of in this way. Failure to appreciate those direct perlocutions which are, as I call them, also *associated* perlocutions will in turn obscure the logic of illocutions.

Warning belongs with alerting, and threatening belongs with intimidating. When my warning alerts you, my illocution has led to its associated perlocution. It is not only that my utterance, say 'Watch out for Ronald Reagan', alerts you by way of the illocutionary act it leads to (making the alerting a direct perlocution), but also that the illocution leads to its, so to speak, proper result (making the alerting an associated perlocution). Not every direct perlocution is associated. I might threaten or warn you and succeed only in a-musing or boring you. You may well be amused or bored only because I have threatened or warned, and so these perlocutions are direct, but amusing and boring don't belong with these illocutions, and so they are not associated perlocutions. It seems likely that amusing and boring do not belong with any illocutions, and thus can never be associated perlocutions. There are perlocutions, however, which can be associated in some speech acts and not associated in others. For instance, when intimidation results from a threat, it is an associated perlocution; but you might intimidate me by predicting, or describing, or reminding, and then the perlocution, though still direct, will be unassociated.

I believe that the relation of an associated perlocution to its illocution is not merely causal. I have discussed this relation elsewhere (*ibid.*, part 4), and the only part of that discussion needed here is this rough claim: for an illocution to occur, it must appear possible that its associated perlocution occur. If both of us know that I am powerless to intimidate you, and also both know that we both know this, then I think I cannot threaten you, whatever locution I choose to make. I will develop this point shortly, and try to defend it a bit. Here I want to note that if there is a kind of logical relation between illocutions and perlocutions, then a total speech act can exhibit an internal anomaly that is something like the aberration of a metaphorical sentence whose semantics are awry. This suggests that if odd juxtapositions within a sentence can produce novel meaning, then perhaps odd juxtapositions within a speech act can produce novel performances. Austin may have seen this.

Austin's introduction of locutions, illocutions, and perlocutions follows his discussion of performatives and constatives. In fact the theory of speech acts absorbs and supplants the theory of performative utterances. The discussion of performatives was permanently blocked for Austin when he found it impossible to formulate a satisfactory criterion for distinguishing performatives from other utterances. The criteria Austin tried sometimes failed because they classified nonperformatives as performatives, but their main flaw is their failure to cover utterances that seem significantly like standard examples of performatives. (The move from sentences to their contexts, from utterances to the total speech acts in which they occur, was

Austin's response to his conviction that ultimately all utterances have both performatory and statemental aspects.) Why abandon the search for what Austin rather loosely called a "criterion" of grammar and vocabulary? His last attempt was this:

> An utterance is an explict performative utterance if and only if it possesses one of the characteristic verbs in the characteristic form.[5]
>
> An utterance is a performative utterance if and only if it either is an explicit performative utterance or is reducible to an explicit performative utterance.[6]

This criterion fails, Austin thought, because there are performatives that are not reducible to the canonical form. He was thinking of performatory acts that cannot be rendered explicit because, although there is a verb for the act, the verb does not work properly in the canonical form. Austin gives insulting as an example. Other examples, including hinting, alleging, and insinuating, have been given recently by Zeno Vendler. What these examples seem to show is that performative utterances outrun those utterances which either are or are reducible to explicit performative utterances. They may not, however, reflect a deep flaw in the criterion, for they might be tabulated separately as those performatory acts which cannot be executed by means of an explicit performative utterance. A radical discovery would be that this tabulation is impossible. This would be to discover that illocutionary acts are unpredictable in the way that metaphors are. I am ready to describe how this could be.

III

It will be helpful to use a perhaps oversimple schematic model which ignores any problems in Austin's exposition. I schematize a total speech act in this way:

U is an utterance in the sense of the thing uttered (not the act of uttering), a sentence, Austin thought. The utterance has a meaning M and a force F.[7] Austin sometimes called these "locutionary meaning" and "illocutionary force," though he was not especially detailed or clear about either notion. L, I, and P are, as before, the locution, the illocution, and the perlocution, which Austin also called locutionary, illocutionary, and perlocutionary acts. The dotted arrows indicate that U's meaning and force are realized, respectively, as L and I when U is activated within a normal speech situation. The other arrows indicate that I follows from L, and P in turn follows from I.

The relation of F to I is relatively clear, and trivial. The illocutionary force of an utterance is that utterance's capacity to be the vehicle for the execution of a particular illocutionary act when the circumstances of the uttering are altogether "normal." (Austin thought that F leads to I "by convention.") The relation of M to L is less clear. The best provisional sense I can make of it is this: what is said by the speaker of an utterance is determined in part by the circumstances in which the utterance is produced. The circumstances act upon the bare utterance, for instance to resolve its ambiguities and to settle the referents of its egocentric particulars, to give it the meaning it takes on in the total speech situation. Thus M is realized as L.

It can happen that an uttering transpire in circumstances that are altogether normal and conventionally appropriate and, furthermore, that the relations of M, F, L, I, and P to one another are signaled directly. The result is a total speech act of a kind which I call *transparent*. Those characteristics of a transparent speech act relevant to this discussion are these:

(1) U has one literal meaning.
(2) The meaning of what is said in L is the meaning of U.
(3) The force of U is indicated in U itself.
(4) I is the activation of U's force.
(5) There is at least one perlocution P directly associated with I, and the participants mutually believe it possible that P arise as an effect of I.

These conditions are meant to be simple and untroublesome. Points at which they become vexed need not trouble this discussion. The idea of (1), (2), (3), and (4) is that what is said and what is done by the utterer of U are exactly what are to be expected from U.

The (Gricean) distinctions between what the speaker means, what he means by his utterance, and what his utterance means need not bother us—if we agree to declare a certain kind of case not transparent. In certain kinds of cases—irony may be one—although it is obvious that the discourse is figurative, it is not clear that the sentence uttered has a figurative meaning. If you say of me, 'He's a swell philosopher', thereby communicating your opinion that I can't think my way out of a paper bag, I don't think your utterance means what you communicate. Your opinion is, perhaps, something you mean by saying U, but it is not what U means. If U thus continues to mean that I'm a swell philosopher, then condition (1) is satisfied. I want to count this case nontransparent, and so I declare that it violates condition (2). I interpret Austin's notion of what is said so that what is said is that I'm a crumby philosopher, and hence L is not a transparent realization of U. If you attach ironic meaning to U, then you can claim that U goes transparently to L, but call the whole speech act nontransparent because (1) is violated. I prefer my account, but either way we are rid of irony and, if there are any, similar figures.

Not every case of nontransparency is a case of figuration, in words or in acts. Consider 'a is flat', said of some painting. There are (at least) four things the speaker might be saying: (i) a is essentially two-dimensional, (ii) a contains no piled-up pigment, (iii) a is dull and boring, (iv) a presents no appearance of inward depth. U could mean any of these things, and there is no way to tell simply from examination of U. More will have to be known of the circumstances in which U is said, and it is likely to be especially useful to know what illocution is performed. If the speaker is informing his hearer, then it is unlikely that (i) is what U means—unless he is addressing a very special audience: for instance, very young children or people blind since birth, or, in general, people who don't know what paintings are. (i) might be meant by U for an entirely competent audience. This could happen during an argument over the concept of pictorial representation, with the speaker arguing against the idea that such representation, is mainly a matter of overt physical similarity. But then I think the illocution would not be simply informing. (ii) could be the meaning easily and naturally enough if the speaker were addressing beginning students of brushwork, or even in high-powered discussions between scholars. (i) and (ii) seem to me both literal meanings of U. (iii) may be a figurative meaning, and (iv) probably is.

When either what is meant or what is done cannot be told from U alone, then the speech act is not transparent. Typically, speech acts are not transparent, and the meaning and force of U can be made out only by looking to elements of the speech situation in addition to U. The procedures for uncovering meaning and force are usually straightforward and easily managed even though they look complex when reconstructed in detail. A critical part of the procedure often consists in trying to relate M and F (or possible L's and I's) to one another. For instance, you could infer that I do not mean (i) from the fact that I am attempting to inform you and the fact that because I must know that you are already aware that paintings are two-dimensional, I couldn't be undertaking to inform you of that. Or you might first establish that what I mean is (i) and from that infer that my illocutionary effort is not to inform.

Transparency fails when L or I cannot be identified directly (either because M or F cannot be read straight off from U, or because L and I don't follow immediately from M and F). When L and I are not signaled directly, they are revealed by the influences upon one another of the parts of the speech act—some way is found to allow them to mesh. When these influences are blocked, so that the standard ways of meshing are impossible, then either the whole thing is aborted and the speech act cannot come off, or the speech act does somehow come off despite the fact that it does so nonstandardly. I think of all these successful deviations collectively as figurative speech acts.

In all cases of figuration something prevents M, F, L, I, and P from fitting together. The most insular form this obstacle can take is an impediment within U itself. This kind of impediment is present in certain basic cases of metaphor. Some examples are 'Men are wolves', 'The chairman plowed through the committee', 'All the world's a stage', and 'Norman Bates was his own mother'. These sentences all have extraliteral meanings, and in each case one is led to the figured meaning by finding it impossible to construct a literal meaning. The effort to find a literal meaning is thwarted by the semantics of the sentence, or its syntax, or by both together. An early initial assumption in theories of metaphor has been that all metaphors embody this kind of grammatical perversity. The assumption is wrong, and examples immediately force it to become more general. The assumption may be made to cover an example like 'No man is an island', if one supposes that 'some men are islands' is not simply false but is semantically defective, and that this defect is present in its negation; but it cannot cover 'Rio is cold' when that sentence means that Rio is an uncomfortable, unfriendly city, etc., for 'Rio is cold' is grammatically sound. It is, however, false taken literally, and it might be thought to be, in a phrase of Monroe Beardsley's, "obviously false in its context." But it makes a substantial difference in the mechanism of the speech act whether U is ungrammatical or only obviously false. If U is ungrammatical (when taken literally), then the fact that what is said, L, is extraliteral is determined by that alone. If U is obviously false but grammatical, then the impetus to construct a non-literal L must come from elsewhere. In particular, it is likely to come from the fact that the illocutionary act performed is one governed in part by a constraint against uttering an obvious falsehood in the commission of the act. There is a tendency to suppose that this difference is not substantial because the distinction between semantic defection and obvious falsity is variable and even arbitrary.[8] But the distinction is reinforced by examples in which not falsity but truth is obvious. For instance, 'Anchorage is a cold city'. This sentence is grammatically unexceptionable, even under a view that counts *every* truth about w part of the meaning of 'w'. So how does the sentence acquire and convey the sense that Anchorage is bereft of human feeling? The search for this meaning is not triggered by the discovery that there is no standard literal meaning, nor by the awareness that with its standard meaning the sentence is false. There must be some other influence at work. It is likely to be the conjunction of awareness that the sentence is literally true and recognition of a prohibition in this case against attempting to convey that truth.

The suggestion of this paper is that I and U are related in ways like those which relate L and U: sometimes I can be read directly from U (the transparent cases); sometimes it can't, either because F cannot be found in U itself or because, although F is known, F does not lead directly to I. Among the last cases are those in which there is an illocutionary act, but I does not follow in any standard way and is a transfiguration of F. These I think of as figurative speech acts, the illocutionary analogues of metaphors. I will work up to examples by stages, beginning with some normal illocutions which illustrate the internal dynamics of the total speech act.

The utterance 'There are sharks in the water' could be a warning, but it needn't be. How does one tell? The force of this utterance cannot be found in U alone. Although the properties of U presumably do limit the possibilities, U remains illocutionarily ambiguous, and it is left to other elements of the speech situation to fix U's force. One way in which they do this is by eliminating possibilities, and there is one means of exclusion that is of special interest here. According to me, at least some illocutions have associated with them specific perlocutions, and shared belief in the possible accomplishment of the associated perlocutions is a necessary condition for completing the illocution. The perlocution associated with warning is alerting—more exactly, alerting to some threat or danger, or, in general, to some disagreeable happening. According to me, if this alerting is plainly out of the question, then the illocution cannot be warning. This is meant to explain a bit why there could be no point in warning me in certain circumstances, and if it is plain to both of us that there *could* be no point in doing it, the presumption is that you are not attempting to do it.

If the illocutionary act is warning, however this is determined, then there are actually two analyses of the relation of U to I. One could say that first U's force is determined to be warning, and then this F is actualized as I. I prefer to say that from among U's possible forces, one has been actualized. This account preserves a parallel with the relation of U to L. I want to deny that every utterance has something called its "force," preferring to regard the discovery of what is done as the discovery of which of U's "act potentials" is realized in the current situation. This is similar to my treatment of utterances of undetermined meaning. I identify what is mean by U (in the situation) as L. For other purposes it may be better to understand the relation between illocutionary forces and acts differently. My account avoids having to read I back into F, and that is the principal reason for preferring my account here. In some cases it seems to me that U has a particular force but that the illocutionary act done is not the normal realization of U's F.

Consider the sentences 'I promise that I was in Chicago yesterday' and 'I promise to live past 1992'. I claim that there are almost no sets of circumstances in which to utter either of these could be to promise. But under circumstances that disallow promising, the utterance could still be the vehicle of an illocutionary act. *I* will not be promising, but I wish to say that *U* (which is an explicit performative) has the illocutionary force of promising. On the way to *I*, *F* has been transformed. In noting how promising is blocked for these utterances we begin to uncover the means for figuration in speech acts.

Saying 'I promise that I was in Chicago yesterday' is not to promise, because the concept of promising requires that the thing promised be something in the future. In this case the fact that the thing is not a future thing is revealed by the meaning of the sentence. In this respect the example parallels textbook-type metaphors. When there is a grammatical breakdown within the sentence, *U* itself will signal that, if it is to have any meaning at all, it will not be a meaning constructed out of *U*'s components in the usual ways. It is different with 'I promise to live past 1992', for here the impossibility of promising is not indicated in *U* alone. To be promisable a thing must be within the power of the promiser (in some sense of 'within the power of' in which it is not in one's power to ensure 17 more years of life), but the fact that what is apparently being promised is thus unpromisable is not evident from *U* alone. Recognition of the fact depends upon knowing something (a very little) about the conditions of life. In this way the example is like cases of metaphor in which the search for a nonliteral meaning is triggered not by the fact that *U* is intrinsically unsemantic but by the fact that with its literal meaning *U* is obviously false. Elements of the speech situation besides *U* block promising in this case, and if the speaker succeeds in performing an *I* at all, it will be an *I* figured by those other elements. These mechanisms are similar to those in 'I promise to *v*', where my v-ing is something you wish me not to do; but in another respect 'I promise to *v*' is like 'I promise that I was in Chicago yesterday'.

'I promise to *v*', like 'I promise to live past 1992', does not give rise to promising because the act in question is one which in fact cannot be promised. The only difference is that an outsider might well not know that you don't want my *v*-ing, but virtually everyone knows that I can't control my longevity. On this count both differ from 'I promise that I was in Chicago yesterday', where the unsuitability of the thing in question is evident in the sentence. But 'I promise to v' is like 'I promise that I was in Chicago yesterday' in what happens to the illocutionary force that is blocked and cannot be realized directly as the illocutionary act of promising.

When an illocutionary act is performed in saying 'I promise to v' it is likely to be an act of threatening, or some similar act. To say 'I promise that I was in Chicago yesterday' is to assert something, or to assure, or to guarantee, or some such act. In both cases F has been realized as something other than its normal I. One may think that the I effected is one which could have been executed by using a U whose F could have led directly to I. I am disinclined to believe this, for I think that the acts done in saying 'I promise to v' and 'I promise that I was in Chicago yesterday' are not exactly the same as the acts that could have been done in saying 'I threaten to v' and 'I assure you that I was in Chicago yesterday'. But this is not a sore point. In fact disagreement over it is altogether welcome, for it seems to me to reflect a standardly disputed point in the theory of metaphor. These cases are illocutionary analogues of metaphors that are either frozen or are freezing, or, frozen or not, are easily paraphrased without remainder. How do you regard 'He's low today' said of someone despondent and dejected? As a trivial and obvious metaphor? As something clearly replaceable by 'He's unhappy and pessimistic today'? Perhaps you don't find it metaphorical at all, thinking the phrase so completely frozen that its meaning as a description of mood is now to be found among the literal senses of 'low'. There are equivalent options in choosing how to regard the illocutionary upshot of these blocked promises—including the last option: there are speakers in both England and America who regard 'I promise that p is true' as a standard sentence in the utterance of which one promises. These speakers have a conception of promising that is either different from or an amplification of mine, and I regard "promising" to have been in Chicago yesterday, "promising" to v, and "promising" that p is true, all as figurative acts. I also believe them to be irreplaceable by equivalent acts in which the utterance would signal the act directly. But I give credit to the other opinion, just as I appreciate the opinion that 'He's low today' is either completely frozen or at least synonymous with something like 'He's melancholy today' although I myself find 'He's low today' a (minimally) vital metaphor.

It is different, I think, with 'I promise to live past 1992'. If an illocutionary act is performed in saying this, then I think it is an act performable in no other (linguistic) way. Perhaps you would say this to a friend or a child or a close relative or a lover: to someone who very badly wanted or needed you for a long time into the future. If you said this, what would you be doing? Acknowledging his need for you? Committing yourself to him? Undertaking to do all that you can to gratify him? None of these describes the act without alteration or remainder.

Other examples are 'I promise to love you all the rest of our lives' and 'I beg you to get well' (said to someone who is in no way interfering with his own recuperation). Saying these will not be to promise or to beg.[9] All these cases seem to me, like the most vital and enigmatic metaphors, to be linguistic entities without equivalents. There are things to be said and things to be done which are essentially novel, but the novelties result from normal elements. The semantic resources of the language yield novel meaning when they are made to collide, either with one another or with other parts of the speech situation. The utterance forces at our disposal yield novel acts when they are somehow askew. I have given some examples in which the force collides with meaning, but I have wished to concentrate more on collision between force and perlocutionary possibility. It is because the perlocutionary effects associated with begging are plainly out of the question that saying 'I beg you to get well' is not to beg. It is to do something—but what? I doubt that there is any easy, direct way to describe the act (beyond describing the circumstances and reporting that 'I beg you to get well' was said), and I am fairly certain that there is no way to do that act besides saying 'I beg you to get well'.

Zeno Vendler has recently noticed a group of verbs with these characteristics: for various reasons they seem to be what Vendler calls performatives, and they are used to describe illocutionary acts; but when put into explicit performative form they result in utterances that cannot be used to perform the relevant acts.[10] Thus, says Vendler, in saying 'I allege [or insinuate, or hint, or incite]' I cannot be alleging (or insinuating, or hinting, or inciting). Such an attempt would be illocutionary suicide. If Vendler's examples succed, then they are cases in which the utterance's F cannot go to the obvious I. My examples have been of cases in which F cannot go to I *in the particular situation at hand* although an explicit performative of force F —perhaps the same utterance as that which misses I in this case—can go to I in other circumstances. In both kinds of case, the failure of F to be realized as the obvious I is not the last word. F may still be realized as some other, unobvious, I. I shall not construct examples here (I invite you to try), but I find it conceivable that illocutionary acts be done in saying 'I allege . . .', 'I hint . . .', and the rest, though perhaps not acts of alleging, hinting, etc. The attempt to allege or hint may be necessarily suicidal, but it is not necessary that F be simply aborted. If an I comes forth, F has not died, but it has been transfigured.

This is one reason why our illocutionary resources cannot be tabulated. Our semantic resources outrun grammatical tabulation because, however the meaning is set for some term '*b*', there will remain sentences of the form '*a* is *b*' which are thereby ruled out on grammatical grounds but which are successful figures. These sentences are unpredictable. Similarly, however illocutionary acts are catalogued, there will be an utterance whose force signals one of those acts but which when placed in a speech situation that blocks I's associated perlocution, will have its force realized as some other, uncatalogued I. These acts are unpredictable. It takes ingenuity to make metaphors, and to understand them. It takes a related but different kind of ingenuity to conceive and execute figurative illocutions, and to take up on them. These special illocutions are at least as significant in our lives as metaphors, for they are forms of action and as such they can be direct relevations of character.

Grammar has to come to terms with figurative language. If, as I think, grammar cannot long confine itself to sentences but must soon look into total speech acts in total speech situations (as Austin designated what he called "the *only actual* phenomenon"), then it must soon come to terms with figuration of illocutionary force. That is not bad at all, for it seems to me that figurative speech and figurative illocutions are two forms of what is, generically, successful aberration within total speech acts, and so I think they are likely to be understood together or not at all.

NOTES

1. Some of this is in "Notes on Metaphor," forthcoming in *The Journal of Aesthetics and Art Criticism*, XXXIV (1976).

2. Seen in this way a metaphor may be the best available example of what Kant called products of *genius*. Genius, according to Kant, is the capacity to produce things which are "original," and hence things which cannot be made sense of by means of any rules of explication, but which nevertheless do make sense. This characterization is developed by Kant in sections 46-50 of the *Critique of Judgment*.

3. Austin presented this material in his 1955 William James Lectures at Harvard, published posthumously as *How to Do Things with Words*, edited by J. O. Urmson (Cambridge, Mass.: Harvard, 1962). The text has recently been re-edited by J. O. Urmson and Marina Sbisa and published as a second edition, 1975.

4. This emendation, the introduction of the notions of direct and associated perlocutions, is given in my "Illocutions and Perlocutions," *Foundations of Language*, IX, 4 (March 1973): 492-503.

5. It will not be necessary to go into Austin's characterizations of these verbs and this form. Put briefly, and uncritically, they are this: The form is first-person, singular, present, indicative, active. Performative verbs display an asymmetry between this form and other forms, which amounts to the fact that to utter sentences with the verb in the characteristic form is to do the act of the verb, but to utter sentences with the verb in other forms is not (typically) to do that act.

6. I reconstruct this two-part criterion from Austin's discussion in lectures V-VII of *How to Do Things with Words, op. cit.*

7. There has been considerable discussion of whether Austin regarded meaning and force as fundamentally different kinds of characteristics, and, if he did, whether he was right to do so. In this paper I have no objection to regarding force as an aspect of meaning so long as it can be distinguished from other aspects. For a skillful, formal treatment of force as a part of meaning, see Jerrold Sadock's *Toward a Linguistic Theory of Speech Acts* (New York: Academic Press, 1974), especially p. 19. The whole book is a very useful effort to bring formal grammar to bear on speech acts. Sadock's work is the most recent and the most helpful I know in a development ironically anticipated by Austin: recently his doctrine of speech acts seems to have lost currency among philosophers just as it has increasingly been found fruitful by linguistics.

8. I am sympathetic to the idea behind this tendency. It is a simple idea. A definition of some word 'w' begins from a consideration of all sentences of the form 'w is p' which are true. From among those predicates 'p' which make 'w is p' true, some group must be declared to be part or all of the meaning of 'w' whereas the remainder are left to be simply empirically true of w. There seems to be no clear, noncircular way of sorting out these predicates, unless it is done arbitrarily by stipulation. In consequence there seems to be no non-arbitrary effective way of deciding whether 'w is not p' is semantically inconsistent or only false.

9. Should you disagree about whether love can be promised, it may be love rather than

promising that you understand differently. What I refer to by 'love' cannot be promised because one is never in a position to guarantee delivery.

10. Vendler has discussed these verbs in the first appendix of *Res Cogitans* (Ithaca: Cornell, 1972), and in "Illocutionary Suicide" (a copy of the typescript was given to me in 1972, and I have been unable to learn of the essay's subsequent publication).

I disagree with some of his examples. For instance, I think it is possible to threaten in saying 'I threaten . . .', to scold in saying 'I scold . . .', and to boast in saying 'I boast . . .'; but most of Vendler's examples seem successful to me. For these cases he gives various subtle and clever analyses of the illocutionary breakdown. I prefer to assimilate all these cases to my general analysis, regarding them as various ways in which illocutionary force is blocked from direct actualization as an illocution by the obvious impossibility of effecting the associated perlocution. I suspect Vendler would not like this. This disagreement, however, is irrelevant to the question of figuration, for Vendler has had the prescience to claim only that 'I allege . . .' and the rest cannot be used to allege and the rest, and not to deny that they are useless for any illocution whatever.

What Metaphors Mean

Donald Davidson

Metaphor is the dreamwork of language and, like all dreamwork, its interpretation reflects as much on the interpreter as on the originator. The interpretation of dreams requires collaboration between a dreamer and a waker, even if they be the same person; and the act of interpretation is itself a work of the imagination. So too understanding a metaphor is as much a creative endeavor as making a metaphor, and as little guided by rules.

These remarks do not, except in matters of degree, distinguish metaphor from more routine linguistic transactions: all communication by speech assumes the interplay of inventive construction and inventive construal. What metaphor adds to the ordinary is an achievement that uses no semantic resources beyond the resources on which the ordinary depends. There are no instructions for devising metaphors; there is no manual for determining what a metaphor "means" or "says"; there is no test for metaphor that does not call for taste.[1] A metaphor implies a kind and degree of artistic success; there are no unsuccessful metaphors, just as there are no unfunny jokes. There are tasteless metaphors, but these are turns that nevertheless have brought something off, even if it were not worth bringing off or could have been brought off better.

Reprinted from *Critical Inquiry* 5, no. 1 (1978): 31-47 by permission of the author.

This paper is concerned with what metaphors mean, and its thesis is that metaphors mean what the words, in their most literal interpretation, mean, and nothing more. Since this thesis flies in the face of contemporary views with which I am familiar, much of what I have to say is critical. But I think the picture of metaphor that emerges when error and confusion are cleared away makes metaphor a more, not a less, interesting phenomenon.

The central mistake against which I shall be inveighing is the idea that a metaphor has, in addition to its literal sense or meaning, another sense or meaning. This idea is common to many who have written about metaphor: it is found in the works of literary critics like Richards, Empson, and Winters; philosophers from Aristotle to Max Black; psychologists from Freud and earlier to Skinner and later; and linguists from Plato to Uriel Weinreich and George Lakoff. The idea takes many forms, from the relatively simple in Aristotle to the relatively complex in Black. The idea appears in writings which maintain that a literal paraphrase of a metaphor can be produced, but it is also shared by those who hold that typically no literal paraphrase can be found. Some stress the special insight metaphor can inspire and make much of the fact that ordinary language, in its usual functioning, yields no such insight. Yet this view too sees metaphor as a form of communication alongside ordinary communication; it conveys truths or falsehoods about the world much as plainer language does, though the message may be considered more exotic, profound, or cunningly garbed.

The concept of metaphor as primarily a vehicle for conveying ideas, even if unusual ones, seems to me as wrong as the parent idea that a metaphor has a special meaning. I agree with the view that metaphors cannot be paraphrased, but I think this is not because metaphors say something too novel for literal expression but because there is nothing there to paraphrase. Paraphrase, whether possible or not, is appropriate to what is *said*: we try, in paraphrase, to say it another way. But if I am right, a metaphor doesn't say anything beyond its literal meaning (nor does its maker say anything, in using the metaphor, beyond the literal). This is not, of course, to deny that a metaphor has a point, nor that that point can be brought out by using further words.

In the past those who have denied that metaphor has a cognitive content in addition to the literal have often been out to show that metaphor is confusing, merely emotive, unsuited to serious, scientific, or philosophic discourse. My views should not be associated with this tradition. Metaphor is a legitimate device not only in literature but in science, philosophy, and the law; it is effective in praise and abuse, prayer and promotion, description and prescription. For the most part I don't disagree with Max Black, Paul Henle, Nelson Goodman, Monroe Beardsley, and the rest in their accounts of what metaphor accomplishes, except that I think it accomplishes more and that what is additional is different in kind.

My disagreement is with the explanation of how metaphor works its wonders. To anticipate: I depend on the distinction between what words mean and what they are used to do. I think metaphor belongs exclusively to the domain of use. It is something brought off by the imaginative employment of words and sentences and depends entirely on the ordinary meanings of those words and hence on the ordinary meanings of the sentences they comprise.

It is no help in explaining how words work in metaphor to posit metaphorical or figurative meanings, or special kinds of poetic or metaphorical truth. These ideas don't explain metaphor, metaphor explains them. Once we understand a metaphor we can call what we grasp the "metaphorical truth" and (up to a point) say what the "metaphorical meaning" is. But simply to lodge this meaning in the metaphor is like explaining why a pill puts you to sleep by saying it has a dormative power. Literal meaning and literal truth conditions can be assigned to words and sentences apart from particular contexts of use. This is why adverting to them has genuine explanatory power.

I shall try to establish my negative views about what metaphors mean and introduce my limited positive claims by examining some false theories of the nature of metaphor.

A metaphor makes us attend to some likeness, often a novel or surprising likeness, between two or more things. This trite and true observation leads, or seems to lead, to a conclusion concerning the meaning of metaphors. Consider ordinary likeness or similarity: two roses are similar because they share the property of being a rose; two infants are similar by virtue of their infanthood. Or, more simply, roses are similar because each is a rose, infants, because each is an infant.

Suppose someone says "Tolstoy was once an infant." How is the infant Tolstoy like other infants? The answer comes pat: by virtue of exhibiting the property of infanthood, that is, leaving out some of the wind, by virtue of being an infant. If we tire of the phrase "by virtue of," we can, it seems, be plainer still by saying the infant Tolstoy shares with other infants the fact that the predicate "is an infant" applies to him; given the word "infant," we have no trouble saying exactly how the infant Tolstoy resembles other infants. We could do it without the word "infant"; all we need is other words that mean the same. The end result is the same. Ordinary similarity depends on groupings established by the ordinary meanings of words. Such similarity is natural and unsurprising to the extent that familiar ways of grouping objects are tied to usual meanings of usual words.

A famous critic said that Tolstoy was "a great moralizing infant." The Tolstoy referred to here is obviously not the infant Tolstoy but Tolstoy the adult writer; this is metaphor. Now in what sense is Tolstoy the writer similar to an infant? What we are to do, perhaps, is think of the class of objects which includes all ordinary infants and, in addition, the adult Tolstoy and then ask ourselves what special, surprising property the members of this class have in common. The appealing thought is that given patience we could come as close as need be to specifying the appropriate property. In any case, we could do the job perfectly if we found words that meant exactly what the metaphorical "infant" means. The important point, from my perspective, is not whether we can find the perfect other words but the assumption that there is something to be attempted, a metaphorical meaning to be matched. So far I have been doing no more than crudely sketching how the concept of meaning may have crept into the analysis of metaphor, and the answer I have suggested is that since what we think of as garden variety similarity goes with what we think of as garden variety meanings, it is natural to posit unusual or metaphorical meanings to help explain the similarities metaphor promotes.

The idea, then, is that in metaphor certain words take on new, or what are often called "extended," meanings. When we read, for example, that "the Spirit of God moved upon the face of the waters," we are to regard the word "face" as having an extended meaning (I disregard further metaphor in the passage). The extension applies, as it happens, to what philosophers call the extension of the word, that is, the class of entities to which it refers. Here the word "face" applies to ordinary faces, and to waters in addition.

This account cannot, at any rate, be complete, for if in these contexts the words "face" and "infant" apply correctly to waters and to the adult Tolstoy, then waters really do have faces and Tolstoy literally was an infant, and all sense of metaphor evaporates. If we are to think of words in metaphors as directly going about their business of applying to what they properly do apply to, there is no difference between metaphor and the introduction of a new term into our vocabulary: to make a metaphor is to murder it.

What has been left out is any appeal to the original meaning of the word. Whether or not metaphor depends on new or extended meanings, it certainly depends in some way on the original meanings; an adequate account of metaphor must allow that the primary or original meanings of words remain active in their metaphorical setting.

Perhaps, then, we can explain metaphor as a kind of ambiguity: in the context of a metaphor, certain words have either a new or an original meaning, and the force of the metaphor depends on our uncertainty as we waver between the two meanings. Thus when Melville writes that "Christ was a chronometer," the effect of metaphor is produced by our taking "chronometer" first in its ordinary sense and then in some extraordinary or metaphorical sense.

It is hard to see how this theory can be correct. For the ambiguity in the word, if there is any, is due to the fact that in ordinary contexts it means one thing and in the metaphorical context it means something else; but in the metaphorical context we do not necessarily hesitate over its meaning. When we do hesitate, it is usually to decide which of a number of metaphorical interpretations we shall accept; we are seldom in doubt that what we have is a metaphor. At any rate, the effectiveness of the metaphor easily outlasts the end of uncertainty over the interpretation of the metaphorical passage. Metaphor cannot, therefore, owe its effect to ambiguity of this sort.[2]

Another brand of ambiguity may appear to offer a better suggestion. Sometimes a word will, in a single context, bear two meanings where we are meant to remember and to use both. Or, if we think of wordhood as implying sameness of meaning, then we may describe the situation as one in which what appears as a single word is in fact two. When Shakespeare's Cressida is welcomed bawdily into the Grecian camp, Nestor says, "Our general doth salute you with a kiss." Here we are to take "general" two ways: once as applying to Agamemnon, who is the general; and once, since she is kissing everyone, as applying to no one in particular, but everyone in general. We really have a conjunction of two sentences: our general, Agamemnon, salutes you with a kiss; and everyone in general is saluting you with a kiss.

This is a legitimate device, a pun, but it is not the same device as metaphor. For in metaphor there is no essential need of reiteration; whatever meanings we assign the words, they keep through every correct reading of the passage.

A plausible modification of the last suggestion would be to consider the key word (or words) in a metaphor as having two different kinds of meaning at once, a literal and a figurative meaning. Imagine the literal meaning as latent, something that we are aware of, that can work on us without working in the context, while the figurative meaning carries the direct load. And finally, there must be a rule which connects the two meanings, for otherwise the explanation lapses into a form of the ambiguity theory. The rule, at least for many typical cases of metaphor, says that in its metaphorical role the word applies to everything that it applies to in its literal role, and then some.[3]

This theory may seem complex, but it is strikingly similar to what Frege proposed to account for the behavior of referring terms in modal sentences and sentences about propositional attitudes like belief and desire. According to Frege, each referring term has two (or more) meanings, one which fixes its reference in ordinary contexts and another which fixes its reference in the special contexts created by modal operators or psychological verbs. The rule connecting the two meanings may be put like this: the meaning of the word in the special contexts makes the reference in those contexts to be identical with the meaning in ordinary contexts.

Here is the whole picture, putting Frege together with a Fregean view of metaphor: we are to think of a word as having, in addition to its mundane field of application or reference, two special or supermundane fields of application, one for metaphor and the other for modal contexts and the like. In both cases the original meaning remains to do its work by virtue of a rule which relates the various meanings.

Having stressed the possible analogy between metaphorical meaning and the Fregean meanings for oblique contexts, I turn to an imposing difficulty in maintaining the analogy. You are entertaining a visitor from Saturn by trying to teach him how to use the word "floor." You go through the familiar dodges, leading him from floor to floor, pointing and stamping and repeating the word. You prompt him to make experiments, tapping objects tentatively with his tentacle while rewarding his right and wrong tries. You want him to come out knowing not only that these particular objects or surfaces are floors but also how to tell a floor when one is in sight or touch. The skit you are putting on doesn't *tell* him what he needs to know, but with luck it helps him to learn it.

Should we call this process learning something about the world or learning something about language? An odd question, since what is learned is that a bit of language refers to a bit of the world. Still, it is easy to distinguish between the business of learning the meaning of a word and using the word once the meaning is learned. Comparing these two activities, it is natural to say that the first concerns learning something about language, while the second is typically learning something about the world. If your Saturnian has learned how to use the word "floor," you may try telling him something new, that *here* is a floor. If he has mastered the word trick, you have told him something about the world.

Your friend from Saturn now transports you through space to his home sphere, and looking back remotely at earth you say to him, nodding at the earth, "floor." Perhaps he will think this is still part of the lesson and assume that the word "floor" applies properly to the earth, at least as seen from Saturn. But what if you thought he already knew the meaning of "floor," and you were remembering how Dante, from a similar place in the heavens, saw the inhabited earth as "the small round floor that makes us passionate"? Your purpose was metaphor, not drill in the use of language. What difference would it make to your friend which way he took it? With the theory of metaphor under consideration, very little difference, for according to that theory a word has a new meaning in a metaphorical context; the occasion of the metaphor would, therefore, be the occasion for learning the new meaning. We should agree that in some ways it makes relatively little difference whether, in a given context, we think a word is being used metaphorically or in a previously unknown, but literal way. Empson, in *Some Versions of Pastoral*, quotes these lines from Donne: "As our blood labours to beget / Spirits, as like souls as it can, . . . / So must pure lover's soules descend. . . ." The modern reader is almost certain, Empson points out, to take the word "spirits" in this passage metaphorically, as applying only by extension to something spiritual. But for Donne there was no metaphor. He writes in his *Sermons*, "The spirits . . . are the thin and active part of the blood, and are a kind of middle nature, between soul and body." Learning this does not matter much; Empson is right when he says, "It is curious how the change in the word [that is, in what we think it means] leaves the poetry unaffected."[4]

The change may be, in some cases at least, hard to appreciate, but unless there is a change, most of what is thought to be interesting about metaphor is lost. I have been making the point by contrasting learning a new use for an old word with using a word already understood; in one case, I said, our attention is directed to language, in the other, to what language is about. Metaphor, I suggested, belongs in the second category. This can also be seen by considering dead metaphors. Once upon a time, I suppose, rivers and bottles did not, as they do now, literally have mouths. Thinking of present usage, it doesn't matter whether we take the word "mouth" to be ambiguous because it applies to entrances to rivers and openings of bottles as well as to animal apertures, or we think there is a single wide field of application that embraces both. What does matter is that when "mouth" applied only metaphorically to bottles, the application made the hearer *notice* a likeness between animal and bottle openings. (Consider Homer's reference to wounds as mouths.) Once one has the present use of the word, with literal application to bottles, there is nothing left to notice. There is no similarity to seek because it consists simply in being referred to by the same word.

Novelty is not the issue. In its context a word once taken for a metaphor remains a metaphor on the hundredth hearing, while a word may easily be appreciated in a new literal role on a first encounter. What we call the element of novelty or surprise in a metaphor is a built-in aesthetic feature we can experience again and again, like the surprise in Haydn's Symphony no. 94, or a familiar deceptive cadence.

If metaphor involved a second meaning, as ambiguity does, we might expect to be able to specify the special meaning of a word in a metaphorical setting by waiting until the metaphor dies. The figurative meaning of the living metaphor should be immortalized in the literal meaning of the dead. But although some philosophers have suggested this idea, it seems plainly wrong. "He was burned up" is genuinely ambiguous (since it may be true in one sense and false in another), but although the slangish idiom is no doubt the corpse of a metaphor, "He was burned up" now suggests no more than that he was very angry. When the metaphor was active, we would have pictured fire in the eyes or smoke coming out of the ears.

We can learn much about what metaphors mean by comparing them with similes, for a simile tells us, in part, what a metaphor merely nudges us into noting. Suppose Goneril had said, thinking of Lear, "Old fools are like babes again"; then she would have used the words to assert a similarity between old fools and babes. What she did say, of course, was "Old fools are babes again," thus using the words to intimate what the simile declared. Thinking along these lines may inspire another theory of the figurative or special meaning of metaphors: the figurative meaning of a metaphor is the literal meaning of the corresponding simile. Thus "Christ was a chronometer" in its figurative sense is synonymous with "Christ was like a chronometer," and the metaphorical meaning once locked up in "He was burned up" is released in "He was like someone who was burned up" (or perhaps "He was like burned up").

There is, to be sure, the difficulty of identifying the simile that corresponds to a given metaphor. Virginia Woolf said that a highbrow is "a man or woman of thoroughbred intelligence who rides his mind at a gallop across country in pursuit of an idea." What simile corresponds? Something like this, perhaps: "A highbrow is a man or woman whose intelligence is like a thoroughbred horse and who persists in thinking about an idea like a rider galloping across country in pursuit of . . . well, something."

The view that the special meaning of a metaphor is identical with the literal meaning of a corresponding simile (however "corresponding" is spelled out) should not be confused with the common theory that a metaphor is an elliptical simile.[5] This theory makes no distinction in meaning between a metaphor and some related simile and does not provide any ground for speaking of figurative, metaphorical, or special meanings. It is a theory that wins hands down so far as simplicity is concerned, but it also seems too simple to work. For if we make the literal meaning of the metaphor to be the literal meaning of a matching simile, we deny access to what we originally took to be the literal meaning of the metaphor, and we agreed almost from the start that *this* meaning was essential to the working of the metaphor, whatever else might have to be brought in in the way of a nonliteral meaning.

Both the elliptical simile theory of metaphor and its more sophisticated variant, which equates the figurative meaning of the metaphor with the literal meaning of a simile, share a fatal defect. They make the hidden meaning of the metaphor all too obvious and accessible. In each case the hidden meaning is to be found simply by looking to the literal meaning of what is usually a painfully trivial simile. This is like that—Tolstoy like an infant, the earth like a floor. It is trivial because everything is like everything, and in endless ways. Metaphors are often very difficult to interpret and, so it is said, impossible to paraphrase. But with this theory, interpretation and paraphrase typically are ready to the hand of the most callow.

These simile theories have been found acceptable, I think, only because they have been confused with a quite different theory. Consider this remark by Max Black:

> When Schopenhauer called a geometrical proof a mousetrap, he was, according to such a view, saying (though not explicitly): "A geometrical proof is *like* a mousetrap, since both offer a delusive reward, entice their victims by degrees, lead to disagreeable surprise, etc." This is a view of metaphor as a condensed or elliptical *simile*.[6]

Here I discern two confusions. First, if metaphors are elliptical similes, they say *explicitly* what similes say, for ellipsis is a form of abbreviation, not of paraphrase or indirection. But, and this is the more important matter, Black's statement of what the metaphor says goes far beyond anything given by the corresponding simile. The simile simply says a geometrical proof is like a mousetrap. It no more *tells* us what similarities we are to notice than the metaphor does. Black mentions three similarities, and of course we could go on adding to the list forever. But is this list, when revised and supplemented in the right way, supposed to give the *literal* meaning of the simile? Surely not, since the simile declared no more than the similarity. If the list is supposed to provide the figurative meaning of the simile, then we learn nothing about metaphor from the comparison with simile—only that both have the same figurative meaning. Nelson Goodman does indeed claim that "the difference between simile and metaphor is negligible," and he continues, "Whether the locution be 'is like' or 'is,' the figure *likens* picture to person by picking out a certain common feature. . . ."[7] Goodman is considering the difference between saying a picture is sad and saying it is like a sad person. It is clearly true that both sayings liken picture to person, but it seems to me a mistake to claim that either way of talking "picks out" a common feature. The simile says there is a likeness and leaves it to us to pick out some common feature or features; the metaphor does not explicitly assert a likeness, but if we accept it as a metaphor, we are again led to seek common features (not necessarily the same features the associated simile suggests; but that is another matter).

Just because a simile wears a declaration of similitude on its sleeve, it is, I think, far less plausible than in the case of metaphor to maintain that there is a hidden second meaning. In the case of simile, we note what it literally says, that two things resemble one another; we then regard the objects and consider what similarity would, in the context, be to the point. Having decided, we might then say the author of the simile intended us—that is, meant us—to notice that similarity. But having appreciated the difference between what the words meant and what the author accomplished by using those words, we should feel little temptation to explain what has happened by endowing the words themselves with a second, or figurative, meaning. The point of the concept of linguistic meaning is to explain what can be done with words. But the supposed figurative meaning of a simile explains nothing; it is not a feature of the word that the word has prior to and independent of the context of use, and it rests upon no linguistic customs except those that govern ordinary meaning.

What words do do with their literal meaning in simile must be possible for them to do in metaphor. A metaphor directs attention to the same sorts of similarity, if not the same similarities, as the corresponding simile. But then the unexpected or subtle parallels and analogies it is the business of metaphor to promote need not depend, for their promotion, on more than the literal meanings of words.

Metaphor and simile are merely two among endless devices that serve to alert us to aspects of the world by inviting us to make comparisons. I quote a few stanzas of T. S. Eliot's "The Hippopotamus":

> The broad-backed hippopotamus
> Rests on his belly in the mud;
> Although he seems so firm to us
> He is merely flesh and blood.
>
> Flesh and blood is weak and frail,
> Susceptible to nervous shock;
> While the True Church can never fail
> For it is based upon a rock.
>
> The hippo's feeble steps may err
> In compassing material ends,
> While the True Church need never stir
> To gather in its dividends.
>
> The 'potamus can never reach
> The mango on the mango-tree;
> But fruits of pomegranate and peach
> Refresh the Church from over sea.

Here we are neither told that the Church resembles a hippopotamus (as in simile) nor bullied into making this comparison (as in metaphor), but there can be no doubt the words are being used to direct our attention to similarities between the two. Nor should there be much inclination, in this case, to posit figurative meanings, for in what words or sentences would we lodge them? The hippopotamus really does rest on his belly in the mud; the True Church, the poem says literally, never can fail. The poem does, of course, intimate much that goes beyond the literal meanings of the words. But intimation is not meaning.

The argument so far has led to the conclusion that as much of metaphor as can be explained in terms of meaning may, and indeed must, be explained by appeal to the literal meanings of words. A consequence is that the sentences in which metaphors occur are true or false in a normal, literal way, for if the words in them don't have special meanings, sentences don't have special truth. This is not to deny that there is such a thing as metaphorical truth, only to deny it of sentences. Metaphor does lead us to notice what might not otherwise be noticed, and there is no reason, I suppose, not to say these visions, thoughts, and feelings inspired by the metaphor, are true or false.

If a sentence used metaphorically is true or false in the ordinary sense, then it is clear that it is usually false. The most obvious semantic difference between simile and metaphor is that all similes are true and most metaphors are false. The earth is like a floor, the Assyrian did come down like a wolf on the fold, because everything is like everything. But turn these sentences into metaphors, and you turn them false; the earth is like a floor, but it is not a floor; Tolstoy, grown up, was like an infant, be he wasn't one. We use a simile ordinarily only when we know the corresponding metaphor to be false. We say Mr. S. is like a pig because we know he isn't one. If we had used a metaphor and said he was a pig, this would not be because we changed our mind about the facts but because we chose to get the idea across a different way.

What matters is not actual falsehood but that the sentence be taken to be false. Notice what happens when a sentence we use as a metaphor, believing it false, comes to be thought true because of a change in what is believed about the world. When it was reported that Hemingway's plane had been sighted, wrecked, in Africa, the New York *Mirror* ran a headline saying, "Hemingway Lost in Africa," the word "lost" being used to suggest he was dead. When it turned out he was alive, the *Mirror* left the headline to be taken literally. Or consider this case: a woman sees herself in a beautiful dress and says, "What a dream of a dress!"—and then wakes up. The point of the metaphor is that the dress is like a dress one would dream of and therefore isn't a dream-dress. Henle provides a good example from *Antony and Cleopatra* (2.2):

> The barge she sat in, like a burnish'd throne
> Burn'd on the water

Here simile and metaphor interact strangely, but the metaphor would vanish if a literal conflagration were imagined. In much the same way the usual effect of a simile can be sabotaged by taking the comparison too earnestly. Woody Allen writes, "The trial, which took place over the following weeks, was like a circus, although there was some difficulty getting the elephants into the courtroom."[8]

Generally it is only when a sentence is taken to be false that we accept it as a metaphor and start to hunt out the hidden implication. It is probably for this reason that most metaphorical sentences are *patently* false, just as all similes are trivially true. Absurdity or contradiction in a metaphorical sentence guarantees we won't believe it and invites us, under proper circumstances, to take the sentence metaphorically.

Patent falsity is the usual case with metaphor, but on occasion patent truth will do as well. "Business is business" is too obvious in its literal meaning to be taken as having been uttered to convey information, so we look for another use; Ted Cohen reminds us, in the same connection, that no man is an island.[9] The point is the same. The ordinary meaning in the context of use is odd enough to prompt us to disregard the question of literal truth.

Now let me raise a somewhat Platonic issue by comparing the making of a metaphor with telling a lie. The comparison is apt because lying, like making a metaphor, concerns not the meaning of words but their use. It is sometimes said that telling a lie entails saying what is false; but this is wrong. Telling a lie requires not that what you say be false but that you think it false. Since we usually believe true sentences and disbelieve false, most lies are falsehoods; but in any particular case this is an accident. The parallel between making a metaphor and telling a lie is emphasized by the fact that the same sentence can be used, with meaning unchanged, for either purpose. So a woman who believed in witches but did not think her neighbor a witch might say, "She's a witch," meaning it metaphorically; the same woman, still believing the same of witches and her neighbor but intending to deceive, might use the same words to very different effect. Since sentence and meaning are the same in both cases, it is sometimes hard to prove which intention lay behind the saying of it; thus a man who says "Lattimore's a Communist" and means to lie can always try to beg off by pleading a metaphor.

What makes the difference between a lie and a metaphor is not a difference in the words used or what they mean (in any strict sense of meaning) but in how the words are used. Using a sentence to tell a lie and using it to make a metaphor are, of course, totally different uses, so different that they do not interfere with one another, as say, acting and lying do. In lying, one must make an assertion so as to represent oneself as believing what one does not; in acting, assertion is excluded. Metaphor is careless to the difference. It can be an insult, and so be an assertion, to say to a man "You are a pig." But no metaphor was involved when (let us suppose) Odysseus addressed the same words to his companions in Circe's palace; a story, to be sure, and so no assertion—but the word, for once, was used literally of men.

No theory of metaphorical meaning or metaphorical truth can help explain how metaphor works. Metaphor runs on the same familiar linguistic tracks that the plainest sentences do; this we saw from considering simile. What distinguishes metaphor is not meaning but use—in this it is like assertion, hinting, lying, promising, or criticizing. And the special use to which we put language in metaphor is not—cannot be—to "say something" special, no matter how indirectly. For a metaphor *says* only what shows on its face—usually a patent falsehood or an absurd truth. And this plain truth or falsehood needs no paraphrase—it is given in the literal meaning of the words.

What are we to make, then, of the endless energy that has been, and is being, spent on methods and devices for drawing out the content of a metaphor? The psychologists Robert Verbrugge and Nancy McCarrell tell us that:

> Many metaphors draw attention to common systems of relationships or common transformations, in which the identity of the participants is secondary. For example, consider the sentences: *A car is like an animal, Tree trunks are straws for thirsty leaves and branches.* The first sentence directs attention to systems of relationships among energy consumption, respiration, self-induced motion, sensory systems, and, possibly, a homunculus. In the second sentence, the resemblance is a more constrained type of transformation: suction of fluid through a vertically oriented cylindrical space from a source of fluid to a destination.[10]

Verbrugge and McCarrell don't believe there is any sharp line between the literal and metaphorical uses of words; they think many words have a "fuzzy" meaning that gets fixed, if fixed at all, by a context. But surely this fuzziness, however it is illustrated and explained, cannot erase the line between what a sentence literally means (given its context) and what it "draws our attention to" (given its literal meaning as fixed by the context). The passage I have quoted is not employing such a distinction: what it says the sample sentences direct our attention to are facts expressed by paraphrases of the sentences. Verbrugge and McCarrell simply want to insist that a correct paraphrase may emphasize "systems of relationships" rather than resemblances between objects.

According to Black's interaction theory, a metaphor makes us apply a "system of commonplaces" associated with the metaphorical word to the subject of the metaphor: in "Man is a wolf" we apply commonplace attributes (stereotypes) of the wolf to man. The metaphor, Black says, thus "selects, emphasizes, suppresses, and organizes features of the principal subject by implying statements about it that normally apply to the subsidiary subject."[11] If paraphrase fails, according to Black, it is not because the metaphor does not have a special cognitive content, but because the paraphrase "will not have the same power to inform and enlighten as the original. . . . One of the points I most wish to stress is that the loss in such cases is a loss in cognitive content; the relevant weakness of the literal paraphrase is not that it may be tiresomely prolix or boringly explicit; it fails to be a translation because it fails to give the insight that the metaphor did."[12]

How can this be right? If a metaphor has a special cognitive content, why should it be so difficult or impossible to set it out? If, as Owen Barfield claims, a metaphor "says one thing and means another," why should it be that when we try to get explicit about what it means, the effect is so much weaker—"put it that way," Barfield says, "and nearly all the tarning, and with it half the poetry, is lost."[13] Why does Black think a literal paraphrase "inevitably says too much—and with the wrong emphasis"? Why inevitably? Can't we, if we are clever enough, come as close as we please?

For that matter, how is it that a simile gets along without a special intermediate meaning? In general, critics do not suggest that a simile says one thing and means another—they do not suppose it *means* anything but what lies on the surface of the words. It may make us think deep thoughts, just as a metaphor does; how come, then, no one appeals to the "special cognitive content" of the simile? And remember Eliot's hippopotamus; there there was neither simile nor metaphor, but what seemed to get done was just like what gets done by similes and metaphors. Does anyone suggest that the *words* in Eliot's poem have special meanings?

Finally, if words in metaphor bear a coded meaning, how can this meaning differ from the meaning those same words bear in the case where the metaphor *dies*—that is, when it comes to be part of the language? Why doesn't "He was burned up" as now used and meant mean *exactly* what the fresh metaphor once meant? Yet all that the dead metaphor means is that he was very angry—a notion not very difficult to make explicit.

There is, then, a tension in the usual view of metaphor. For on the one hand, the usual view wants to hold that a metaphor does something no plain prose can possibly do and, on the other hand, it wants to explain what a metaphor does by appealing to a cognitive content —just the sort of thing plain prose is designed to express. As long as we are in this frame of mind, we must harbor the suspicion that it *can* be done, at least up to a point.

There is a simple way out of the impasse. We must give up the idea that a metaphor carries a message, that it has a content or meaning (except, of course, its literal meaning). The various theories we have been considering mistake their goal. Where they think they provide a method for deciphering an encoded content, they actually tell us (or try to tell us) something about the *effects* metaphors have on us. The common error is to fasten on the contents of the thoughts a metaphor provokes and to read these contents into the metaphor itself. No doubt metaphors often make us notice aspects of things we did not notice before; no doubt they bring surprising analogies and similarities to our attention; they do provide a kind of lens or lattice, as Black says, through which we view the relevant phenomena. The issue does not lie here but in the question of how the metaphor is related to what it makes us see.

It may be remarked with justice that the claim that a metaphor provokes or invites a certain view of its subject rather than saying it straight out is a commonplace; so it is. Thus Aristotle says metaphor leads to a "perception of resemblances." Black, following Richards, says a metaphor "evokes" a certain response: "a suitable hearer will be led by a metaphor to construct a . . . system.''[14] This view is neatly summed up by what Heracleitus said of the Delphic oracle: ''It does not say and it does not hide, it intimates.''[15]

I have no quarrel with these descriptions of the effects of metaphor, only with the associated views as to *how* metaphor is supposed to produce them. What I deny is that metaphor does its work by having a special meaning, a specific cognitive content. I do not think, as Richards does, that metaphor produces its result by having a meaning which results from the interaction of two ideas; it is wrong, in my view, to say, with Owen Barfield, that a metaphor ''says one thing and means another''; or with Black that a metaphor asserts or implies certain complex things by dint of a special meaning and *thus* accomplishes its job of yielding an ''insight.'' A metaphor does its work through other intermediaries—to suppose it can be effective only by conveying a coded message is like thinking a joke or a dream makes some statement which a clever interpreter can restate in plain prose. Joke or dream or metaphor can, like a picture or a bump on the head, make us appreciate some fact—but not by standing for, or expressing, the fact.

If this is right, what we attempt in ''paraphrasing'' a metaphor cannot be to give its meaning, for that lies on the surface; rather we attempt to evoke what the metaphor brings to our attention. I can imagine someone granting this and shrugging it off as no more than an insistence on restraint in using the word ''meaning.'' This would be wrong. The central error about metaphor is most easily attacked when it takes the form of a theory of metaphorical meaning, but behind that theory, and statable independently, is the thesis that associated with a metaphor is a cognitive content that its author wishes to convey and that the interpreter must grasp if he is to get the message. This theory is false, whether or not we call the purported cognitive content a meaning.

It should make us suspect the theory that it is so hard to decide, even in the case of the simplest metaphors, exactly what the content is supposed to be. The reason it is often so hard to decide is, I think, that we imagine there is a content to be captured when all the while we are in fact focusing on what the metaphor makes us notice. If what the metaphor makes us notice were finite in scope and propositional in nature, this would not in itself make trouble; we would simply project the content the metaphor brought to mind onto the metaphor. But in fact there is no limit to what a metaphor calls to our attention, and much of what we are caused to notice is not propositional in character. When we try to say what a metaphor "means," we soon realize there is no end to what we want to mention.[16] If someone draws his finger along a coastline on a map, or mentions the beauty and deftness of a line in a Picasso etching, how many things are drawn to your attention? You might list a great many, but you could not finish since the idea of finishing would have no clear application. How many facts or propositions are conveyed by a photograph? None, an infinity, or one great unstatable fact? Bad question. A picture is not worth a thousand words, or any other number. Words are the wrong currency to exchange for a picture.

It's not only that we can't provide an exhaustive catalogue of what has been attended to when we are led to see something in a new light; the difficulty is more fundamental. What we notice or see is not, in general, propositional in character. Of course it *may* be, and when it is, it usually may be stated in fairly plain words. But if I show you Wittgenstein's duck-rabbit, and I say, "It's a duck," then with luck you see it as a duck; if I say, "It's a rabbit," you see it as a rabbit. But no proposition expresses what I have led you to see. Perhaps you have come to realize that the drawing can be seen as a duck or as a rabbit. But one could come to know this without ever seeing the drawing as a duck or as a rabbit. Seeing as is not seeing that. Metaphor makes us see one thing as another by making some literal statement that inspires or prompts the insight. Since in most cases what the metaphor prompts or inspires is not entirely, or even at all, recognition of some truth or fact, the attempt to give literal expression to the content of the metaphor is simply misguided.

The theorist who tries to explain a metaphor by appealing to a hidden message, like the critic who attempts to state the message, is then fundamentally confused. No such explanation or statement can be forthcoming because no such message exists.

Not, of course, that interpretation and elucidation of a metaphor are not in order. Many of us need help if we are to see what the author of a metaphor wanted us to see and what a more sensitive or educated reader grasps. The legitimate function of so-called paraphrase is to make the lazy or ignorant reader have a vision like that of the skilled critic. The critic is, so to speak, in benign competition with the metaphor maker. The critic tries to make his own art easier or more transparent in some respects than the original, but at the same time he tries to reproduce in others some of the effects the original had on him. In doing this the critic also, and perhaps by the best method at his command, calls attention to the beauty or aptness, the hidden power, of the metaphor itself.

NOTES

1. I think Max Black is wrong when he says, "The rules of our language determine that some expressions must count as metaphors." He allows, however, that what a metaphor "means" depends on much more: the speaker's intention, tone of voice, verbal setting, etc. "Metaphor," in his *Models and Metaphors* (Ithaca, N.Y., 1962), p. 29.

2. Nelson Goodman says metaphor and ambiguity differ chiefly "in that the several uses of a merely ambiguous term are coeval and independent" while in metaphor "a term with an extension established by habit is applied elsewhere under the influence of that habit"; he suggests that as our sense of the history of the "two uses" in metaphor fades, the metaphorical word becomes merely ambiguous (*Languages of Art* [Indianapolis, Ind., 1968], p. 71). In fact in many cases of ambiguity, one use springs from the other (as Goodman says) and so cannot be coeval. But the basic error, which Goodman shares with others, is the idea that two "uses" are involved in metaphor in anything like the way they are in ambiguity.

3. The theory described is essentially that of Paul Henle, "Metaphor," in *Language, Thought, and Culture*, ed. Henle (Ann Arbor, Mich., 1958).

4. William Empson, *Some Versions of Pastoral* (London, 1935), p. 133.

5. J. Middleton Murray says a metaphor is a "compressed simile," *Countries of the Mind*, 2d ser. (Oxford, 1931), p. 3. Max Black attributes a similar view of Alexander Bain, *English Composition and Rhetoric*, enl. ed. (London, 1887).

6. Black, p. 35.

7. Goodman, pp. 77-78.

8. Woody Allen, *New Yorker*, 21 November 1977, p. 59.

9. Ted Cohen, "Figurative Speech and Figurative Acts," *Journal of Philosophy* 72 (1975): 671. Since the negation of a metaphor seems always to be a potential metaphor, there may be as many platitudes among the potential metaphors as there are absurds among the actuals.

10. Robert R. Verbrugge and Nancy S. McCarrell, "Metaphoric Comprehension: Studies in Reminding and Resembling," *Cognitive Psychology* 9 (1977): 499.

11. Black, pp. 44-45.

12. Ibid., p. 46.

13. Owen Barfield, "Poetic Diction and Legal Fiction," in *The Importance of Language*, ed. Max Black (Englewood Cliffs, N.J., 1962), p. 55.

14. Black, p. 41.

15. I use Hannah Arendt's attractive translation of "σημαίνει"; it clearly should not be rendered as "mean" in this context.

16. Stanley Cavell mentions the fact that most attempts at paraphrase end with "and so on" and refers to Empson's remark that metaphors are "pregnant" (*Must We Mean What We Say?* [New York, 1969], p. 79). But Cavell doesn't explain the endlessness of paraphrase as I do, as can be learned from the fact that he thinks it distinguishes metaphor from some ("but perhaps not all") literal discourse. I hold that the endless character of what we call the paraphrase of a metaphor springs from the fact that it attempts to spell out what the metaphor makes us notice, and to this there is no clear end. I would say the same for any use of language.

Metaphor as Moonlighting

Nelson Goodman

I

The present symposium is evidence of a growing sense that metaphor is both important and odd—its importance odd and its oddity important—and that its place in a general theory of language and knoweldge needs study.

Metaphorical use of language differs in significant ways from literal use but is no less comprehensible, nor more recondite, no less practical, and no more independent of truth and falsity than its literal use. Far from being a mere matter of ornament, it participates fully in the progress of knowledge: in replacing some stale "natural" kinds with novel and illuminating categories, in contriving facts, in revising theory, and in bringing us new worlds. The oddity is that metaphorical truth is compatible with literal falsity;[1] a sentence false when taken literally may be true when taken metaphorically, as in the case of "The joint is jumping" or "The lake is a sapphire".

The oddity vanishes upon recognition that a metaphorical application of a term is normally quite different from the literal application.

Reprinted from *On Metaphor*, edited by Sheldon Sacks, pp. 175-180, by permission of the author and The University of Chicago Press. Copyright © 1978, 1979 by The University of Chicago. All rights reserved. Published 1979. Printed in the United States of America.

Applied literally, the noun "sapphire" sorts out various things including a certain gem but no lake; applied metaphorically (in the way here in question) it sorts out various things including a certain lake but no gem. "The lake is a sapphire" is thus literally false but metaphorically true, while "Muddy Pond is a sapphire" is both literally and metaphorically false. Metaphorical truth and falsity are as distinct from—and as opposite to—each other as are literal truth and falsity. And "The lake is a sapphire" is metaphorically true if and only if "The lake is metaphorically a sapphire" is literally true.

Obviously, metaphor and ambiguity are closely akin in that ambiguous terms likewise have two or more different applications. But metaphor differs from ambiguity in that a literal application precedes and influences a correlative metaphorical application. Words often have many different metaphorical as well as many different literal applications. In an ironic metaphorical use, "Muddy Pond is a sapphire" is true while "The lake is a sapphire" is false. The two metaphorical applications here derive in different ways from the literal application of "sapphire" to gems.

II

Donald Davison[2] disputes this straightforward account, denying that a term may have a metaphorical application different from its literal one, and scorning the notions of metaphorical truth and falsity. A sentence is true or false, he maintains, only as taken literally; to take a literally false sentence metaphorically is not to take it as saying something else that may be true, but merely to bring out certain suggestions of that false sentence, to invite comparisons or evoke thoughts or feelings. What can be said for this position?

The acknowledged difficulty and even impossibility of finding a literal paraphrase for most metaphors is offered by Davidson as evidence that there is nothing to be paraphrased—that a sentence says nothing metaphorically that it does not say literally, but rather functions differently, inviting comparisons and stimulating thought. But paraphrase of many literal sentences also is exceedingly difficult, and indeed we may seriously question whether any sentence can be translated exactly into other words in the same or any other language. Let's agree, though, that literal paraphrase of metaphor is on the whole especially hard. That is easily understood since the metaphorical application of terms has the effect, and usually the purpose, of drawing significant boundaries that cut across ruts worn by habit, of picking out new relevant kinds for which we have no simple and familiar literal descriptions. We must note in passing, though, that the metaphorical application may nevertheless be quite clear. For just as inability to define "desk" is compatible with knowing which articles are desks, so inability to paraphrase a metaphorical term is compatible with knowing what it applies to. And as I have remarked elsewhere,[3] whether a man is metaphorically a Don Quixote or a Don Juan is perhaps even easier to decide than whether he is literally a schizoid or a paranoiac.

In a second argument, Davidson considers the example of a term, "burned up", that after being used metaphorically later loses its metaphorical force through overuse. His argument runs somewhat as follows: "burned up" does not change its application when it ceases to be metaphorical; what is lost is the way it functions in inviting and this shows that metaphor is a matter of function—rather than of application. Now I agree that when a metaphor wilts, it no longer instigates such comparison—comparison, I would say, between two different applications of the term. But Davidson's argument seems at odds with his thesis that the metaphorical and literal applications of a term cannot be different. For if when "burned up" becomes a literal term for angry people, it has the same application as when metaphorical, then its metaphorical application must have been different from its other (original) literal application to things consumed by flame. When "burned up" retires as a metaphor, it becomes ambiguous; one literal application no longer suggests or is influenced by the other, but neither one is newly established.

Incidentally, if "burned up" retains its metaphorical application when its metaphorical force vanishes and is, as Davidson claims, in that application coextensive with "angry", we may well ask: Why, then, is there any difficulty about paraphrasing "burned up" when metaphorical by "angry"? I think that "burned up" was an effective metaphor in being not quite coextensive with "angry"; that, for example, "burned up" and "come to a boil" did not apply metaphorically in exactly the same cases; and that for a while after the metaphor fades, the second literal application of "burned up" still departs somewhat from that of "angry". Of course, as with words in general, such differences tend to rub off with frequent careless use.

Davidson, in a further argument, cites T. S. Eliot's "The Hippopotamus" to show that a nonmetaphorical text can invite comparison as pointedly as does a metaphor. That seems obvious enough also from simpler examples. The nonmetaphorical sentences "Compare the True Church with the hippopotamus" and "The True Church has important features in common with the hippopotamus" are quite as explicit invitations as the metaphorical "The True Church is a hippopotamus"; and in general, metaphorical and nonmetaphorical sentences alike can be put to such uses as inviting, warning, shocking, enticing, misleading, inquiring, informing, persuading, etc. Plainly, then, no such function is peculiar to metaphor, and metaphor cannot be defined in terms of the performance of, or the capacity to perform, any such function. Davidson's argument here seems a conclusive refutation of his own thesis.

Metaphor in my view involves withdrawing a term or rather a schema of terms from an initial literal application and applying it in a new way to effect a new sorting either of the same or of a different realm. Davidson's denial that the metaphorical and literal applications of a term can be distinct and that a statement false when taken literally may be true when taken metaphorically seems to me to constitute a fundamental confusion about metaphor.

III

As Ted Cohen has often stressed,[4] and as I illustrated in *Languages of Art*[5] by the case of a picture that is both metaphorically and literally blue, a metaphorical truth is not always a literal falsehood. Wherein then, Davidson asks in effect, lies the metaphorical character of the literally true "No man is an island"? Quite clearly, the metaphorical reading is different from the literal one: in the metaphorical reading, a schema of terms that taken literally sort geographical units is applied to sorting organisms, with the result that no men fall under "island". "No man is an island" is metaphorical insofar as it implicitly continues "; rather, every man is part of a mainland". Likewise "No lake is a ruby" is as metaphorical as "That lake is a sapphire"; for in both cases a schema of terms for sorting jewels is being applied to bodies of water.

Furthermore, as shown by our doubly blue picture, a literal extension of a term and a correlative metaphorical extension need not be altogether separate; they may, though different, have items in common. Although "blue" applies both literally and metaphorically to the picture in question, many other things that are either literally or metaphorically blue in this way are not both.

But what if all and only things literally blue were also metaphorically blue? Still the distinction between literal and metaphorical use, in the face of extensional equivalence, will not require resort to non-extensional "meanings" or "senses". Difference in meaning between two extensionally equivalent terms amounts to difference between their secondary extensions—that is, the extensions of parallel compounds of those terms. For example, although all and only unicorns are centaurs, not all and only (or indeed many) unicorn pictures are centaur pictures; and although all and only featherless bipeds are laughing animals, not all and only featherless-biped descriptions are laughing-animal descriptions. Likewise, when a literal and a correlative metaphorical use coincide extensionally, the significant difference is between secondary extensions: the literally-blue descriptions (descriptions as literally blue) are not all and only the metaphorically-blue descriptions (descriptions as metaphorically blue).[6]

Ordinarily, I have said, a term effects a literal sorting that upon metaphorical transfer is reflected in a new sorting. But where a term with a null literal extension—a term such as "unicorn" that does not apply literally to anything—is applied metaphorically, the new sorting cannot of course thus reflect any literal sorting by that term. Here again, secondary extensions are involved. The metaphorical sorting reflects, rather, the literal sorting of descriptions that is effected by such a compound of the term as "literally-unicorn description (or picture)".

A different and curious case was inadvertently introduced in the course of a recent paper of mine on another topic.[7] I suggested that Sir Agilulf, the hero of Italo Calvino's novel *The Nonexistent Knight*, is, among other things, a metaphor for "the real world": as the mythical knight existed only in and as some sort of armor, the chimerical one-real-world exists only in various versions. But how can a literally null term have a different, metaphorical application that is also null, since there is at most one null extension? The answer is

that there are many null labels—that is labels with null extension—
and that the compound term "Sir Agilulf description", taken literally, sorts out certain from other null labels. This sorting is reflected
in the sorting of one-real-world descriptions from other null labels
when we take "Sir Agilulf" to be a metaphor for the nonexistent
one-real-world.

IV

Such special cases, though, must not leave the impression that metaphor is a mere literary luxury, a rare or esoteric or purely decorative
device. By so putting old words to new work, we save enormously on
vocabulary and take advantage of established habits in the process of
transcending them. Metaphor permeates nearly all discourse; thor-
oughly literal paragraphs without fresh or frozen metaphors are hard
to find in even the least literary texts. In terms of multiple application of words—and other symbols—and of schemata consisting of
them, we can understand how various figures of speech are related to
each other and to literal discourse, and also how metaphor constitutes
so economical, practical, and creative a way of using symbols.[8]

In metaphor, symbols moonlight.

NOTES

1. "Metaphorical truth" does not mean that the truth of the sentence is metaphorical
but that the sentence taken metaphorically is true. The same sort of ellipsis is to be understood in many like locutions. Furthermore, in what follows I have usually avoided the confusing word "meaning"; and for readers not familiar with philosophical terminology, I have
ordinarily written "application" rather than "extension" for the collection of things denoted by a word or other label. I have also often kept clear of an ambiguity of "use" by
writing either "application" or "function" as the case may be.

2. In "What Metaphors Mean", pp. 201-20 in this volume.

3. In "Stories upon Stories: or Reality in Tiers", delivered at the conference Levels of
Reality in Florence, Italy, September 1978.

4. E.g., "Notes on Metaphor", *Journal of Aesthetics and Art Criticism* 34 (1976):
358-59.

5. *Languages of Art*, 2d ed. (Indianapolis, 1976), p. 83. However, in some other passages in that book, I have not taken this sufficiently into account. For further interesting discussion of this and related matters, see Israel Scheffler's forthcoming *Beyond the Letter* (London, 1979).

6. On the notion of secondary extensions and parallel compounds, see my "On Likeness of Meaning" and "Some Differences about Meaning" in *Problems and Projects* (Indianapolis, 1976), pp. 221-38; see also pp. 204-6. As Israel Scheffler has pointed out to me, I assume here that the modifiers "literally" and "metaphorically" are incorporated in the original terms; otherwise, an intermediate step is needed. Incidentally, were "literally blue" and "metaphorically blue" coextensive, there might also be this further difference: that the sorting of pictures by feeling under color terms might still differ from the literal sorting under these terms in what falls under some term other than "blue."

7. See n. 3 above.

8. On the ways, metaphorical and otherwise, of making worlds, see my *Ways of Worldmaking* (Indianapolis, 1978).

The Metaphorical Process as Cognition, Imagination, and Feeling

Paul Ricoeur

This paper will focus on a specific problem in the somewhat bound-less field of metaphor theory. Although this problem may sound merely psychological, insofar as it includes such terms as "image" and "feeling," I would rather characterize it as a problem arising on the boundary between a *semantic* theory of metaphor and a *psychological* theory of imagination and feeling. By a semantic theory, I mean an inquiry into the capacity of metaphor to provide untrans-latable information and, accordingly, into metaphor's claim to yield some true insight about reality. The question to which I will address myself is whether such an inquiry may be completed without in-cluding as a necessary component a psychological moment of the kind usually described as "image" or "feeling."

At first glance, it seems that it is only in theories in which meta-phorical phrases have no informative value and consequently no truth claim that the so-called images or feelings are advocated as substitu-tive explanatory factors. By substitutive explanation I mean the attempt to derive the alleged significance of metaphorical phrases from their capacity to display streams of images and to elicit feelings

Reprinted from *Critical Inquiry* 5, no. 1 (1978):143-159 by permission of the author and The University of Chicago Press. Copyright © 1978 by The University of Chicago. All rights reserved. Printed in U.S.A.

that we mistakenly hold for genuine information and for fresh insight into reality. My thesis is that it is not only for theories which deny metaphors any informative value and any truth claim that images and feelings have a *constitutive* function. I want instead to show that the kind of theory of metaphor initiated by I. A. Richards in *Philosophy of Rhetoric,* Max Black in *Models and Metaphors,* Beardsley, Berggren, and others cannot achieve its own goal without including imagining and feeling, that is, without assigning a *semantic* function to what seems to be mere *psychological* features and without, therefore, concerning itself with some accompanying factors extrinsic to the informative kernel of metaphor. This contention seems to run against a well-established—at least since Frege's famous article "Sinn und Bedeutung" and Husserl's *Logical Investigations*—dichotomy, that between *Sinn* or sense and *Vorstellung* or representation, if we understand "sense" as the objective content of an expression and "representation" as its mental actualization, precisely in the form of image and feeling. But the question is whether the functioning of metaphorical sense does not put to the test and even hold at bay this very dichotomy.

The first articulate account of metaphor, that of Aristotle, already provides some hints concerning what I will call the semantic role of imagination (and by implication, feeling) in the establishment of metaphorical sense. Aristotle says of the *lexis* in general—that is, of diction, elocution, (logos) *appear* as such and such. He also says that the gift of making good metaphors relies on the capacity to contemplate similarities. Moreover, the vividness of such good metaphors consists in their ability to "set before the eyes" the sense that they display. What is suggested here is a kind of pictorial dimension, which can be called the *picturing function* of metaphorical meaning.

The tradition of rhetoric confirms that hint beyond any specific theory concerning the semantic status of metaphor. The very expression "figure of speech" implies that in metaphor, as in the other tropes or turns, discourse assumes the nature of a body by displaying forms and traits which usually characterize the human face, man's "figure"; it is as though the tropes gave to discourse a quasi-bodily externalization. By providing a kind of figurability to the message, the tropes make discourse appear.

Roman Jakobson suggests a similar interpretation when he characterizes the "poetic" function in his general model of communication as the valorization of the message *for its own sake.* In the same way, Tzvetan Todorov, the Bulgarian theoretician of neo-rhetorics, defines "figure" as the visibility of discourse. Gérard Genette, in *Figures I,* speaks of deviance as an "inner space of language." "Simple and common expressions," he says, "have no form, figures [of speech] have some."

I am quite aware that these are only hints which point toward a problem rather than toward a statement. Furthermore, I am quite aware that they add to this difficulty the fact that they tend to speak metaphorically about metaphor and thus introduce a kind of circularity which obscures the issue. But is not the word "metaphor" itself a metaphor, the metaphor of a displacement and therefore of a transfer in a kind of space? What is at stake is precisely the necessity of these *spatial* metaphors about metaphor included in our talk about "figures" of speech.

Such being the problem, in what direction are we to look for a correct assessment of the *semantic* role of imagination and eventually of feeling? It seems that it is in the *work of resemblance* that a pictorial or iconic moment is implied, as Aristotle suggests when he says that to make good metaphors is to contemplate similarities or (according to some other translations) to have an insight into likeness.

But in order to understand correctly the work of resemblance in metaphor and to introduce the pictorial or iconic moment at the right place, it is necessary briefly to recall the mutation undergone by the theory of metaphor at the level of semantics by contrast with the tradition of classical rhetoric. In this tradition, metaphor was correctly described in terms of *deviance,* but this deviance was mistakenly ascribed to denomination only. Instead of giving a thing its usual common *name,* one designates it by means of a borrowed name, a "foreign" name in Aristotle's terminology. The rationale of this transfer of name was understood as the objective similarity between the things themselves or the subjective similarity between the attitudes linked to the grasping of these things. As concerns the goal of this transfer, it was supposed either to fill up a lexical lacuna, and therefore to serve the principle of economy which rules the endeavor of giving appropriate names to new things, new ideas, or new experiences, or to decorate discourse, and therefore to serve the main purpose of rhetorical discourse, which is to persuade and to please.

The problem of resemblance receives a new articulation in the semantic theory characterized by Max Black as an interaction theory (as opposed to a substitutive theory). The bearer of the metaphorical meaning is no longer the word but the sentence as a whole. The interaction process does not merely consist of the substitution of a word for a word, of a name for a name—which, strictly speaking, defines only metonymy—but in an interaction between a logical subject and a predicate. If metaphor consists in some deviance—this feature is not denied but is described and explained in a new way—this deviance concerns the predicative structure itself. Metaphor, then, has to be described as a deviant predication rather than a deviant denomination. We come closer to what I called the work of resemblance if we ask *how* this deviant predication obtains. A French theoretician in the field of poetics, Jean Cohen, in *Structure du langage poétique,* speaks of this deviance in terms of a semantic impertinence, meaning by that the violation of the code of pertinence or relevance which rules the ascription of predicates in ordinary use.[1] The metaphorical statement works as the reduction of this syntagmatic deviance by the establishment of a new semantic pertinence. This new pertinence in turn is secured by the production of a lexical deviance, which is therefore a paradigmatic deviance, that is, precisely the kind of deviance described by classical rhetoricians. Classical rhetoric, in that sense, was not wrong, but it only described the "effect of sense" at the level of the word while it overlooked the production of this semantic twist at the level of sense. While it is true that the effect of sense is focused on the word, the production of sense is borne by the whole utterance. It is in that way that the theory of metaphor hinges on a semantics of the sentence.

Such is the main presupposition of the following analysis. The first question is to understand *how* resemblance works in this production of meaning. The next step will be to connect in the right way the pictorial or iconic moment to this work of resemblance.

As concerns the first step, the work of resemblance as such, it seems to me that we are still only halfway to a full understanding of the semantic innovation which characterizes metaphorical phrases or sentences if we underline only the aspect of deviance in metaphor, even if we distinguish the semantic impertinence which requires the lexical deviance from this lexical deviance itself, as described by Aristotle and all classical rhetoricians. The decisive feature is the semantic innovation, thanks to which a new pertinence, a new congruence, is established in such a way that the utterance "makes sense" as a whole. The *maker* of metaphors is this craftsman with verbal skill *who*, from an inconsistent utterance for a literal interpretation, draws a significant utterance for a new interpretation which deserves to be called metaphorical because it generates the metaphor not only as deviant but as acceptable. In other words, metaphorical meaning does not merely consist of a semantic clash but of the *new* predicative meaning which emerges from the collapse of the literal meaning, that is, from the collapse of the meaning which obtains if we rely only on the common or usual lexical values of our words. The metaphor is not the enigma but the solution of the enigma.

It is here, in the mutation characteristic of the semantic innovation, that similarity and accordingly imagination play a role. But which role? I think that this role cannot be but misunderstood as long as one has in mind the Humean theory of image as a faint impression, that is, as a perceptual residue. It is no better understood if one shifts to the other tradition, according to which imagination can be reduced to the alternation between two modalities of association, either by contiguity or by similarity. Unfortunately, this prejudice has been assumed by such important theoreticians as Jakobson, for whom the metaphoric process is opposed to the metonymic process in the same way as the substitution of one sign for another within a sphere of similarity is opposed to the concatenation between signs along a string of contiguity. What must be understood and underscored is a mode of functioning of similarity and accordingly of imagination which is immanent—that is, nonextrinsic—to the predicative process itself. In other words, the work of resemblance has to be appropriate and homogeneous to the deviance and the oddness and the freshness of the semantic innovation itself.

How is this possible? I think that the decisive problem that an interaction theory of metaphor has helped to delineate but not to solve is the transition from literal incongruence to metaphorical congruence between two semantic fields. Here the metaphor of space is useful. It is as though a change of distance between meanings occurred within a logical space. The *new* pertinence or congruence proper to a meaningful metaphoric utterance proceeds from the kind of semantic proximity which suddenly obtains between terms in spite of their distance. Things or ideas which were remote appear now as close. Resemblance ultimately is nothing else than this rapprochement which reveals a generic kinship between heterogeneous ideas. What Aristotle called the *epiphora* of the metaphor, that is, the transfer of meaning, is nothing else than this move or shift in the logical distance, from the far to the near. The lacuna of some recent theories of metaphor, including Max Black's, concerns precisely the innovation proper to this shift.[2]

It is the first task of an appropriate theory of imagination to plug this hole. But this theory of imagination must deliberately break with Hume and draw on Kant, specifically on Kant's concept of productive imagination *as schematizing a synthetic operation.* This will provide us with the first step in our attempt to adjust a psychology of imagination to a semantics of metaphor or, if you prefer, to complete a semantics of metaphor by having recourse to a psychology of imagination. There will be three steps in this attempt of adjustment and of completion.

In the first step, imagination is understood as the "seeing," still homogeneous to discourse itself, which effects the shift in logical distance, the rapprochement itself. The place and the role of productive imagination is there, in the *insight*, to which Aristotle alluded when he said that to make good metaphors is to contemplate likeness —*theorein to omoion.* This insight into likeness is both a thinking and a seeing. It is a thinking to the extent that it effects a restructuration of semantic fields; it is transcategorical because it is categorical. This can be shown on the basis of the kind of metaphor in which the logical aspect of this restructuration is the most conspicuous, the metaphor which Aristotle called metaphor by analogy, that is, the proportional metaphor: A is to B what C is to D. The cup is to Dionysus what the shield is to Ares. Therefore we may say, by shifting terms, Dionysis' shield or Ares' cup. But this thinking is a seeing, to the extent that the insight consists of the instantaneous grasping of the combinatory possibilities offered by the proportionality and consequently the establishment of the proportionality by the rapprochement between the two ratios. I suggest we call this *productive* character of the insight *predicative assimilation.* But we miss entirely its semantic role if we interpret it in terms of the old association by re-semblance. A kind of mechanical attraction between mental atoms is thereby substituted for an operation homogeneous to language and to its nuclear act, the predication act. The assimilation consists pre-cisely in *making* similar, that is, semantically proximate, the terms that the metaphorical utterance brings together.

Some will probably object to my ascribing to the imagination this predicative assimilation. Without returning to my earlier critique of the prejudices concerning the imagination itself which may prevent the analysts from doing justice to productive imagination, I want to underscore a trait of predicative assimilation which may support my contention that the rapprochement characteristic of the metaphorical process offers a typical kinship to Kant's *schematism.* I mean the *paradoxical* character of the predicative assimilation which has been compared by some authors to Ryle's concept of "category mistake," which consists in presenting the facts pertaining to one category in the terms appropriate to another. All new rapprochement runs against a previous categorization which resists, or rather which yields while resisting, as Nelson Goodman says. This is what the idea of a semantic impertinence or incongruence preserves. In order that a metaphor obtains, one must continue to identify the previous in-compatibility *through* the new compatibility. The predicative assimi-lation involves, in that way, a specific kind of tension which is not so much between a subject and a predicate as between semantic incon-gruence and congruence. The insight into likeness is the perception of the conflict between the previous incompatibility and the new compatibility. "Remoteness" is preserved within "proximity." To see *the like* is to see the same in spite of, and through, the different. This tension between sameness and difference characterizes the log-ical structure of likeness. Imagination, accordingly, is this *ability* to produce new kinds by assimilation and to produce them not *above* the differences, as in the concept, but in spite of and through the dif-ferences. Imagination is this stage in the production of genres where generic kinship has not reached the level of conceptual peace and rest but remains caught in the war between distance and proximity, be-tween remoteness and nearness. In that sense, we may speak with Gadamer of the fundamental metaphoricity of thought to the extent that the figure of speech that we call "metaphor" allows us a glance

at the general procedure by which we produce concepts. This is because in the metaphoric process the movement toward the genus
is arrested by the resistance of the difference and, as it were, inter-
cepted by the figure of rhetoric.

Such is the first function of imagination in the process of semantic
innovation. Imagination has not yet been considered under its sensible, quasi-optic aspect but under its quasi-verbal aspect. However,
the latter is the condition of the former. We first have to understand
an image, according to Bachelard's remark in the *Poetics of Space,* as
"a being pertaining to language."[3] Before being a fading perception,
the image is an emerging meaning. Such is, in fact, the tradition of
Kant's productive imagination and schematism. What we have above
described is nothing else than the schematism of metaphorical attribution.

The next step will be to incorporate into the semantics of metaphor the second aspect of imagination, its *pictorial* dimension. It is
this aspect which is at stake in the *figurative* character of metaphor.
It is also this aspect which was intended by I. A. Richards' distinction between tenor and vehicle. This distinction is not entirely ab-
sorbed in the one Black makes between frame and focus. Frame and
focus designate only the contextual setting—say, the sentence as a
whole—and the term which is the bearer of the shift of meaning,
whereas tenor and vehicle designate the conceptual import and its
pictorial envelope. The first function of imagination was to give an
account of the frame/focus interplay; its second function is to give
an account of the difference of level between tenor and vehicle or,
in other words, of the way in which a semantic innovation is not
only schematized but pictured. Paul Henle borrows from Charles
Sanders Peirce the distinction between sign and icon and speaks of
the *iconic* aspect of metaphor.[4] If there are two thoughts in one in
a metaphor, there is one which is intended; the other is the concrete
aspect *under* which the first one is presented. In Keats' verse "When
by my solitary hearth I sit / And hateful thoughts enwrap my soul in
gloom," the metaphorical expression "enwrap" consists in presenting
sorrow as if it were capable of enveloping the soul in a cloak. Henle
comments: "We are led [by figurative discourse] to think of something by a consideration of something like it, and this is what constitutes the iconic mode of signifying."

Someone might object at this point that we are in danger of re-introducing an obsolete theory of the image, in the Humean sense of a weakened sensorial impression. This is therefore the place to recall a remark made by Kant that one of the functions of the schema is to provide images for a concept. In the same vein, Henle writes: "If there is an iconic element in metaphor it is equally clear that the icon is not presented, but merely described." And further: "What is presented is a formula for the construction of icons." What we have therefore to show is that if this new extension of the role of imagination is not exactly included in the previous one, it makes sense for a semantic theory only to the extent that it is controlled by it. What is at issue is the development from schematization to iconic presentation.

The enigma of iconic presentation is the way in which depiction occurs in predicative assimilation: something appears on which we read the new connection. The enigma remains unsolved as long as we treat the image as a mental picture, that is, as the replica of an absent thing. Then the image must remain foreign to the process, extrinsic to predicative assimilation.

We have to understand the process by which a certain production of images channels the schematization of predicative assimilation. By displaying a flow of images, discourse initiates changes of logical distance, generates rapprochement. Imaging or imagining, thus, is the concrete milieu in which and through which we see similarities. To imagine, then, is not to have a mental picture of something but to display relations in a depicting mode. Whether this depiction concerns unsaid and unheard similarities or refers to qualities, structures, localizations, situations, attitudes, or feelings, each time the new intended connection is grasped as what the icon describes or depicts.

It is in this way, I think, that one can do justice within a semantic theory of metaphor to the Wittgensteinian concept of "seeing as." Wittgenstein himself did not extend this analysis beyond the field of perception and beyond the process of interpretation made obvious by the case of ambiguous "Gestalten," as in the famous duck/rabbit drawing. Marcus B. Hester, in his *The Meaning of Poetic Metaphor,* has attempted to extend the concept of "seeing as" to the functioning of poetic images.[5] Describing the experience of *reading*, he shows that the kind of images which are interesting for a theory of poetic language are not those that interrupt reading and distort or divert it. These images—these "wild" images, if I may say so—are properly extrinsic to the fabric of sense. They induce the reader, who has become a dreamer rather than a reader, to indulge himself in the delusive attempt, described by Sartre as fascination, to possess magically the absent thing, body, or person. The kind of images which still belong to the production of sense are rather what Hester calls "bound" images, that is, concrete representations aroused by the verbal element and controlled by it. Poetic language, says Hester, is this language which not only merges sense and sound, as many theoreticians have said, but sense and senses, meaning by that the flow of bound images displayed by the sense. We are not very far from what Bachelard called *retentissement* [reverberation]. In reading, Bachelard says, the verbal meaning generates images which, so to speak, rejuvenate and reenact the traces of sensorial experience. Yet it is not the process of reverberation which expands the schematization and, in Kant's words, provides a concept with an image. In fact, as the experience of reading shows, this display of images ranges from schematization without full-blown images to wild images which distract thought more than they instruct it. The kind of images which are relevant for a semantics of the poetic image are those which belong to the intermediary range of the scale, which are, therefore, the bound images of Hester's theory. These images bring to concrete completion the metaphorical process. The meaning is then depicted under the features of ellipsis. Through this depiction, the meaning is not only schematized but lets itself be read *on* the image in which it is inverted. Or, to put it another way, the metaphorical sense is generated in the thickness of the imagining scene displayed by the verbal structure of the poem. Such is, to my mind, the functioning of the intuitive grasp of a predicative connection.

I do not deny that this second stage of our theory of imagination has brought us to the borderline between pure semantics and psychology or, more precisely, to the borderline between a semantics of productive imagination and a psychology of reproductive imagination. But the metaphorical meaning, as I said in the introduction, is precisely this kind of meaning which denies the well-established distinction between sense and representation, to evoke once more Frege's opposition between *Sinn* and *Vorstellung*. By blurring this distinction, the metaphorical meaning compels us to explore the borderline between the verbal and the non-verbal. The process of schematization and that of the bound images aroused and controlled by schematization obtain precisely on that borderline between a semantics of metaphorical utterances and a psychology of imagination.

The third and final step in our attempt to complete a semantic theory of metaphor with a proper consideration of the role of imagination concerns what I shall call the "suspension" or, if you prefer, the moment of negativity brought by the image in the metaphorical process.

In order to understand this new contribution of the image to this process, we have to come back to the basic notion of meaning as applied to a metaphorical expression. By meaning we may understand —as we have in the preceding as well—the inner functioning of the proposition as a predicative operation, for example, in Black's vocabulary, the "filter" or the "screen" effect of the subsidiary subject on the main subject. Meaning, then, is nothing else than what Frege called *Sinn* [sense], in contradistinction to *Bedeutung* [reference or denotation]. But to ask *about what* a metaphorical statement is, is something other and something more than to ask *what* it says.

The question of reference in metaphor is a particular case of the more general question of the truth claim of poetic language. As Goodman says in *Languages of Art,* all symbolic systems are denotative in the sense that they "make" and "remake" reality. To raise the question of the referential value of poetic language is to try to show how symbolic systems *reorganize* "the world in terms of works and works in terms of the world."[6] At that point the theory of metaphor tends to merge with that of models to the extent that a metaphor may be seen as a model for changing our way of looking at things, of perceiving the world. The word "insight," very often applied to the *cognitive* import of metaphor, conveys in a very appropriate manner this move from sense to reference which is no less obvious in poetic discourse than in so-called descriptive discourse. Here, too, we do not restrict ourselves to talking about ideas nor, as Frege says of proper names, "are we satisfied with the sense alone." "We presuppose besides a reference," the "striving for truth," which prompts "our intention in speaking or thinking" and "drives us always to advance from the sense of the reference."[7]

But the paradox of metaphorical reference is that its functioning is as odd as that of the metaphorical sense. At first glance, poetic language refers to nothing but itself. In a classic essay entitled "Word and Language," which defines the poetic function of language in relation to the other functions implied in any communicative transaction, Jakobson bluntly opposes the poetic function of the message to its referential function. On the contrary, the referential function prevails in descriptive language, be it ordinary or scientific. Descriptive language, he says, is not about itself, not inwardly oriented, but outwardly directed. Here language, so to speak, effaces itself for the sake of what is said about reality. "The poetic function—which is more than mere poetry—lays the stress on the palpable side of the signs, underscores the message for its own sake and deepens the fundamental dichotomy between signs and objects."[8] The poetic function and the referential function, accordingly, seem to be polar opposites. The latter directs language toward the nonlinguistic context, the former directs message toward itself.

This analysis seems to strengthen some other classical arguments among literary critics and more specifically in the structuralist camp according to which not only poetry but literature in general implies a mutation in the use of language. This redirects language toward itself to the point that language may be said, in Roland Barthes' words, to "celebrate itself" rather than to celebrate the world.

My contention is that these arguments are not false but give an incomplete picture of the whole process of reference in poetic discourse. Jakobson himself acknowledged that what happens in poetry is not the suppression of the referential function but its profound alteration by the workings of the ambiguity of the message itself. "The supremacy of poetic function over referential function," he says, "does not obliterate the reference but makes it ambiguous. The double-sensed message finds correspondence in a split addresser, in a split addressee, and what is more, in a split reference, as is cogently exposed in the preambles to fairy tales of various people, for instance, in the usual exortation of the Majorca story tellers: *Aixo era y no era* (it was and it was not)."[9]

I suggest that we take the expression "split reference" as our leading line in our discussion of the referential function of the metaphorical statement. This expression, as well as the wonderful "it was and it was not," contains *in nuce* all that can be said about metaphorical reference. To summarize, poetic language is no less *about* reality than any other use of language but refers to it by the means of a complex strategy which implies, as an essential component, a suspension and seemingly an abolition of the ordinary reference attached to descriptive language. This suspension, however, is only the negative condition of a second-order reference, of an indirect reference built on the ruins of the direct reference. This reference is called second-order reference only with respect to the primacy of the reference of ordinary language. For, in another respect, it constitutes the primordial reference to the extent that it suggests, reveals, unconceals—or whatever you say—the deep structures of reality to which we are related as mortals who are born into this world and who *dwell* in it for a while.

This is not the place to discuss the ontological implications of this contention nor to ascertain its similarities and dissimilarities with Husserl's concept of *Lebenswelt* or with Heidegger's concept of *In-der-Welt-Sein*. I want to emphasize, for the sake of our further discussion of the role of imagination in the completion of the *meaning* of metaphor, the mediating role of the *suspension*—or *epoché*—of ordinary descriptive reference in connection with the ontological claims of poetic discourse. This mediating role of the *epoché* in the functioning of the reference in metaphor is in complete agreement with the interpretation we have given to the functioning of sense. The sense of a novel metaphor, we said, is the emergence of a new semantic congruence or pertinence from the ruins of the literal sense shattered by semantic incompatibility or absurdity. In the same way as the self-abolition of literal sense is the negative condition for the emergence of the metaphorical sense, the suspension of the reference proper to ordinary descriptive language is the negative condition for the emergence of a more radical way of looking at things, whether it is akin or not to the unconcealing of that layer of reality which phenomenology calls preobjective and which, according to Heidegger, constitutes the horizon of all our modes of dwelling in the world. Once more, what interests me here is the parallelism between the suspension of literal sense and the suspension of ordinary descriptive reference. This parallelism goes very far. In the same way as the metaphorical sense not only abolishes but preserves the literal sense, the metaphorical reference maintains the ordinary vision in tension with the new one it suggests. As Berggren says in "The Use and Abuse of Metaphor": "The possibility or comprehension of metaphorical construing requires, therefore, a peculiar and rather sophisticated intellectual ability which W. Bedell Stanford metaphorically labels 'stereoscopic vision': the ability to entertain two different points of view at the same time. That is to say, the perspective prior to and subsequent to the transformation of the metaphor's principle and subsidiary subjects must both be conjointly maintained."[10]

But what Bedell Stanford called stereoscopic vision is nothing else than what Jakobson called split reference: ambiguity in reference.

My contention now is that one of the functions of imagination is to give a concrete dimension to the suspension or *epoché* proper to split reference. Imagination does not merely *schematize* the predicative assimilation between terms by its synthetic insight into similarities nor does it merely *picture* the sense thanks to the display of images aroused and controlled by the cognitive process. Rather, it contributes concretely to the *epoché* of ordinary reference and to the *projection* of new possibilities of redescribing the world.

In a sense, all *epoché* is the work of the imagination. Imagination *is epoché*. As Sartre emphasized, to imagine is to address oneself to what is not. More radically, to imagine is to make oneself absent to the whole of things. Yet I do not want to elaborate further this thesis of the negativity proper to the image. What I do want to underscore is the solidarity between the *epoché* and the capacity to project new possibilities. Image as absence is the negative side of image as fiction. It is to this aspect of the image as fiction that is attached the power of symbolic systems to "remake" reality, to return to Goodman's idiom. But this productive and projective function of fiction can only be acknowledged if one sharply distinguishes it from the reproductive role of the so-called mental image which merely provides us with a re-presentation of things already perceived. *Fiction* addresses itself to deeply rooted potentialities of reality to the extent that they are absent from the actualities with which we deal in everyday life under the mode of empirical control and manipulation. In that sense, fiction presents under a concrete mode the split structure of the reference pertaining to the metaphorical statement. It both reflects and completes it. It reflects it in the sense that the mediating role of the *epoché* proper to the image is homogeneous to the paradoxical structure of the cognitive process of reference. The "it was and it was not" of the Majorca storytellers rules both the split reference of the metaphorical statement and the contradictory structure of fiction. Yet, we may say as well that the structure of the fiction not only reflects but completes the logical structure of the split reference. The poet is this genius who generates split references *by* creating fictions. It is in fiction that the "absence" proper to the power of suspending what we call "reality" in ordinary language concretely coalesces and fuses with the *positive insight* into the potentialities of our being in the world which our everyday transactions with manipulatable objects tend to conceal.

You may have noticed that until now I have said nothing concerning feelings in spite of the commitment implied in this paper's title to deal with the problem of the connection between cognition, imagination, *and* feeling. I have no intention to elude this problem.

Imagination and feeling have always been closely linked in classical theories of metaphor. We cannot forget that rhetoric has always been defined as a strategy of discourse aiming at persuading and pleasing. And we know the central role played by pleasure in the aesthetics of Kant. A theory of metaphor, therefore, is not complete if it does not give an account of the place and role of feeling in the metaphorical process.

My contention is that feeling has a place not just in theories of metaphor which deny the *cognitive* import of metaphor. These theories ascribe a substitutive role of image and feeling due to the metaphor's lack of informative value. In addition, I claim that feeling as well as imagination are genuine components in the process described in an interaction theory of metaphor. They both *achieve* the semantic bearing of metaphor.

I have already tried to show the way in which a *psychology* of imagination has to be integrated into a semantics of metaphor. I will now try to extend the same kind of description to feeling. A bad psychology of imagination in which imagination is conceived as a residue of perception prevents us from acknowledging the constructive role of imagination. In the same way, a bad psychology of feeling is responsible for a similar misunderstanding. Indeed, our natural inclination is to speak of feeling in terms appropriate to emotion, that is, to affections conceived as (1) inwardly directed states of mind, and (2) mental experiences closely tied to bodily disturbances, as is the case in fear, anger, pleasure, and pain. In fact both traits come together. To the extent that in emotion we are, so to speak, under the spell of our body, we are delivered to mental states with little intentionality, as though in emotion we "lived" our body in a more intense way.

Genuine feelings are not emotions, as may be shown by feelings which are rightly called *poetic feelings.* Just like the corresponding images which they reverberate, they enjoy a specific kinship with language. They are properly displayed by the poem as a verbal texture. But how are they linked to its meaning?

I suggest that we construe the role of feeling according to the three similar moments which provided an articulation to my theory of imagination.

Feelings, first, accompany and complete imagination in its function of *schematization* of the new predicative congruence. This schematization, as I said, is a kind of insight into the mixture of "like" and "unlike" proper to similarity. Now we may say that this instantaneous grasping of the new congruence is "felt" as well as "seen." By saying that it is felt, we underscore the fact that we are included in the process as knowing subjects. If the process can be called, as I called it, predicative *assimilation*, it is true that *we* are assimilated, that is, made similar, to what is seen as similar. This self-assimilation is a part of the commitment proper to the "illocutionary" force of the metaphor as speech act. We feel *like* what we see *like*.

If we are somewhat reluctant to acknowledge this contribution of feeling to the illocutionary act of metaphorical statements, it is because we keep applying to feeling our usual interpretation of emotion as both inner and bodily states. We then miss the specific structure of feeling. As Stephan Strasser shows in *Das Gemut* [The heart], a feeling is a second-order intentional structure.[11] It is a process of interiorization succeeding a movement of intentional transcendence directed toward some objective state of affairs. To *feel*, in the emotional sense of the word, is to make *ours* what has been put at a distance by thought in its objectifying phase. Feelings, therefore, have a very complex kind of intentionality. They are not merely inner states but interiorized thoughts. It is as such that they accompany and complete the work of imagination as schematizing a synthetic operation: they make the schematized thought ours. Feeling, then, is a case of *Selbst-Affektion*, in the sense Kant used it in the second edition of the *Critique*. This *Selbst-Affektion*, in turn, is a part of what we call poetic feeling. Its function is to abolish the distance between knower and known without canceling the cognitive structure of thought and the intentional distance which it implies. Feeling is not contrary to thought. It is thought made ours. This felt participation is a part of its complete meaning as poem.

Feelings, furthermore, accompany and complete imagination as *picturing* relationships. This aspect of feeling has been emphasized by Northrop Frye in *Anatomy of Criticism* under the designation of "mood." Each poem, he says, structures a mood which is *this* unique mood generated by *this* unique string of words. In that sense, it is co-extensive to the verbal structure itself. The mood is nothing other than the way in which the poem affects us as an *icon*. Frye offers strong expression here: "The unity of a poem is the unity of a mood"; the poetic images "express or articulate this mood. This mood is the poem and nothing else behind it."[12] In my own terms, I would say, in a tentative way, that the mood is *the iconic as felt.* Perhaps we could arrive at the same assumption by starting from Goodman's concept of *dense* vs. *discrete* symbols. Dense symbols are felt as dense. That does not mean, once more, that feelings are radically opaque and ineffable. "Density" is a mode of articulation just as discreteness is. Or, to speak in Pascal's terms, the "esprit de finesse" is no less thought than the "esprit géometrique." However, I leave these suggestions open to discussion.

Finally, the most important function of feelings can be construed according to the third feature of imagination, that is, its contribution to the split reference of poetic discourse. The imagination contributes to it, as I said, owing to its split structure. On the one hand, imagination entails the *epoché*, the suspension, of the direct reference of thought to the objects of our ordinary discourse. On the other hand, imagination provides *models for* reading reality in a new way. This split structure is the structure of imagination as fiction.

What could be the counterpart and the complement of this split structure at the level of feelings? My contention is that feelings, too, display a split structure which completes the split structure pertaining to the cognitive component of metaphor.

On the one hand, feelings—I mean poetic feelings—imply a kind of *epoché* of our bodily emotions. Feelings are negative, suspensive experiences in relation to the literal emotions of everyday life. When we read, we do not literally feel fear or anger. Just as poetic language denies the first-order reference of descriptive discourse to ordinary objects of our concern, feelings deny the first-order feelings which tie us to these first-order objects of reference.

But this denial, too, is only the reverse side of a more deeply rooted operation of feeling which is to insert us within the world in a nonobjectifying manner. That feelings are not merely the denial of emotions but their metamorphosis has been explicitly asserted by Aristotle in his analysis of catharsis. But this analysis remains trivial as long as it is not interpreted in relation to the split reference of the cognitive and the imaginative function of poetic discourse. It is the tragic poem itself, as thought (*dianoia*), which displays specific feelings which are the poetic transposition—I mean the transposition by means of poetic *language*—of fear and compassion, that is, of feelings of the first order, of emotions. The tragic *phobos* and the tragic *eleos* (terror and pity, as some translators say) are both the denial and the transfiguration of the literal feelings of fear and compassion.

On the basis of this analysis of the split structure of poetic feeling, it is possible to do justice to a certain extent to a claim of Heidegger's analytic of the *Dasein* that feelings have *ontological* bearing, that they are ways of "being-there," of "finding" ourselves within the world, to keep something of the semantic intent of the German *Befindlichkeit*. Because of feelings we are "attuned to" aspects of reality which cannot be expressed in terms of the objects referred to in ordinary language. Our entire analysis of the split reference of both language and feeling is in agreement with this claim. But it must be underscored that this analysis of *Befindlichkeit* makes sense only to the extent that it is paired with that of split reference both in verbal and imaginative structures. If we miss this fundamental connection, we are tempted to construe this concept of *Befindlichkeit* as a new kind of intuitionism—and the worst kind!—in the form of a new emotional realism. We miss, in Heidegger's *Daseinanalyse* itself, the close connections between *Befindlichkeit* and *Verstehen*, between situation and project, between anxiety and interpretation. The onto-logical bearing of feeling cannot be separated from the negative pro-cess applied to the first-order emotions, such as fear and sympathy, according to the Aristotelian paradigm of catharsis. With this quali-fication in mind, we may assume the Heideggerian thesis that it is mainly through feelings that we are attuned to reality. But this attunement is nothing else than the reverberation in terms of feel-ings of the split reference of both verbal and imaginative structure.

To conclude, I would like to emphasize the points which I submit to discussion:

1. There are three main *presuppositions* on which the rest of my analysis relies: (*a*) metaphor is an act of *predication* rather than of *denomination*; (*b*) a theory of deviance is not enough to give an account of the emergence of a *new congruence* at the predicative level; and (*c*) the notion of metaphorical sense is not complete without a description of the *split reference* which is specific to poetic discourse.

2. On this threefold basis, I have tried to show that imagination and feeling are not extrinsic to the emergence of the metaphorical sense and of the split reference. They are not substitutive for a lack of informative content in metaphorical statements, but they complete their full cognitive intent.

3. *But* the price to pay for the last point is a theory of imagination and of feeling which is still in infancy. The burden of my argument is that the notion of *poetic image* and of *poetic feeling* has to be construed in accordance with the cognitive component, under-stood itself as a tension between congruence and incongruence at the level of sense, between *epoché* and commitment at the level of reference.

4. My paper suggests that there is a *structural analogy* between the cognitive, the imaginative, and the emotional components of the complete metaphorical act and that the metaphorical process draws its concreteness and its completeness from this structural analogy and this complementary functioning.

NOTES

1. Jean Cohen, *Structure du langage poétique* (Paris, 1966).

2. Black's explanation of the metaphorical process by the "system of associated commonplaces" leaves unsolved the problem of innovation, as the following reservations and qualifications suggest: "Metaphors," he says, "can be supported by specifically constructed systems of implications as well as by accepted commonplaces" (*Models and Metaphors* [Ithaca, N.Y., 1962], p. 43). And further: "These implications usually consist of commonplaces about the subsidiary subject; but may, in suitable cases, consist of deviant implications established *ad hoc* by the writer" (p. 44). How are we to think of these implications that are created on the spot?

3. Gaston Bachelard, *The Poetics of Space*, trans. Maria Jolas (New York, 1964).

4. Paul Henle, "Metaphor," in *Language, Thought, and Culture*, ed. Henle (Ann Arbor, Mich., 1958).

5. Marcus B. Hester, *The Meaning of Poetic Metaphor* (The Hague, 1967).

6. Nelson Goodman, *Languages of Art* (Indianapolis, Ind., 1968), p. 241.

7. As quoted from Frege's "Sense and Reference" in my *The Rule of Metaphor: Multidisciplinary Studies of the Creation of Meaning in Language* (Toronto, 1978), pp. 217-18.

8. Jakobson, *Selected Writings*, 2 vols. (The Hague, 1962), 2:356.

9. As found in my *The Rule of Metaphor*, p. 224.

10. Douglas Berggren, "The Use and Abuse of Metaphor," *Review of Metaphysics* 16 (December 1962): 243.

11. Stephan Strasser, *Das Gemut* (Freiberg, 1956).

12. Northrop Frye, *Anatomy of Criticism: Four Essays* (Princeton, 1957).

Metaphor

John R. Searle

Formulating the Problem

If you hear somebody say, "Sally is a block of ice", or "Sam is a pig", you are likely to assume that the speaker does not mean what he says literally, but that he is speaking metaphorically. Furthermore, you are not likely to have very much trouble figuring out what he means. If he says, "Sally is a prime number between 17 and 23", or "Bill is a barn door", you might still assume he is speaking metaphorically, but it is much harder to figure out what he means. The existence of such utterances—utterances in which the speaker means metaphorically something different from what the sentence means literally —poses a series of questions for any theory of language and communication: What is metaphor, and how does it differ from both literal and other forms of figurative utterances? Why do we use expressions metaphorically instead of saying exactly and literally what we mean? How do metaphorical utterances work, that is, how is it possible for speakers to communicate to hearers when speaking metaphorically inasmuch as they do not say what they mean? And why do some metaphors work and others do not?

Reprinted from *Expression and Meaning* by John R. Searle, Cambridge University Press, 1979, pp. 76-116, by permission of the author and Cambridge University Press.

In my discussion, I propose to tackle this latter set of questions —those centering around the problem of how metaphors work—both because of its intrinsic interest, and because it does not seem to me that we shall get an answer to the others until this fundamental question has been answered. Before we can begin to understand it, however, we need to formulate the question more precisely.

The problem of explaining how metaphors work is a special case of the general problem of explaining how speaker's meaning and sentence or word meaning come apart. It is a special case, that is, of the problem of how it is possible to say one thing and mean something else, occasions where one succeeds in communicating what one means even though both the speaker and the hearer know that the meanings of the words uttered by the speaker do not exactly and literally express what the speaker meant. Some other instances of the break between speaker's utterance meaning and literal sentence meaning are irony and indirect speech acts. In each of these cases, what the speaker means is not identical with what the sentence means, and yet what he means is in various ways dependent on what the sentence means.

It is essential to emphasize at the very beginning that the problem of metaphor concerns the relations between word and sentence meaning, on the one hand, and speaker's meaning or utterance meaning, on the other. Many writers on the subject try to locate the metaphorical element of a metaphorical utterance in the sentence or expressions uttered. They think there are two kinds of sentence meaning, literal and metaphorical. However, sentences and words have only the meanings that they have. Strictly speaking, whenever we talk about the metaphorical meaning of a word, expression, or sentence, we are talking about what a speaker might utter it to mean, in a way that departs from what the word, expression, or sentence actually means. We are, therefore, talking about possible speaker's intentions. Even when we discuss how a nonsense sentence, such as Chomsky's example, "Colorless green ideas sleep furiously", could be given a metaphorical interpretation, what we are talking about is how a speaker could utter the sentence and mean something by it metaphorically, even though it is literally nonsensical. To have a brief way of distinguishing what a speaker means by uttering words, sentences, and expressions, on the one hand, and what the words, sentences, and expressions mean, on the other, I shall call the former *speaker's utterance meaning*, and the latter, *word, or sentence, meaning.* Metaphorical meaning is always speaker's utterance meaning.

In order that the speaker can communicate using metaphorical utterances, ironical utterances, and indirect speech acts, there must be some principles according to which he is able to mean more than, or something different from, what he says—principles known to the hearer, who, using this knowledge, can understand what the speaker means. The relation between the sentence meaning and the metaphorical utterance meaning is systematic rather than random or ad hoc. Our task in constructing a theory of metaphor is to try to state the principles which relate literal sentence meaning to metaphorical utterance meaning. Because the knowledge that enables people to use and understand metaphorical utterances goes beyond their knowledge of the literal meanings of words and sentences, the principles we seek are not included, or at least not entirely included, within a theory of semantic competence as traditionally conceived. From the point of view of the hearer, the problem of a theory of metaphor is to explain how he can understand the speaker's utterance meaning given that all he hears is a sentence with its word and sentence meaning. From the point of view of the speaker, the problem is to explain how he can mean something different from the word and sentence meaning of the sentence he utters. In the light of these reflections our original question, How do metaphors work? can be recast as follows: What are the principles that enable speakers to formulate, and hearers to understand, metaphorical utterances? and How can we state these principles in a way that makes it clear how metaphorical utterances differ from other sorts of utterances in which speaker meaning does not coincide with literal meaning?

Because part of our task is to explain how metaphorical utterances differ from literal utterances, to start with we must arrive at a characterization of literal utterances. Most—indeed all—of the authors I have read on the subject of metaphor assume that we know how literal utterances work; they do not think that the problem of literal utterances is worth discussing in their account of metaphor. The price they pay for this is that their accounts often describe metaphorical utterances in ways that fail to distinguish them from literal ones.

In fact, to give an accurate account of literal predication is an extremely difficult, complex, and subtle problem. I shall not attempt anything like a thorough summary of the principles of literal utterance but shall remark on only those features which are essential for a comparison of literal utterance with metaphorical utterance. Also, for the sake of simplicity, I shall confine most of my discussion of both literal and metaphorical utterance to very simple cases, and to sentences used for the speech act of assertion.

Imagine that a speaker makes a literal utterance of a sentence such as

1. Sally is tall
2. The cat is on the mat
3. It's getting hot in here.

Now notice that, in each of these cases, the literal meaning of the sentence determines, at least in part, a set of truth conditions; and because the only illocutionary force indicating devices (see Searle, 1969) in the sentences are assertive, the literal and serious utterance of one of these sentences will commit the speaker to the existence of the set of truth conditions determined by the meaning of that sentence, together with the other determinants of truth conditions. Notice, furthermore, that in each case the sentence only determines a definite set of truth conditions relative to a particular context. That is because each of these examples has some indexical element, such as the present tense, or the demonstrative "here", or the occurrence of contextually dependent definite descriptions, such as "the cat" and "the mat".

In these examples, the contextually dependent elements of the sentence are explicitly realized in the semantic structure of the sentence: One can see and hear the indexical expressions. But these sentences, like most sentences, only determine a set of truth conditions against a background of assumptions that are not explicitly realized in the semantic structure of the sentence. This is most obvious for 1 and 3, because they contain the relative terms "tall" and "hot". These are what old-fashioned grammarians called "attributive" terms, and they only determine a definite set of truth conditions against a background of factual assumptions about the sort of things referred to by the speaker in the rest of the sentence.

Moreover, these assumptions are not explicitly realized in the semantic structure of the sentence. Thus, a woman can be correctly described as "tall" even though she is shorter than a giraffe that could correctly be described as "short".

Though this dependence of the application of the literal meaning of the sentence on certain factual background assumptions that are not part of the literal meaning is most obvious for sentences containing attributive terms, the phenomenon is quite general. Sentence 2 only determines a definite set of truth conditions given certain assumptions about cats, mats, and the relation of being on. However, these assumptions are not part of the semantic content of the sentence. Suppose, for example, that the cat and mat are in the usual cat-on-mat spatial configuration, only both cat and mat are in outer space, outside any gravitational field relative to which one could be said to be "above" or "over" the other. Is the cat still *on* the mat? Without some further assumptions, the sentence does not determine a definite set of truth conditions in this context. Or suppose all cats suddenly became lighter than air, and the cat went flying about with the mat stuck to its belly. Is the cat still on the mat?

We know without hesitation what are the truth conditions of, "The fly is on the ceiling", but not of, "The cat is on the ceiling," and this difference is not a matter of meaning, but a matter of how our factual background information enables us to apply the meanings of sentences. In general, one can say that in most cases a sentence only determines a set of truth conditions relative to a set of assumptions that are not realized in the semantic content of the sentence. Thus, even in literal utterances, where speaker's meaning coincides with sentence meaning, the speaker must contribute more to the literal utterance than just the semantic content of the sentence, because that semantic content only determines a set of truth conditions relative to a set of assumptions made by the speaker, and if communication is to be successful his assumptions must be shared by the hearer. (For further discussion on this point, see Searle, 1978.)

Notice finally that the notion of similarity plays a crucial role in any account of literal utterance. This is because the literal meaning of any general term, by determining a set of truth conditions, also determines a criterion of similarity between objects. To know that a general term is true of a set of objects is to know that they are similar with respect to the property specified by that term. All tall women are similar with respect to being tall, all hot rooms similar with respect to being hot, all square objects similar with respect to being square, and so on.

To summarize this brief discussion of some aspects of literal utterance, there are three features we shall need to keep in mind in our account of metaphorical utterance. First, in literal utterance the speaker means what he says; that is, literal sentence meaning and speaker's utterance meaning are the same; second, in general the literal meaning of a sentence only determines a set of truth conditions relative to a set of background assumptions which are not part of the semantic content of the sentence; and third, the notion of similarity plays an essential role in any account of literal predication.

When we turn to cases where utterance meaning and sentence meaning are different, we find them quite various. Thus, for example, 3 could be uttered not only to tell somebody that it is getting hot in the place of utterance (literal utterance), but it could also be used to request somebody to open a window (indirect speech act), to complain about how cold it is (ironical utterance), or to remark on the increasing vituperation of an argument that is in progress (metaphorical utterance). In our account of metaphorical utterance, we shall need to distinguish it not only from literal utterance, but also from these other forms in which literal utterance is departed from, or exceeded, in some way.

Because in metaphorical utterances what the speaker means differs from what he says (in one sense of "say"), in general we shall need two sentences for our examples of metaphor—first the sentence uttered metaphorically, and second a sentence that expresses literally what the speaker means when he utters the first sentence and means it metaphorically. Thus 3, the metaphor (MET):

3. (MET) It's getting hot in here

corresponds to 3, the paraphrase (PAR):

3. (PAR) The argument that is going on is becoming more vituperative

and similarly with the pairs:

4. (MET) Sally is a block of ice

4. (PAR) Sally is an extremely unemotional and unresponsive person

5. (MET) I have climbed to the top of the greasy pole (Disraeli)

5. (PAR) I have after great difficulty become prime minister

6. (MET) Richard is a gorilla

6. (PAR) Richard is fierce, nasty, and prone to violence.

Notice that in each case we feel that the paraphrase is somehow inadequate, that something is lost. One of our tasks will be to explain this sense of dissatisfaction that we have with paraphrases of even feeble metaphors. Still, in some sense, the paraphrases must approximate what the speaker meant, because in each case the speaker's metaphorical assertion will be true if, and only if, the corresponding assertion using the "PAR" sentence is true. When we get to more elaborate examples, our sense of the inadequacy of the paraphrase becomes more acute. How would we paraphrase

7. (MET) My Life had stood—a Loaded Gun—
   In Corners—till a Day
   The Owner passed—identified—
   And carried Me away—(Emily Dickinson)?

Clearly a good deal is lost by

7. (PAR) My life was one of unrealized but readily realizable potential (a loaded gun) in mediocre surroundings (corners) until such time (a day) when my destined lover (the owner) came (passed), recognized my potential (identified), and took (carried) me away.

Yet, even in this case, the paraphrase or something like it must express a large part of speaker's utterance meaning, because the truth conditions are the same.

Sometimes we feel that we know exactly what the metaphor means and yet would not be able to formualte a literal "PAR" sentence because there are no literal expressions that convey what it means. Thus even for such a simple case as

8. (MET) The ship ploughed the sea,

we may not be able to construct a simple paraphrase sentence even tough there is no obscurity in the metaphorical utterance. And indeed metaphors often serve to plug such semantic gaps as this. In other cases, there may be an indefinite range of paraphrases. For example, when Romeo says:

9. (MET) Juliet is the sun,

there may be a range of things he might mean. But while lamenting the inadequacy of paraphrases, let us also recall that paraphrase is a symmetrical relation. To say that the paraphrase is a poor paraphrase of the metaphor is also to say that the metaphor is a poor paraphrase of its paraphrase. Furthermore, we should not feel apologetic about the fact that some of our examples are trite or dead metaphors. Dead metaphors are especially interesting for our study, because, to speak oxymoronically, dead metaphors have lived on. They have become dead through continual use, but their continual use is a clue that they satisfy some semantic need.

Confining ourselves to the simplest subject-predicate cases, we can say that the general form of the metaphorical utterance is that a speaker utters a sentence of the form "S is P" and means metaphorically that S is R. In analyzing metaphorical predication, we need to distinguish, therefore, between three sets of elements. Firstly, there is the subject expression "S" and the object or objects it is used to refer to. Secondly, there is a predicate expression "P" that is uttered and the literal meaning of that expression with its corresponding truth conditions, plus the denotation if there is any. And thirdly, there is the speaker's utterance meaning "S is R" and the truth conditions determined by that meaning. In its simplest form, the problem of metaphor is to try to get a characterization of the relations between the three sets, S, P, and R,[1] together with a specification of other information and principles used by speakers and hearers, so as to explain how it is possible to utter "S is P" and mean "S is R", and how it is possible to communicate that meaning from speaker to hearer. Now, obviously, that is not all there is to understand about metaphorical utterances; the speaker does more than just assert that S is R, and the peculiar effectiveness of metaphor will have to be explained in terms of how he does more than just assert that S is R and why he should choose this roundabout way of asserting that S is R in the first place. But at this stage we are starting at the beginning. At the very minimum, a theory of metaphor must explain how it is possible to utter "*S* is *P*" and both mean and communicate that *S* is *R*.

We can now state one of the differences between literal and metaphorical utterances as applied to these simple examples: In the case of literal utterance, speaker's meaning and sentence meaning are the same; therefore the assertion made about the object referred to will be true if and only if it satisfies the truth conditions determined by the meaning of the general term as applied against a set of shared background assumptions. In order to understand the utterance, the hearer does not require any extra knowledge beyond his knowledge of the rules of language, his awareness of the conditions of utterance, and a set of shared background assumptions. But, in the case of metaphorical utterance, the truth conditions of the assertion are not determined by the truth conditions of the sentence and its general term. In order to understand the metaphorical utterance, the hearer requires something more than his knowledge of the language, his awareness of the conditions of the utterance, and background assumptions that he shares with the speaker. He must have some other principles, or some other factual information, or some combination of principles and information that enables him to figure out that when the speaker says, "*S* is *P*", he means "*S* is *R*". What is this extra element?

I believe that, at the most general level, the question has a fairly simple answer, but it will take me much of the rest of this discussion to work it out in any detail. The basic principle on which all metaphor works is that the utterance of an expression with its literal meaning and corresponding truth conditions can, in various ways that are specific to metaphor, call to mind another meaning and corresponding set of truth conditions. The hard problem of the .theory of metaphor is to explain what exactly are the principles according to which the utterance of an expression can metaphorically call to mind a different set of truth conditions from the one determined by its literal meaning, and to state those principles precisely and without using metaphorical expressions like "call to mind".

Some Common Mistakes about Metaphor

Before attempting to sketch a theory of metaphor, I want in this section and the next to backtrack a bit and examine some existing theories. Roughly speaking, theories of metaphor from Aristotle to the present can be divided into two types.[2] Comparison theories assert that metaphorical utterances involve a *comparison* or *similarity* between two or more *objects* (e.g., Aristotle; Henle, 1965), and semantic interaction theories claim that metaphor involves a *verbal opposition* (Beardsley, 1962) or *interaction* (Black, 1962) between two *semantic contents*, that of the expression used metaphorically, and that of the surrounding literal context. I think that both of these theories, if one tries to take them quite literally, are in various ways inadequate; nonetheless, they are both trying to say something true, and we ought to try to extract what is true in them. But first I want to show some of the common mistakes they contain and some further common mistakes made in discussions of metaphor. My aim here is not polemical; rather, I am trying to clear the ground for the development of a theory of metaphor. One might say the endemic vice of the comparison theories is that they fail to distinguish between the claim that the statement of the comparison is part of the *meaning*, and hence the *truth conditions* of the metaphorical statement, and the claim that the statement of the similarity is the *principle of inference*, or a step in the process of *comprehending*, on the basis of which speakers produce and hearers understand metaphor. (More about this distinction later.) The semantic interaction theories were developed in response to the weaknesses of the comparison theories, and they have little independent argument to recommend them other than the weakness of their rivals: Their endemic vice is the failure to appreciate the distinction between sentence or word meaning, which is never metaphorical, and speaker or utterance meaning, which can be metaphorical. They usually try to locate metaphorical meaning in the sentence or some set of associations with the sentence. In any event, here are half a dozen mistakes which I believe should be noted:

It is often said that in metaphorical utterances there is a change in meaning of at least one expression. I wish to say that on the contrary, strictly speaking, in metaphor there is never a change of meaning;

diachronically speaking, metaphors do indeed initiate semantic changes, but to the extent that there has been a genuine change in meaning, so that a word or expression no longer means what it previously did, to precisely that extent the locution is no longer metaphorical. We are all familiar with the processes whereby an expression becomes a dead metaphor, and then finally becomes an idiom or acquires a new meaning different from the original meaning. But in a genuine metaphorical utterance, it is only because the expressions have not changed their meaning that there is a metaphorical utterance at all. The people who make this claim seem to be confusing *sentence* meaning with *speaker's* meaning. The metaphorical utterance does indeed mean something different from the meaning of the words and sentences, but that is not because there has been any change in the meanings of the lexical elements, but because the speaker means something different by them; speaker meaning does not coincide with sentence or word meaning. It is essential to see this point, because the main problem of metaphor is to explain how speaker meaning and sentence meaning are different and how they are, nevertheless, related. Such an explanation is impossible if we suppose that sentence or word meaning has changed in the metaphorical utterance.

The simplest way to show that the crude versions of the comparison view are false is to show that, in the production and understanding of metaphorical utterances, there need not be any two objects for comparison. When I say metaphorically

4.   (MET) Sally is a block of ice,

I am not necessarily quantifying over blocks of ice at all. My utterance does not entail literally that

10. $(\exists x)$ (x is a block of ice),

and such that I am comparing Sally to x. This point is even more obvious if we take expressions used as metaphors which have a null extension. If I say

11. Sally is a dragon

that does not entail literally

12. $(\exists x)$ (x is a dragon).

Or, another way to see the same thing is to note that the negative utterance is just as metaphorical as the affirmative. If I say

13. Sally is not a block of ice,

that, I take it, does not invite the absurd question: Which block of ice is it that you are comparing Sally with, in order to say that she is not like it? At its *crudest*, the comparison theory is just muddled about the referential character of expressions used metaphorically.

Now, this might seem a somewhat minor objection to the comparison theorists, but it paves the way for a much more radical objection. Comparison theories which are explicit on the point at all, generally treat the statement of the comparison as part of the meaning and hence as part of the truth conditions of the metaphorical statement. For example, Miller (1979) is quite explicit in regarding metaphorical statements as statements of similarity, and indeed for such theorists the meaning of a *metaphorical* statement is always given by an explicit *statement* of similarity. Thus, in their view, I have not even formulated the problem correctly. According to me, the problem of explaining (simple subject—predicate) metaphors is to explain how the speaker and hearer go from the literal sentence meaning "S is P" to the metaphorical utterance meaning "S is R". But, according to them, that is not the utterance meaning; rather the utterance meaning must be expressible by an explicit statement of similarity, such as "S is like P with respect to R", or in Miller's case, the metaphorical statement "S is P" is to be analyzed as, "There is some property F and some property G such that S's being F is similar to P's being G". I will have more to say about this thesis and its exact formulation later, but at present I want to claim that though similarity often plays a role in the *comprehension* of metaphor, the metaphorical assertion is not necessarily an *assertion* of similarity. The simplest argument that metaphorical assertions are not always assertions of similarity is that given above: there are true metaphorical assertions for which there are no objects to be designated by the P term, hence the true metaphorical statement cannot falsely presuppose the existence of an object of comparison. But even where there are objects of comparison, the metaphorical assertion is not necessarily an assertion of similarity. Similarity, I shall argue, has to do with the production and understanding of metaphor, not with its meaning.

A second simple argument to show that metaphorical assertions are not necessarily assertions of similarity is that often the metaphorical assertion can remain true even though it turns out that the statement of similarity on which the inference to the metaphorical meaning is based is false. Thus, suppose I say,

    6. (MET) Richard is a gorilla

meaning

    6. (PAR) Richard is fierce, nasty, prone to violence, and so forth.

And suppose the hearer's inference to 6 (PAR) is based on the belief that

    14. Gorillas are fierce, nasty, prone to violence, and so forth.

and hence 6 (MET) and 14, on the comparison view, would justify the inference to

    15. Richard and gorillas are similar in several respects; *viz.*, they are fierce, nasty, prone to violence, and so forth.

and this in turn would be part of the inference pattern that enabled the hearer to conclude that when I uttered 6 (MET) I meant 6 (PAR). But suppose ethological investigation shows, as I am told it has, that gorillas are not at all fierce and nasty, but are in fact shy, sensitive creatures, given to bouts of sentimentality. This would definitely show that 15 is false, for 15 is as much an assertion about gorillas as about Richard. But would it show that when I uttered 6 (MET), what I said was false? Clearly not, for what I meant was 6 (PAR), and 6 (PAR) is an assertion about Richard. It can remain true regardless of the actual facts about gorillas; though, of course, what expressions we use to convey metaphorically certain semantic contents will normally depend on what we take the facts to be.

To put it crudely, "Richard is a gorilla", is just about Richard; it is not literally about gorillas at all. The word "gorilla" here serves to convey a certain semantic content other than its own meaning by a set of principles I have yet to state. But 15 is literally about both

Richard and gorillas, and it is true if and only if they both share the properties it claims they do. Now, it may well be true that the hearer employs something like 15 as a step in the procedures that get him from 6 (MET) to 6 (PAR), but it does not follow from this fact about his *procedures of comprehension* that this is part of the *speaker's utterance meaning* of 6 (MET); and, indeed, that it is not part of the utterance meaning is shown by the fact that the metaphorical statement can be *true* even if it turns out that gorillas do not have the traits that the metaphorical occurrence of "gorilla" served to convey. I am not saying that a metaphorical assertion can *never* be equivalent in meaning to a statement of similarity—whether or not it is would depend on the intentions of the speaker, but I am saying that it is not a necessary feature of metaphor—and is certainly not the point of having metaphor—that metaphorical assertions are equivalent in meaning to statements of similarity. My argument is starkly simple: In many cases the metaphorical statement and the corresponding similarity statement cannot be equivalent in meaning because they have different truth conditions. The difference between the view I am attacking and the one I shall espouse is this. According to the view I am attacking, 6 (MET) *means* Richard and gorillas are similar in certain respects. According to the view I shall espouse, similarity functions as a comprehension strategy, not as a component of meaning: 6 (MET) says that Richard has certain traits (and to figure out what they are, look for features associated with gorillas). On my account the *P* term need not figure literally in the statement of the truth conditions of the metaphorical statement at all.

Similar remarks apply incidentally to similes. If I say,

16. Sam acts like a gorilla

that need not commit me to the truth of

17. Gorillas are such that their behaviour resembles Sam's.

For 16 need not be about gorillas at all, and we might say that "gorilla" in 16 has a metaphorical occurrence. Perhaps this is one way we might distinguish between figurative similes and literal statements of similarity. Figurative similes need not necessarily commit the speaker to a literal statement of similarity.

The semantic interaction view, it seems to me, is equally defective. One of the assumptions behind the view that metaphorical meaning is a result of an interaction between an expression used metaphorically and other expressions used literally is that all metaphorical uses of expressions must occur in sentences containing literal uses of expressions, and that assumption seems to me plainly false. It is, incidentally, the assumption behind the terminology of many of the contemporary discussions of metaphor. We are told, for example, that every metaphorical sentence contains a "tenor" and a "vehicle" (Richards, 1936) or a "frame" and a "focus" (Black, 1962). But it is not the case that every metaphorical use of an expression is surrounded by literal uses of other expressions. Consider again our example 4: In uttering, "Sally is a block of ice", we referred to Sally using her proper name literally, but we need not have. Suppose, to use a mixed metaphor, we refer to Sally as "the bad news". We could then say, using a mixed metaphor

18. The bad news is a block of ice.

If you insist that the "is" is still literal, it is easy enough to construct examples of a dramatic change on Sally's part where we would be inclined, in another mixed metaphor, to say

19. The bad news congealed into a block of ice.

Mixed metaphors may be stylistically objectionable, but I cannot see that they are necessarily logically incoherent. Of course, most metaphors do occur in contexts of expressions used literally. It would be very hard to understand them if they did not. But it is not a logical necessity that every metaphorical use of an expression occurs surrounded by literal occurrences of other expressions and, indeed, many famous examples of metaphor are not. Thus Russell's example of a completely nonsensical sentence, "Quadrilaterality drinks procrastination", is often given a metaphorical interpretation as a description of any postwar four-power disarmament conference, but none of the words, so interpreted, has a literal occurrence; that is, for every word the speaker's utterance meaning differs from the literal word meaning.

However, the most serious objection to the semantic interaction view is not that it falsely presupposes that all metaphorical occurrences of words must be surrounded by literal occurrence of other words, but rather that, even where the metaphorical occurrence is within the context of literal occurrences, it is not in general the case that the metaphorical speaker's meaning is a result of any inter- action among the elements of the sentence in any literal sense of "interaction". Consider again our example 4. In its metaphorical utterances, there is no question of any interaction between the meaning of the "principal subject" ("Sally") and the "subsidiary subject" ("block of ice"). "Sally" is a proper name; it does not have a meaning in quite the way in which "block of ice" has a meaning. Indeed, other expressions could have been used to produce the same metaphorical predication. Thus,

20. Miss Jones is a block of ice

or

21. That girl over there in the corner is a block of ice

could have been uttered with the same metaphorical utterance mean- ing.

I conclude that, as general theories, both the object comparison view and the semantic interaction view are inadequate. If we were to diagnose their failure in Fregean terms, we might say that the comparison view tries to explain metaphor as a relation between references, and the interaction view tries to explain it as a relation between senses and beliefs associated with references. The propon- ents of the interaction view see correctly that the mental processes and the semantic processes involved in producing and understanding metaphorical utterances cannot involve references themselves, but must be at the level of intentionality, that is, they must involve re- lations at the level of beliefs, meanings, associations, and so on. How- ever, they then say incorrectly that the relations in question must be some unexplained, but metaphorically described, relations of "inter- action"[3] between a literal frame and a metaphorical focus.

Two final mistakes I wish to note are not cases of saying something false about metaphors but of saying something true which fails to distinguish metaphor from literal utterance. Thus it is sometimes said that the notion of similarity plays a crucial role in the analysis of a metaphor, or that metaphorical utterances are dependent on the context for their interpretation. But, as we saw earlier, both of these features are true of literal utterances as well. An analysis of metaphor must show how similarity and context play a role in metaphor different from their role in literal utterance.

A Further Examination of the Comparison Theory

One way to work up to a theory of metaphor would be to examine the strengths and weaknesses of one of the existing theories. The obvious candidate for this role of stalking horse is a version of the comparison theory that goes back to Aristotle and can, indeed, probably be considered the commonsense view—the theory that says all metaphor is really literal simile with the "like" or "as" deleted and the respect of the similarity left unspecified. Thus, according to this view, the metaphorical utterance, "Man is a wolf", means "Man is like a wolf in certain unspecified ways"; the utterance, "You are my sunshine", means "You are like sunshine to me in certain respects", and "Sally is a block of ice", means "Sally is like a block of ice in certain but so far unspecified ways".

The principles on which metaphors function, then, according to this theory are the same as those for literal statements of similarity together with the principle of ellipsis. We understand the metaphor as a shortened version of the literal simile.[4] Since literal simile requires no special extralinguistic knowledge for its comprehension, most of the knowledge necessary for the comprehension of metaphor is already contained in the speaker's and hearer's semantic competence, together with the general background knowledge of the world that makes literal meaning comprehensible.

We have already seen certain defects of this view, most notably that metaphorical statements cannot be equivalent in meaning to literal statements of similarity because the truth conditions of the two sorts of statements are frequently different. Furthermore, we must emphasize that even as a theory of metaphorical comprehension —as opposed to a theory of metaphorical meaning—it is important for the simile theory that the alleged underlying similes be literal statements of similarity. If the simile statements which are supposed to explain metaphor are themselves metaphorical or otherwise figurative, our explanation will be circular.

Still, treated as a theory of comprehension, there do seem to be a large number of cases where for the metaphorical utterance we can construct a simile sentence that does seem in some way to explain how its metaphorical meaning is comprehended. And, indeed, the fact that the specification of the values of R is left vague by the simile statement may, in fact, be an advantage of the theory, inasmuch as metaphorical utterances are often vague in precisely that way: it is not made *exactly* clear what the R is supposed to be when we say that "S is P" meaning metaphorically that "S is R". Thus, for example, in analyzing Romeo's metaphorical statement, "Juliet is the sun", Cavell (1976, pp. 78-9) gives as part of its explanation that Romeo means that his day begins with Juliet. Now, apart from the special context of the play, that reading would never occur to me. I would look for other properties of the sun to fill in the values of R in the formula. Saying this is not objecting to either Shakespeare or Cavell, because the metaphor in question, like most metaphors, is open-ended in precisely that way.

Nonetheless, the simile theory, in spite of its attractiveness, has serious difficulties. First, the theory does more — or rather, less — than fail to tell us how to compute the value of R exactly: So far it fails to tell us how to compute it at all. That is, the theory still has almost no explanatory power, because the task of a theory of metaphor is to explain how the speaker and hearer are able to go from "S is P" to "S is R", and it does not explain that process to tell us that they go from "S is P" to "S is R" by first going through the stage "S is like P with respect to R" because we are not told how we are supposed to figure out which values to assign to R. Similarity is a vacuous predicate: any two things are similar in some respect or other. Saying that the metaphorical "S is P" implies the literal "S is like P" does not solve our problem. It only pushes it back a step. The problem of understanding literal similes with the respect of the similarity left unspecified is only a part of the problem of understanding metaphor. How are we supposed to know, for example, that the utterance, "Juliet is the sun", does not mean "Juliet is for the most part gaseous", or "Juliet is 90 million miles from the earth", both of which properties are salient and well-known features of the sun.

Yet another objection is this: It is crucial to the simile thesis that the simile be taken literally; yet there seem to be a great many

metaphorical utterances where there is no relevant literal corresponding similarity between S and P. If we insist that there are always such
similes, it looks as if we would have to interpret them metaphorically,
and thus our account would be circular. Consider our example 4,
"Sally is a block of ice". If we were to enumerate quite literally the
various distinctive qualities of blocks of ice, none of them would be
true of Sally. Even if we were to throw in the various beliefs that
people have about blocks of ice, they still would not be literally true
of Sally. There simply is no class of predicates, R, such that Sally is
literally like a block of ice with respect to R where R is what we intended to predicate metaphorically of Sally when we said she was a
block of ice. Being unemotional is not a feature of blocks of ice because blocks of ice are not in that line of business at all, and if one
wants to insist that blocks of ice are literally unresponsive, then we
need only point out that that feature is still insufficient to explain
the metaphorical utterance meaning of 4, because in that sense bon-
fires are "unresponsive" as well, but

22. Sally is a bonfire

has a quite different metaphorical utterance meaning from 4. Furthermore, there are many similes that are not intended literally.
For example, an utterance of "My love is like a red, red rose" does
not mean that there is a class of literal predicates that are true both
of my love and red, red roses and that express what the speaker was
driving at when he said his love was like a red, red rose.

The defender of the simile thesis, however, need not give up so
easily. He might say that many metaphors are also examples of other
figures as well. Thus, "Sally is a block of ice" is not only an example
of metaphor, but of hyperbole as well.[5] The metaphorical utterance
meaning is indeed derived from the simile, "Sally is like a block of
ice", but then both the metaphor and the simile are cases of *hyperbole*; they are exaggerations, and indeed, many metaphors are exaggerations. According to this reply, if we interpret both the metaphor and the simile hyperbolically, they are equivalent.

Furthermore, the defender of the simile thesis might add that it is
not an objection to the simile account to say that some of the respects in which Sally is like a block of ice will be specified metaphorically, because for each of these metaphorical similes we can specify

another underlying simile until eventually we reach the rock bottom of literal similes on which the whole edifice rests. Thus "Sally is a block of ice" means "Sally is like a block of ice", which means "She shares certain traits with a block of ice, in particular she is very cold". But since "cold" in "Sally is very cold" is also metaphorical, there must be an underlying similarity in which Sally's emotional state is like coldness, and when we finally specify these respects, the metaphor will be completely analyzed.

There are really two stages to this reply: First, it points out that other figures such as hyperbole sometimes combine with metaphor, and, secondly, it concedes that some of the similes that we can offer as translations of the metaphor are still metaphorical, but insists that some recursive procedure of analyzing metaphorical similes will eventually lead us to literal similes.

Is this reply really adequate? I think not. The trouble is that there do not seem to be any literal similarities between objects which are cold and people who are unemotional that would justify the view that when we say metaphorically that someone is cold what we mean is that he or she is unemotional. In what respects exactly are unemotional people like cold objects? Well, there are some things that one can say in answer to this, but they all leave us feeling somewhat dissatisfied.

We can say, for example, that when someone is physically cold it places severe restrictions on their emotions. But even if that is true, it is not what we meant by the metaphorical utterance. I think the only answer to the question, "What is the relation between cold things and unemotional people that would justify the use of 'cold' as a metaphor for lack of emotion?" is simply that as a matter of perceptions, sensibilities, and linguistic practices, people find the notion of coldness associated in their minds with lack of emotion. The notion of being cold just is associated with being unemotional.

There is some evidence, incidentally, that this metaphor works across several different cultures: It is not confined to English speakers (cf. Asch, 1958). Moreover, it is even becoming, or has become, a dead metaphor. Some dictionaries (e.g. the *OED*) list lack of emotion as one of the meanings of "cold". Temperature metaphors for emotional and personal traits are in fact quite common and they are not derived from any literal underlying similarities. Thus we speak of a "heated argument", "a warm welcome", "a lukewarm friendship", and "sexual frigidity". Such metaphors are fatal for the simile thesis, unless the defenders can produce a literal R which S and P have in common, and which is sufficient to explain the precise metaphorical meaning which is conveyed.

Because this point is bound to be contested, it is well to emphasize exactly what is at stake. In claiming that there are not sufficient similarities to explain utterance meaning, I am making a negative existential claim, and thus not one which is demonstrable from an examination of a finite number of instances. The onus is rather on the similarity theorist to state the similarities and show how they exhaust utterance meaning. But it is not at all easy to see how he could do that in a way that would satisfy the constraints of his own theory.

Of course, one can think of lots of ways in which any S is like any P, e.g. ways in which Sally is like a block of ice, and one can think of lots of Fs and Gs such that Sally's being F is like a block of ice's being G. But that is not enough. Such similarities as one can name do not exhaust utterance meaning and if there are others that do, they are certainly not obvious.

But suppose with some ingenuity one could think up a similarity that would exhaust utterance meaning. The very fact that it takes so much ingenuity to think it up makes it unlikely that it is the underlying principle of the metaphorical interpretation, inasmuch as the metaphor is obvious: There is no difficulty for any native speaker to explain what it means. In "Sam is a pig", both utterance meaning and similarities are obvious, but in "Sally is a block of ice", only the utterance meaning is obvious. The simpler hypothesis, then, is that this metaphor like several others I shall now discuss, functions on principles other than similarity.

Once we start looking for them, this class of metaphors turns out to be quite large. For example, the numerous spatial metaphors for temporal duration are not based on literal similarities. In "time flies", or "the hours crawled by", what is it that time does and the hours did which is literally like flying or crawling? We are tempted to say they went rapidly or slowly respectively, but of course "went rapidly" and "went slowly" are further spatial metaphors. Similarly, taste metaphors for personal traits are not based on properties in common. We speak of a "sweet disposition" or a "bitter person", without implying that the sweet disposition and the bitter person have literal traits in common with sweet and bitter tastes which exhaust the utterance meaning of the metaphorical utterance. Of course, sweet dispositions and sweet things are both pleasant, but much more is conveyed by the metaphor than mere pleasantness.

So deeply embedded in our whole mode of sensibility are certain metaphorical associations that we tend to think there *must* be a similarity, or even that the association itself is a form of similarity. Thus, we feel inclined to say that the passage of time *just is like* spatial movement, but when we say this we forget that "passage" is only yet another spatial metaphor for time and that the bald assertion of similarity, with no specification of the respect of similarity, is without content.

The most sophisticated version of the simile thesis I have seen is by George Miller (1979), and I shall digress briefly to consider some of its special features. Miller, like other simile theorists, believes that the meanings of metaphorical statements can be expressed as statements of similarity, but he offers a special kind of similarity statement (rather like one of Aristotle's formulations, by the way) as the form of "reconstruction" of metaphorical statements. According to Miller, metaphors of the form "S is P", where both S and P are noun phrases, are equivalent to sentences of the form

23. $(\exists F)(\exists G)(\text{SIM}(F(S),G(P)))$.

Thus, for example, "Man is a wolf", according to Miller would be analyzed as

24. There is some property F and some property G such that man's being F is similar to a wolf's being G.

And when we have metaphors where a verb or predicate adjective F is used metaphorically in a sentence of the form "x is F" or "xFs", the analysis is of the form

25. $(\exists G)\,(\exists y)\,(\text{SIM}(G(x),F(y)))$.

Thus, for example, "The problem is thorny" would be analyzed as

26. There is some property G and some object y such that the problem's being G is similar to y's being thorny.

I believe this account has all the difficulties of the other simile theories—namely, it mistakenly supposes that the use of a meta-phorical predicate commits the speaker to the existence of objects of which that predicate is literally true; it confuses the truth con-ditions of the metaphorical statement with the principles under which it is comprehended; it fails to tell us how to compute the values of the variables (Miller is aware of this problem, he calls it the problem of "interpretation" and sees it as different from the problem of "reconstruction"); and it is refuted by the fact that not all metaphors have literal statements of similarity under-lying them. But it has some additional problems of its own. In my view, the most serious weakness of Miller's account is that ac-cording to it the semantic contents of most metaphorical utter-ances would have too many predicates, and, in fact, rather few metaphors really satisfy the formal structure he provides us with. Consider, for example, "Man is a wolf". On what I believe is the most plausible version of the simile thesis, it means something of the form

27. Man is like a wolf in certain respects R.

We could represent this as

28. SIM_R (man, wolf).

The hearer is required to compute only one set of predicates, the values for R. But according to Miller's account, the hearer is requir-ed to compute no less than three sets of predicates. Inasmuch as sim-ilarity is a vacuous predicate, we need to be told in which respect two things are similar for the statement that they are similar to have any informative content. His formalization of the above metaphorical utterance is

29. $(\exists F) (\exists G) (SIM(F(man),G(wolf)))$.

In order to complete this formula in a way that would specify the respect of the similarity we would have to rewrite it as

30. $(\exists F) (\exists G) (\exists H)(SIM_H (F(man),G(wolf)))$.

But both the reformulation 30, and Miller's 29, contain too many predicate variables. When I say, "Man is a wolf", I am not saying that there are some *different* sets of properties that men have from those that wolves have, I am saying they have the *same* set of properties (at least on a sympathetic construal of the simile thesis, that is what I am saying). But according to Miller's account, I am saying that man has one set of properties F, wolves have a different set of properties G, and man's having F is similar to wolves having G with respect to some other properties H. I argue that this "reconstruction" is (a) counterintuitive, (b) unmotivated, and (c) assigns an impossible computing task to the speaker and hearer. What are these Fs, Gs and Hs supposed to be? and how is the hearer supposed to figure them out? It is not surprising that his treatment of the interpretation problem is very sketchy. Similar objections apply to his accounts of other syntactical forms of metaphorical utterances.

There is a class of metaphors, that I shall call "relational metaphors", for which something like his analysis might be more appropriate. Thus, if I say

8. The ship ploughed the sea

or

31. Washington is the father of his country,

these might be interpreted using something like his forms. We might treat 8 as equivalent to

32. There is some relation R which the ship has to the sea and which is similar to the relation that ploughs have to fields when they plough fields;

and 31 as

33. There is some relation R which Washington has to his country and which is like the relation that fathers have to their offspring.

And 32 and 33 are fairly easily formalized *à la* Miller. However, even these analyses seem to me to concede too much to his approach: 8 makes no reference either implicitly or explicitly to fields and 31 makes no reference to offspring. On the simplest and most plausible version of the simile thesis 8 and 31 are equivalent to:

34. The ship does something to the sea which is like ploughing

and

35. Washington stands in a relation to his country which is like the relation of being a father.

And the hearer's task is simply to compute the intended relations in the two cases. By my account, which I shall develop in the next section, similarity does not in general function as part of the truth conditions either in Miller's manner or in the simpler version; rather, when it functions, it functions as a strategy for interpretation. Thus, very crudely, the way that similarity figures in the interpretation of 8 and 31 is given by

36. The ship does something to the sea (to figure out what it is, find a relationship like ploughing)

and

37. Washington stands in a certain relationship to his country (to figure out what it is, find a relationship like that of being a father).

But the hearer does not have to compute any respects in which these relations are similar, since that is not what is being asserted. Rather, what is being asserted is that the ship is doing something to the sea and that Washington stands in a certain set of relations to his country, and the hearer is to figure out what it is that the ship does and what the relations are that Washington stands in by looking for relations similar to *ploughing* and *being a father of*.

To conclude this section: The problem of metaphor is either very difficult or very easy. If the simile theory were true, it would be very easy, because there would be no separate semantic category of metaphors—only a category of *elliptical utterances* where "like" or "as" had been deleted from the uttered sentence. But alas, the simile theory is not right, and the problem of metaphor remains very difficult. I hope our rather lengthy discussion of the simile theory has been illuminating in at least these respects. First, there are many metaphors in which there is no underlying literal similarity adequate to explain the metaphorical utterance meaning. Second, even where there is a correlated literal statement of similarity, the truth conditions, and hence the meaning of the metaphorical statement and the similarity statements, are not, in general, the same. Third, what we should salvage from the simile theory is a set of strategies for producing and understanding metaphorical utterances, using similarity. And fourth, even so construed, that is, construed as a theory of interpretation rather than of meaning, the simile theory does not tell us how to compute the respects of similarity or which similarities are metaphorically intended by the speaker.

The Principles of Metaphorical Interpretations

The time has now come to try to state the principles according to which metaphors are produced and understood. To reiterate, in its simplest form, the question we are trying to answer is, How is it possible for the speaker to say metaphorically "S is P" and mean "S is R", when P plainly does not mean R? Furthermore, How is it possible for the hearer who hears the utterance "S is P" to know that the speaker means "S is R"? The short and uninformative answer is that the utterance of P calls to mind the meaning and, hence, truth conditions associated with R, in the special ways that metaphorical utterances have of calling other things to mind. But that answer remains uninformative until we know what are the principles according to which the utterance calls the metaphorical meaning to mind, and until we can state these principles in a way which does not rely on metaphorical expressions like "calls to mind". I believe that there is no single principle on which metaphor works.

The question, "How do metaphors work?" is a bit like the question, "How does one thing remind us of another thing?" There is no single answer to either question, though similarity obviously plays a major role in answering both. Two important differences between them are that metaphors are both restricted and systematic; restricted in the sense that not every way that one thing can remind us of something else will provide a basis for metaphor, and systematic in the sense that metaphors must be communicable from speaker to hearer in virtue of a shared system of principles.

Let us approach the problem from the hearer's point of view. If we can figure out the principles according to which hearers understand

metaphorical utterances, we shall be a long way toward understanding how it is possible for speakers to make metaphorical utterances,
because for communication to be possible, speaker and hearer must
share a common set of principles. Suppose a hearer hears an utterance such as, "Sally is a block of ice", or "Richard is a gorilla", or
"Bill is a barn door". What are the steps he must go through in order
to comprehend the metaphorical meaning of such utterances? Obviously an answer to that question need not specify a set of steps
that he goes through consciously; instead it must provide a rational
reconstruction of the inference patterns that underlie our ability to
understand such metaphors. Furthermore, not all metaphors will be
as simple as the cases we shall be discussing; nonetheless, a model
designed to account for the simple cases should prove to be of more
general application.

I believe that for the simple sorts of cases that we have been discussing, the hearer must go through at least three sets of steps. First,
he must have some strategy for determining whether or not he has to
seek a metaphorical interpretation of the utterance in the first place.
Second, when he has decided to look for a metaphorical interpretation, he must have some set of strategies, or principles, for computing possible values of R, and third, he must have a set of strategies,
or principles, for restricting the range of Rs—for deciding which Rs
are likely to be the ones the speaker is asserting of S.

Suppose he hears the utterance, "Sam is a pig". He knows that
that cannot be literally true, that the utterance, if he tries to take it
literally, is radically defective. And, indeed, such defectiveness is a
feature of nearly all of the examples that we have considered so far.
The defects which cue the hearer may be obvious falsehood, semantic nonsense, violations of the rules of speech acts, or violations of
conversational principles of communication. This suggests a strategy
that underlies the first step:

*Where the utterance is defective if taken literally, look for an utter-
ance meaning that differs from sentence meaning.*

This is not the only strategy on which a hearer can tell that an
utterance probably has a metaphorical meaning, but it is by far the
most common. (It is also common to the interpretation of poetry. If
I hear a figure on a Grecian Urn being addressed as a "still unravish'd

bride of quietness", I know I had better look for alternative meanings.) But it is certainly not a necessary condition of a metaphorical
utterance that it be in any way defective if construed literally.
Disraeli might have said metaphorically

5.   (MET) I have climbed to the top of the greasy pole,

though he had in fact climbed to the top of a greasy pole. There are
various other clues that we employ to spot metaphorical utterances.
For example, when reading Romantic poets, we are on the lookout
for metaphors, and some people we know are simply more prone to
metaphorical utterances than others.

Once our hearer has established that he is to look for an alternative meaning, he has a number of principles by which he can
compute possible values of R. I will give a list of these shortly, but
one of them is this.

*When you hear "S is P", to find possible values of R look for ways
in which S might be like P, and to fill in the respect in which S
might be like P, look for salient, well known, and distinctive
features of P things.*

In this case, the hearer might invoke his factual knowledge to
come up with such features as that pigs are fat, gluttonous, slovenly,
filthy, and so on. This indefinite range of features provides possible
values of R. However, lots of other features of pigs are equally distinctive and well known, for example, pigs have a distinctive shape
and distinctive bristles. So, in order to understand the utterance, the
hearer needs to go through the third step where he restricts the range
of possible Rs. Here again the hearer may employ various strategies
for doing that but the one that is most commonly used is this.

*Go back to the S term and see which of the many candidates for
the values of R are likely or even possible properties of S.*

Thus, if the hearer is told, "Sam's car is a pig", he will interpret
that metaphor differently from the utterance, "Sam is a pig". The
former, he might take to mean that Sam's car consumes gas the way
pigs consume food, or that Sam's car is shaped like a pig. Though, in
one sense, the metaphor is the same in the two cases, in each case it
is restricted by the S term in a different way. The hearer has to use

his knowledge of S things and P things to know which of the possible values of R are plausible candidates for metaphorical predication.

Now, much of the dispute between the interaction theories and the object comparison theories derives from the fact that they can be construed as answers to different questions. The object comparison theories are best construed as attempts to answer the question of stage two: "How do we compute the possible values of R?" The interaction theories are best construed as answers to the question of stage three: "Given a range of possible values of R, how does the relationship between the S term and the P term restrict that range?" I think it is misleading to describe these relations as "interactions", but it seems correct to suppose that the S term must play a role in metaphors of the sort we have been considering. In order to show that the interaction theory was also an answer to the question of stage two, we would have to show that there are values of R that are specifiable, given S and P together, that are not specifiable given P alone; one would have to show that S does not *restrict* the range of Rs but in fact, creates new Rs. I do not believe that can be shown, but I shall mention some possibilities later.

I said that there were a variety of principles for computing R, given P—that is, a variety of principles according to which the utterance of P can call to mind the meaning R in ways that are peculiar to metaphor. I am sure I do not know all of the principles that do this, but here are several (not necessarily independent) for a start.

Principle 1. Things which are P are by definition R. Usually, if the metaphor works, R will be one of the salient defining characteristics of P. Thus, for example,

    38. (MET) Sam is a giant

will be taken to mean

    38. (PAR) Sam is big,

because giants are by definition big. That is what is special about them.

Principle 2. Things which are P are contingently R. Again, if the metaphor works, the property *R* should be a salient or well known property of *P* things.

39. (MET) Sam is a pig

will be taken to mean

39. (PAR) Sam is filthy, gluttonous, and sloppy, etc.

Both principles 1 and 2 correlate metaphorical utterances with literal similes, "Sam is like a giant", "Sam is like a pig", and so on. Notice in connection with this principle and the next that small variations in the *P* term can create big differences in the *R* terms. Consider the differences between "Sam is a pig", "Sam is a hog", and "Sam is a swine".

Principle 3. Things which are *P* are often said or believed to be *R*, even though both speaker and hearer may know that *R* is false of *P*. Thus,

7. (MET) Richard is a gorilla

can be uttered to mean

7. (PAR) Richard is mean, nasty, prone to violence, and so on,

even though both speaker and hearer know that in fact gorillas are shy, timid, and sensitive creatures, but generations of gorilla mythology have set up associations that will enable the metaphor to work even though both speaker and hearer know these beliefs to be false.

Principle 4. Things which are *P* are not *R*, nor are they like *R* things, nor are they believed to be *R*; nonetheless it is a fact about our sensibility, whether culturally or naturally determined, that we just do perceive a connection, so that *P* is associated in our minds with *R* properties. Thus,

4. (MET) Sally is a block of ice
40. (MET) I am in a black mood
41. (MET) Mary is sweet
42. (MET) John is bitter

43. (MET) The hours $\begin{cases} \text{crept} \\ \text{crawled} \\ \text{dragged} \\ \text{sped} \\ \text{whizzed} \end{cases}$ by as we waited

        for the plane

are sentences that could be uttered to mean metaphorically that: Sally is unemotional; I am angry and depressed; Mary is gentle, kind, pleasant, and so on; John is resentful; and the hours seemed (of varying degrees of duration) as we waited for the plane; even though there are no literal similarities on which these metaphors are based. Notice that the associations tend to be scalar: degrees of temperature with ranges of emotion, degrees of speed with temporal duration, and so forth.

Principle 5. P things are not like R things, and are not believed to be like R things; nonetheless the condition of being P is like the condition of being R. Thus, I might say to someone who has just received a huge promotion

44. You have become an aristocrat,

meaning not that he has personally become *like* an aristocrat, but that his new status or condition is like that of being an aristocrat.

Principle 6. There are cases where P and R are the same or similar in meaning, but where one, usually P, is restricted in its application, and does not literally apply to S. Thus, "addled" is only said literally of eggs, but we can metaphorically say

45. This soufflé is addled
46. That parliament was addled

and

47. His brain is addled.

Principle 7. This is not a separate principle but a way of applying principles 1-6 to simple cases which are not of the form "S is P" but relational metaphors, and metaphors of other syntactical forms such as those involving verbs and predicate adjectives. Consider such relational metaphors as

48. Sam devours books
8. The ship ploughs the sea
31. Washington was the father of his country.

In each case, we have a literal utterance of two noun phrases surrounding a metaphorical utterance of a relational term (it can be a transitive verb, as in 48 and 8 but it need not be, as in 31). The hearer's task is not to go from "*S* is *P*" to "*S* is *R*" but to go from "*S* *P*-relation *S'*" to "*S* *R*-relation *S'*" and the latter task is formally rather different from the former because, for example, our similarity principles in the former case will enable him to find a property that *S* and *P* things have in common, namely, *R*. But in the latter, he cannot find a relation in common; instead he has to find a relation *R* which is different from relation *P* but similar to it in some respect. So, as applied to these cases, principle 1, for example, would read

P-relations are by definition *R*-relations.

For example, *ploughing* is by definition partly a matter of moving a substance to either side of a pointed object while the object moves forward; and though this definitional similarity between the *P*-relation and the *R*-relation would provide the principle that enables the hearer to infer the *R*-relation, the respect of similarity does not exhaust the content of the *R*-relation, as the similarity exhausts the content of the *R* term in the simplest of the "*S* is *P*" cases. In these cases, the hearer's job is to find a relation (or property) that is similar to, or otherwise associated with, the relation or property literally expressed by the metaphorical expression *P*; and the principles function to enable him to select that relation or property by giving him a respect in which the *P*-relation and the *R*-relation might be similar or otherwise associated.

Principle 8. According to my account of metaphor, it becomes a matter of terminology whether we want to construe metonymy and synecdoche as special cases of metaphor or as independent tropes.

When one says, "S is P", and means that "S is R", P and R may be associated by such relations as the part-whole relation, the container-contained relation, or even the clothing and wearer relation. In each case, as in metaphor proper, the semantic content of the P term conveys the semantic content of the R term by some principle of association. Since the principles of metaphor are rather various anyway, I am inclined to treat metonymy and synecdoche as special cases of metaphor and add their principles to my list of metaphorical principles. I can, for example, refer to the British monarch as "the Crown", and the executive branch of the US government as "the White House" by exploiting systematic principles of association. However, as I said, the claim that these are special cases of metaphor seems to me purely a matter of terminology, and if purists insist that the principles of metaphor be kept separate from those of metonymy and synecdoche, I can have no nontaxonomical objections.

In addition to these eight principles, one might wonder if there is a ninth one. Are there cases where an association between P and R that did not previously exist can be created by the juxtaposition of S and P in the original sentence? This, I take it, is the thesis of the interaction theorists. However, I have never seen any convincing examples, nor any even halfway clear account, of what "interaction" is supposed to mean. Let us try to construct some examples. Consider the differences between

49. Sam's voice is $\begin{Bmatrix} \text{mud} \\ \text{gravel} \\ \text{sandpaper} \end{Bmatrix}$

and

50. Kant's second argument for the transcendental deduction is so much $\begin{Bmatrix} \text{mud} \\ \text{gravel} \\ \text{sandpaper} \end{Bmatrix}$.

The second set clearly gives us different metaphorical meanings— different values for R—than the first trio, and one might argue that this is due not to the fact that the different S terms restrict the range of possible Rs generated by the P terms, but to the fact that the different combinations of S and P create new Rs. But that explanation seems implausible. The more plausible explanation is this. One has a set of associations with the P terms, "mud", "gravel", and "sandpaper". The principles of these associations are those of principles 1-7. The different S terms restrict the values of R differently, because different Rs can be true of voices than can be true of arguments for transcendental deductions. Where is the interaction?

Since this section contains my account of metaphorical predication, it may be well to summarize its main points. Given that a speaker and a hearer have shared linguistic and factual knowledge sufficient to enable them to communicate literal utterances, the following strategies and principles are individually necessary and collectively sufficient to enable speaker and hearer to form and comprehend utterances of the form "S is P", where the speaker means metaphorically that S is R (where $P \neq R$).

First, there must be some shared strategies on the basis of which the hearer can recognize that the utterance is not intended literally. The most common, but not the only strategy, is based on the fact that the utterance is obviously defective if taken literally.

Second, there must be some shared principles that associate the P term (whether the meaning, the truth conditions, or the denotation if there is any) with a set of possible values of R. The heart of the problem of metaphor is to state these principles. I have tried to state several of them, but I feel confident that there must be more.

Third, there must be some shared strategies that enable the speaker and the hearer, given their knowledge of the S term (whether the meaning of the expression, or the nature of the referent, or both), to restrict the range of possible values of R to the actual value of R. The basic principle of this step is that only those possible values of R which determine possible properties of S can be actual values of R.

Metaphor, Irony, and Indirect Speech Acts

To conclude, I wish to compare briefly the principles on which metaphor works with those on which irony and indirect speech acts work. Consider first a case of irony. Suppose you have just broken a priceless K'ang Hsi vase and I say ironically, "That was a brilliant thing to do." Here, as in metaphor, the speaker's meaning and sentence meaning are different. What are the principles by which the hearer is able to infer that the speaker meant, "That was a stupid thing to do", when what he heard was the sentence, "That was a brilliant thing to do"? Stated very crudely, the mechanism by which irony works is that the utterance, if taken literally, is obviously inappropriate to the situation. Since it is grossly inappropriate, the hearer is compelled to reinterpret it in such a way as to render it appropriate, and the most natural way to interpret it is as meaning the *opposite* of its literal form.

I am not suggesting that this is by any means the whole story about irony. Cultures and subcultures vary enormously in the extent and degree of the linguistic and extralinguistic cues provided for ironical utterances. In English, in fact, there are certain characteristic intonational contours that go with ironical utterances. However, it is important to see that irony, like metaphor, does not require any conventions, extralinguistic or otherwise. The principles of conversation and the general rules for performing speech acts are sufficient to provide the basic principles of irony.

Now consider a case of an indirect speech act. Suppose that in the usual dinner-table situation, I say to you, "Can you pass the salt?" In this situation you will normally take that as meaning, "Please pass the salt." That is, you will take the question about your ability as a request to perform an action. What are the principles on which this inference works? There is a radical difference between indirect speech acts, on the one hand, and irony and metaphor, on the other. In the indirect speech act, the speaker means what he says. However, in addition, he means something more. Sentence meaning is part of utterance meaning, but it does not exhaust utterance meaning. In a very simplified form (for a more detailed account, see Searle, 1975b), the principles on which the inference works in this case are: First, the hearer must have some device for recognizing that the utterance might be an indirect speech act. This requirement is satisfied by the fact that in the context, a question about the hearer's ability lacks any conversational point. The hearer, therefore, is led to seek an alternative meaning. Second, since the hearer knows the rules of speech acts, he knows that the ability to pass the salt is a preparatory condition on the speech act of requesting him to do so. Therefore, he is able to infer that the question about his ability is likely to be a polite request to perform the act.

The differences and similarities between literal utterances, metaphorical utterances, ironical utterances, and indirect speech acts are illustrated in Figure 2.

The question of whether all metaphorical utterances can be given a literal paraphrase is one that must have a trivial answer. Interpreted one way, the answer is trivially yes; interpreted another way, it is trivially no. If we interpret the question as, "Is it possible to find or to invent an expression that will exactly express the intended metaphorical meaning R, in the sense of the truth conditions of R, for any metaphorical utterance of 'S is P', where what is meant is that S is R?" the answer to that question must surely be yes. It follows trivially from the Principle of Expressibility (see Searle, 1969) that any meaning whatever can be given an exact expression in the language.

If the question is interpreted as meaning, "Does every existing language provide us exact devices for expressing literally whatever we wish to express in any given metaphor?" then the answer is obviously no. It is often the case that we use metaphor precisely because there is no literal expression that expresses exactly what we mean. Furthermore, in metaphorical utterances, we do more than just state that S is R; as Figure 2 shows, we state that S is R by way of going through the meaning of "S is P". It is in this sense that we feel that metaphors somehow are intrinsically not paraphrasable. They are not paraphrasable, because without using the metaphorical expression we will not reproduce the semantic content which occurred in the hearer's comprehension of the utterance.

The best we can do in the paraphrase is reproduce the truth conditions of the metaphorical utterance, but the metaphorical utterance does more than just convey its truth conditions. It conveys its truth conditions by way of another semantic content, whose truth conditions are not part of the truth conditions of the utterance. The expressive power that we feel is part of good metaphors is largely a matter of two features. The hearer has to figure out what the speaker means—he has to contribute more to the communication than just passive uptake—and he has to do that by going through another and related semantic content from the one which is communicated. And that, I take it, is what Dr. Johnson meant when he said metaphor gives us two ideas for one.

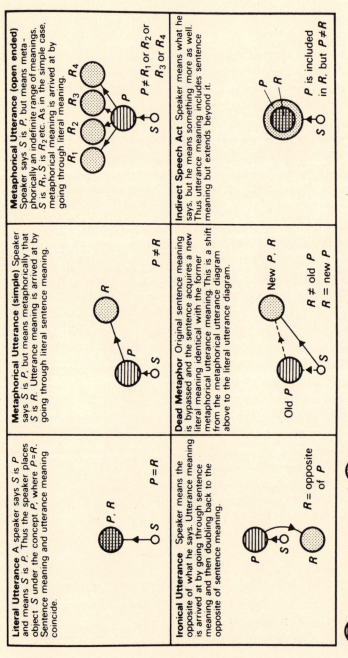

Sentence meaning, P ◉ Utterance meaning, R ○ Object, S

Fig. 2. A graphic comparison of the relations between sentence meaning and utterance meaning, where the sentence meaning is "S is P", and the utterance meaning is "S is R", that is, where the speaker utters a sentence that means literally that the object S falls under the concept P, but where the speaker means by his utterance that the object S falls under the concept R.

NOTES

I am indebted to several people for helpful comments on earlier drafts of this article, and I especially want to thank Jerry Morgan, Andrew Ortony, Paul Rauber, and Dagmar Searle.

1. It is essential to avoid any use—mention confusions when talking about these sets. Sometimes we will be talking about the words, other times about meanings, other times about references and denotations, and still other times about truth conditions.

2. I follow Beardsley (1962) in this classification.

3. Even in Black's (1979) clarification of interaction in terms of "implication-complexes" there still does not seem to be any precise statement of the principles on which interaction works. And the actual example he gives, "Marriage is a zero-sum game," looks distressingly like a comparison metaphor: "Metaphor is *like* a zero-sum game in that it is an adversary relationship between two parties in which one side can benefit only at the expense of the other." It is hard to see what the talk about interaction is supposed to add to this analysis.

4. By "literal simile," I mean literal statement of similarity. It is arguable that one should confine "simile" to nonliteral comparisons, but that is not the usage I follow here.

5. Furthermore, it is at least arguable that "block of ice" functions metonymously in this example.

Conceptual Metaphor
in Everyday Language

George Lakoff and Mark Johnson

Until recently philosophers have tended to berate metaphor as irrational and dangerous, or to ignore it, reducing it to the status of a subsidiary problem in the philosophy of language. Literal language, assumed to be mutually exclusive with metaphor, has been taken to be the real stuff of philosophy, the domain where issues of meaning and truth arise and can be dealt with. At best, metaphor is treated as if it were always the result of some operation performed upon the literal meaning of the utterance. The phenomenon of "conventional metaphor," where much of our ordinary conceptual system and the bulk of our everyday conventional language are structured and understood primarily in metaphorical terms, has gone either unnoticed or undiscussed.

As we will show directly, conventional metaphors are pervasive in our ordinary everyday way of thinking, speaking, and acting. We feel that an understanding of conventional metaphor and the way that metaphor structures our ordinary conceptual system will ultimately provide a new "experientialist" perspective on classical philosophical

Reprinted from *The Journal of Philosophy* 77, no. 8 (1980): 453-486 and later printed, in part, in *Metaphors We Live By* (University of Chicago Press, 1980) by permission of the University of Chicago Press. Copyright © 1980 by The University of Chicago. All rights reserved. Published 1980. Printed in the United States of America.

problems, such as the nature of meaning, truth, rationality, logic, and knowledge. In this present paper we can only focus on the nature and role of metaphor in our conceptual system, with a few suggestions concerning the larger implications of our account.[1]

I. Concepts that We Live By

Metaphor is for most people a device of the poetic imagination and the rhetorical flourish—a matter of extraordinary rather than ordinary language. Moreover, metaphor is typically viewed as characteristic of language alone, a matter of words rather than thought or action. For this reason, most people think they can get along perfectly well without metaphor. We have found, on the contrary, that metaphor is pervasive in everyday life, not just in language, but in thought and action. Our ordinary conceptual system, in terms of which we both think and act, is fundamentally metaphorical in nature.

The concepts that govern our thought are not just matters of the intellect. They also govern our everyday functioning, down to the most mundane details. Our concepts structure what we perceive, how we get around in the world, and how we relate to other people. Our conceptual system thus plays a central role in defining our everyday realities. If we are right in suggesting that our conceptual system is largely metaphorical, then the way we think, what we experience, and what we do every day is very much a matter of metaphor.

But our conceptual system is not something that we are normally aware of. In most of the little things we do every day, we simply think and act more or less automatically along certain lines. Just what these lines are is by no means obvious. One way to find out is by looking at language. Since communication is based on the same conceptual system in terms of which we think and act, language is an important source of evidence for what that system is like.

Primarily on the basis of linguistic evidence, we have found that most of our ordinary conceptual system is metaphorical in nature. And we have found a way to begin to identify in detail just what the metaphors are that structure how we perceive, how we think, and what we do.

To give some idea of what it could mean for a concept to be

metaphorical and for such a concept to structure an everyday activity, let us start with the concept of an ARGUMENT, and the conceptual metaphor ARGUMENT IS WAR. This metaphor is reflected in our every day language by a wide variety of expressions:

ARGUMENT IS WAR
Your claims are *indefensible.*
He *attacked every weak point* in my argument.
His criticisms were *right on target.*
I *demolished* his argument.
I've never *won* an argument with him.
You disagree? Okay, *shoot!*
If you use that *strategy*, he'll *wipe you out.*
He *shot down* all my arguments.

It is important to see that we don't just *talk* about arguments in terms of war. We can actually win or lose arguments. We see the person we are arguing with as an opponent. We attack his positions and we defend our own. We gain and lose ground. We plan and use strategies. If we find a position indefensible, we can abandon it and take a new line of attack. Many of the things we *do* in arguing are partially structured by the concept of war. Though there is no physical battle, there is a verbal battle, and the structure of an argument—attack, defense, counterattack, etc.—reflects this. It is in this sense that we live by the ARGUMENT IS WAR metaphor in this culture; it structures the actions we perform in arguing.

Try to imagine a culture where arguments were not viewed in terms of war, where no one won or lost, where there was no sense of attacking or defending, gaining or losing ground. Imagine a culture where an argument is viewed as a dance, with the participants as performers, and the goal being to perform in a balanced and aesthetic way. In such a culture, people would view arguments differently, experience them differently, carry them out differently, and talk about them differently. But *we* would probably not view them as arguing at all. It would be strange even to call what they were doing "arguing." Perhaps the most neutral way of describing this difference between their culture and ours would be to say that we have a discourse form structured in terms of battle and they have one structured in terms of dance.

This is an example of what it means for a metaphorical concept, namely, ARGUMENT IS WAR, partially to structure what we do and how we understand what we do when we argue. *The essence of metaphor is understanding and experiencing one kind of thing or experience in terms of another.* It is not that arguments are a subspecies of wars. Arguments and wars are different kinds of things—verbal discourse and armed conflict—and the actions performed are different kinds of actions. But ARGUMENT is partially structured, understood, performed, and talked about in terms of WAR. The concept is metaphorically structured, the activity is metaphorically structured, and consequently, the language is metaphorically structured.

Moreover, this is the *ordinary* way of having an argument and talking about one. The normal way *for us* to talk about attacking a position is to use the words 'attack a position'. Our conventional ways of talking about arguments presuppose a metaphor we are hardly ever conscious of. The metaphor is not merely in the words we use—it is in our very concept of an argument. The language of argument is not poetic, fanciful, or rhetorical, but rather literal. We talk about arguments that way because we conceive of them that way—and we act according to the way we conceive of things.

II. The Systematicity of Metaphorical Concepts

Arguments usually follow patterns; that is, there are certain things we typically do and do not do in arguing. The fact that we in part conceptualize arguments in terms of battle systematically influences the shape arguments take and the way we talk about what we do in arguing. Because the metaphorical concept is sytematic, the language we use to talk about that aspect of the concept is systematic.

We saw in the ARGUMENT IS WAR metaphor that expressions from the vocabulary of war, e.g., 'attack a position', 'indefensible', 'strategy', 'new line of attack', 'win', 'gain ground', etc. form a systematic way of talking about the battling aspects of arguing. It is no accident that these expressions mean what they mean when we use them to talk about arguments. A portion of the conceptual network of battle partially characterizes the concept of an argument, and the language follows suit. Since metaphorical expressions in our language are tied to metaphorical concepts in a systematic way, we can use metaphorical linguistic expressions to study the nature of metaphorical concepts and to gain an understanding of the metaphorical nature of our activities.

To get an idea of how metaphorical expressions in everyday language can give us insight into the metaphorical nature of the concepts that structure our everyday activities, let us consider the metaphorical concept TIME IS MONEY as it is reflected in contemporary English:

> TIME IS MONEY
> You're *wasting* my time.
> This gadget will *save* you hours.
> I don't *have* the time to *give* you.
> How do you *spend* your time these days?
> That flat tire *cost* me an hour.
> I've *invested* a lot of time in her.
> I don't *have enough* time to *spare* for that.
> You're *running out* of time.
> You need to *budget* your time.
> *Put aside* some time for ping pong.
> Is that *worth your while?*
> Do you *have* much time *left?*
> You don't *use* your time *profitably.*
> I *lost* a lot of time when I got sick.
> *Thank you for* your time.

Time in our culture is a valuable commodity. It is a limited resource that we use to accomplish our goals. Because of the way that the concept of work has developed in modern Western culture, where work is typically associated with the time it takes and time is precisely quantified, it has become customary to pay people by the hour, week, or year. In our culture TIME IS MONEY in many ways: telephone message units, hourly wages, hotel room rates, yearly budgets, interest on loans, and paying your debt to society by serving time. These practices are relatively new in the history of the human race and by no means exist in all cultures. They have arisen in modern industrialized societies and structure our basic everyday activities in a very profound way. Corresponding to the fact that we *act* as if time were a valuable commodity, a limited resource, even money, so we *conceive* of time that way. Thus we understand and experience time as the kind of thing that can be spent, wasted, budgeted, invested wisely or poorly, saved or squandered.

TIME IS MONEY, TIME IS A LIMITED RESOURCE, and TIME IS A VALUABLE COMMODITY are all metaphorical concepts. They are metaphorical since we are using our everyday experience with money, limited resources, and valuable commodities to conceptualize time. This isn't a necessary way for human beings to conceptualize time; it is tied to our culture. There are cultures where time is none of these things.

The metaphorical concepts TIME IS MONEY, TIME IS A RESOURCE, and TIME IS A VALUABLE COMMODITY form a single system based on subcategorization, since in our society money is a limited resource and limited resources are valuable commodities. These subcategorization relationships characterize what we will call "entailment relationships" between the metaphors. TIME IS MONEY entails that TIME IS A LIMITED RESOURCE, which entails that TIME IS A VALUABLE COMMODITY. We can see the relationship in the following diagram:

MONEY	TIME IS MONEY
is	entails
A LIMITED RESOURCE	TIME IS A LIMITED RESOURCE
is	entails
A VALUABLE COMMODITY	TIME IS A VALUABLE COMMODITY

We are adopting the practice of using the most specific metaphorical concept, in this case TIME IS MONEY, to characterize the entire system, since TIME IS MONEY entails TIME IS A LIMITED RESOURCE and TIME IS A VALUABLE COMMODITY. Of the expressions listed under the TIME IS MONEY metaphor, some refer specifically to money ('spend', 'invest', 'budget', 'profitably', 'cost'), others to limited resources ('use', 'use up', 'have enough of', 'run out of'), and still others to valuable commodities ('have', 'give', 'lose', 'thank you for'). This is an example of the way in which metaphorical entailments can characterize a coherent system of metaphorical concepts and a corresponding coherent system of metaphorical expressions for those concepts.[2]

III. Metaphorical Systematicity: Highlighting and Hiding

The very systematicity that allows us to comprehend one aspect of a concept in terms of another (e.g., comprehending an aspect of arguing in terms of battle) will necessarily hide other aspects of the concept. In allowing us to focus on one aspect of a concept (e.g., the battling aspects of arguing), a metaphorical concept can keep us from focusing on other aspects of the concept which are not coherent with that metaphor. For example, in the midst of a heated argument, where we are intent on attacking our opponent's position and defending our own, we can lose sight of the more cooperative aspects involved in an argument. Someone who is arguing with you can be viewed as giving you his time, a valuable commodity, in an effort at mutual understanding. But when we are preoccupied with the battle aspects, we will most often lose sight of the cooperative aspects.

A far more subtle case of how a metaphorical concept can hide an aspect of our experience can be seen in what Michael Reddy[3] has called the "conduit metaphor." Reddy observes that our language about language is structured roughly by the following complex metaphor: (i) ideas (or meanings) are objects; (ii) linguistic expressions are containers; (iii) communication is sending—the speaker puts ideas (objects) into words (containers) and sends them (along a conduit) to a hearer who takes the idea-objects out of the word-containers. Reddy documents this with over one hundred *types* of expressions in English, which he estimates account for at least seventy per cent of the expressions we use to talk about language. Here are some examples:

THE CONDUIT METAPHOR
It's hard to *get* that *idea* across to him.
I *gave* you that idea.
Your reasons *came through* to us.
It's difficult to *put* my ideas *into* words.

When you *have* a good idea, try to *capture* it immediately
  in words.
Try to *pack* more thought *into* fewer words.
You can't simply *stuff* ideas *into* a sentence any old way.
The meaning is right there *in* the words.
Don't *force* your meanings *into* the wrong words.
His words *carry* little meaning.
The introduction *has* a great deal of thought-*content.*
Your words seem *hollow.*
The sentence is *without* meaning.
The idea is *buried in* terribly dense paragraphs.

In examples like these it is far more difficult to see that there is anything hidden by the metaphor, or even to see that there is a metaphor here at all. This is so much the conventional way of thinking about language that it is sometimes hard to imagine that it might not fit reality. But if we look at what the conduit metaphor entails, we can see some of the ways in which it masks aspects of the communicative process.

First, the LINGUISTIC EXPRESSIONS ARE CONTAINERS FOR MEANINGS aspect of the metaphor entails that words and sentences have meanings in themselves, independent of any context or speaker. The MEANINGS ARE OBJECTS part of the metaphor, for example, entails that meanings have an existence independent of people and contexts. The part of the metaphor that says that LINGUISTIC EXPRESSIONS ARE CONTAINERS FOR MEANING entails that words (and sentences) have meanings, again independent of contexts and speakers. These metaphors are appropriate in many situations—those where context differences don't matter and where all the participants in the conversation understand the sentences in the same way. These two entailments are exemplified by sentences like "The meaning is *right there in* the words," which, according to the conduit metaphor, can correctly be said of any sentence. But there are many cases where context does matter. Here is a celebrated example recorded in actual conversation by Pamela Downing: "Please sit in the apple-juice seat." In isolation this sentence has no meaning at all, since the compound 'apple-juice seat' is not a conventional way of referring to any kind of object. But the sentence made perfect sense in the context in which it was uttered: An overnight guest came down to breakfast. There were four place settings, three with orange juice and one with apple juice. It was clear what the apple-juice seat was. And even the next morning, when there was no apple juice, it was still clear which seat was the apple-juice seat.

In addition to sentences that have no meaning without context, there are cases where a single sentence will mean different things to different people. Consider: "We need new alternative sources of energy." This means something very different to the president of Mobil Oil than it does to the president of Friends of the Earth. The meaning is not right there in the sentence—it matters a lot who is saying or listening to the sentence and what his social and political attitudes are. The conduit metaphor does not fit cases where context is required to determine whether the sentence has any meaning at all, and, if so, what meaning it has.

These examples show that the metaphorical concepts we have looked at provide us with a partial understanding of what communication, argument, and time are, and that in so doing they hide other aspects of these concepts. It is important to see that the metaphorical structuring involved here is partial, not total. If it were total, one concept would *be* the other, would not merely be understood in terms of it. For example, time isn't actually money. If you *spend your time* trying to do something and it doesn't work, you can't *get your time back*. There are no *time banks*. I can *give* you *a lot of time*, but you can't *give me back the same time*, though you can *give me back the same amount of time*. And so on. Thus, part of a metaphorical concept does not and cannot fit.

On the other hand, metaphorical concepts can be extended beyond the range of ordinary literal ways of thinking and talking into the range of what is called figurative, poetic, colorful, or fanciful thought and language. Thus, if ideas are objects, we can *dress them up in fancy clothes, juggle them, line them up nice and neat*, etc. So when we say that a concept is structured by a metaphor, we mean that it is partially structured, and that it can be extended in some ways but not others.

IV. Types of Metaphor: Structural, Orientational, Physical

In order to see in more detail what is involved in the metaphorical structuring of a concept or system of concepts, it is useful to identify three basic domains of conceptual structure and to trace some of the systematic connections among and within them. These three domains —physical, cultural, and intellectual—are only roughly divided, because they cannot be sharply delineated and usually interact in significant ways.

So far we have examined what we might call "structural" metaphors, cases where one concept is metaphorically structured in terms of another (e.g., ARGUMENT is structured in terms of WAR). Structural metaphors often involve using a concept from one domain (WAR as a physical or cultural phenomenon) to structure a concept from another domain (ARGUMENT as primarily an intellectual concept, but with cultural content). But before we can look more closely at the various domains of conceptual structure, it is important to see that there are what might be called "physical" and "orientational" metaphors, in addition to structural metaphors of the conventional type. Briefly, "physical" metaphors involve the projection of entity or substance status upon something that does not have that status inherently. Such conventional metaphors allow us to view events, activities, emotions, ideas, etc., as entities for various purposes (e.g., in order to refer to them, categorize them, group them, or quantify them). For example, we find physical metaphors such as:

My *fear of insects* is driving my wife crazy. (referring)
You've got *too much hostility* in you. (quantifying)
The *brutality of war* dehumanizes us all. (identifying aspects)
The *pressures of his responsibilities* caused his breakdown.
    (identifying causes)
Here's what to do to ensure *fame and fortune*. (setting goals
    and motivating actions)

Physical metaphors such as these are hardly ever noticed, because they are so basic to our everyday conceptualizing and functioning. But they are, nevertheless, conventional metaphors by means of which we understand either nonphysical or not clearly bounded things as entities. In most cases such metaphors involve the use of a concept from the physical domain to structure a concept from the cultural or intellectual domains.

A third kind of conventional metaphor is the "orientational" metaphor, which does not structure one concept in terms of another, but instead organizes a whole system of concepts with respect to one another. We call them "orientational" metaphors because most of them have to do with spatial orientation: UP-DOWN, FRONT-BACK, IN-OUT, ON-OFF, DEEP-SHALLOW, CENTRAL-PERIPHERAL. These spatial orientations arise from the facts that we have bodies of the sort we have and that they function as they do in our physical environment. Orientational metaphors give a concept a spatial orientation, for example, HAPPY IS UP. The fact that the concept HAPPY is oriented UP leads to English expressions like "I'm feeling up today."

In order to examine the way in which metaphors provide structure across the different domains of concepts (physical, cultural, intellectual) we shall focus briefly on orientational metaphors, as representative examples. Such metaphorical orientations are not arbitrary. They have a basis in our physical and cultural experience. Though the polar oppositions UP-DOWN, IN-OUT, etc. are physical in nature, the orientational metaphors can vary from culture to culture. For example, some cultures orient the future in front of us; others orient it in back. We will be looking at UP-DOWN spatialization metaphors, which have been studied intensively by William Nagy,[4] as an illustration. In each case, we will give a brief hint of how each metaphorical concept might have arisen from our physical and cultural experience. These accounts are meant to be suggestive and plausible, rather than definitive.

(1) HAPPY IS UP; SAD IS DOWN

I'm feeling up. That boosted my spirits. My spirits rose. You're in high spirits. Thinking about her always gives me a lift. I'm feeling down. I'm depressed. He's really low these days. I fell into a depression. My spirits sank.

Physical basis: Drooping posture typically goes along with sadness and depression, erect posture with a positive emotional state.

(2) CONSCIOUS IS UP; UNCONSCIOUS IS DOWN

Get up. Wake up. I'm up already. He rises early in the morning. He fell asleep. He dropped off to sleep. He's under hypnosis. He sank down into a coma.

Physical basis: Humans and most animals sleep lying down and stand erect when they wake up.

(3) HEALTH AND LIFE ARE UP; SICKNESS AND DEATH ARE DOWN

He's at the peak of health. Lazarus rose from the dead. He's in top shape. As to his health, he's way up there. He fell ill. He's sinking fast. He came down with the flu. His health is declining. He dropped dead.

Physical basis: Serious illness forces us physically to lie down. When you're dead you are physically down.

(4) HAVING CONTROL OR FORCE IS UP; BEING SUBJECT TO CONTROL OR FORCE IS DOWN

I have control over her. I am on top of the situation. He's in a superior position. He's at the height of his power. He's in the high command. His power rose. He's in a dominating position. He ranks above me in strength. He is under my control. He fell from power. His power is on the decline. He's in an inferior position.

Physical basis: Physical size typically correlates with physical strength, and the victor in a fight is typically on top.

(5) MORE IS UP; LESS IS DOWN

The number of books printed each year keeps going up. You made a high number of mistakes. My income rose last year. There is an overabundance of food in this country. My knowledge keeps increasing. The amount of artistic activity in this state has gone down in the past year. His number of errors is incredibly low. His income fell last year. He is underage. If you're too hot, turn the heat down.

Physical basis: If you add more of a substance or of physical objects to a container or pile, the level goes up.

(6) FORESEEABLE FUTURE EVENTS ARE UP (AND AHEAD)

The up-and-coming events are listed in the paper. What's coming up this week? I'm afraid of what's up ahead of us. What's up?

Physical basis: Normally our eyes are in the direction in which we typically move (ahead, forward). As an object approaches a person (or the person approaches the object), the object appears larger. Since the ground is perceived as being fixed, the top of the object appears to be moving *upward* in the person's field of vision.

(7) HIGH STATUS IS UP; LOW STATUS IS DOWN

He has a high position. She'll rise to the top. He's at the peak of his career. He's climbing the ladder. He has little upward mobility. He has a low position. She fell in status.

Social and physical basis: Status is correlated with power (social) and power is UP (physical).

(8) GOOD IS UP; BAD IS DOWN

Things are looking up. We hit a peak last year, but it's been going downhill ever since. Things are at an all-time low. The quality of life is high these days.

Physical basis for personal well-being: HAPPINESS, HEALTH, LIFE, and CONTROL—the things that principally characterize what is GOOD for a person—are all UP.

(9) VIRTUE IS UP; DEPRAVITY IS DOWN

He is high-minded. She has high standards. She is upright. She is an upstanding citizen. That was a low trick. Don't be underhanded. I wouldn't stoop to that. That would be beneath me. He fell into the abyss of depravity. That was a low-down thing to do.

Physical and social basis: GOOD IS UP for a person (physical basis), together with the SOCIETY IS A PERSON metaphor (in the version where you are *not* identifying with your society). To be virtuous is to act in accordance with the standards set by the society-person to maintain its well-being. VIRTUE IS UP because virtuous actions correlate with social well-being from the society-person's point of view. Since socially based metaphors are part of the culture, it's the society-person's point of view that counts.

(10) RATIONAL IS UP; EMOTIONAL IS DOWN

The discussion fell to the emotional level, but I raised it back up to the rational plane. We put our feelings aside and had a high-level intellectual discussion of the matter. He couldn't rise above his emotions.

Physical and cultural basis: In this culture people view themselves as being in control over animals, plants, and their physical environment, and it is their unique ability to reason that places human beings above other animals and gives them this control. CONTROL IS UP, which has a physical basis, thus provides a basis for MAN IS UP, and therefore for RATIONAL IS UP.

On the basis of these examples, we suggest the following conclusions about the experiential grounding, the coherence, and the systematicity of metaphorical concepts:

(i) Most of our fundamental concepts are organized in terms of one or more spatialization metaphors.

(ii) There is an internal systematicity to each spatialization metaphor. For example, HAPPY IS UP defines a coherent system, rather than a number of isolated and random cases. (An example of an incoherent system would be one where, say, "I'm feeling up" meant "I'm feeling happy," but "My spirits rose" meant "I became sadder").

(iii) There is an over-all external systematicity among the various spatialization metaphors, which defines coherence among them. Thus, GOOD IS UP gives an UP orientation to general well-being, which is coherent with special cases like HAPPY IS UP, HEALTHY IS UP, ALIVE IS UP, CONTROL IS UP. STATUS IS UP is coherent with CONTROL IS UP.

(iv) Spatialization metaphors are rooted in physical and cultural experience. They are not randomly assigned.

(v) There are many possible physical and social bases for metaphors. Coherence within the over-all system seems to be part of the reason why one is chosen and not another. For example, happiness also tends to correlate physically with a smile and a general feeling of expansiveness. This could in principle form the basis for a metaphor HAPPY IS WIDE; SAD IS NARROW. And in fact there are minor metaphorical expressions like "I'm feeling expansive" which pick out a different aspect of happiness than does "I'm feeling up." But the major metaphor *in our culture* is HAPPY IS UP; there is a reason why we speak of the height of ecstasy rather than the breadth of ecstasy. HAPPY IS UP is maximally coherent with GOOD IS UP, HEALTHY IS UP, etc.

(vi) In some cases spatialization is so essential a part of a concept that it is difficult for us to imagine any alternative metaphor that might structure the concept. In our society "high status" is such a concept. Other cases, like happiness, are less clear. Is the concept of happiness independent of the HAPPY IS UP metaphor, or is the up-down spatialization of happiness a part of the concept? We believe that it is a part of the concept within a given conceptual system. The HAPPY IS UP metaphor places happiness within a coherent metaphorical system, and part of its meaning comes from its role in that system.

(vii) So-called "purely intellectual" concepts, e.g., the concepts in a scientific theory, are often—and maybe even always—based on metaphors that have a physical or cultural basis. The 'high' in 'high-energy particles' is based on MORE IS UP. The 'high' in 'high-level functions', as in physiological psychology, is based on RATIONAL IS UP. The 'low' in 'low-level phonology' (which refers to detailed phonetic aspects of the sound systems of languages) is based on MUNDANE REALITY IS DOWN (as in 'down to earth'). The intuitive appeal of a scientific theory has to do with how well its metaphors fit one's experience.

(viii) Our physical and cultural experience provides many possible bases for spatialization metaphors. Which ones are chosen, and which ones are major, may vary from culture to culture.

(ix) It is hard to distinguish the physical from the cultural basis of a metaphor, since the choice of one from among many possible physical bases has to do with cultural coherence. It is to this connection between metaphor and cultural coherence that we now turn.

V. Metaphor and Cultural Coherence

The most fundamental values in a culture will be coherent with the metaphorical structure of the most fundamental concepts in the culture. As an example, let us consider some cultural values in our society which are coherent with our UP-DOWN spatialization metaphors and whose opposites would not be.

1. MORE IS BETTER is coherent with MORE IS UP and GOOD IS UP. LESS IS BETTER is not coherent with them.
2. BIGGER IS BETTER is coherent with MORE IS UP and GOOD IS UP; SMALLER IS BETTER is not coherent with them.
3. THE FUTURE WILL BE BETTER is coherent with THE FUTURE IS UP and GOOD IS UP; THE FUTURE WILL BE WORSE is not.
4. THERE WILL BE MORE IN THE FUTURE is coherent with MORE IS UP and THE FUTURE IS UP.
5. YOUR STATUS SHOULD BE HIGHER IN THE FUTURE is coherent with HIGH STATUS IS UP and THE FUTURE IS UP.

These are values deeply embedded in our culture. THE FUTURE WILL BE BETTER is a statement of the concept of progress. THERE WILL BE MORE IN THE FUTURE has as special cases the accumulation of goods and wage inflation. YOUR STATUS SHOULD BE HIGHER IN THE FUTURE is a statement of careerism. These are coherent with our present spatialization metaphors; their opposites would not be. So it seems that our values are not independent, but must form a coherent system with the metaphorical concepts we live by. We are not claiming that all cultural values coherent with a metaphorical system will exist, but only that those which do exist and are deeply entrenched will be consistent with the metaphorical system.

The values listed above hold in our culture in general—all things being equal. But because things are usually not equal, there are often conflicts among these values. To resolve such conflicts, one has to give different priorities to these values. There are certain constants. For instance, MORE IS UP seems always to have the highest priority since it has the clearest physical basis. The priority of MORE IS UP over GOOD IS UP can be seen in examples like "Inflation is rising" and "The crime rate is going up." Assuming that inflation and the crime rate are BAD, these sentences mean what they do because MORE IS UP always has top priority.

In general, which values are given priority is partly a matter of the subculture you live in and partly a matter of personal values. The various subcultures of a mainstream culture share basic values, but give them different priorities. For example, the value BIGGER IS BETTER may be in conflict with THERE WILL BE MORE IN THE FUTURE when it comes to the question of whether to buy a big car now with large time payments that will eat up future salary or whether to buy a smaller cheaper car. There are American subcultures where you buy the big car and don't worry about the future, and there are others where the future comes first and you buy the small car. There was a time (before inflation and the energy crisis) when owning a small car had a high status within the subculture where VIRTUE IS UP and SAVING RESOURCES IS VIRTUOUS took priority over BIGGER IS BETTER. Nowadays the number of small car owners has gone up drastically because there is a large subculture where SAVING MORE MONEY IS BETTER has priority over BIGGER IS BETTER.

In addition to subcultures, there are groups whose defining characteristic is that they have certain important values that conflict with those of the mainstream culture. But in less obvious ways they preserve other mainstream values. Take monastic orders like the Trappists. There LESS IS BETTER and SMALLER IS BETTER with respect to material possessions, which are viewed as hindering what is important, namely, spiritual growth. The Trappists share the mainstream value VIRTUE IS UP, though they give it the highest priority and a very different definition. MORE is still BETTER, though it applies to VIRTUE; and STATUS is still UP, though it is not of this world but of a HIGHER one, the Kingdom of God. Moreover, THE FUTURE WILL BE BETTER in terms of spiritual growth (UP) and ultimately salvation (REALLY UP). This is typical of groups that are out of mainstream culture. VIRTUE, GOODNESS, and STATUS may be radically redefined, but they are still UP. It is still BETTER to have MORE of what is important, the FUTURE WILL BE BETTER with respect to what is important, and so on. Relative to what is important for such a monastic group, the value system is both internally coherent and, with respect to what is important for the group, coherent with the major orientational metaphors of the mainstream culture.

Individuals, like groups, will vary in their priorities and in the way they define what is GOOD or VIRTUOUS to them. In this sense, they are like subgroups of one. Relative to what is important for them, their individual value systems are coherent with the major orientational metaphors of their mainstream culture.

Not all cultures give the priorities we do to UP-DOWN orientation. There are cultures where BALANCE or CENTRALITY plays a much more important role than it does in our culture. Or consider the non-spatial orientation ACTIVE-PASSIVE. For us ACTIVE IS UP and PASSIVE IS DOWN in most matters. But there are cultures where passivity is valued more than activity. In general the major orientations UP-DOWN, IN-OUT, CENTRAL-PERIPHERAL, ACTIVE-PASSIVE, etc., seem to cut across all cultures, but which concepts will be oriented which way, and which orientations will be most important, will vary from culture to culture.

VI. An Apparent Metaphorical Contradiction

Charles Fillmore has observed (in conversation) that English appears to have two contradictory organizations of time. In the first the future is in front and the past behind.

In the weeks ahead of us . . . (future)
That's all behind us now . . . (past)

In the second, the future is behind and the past is in front.

In the following weeks . . . (future)
In the preceding weeks . . . (past)

This appears to be a contradiction in the metaphorical organization of time. Moreover, the apparently contradictory metaphors can mix with no ill effect, as in "We're looking *ahead* to the *following* weeks." Here it appears that *ahead* organizes the future in front, while *following* organizes it behind.

To see that there is, in fact, a coherence here, we first have to consider some facts about back and front organization. Some things have inherent fronts and backs, for example, people and cars, but not trees. A rock may receive a front-back organization under certain circumstances. Suppose you are looking at a medium-sized rock and there is a ball between you and the rock, say, a foot from the rock. Then it is appropriate for you to say "The ball is in front of the rock." The rock has received a front-back orientation, as if it had a front that faced you. This is not universal. There are languages, for instance Hausa, where the rock would receive the reverse orientation and you would say that the ball was behind the rock, if it was between you and the rock.

Moving objects generally receive a front-back orientation so that the front is in the direction of motion (or in the canonical direction of motion, so that a car backing up retains its front). A spherical satellite, for example, that has no front while standing still, gets a front while in orbit by virtue of the direction in which it is moving.

Now time in English is structured in terms of the TIME IS A MOVING OBJECT metaphor, with the future moving toward us.

The time will come when . . .
The time has long since gone when . . .
The time for action has arrived.

The proverb "Time flies" is an instance of the TIME IS A MOVING OBJECT metaphor. Since we are facing toward the future, we get:

In the weeks ahead of us . . .
I look forward to doing that.
Before us is a great opportunity.

By virtue of the TIME IS A MOVING OBJECT metaphor, time receives a front-back orientation facing in the direction of motion, just as any moving object would. Thus the future is facing toward us as it moves toward us, and we find expressions like:

I can't face the future.
The face of things to come . . .
Let's meet the future head-on.

Now, although expressions like 'ahead of us', 'I look forward', and 'before us' orient times with respect to people, expressions like 'precede' and 'follow' orient times with respect to times. Thus we get:

Next week and the week following it . . .

but not:

The week following me . . .

Since future times are facing toward us, the times following them are further in the future, and all future times follow the present. That is why the *weeks to follow* are the same as *the weeks ahead of us.*

The point of this example is not merely to show that there is no contradiction, but also to show all the subtle details that are involved in the coherence: the TIME IS A MOVING OBJECT metaphor, the front-back orientation given to time by virtue of its being a moving object, and the consistent application of words like 'follow', 'precede', and 'face' when applied to time on the basis of the metaphor. All of this coherent detailed metaphorical structure is part of our everyday literal language about time, so familiar that we would normally not notice it.

VII. Some Further Examples

We have been claiming that metaphors partially structure our everyday concepts, and that this structure is reflected in our literal language. Before we can get an over-all picture of the philosophical implications of these claims, we need a few more examples. In each of the following cases we give a metaphor and a list of ordinary expressions that are special cases of the metaphor. The English expressions are of two sorts—simple literal expressions and idioms that fit the metaphor and are part of the normal everyday way of talking about the subject.

THEORIES (AND ARGUMENTS) ARE BUILDINGS

Is that the *foundation* for your theory? The theory needs more *support*. The argument is *shaky*. We need some more facts or the arguments will *fall apart*. We need to *construct a strong* argument for that. I haven't figured out yet what the *form* of the argument will be. We need some more facts to *shore up* the theory. We need to *buttress* the theory with *solid* arguments. The theory will *stand* or *fall* on the *strength* of that argument. The argument *collapsed*. They *exploded* his latest theory. We will show that theory is *without foundation*. So far we have only put together the *framework* of the theory.

IDEAS ARE FOOD

What he said *left a bad taste in my mouth*. All this paper has in it are *raw facts, half-baked ideas*, and *warmed-over theories*. There were too many facts in the paper for me to *digest* them all. I just can't *swallow* that claim. That argument *smells fishy*. Let me *stew over* that for a while. Now there's a theory you can really *sink your teeth into*. We need to let that idea *percolate* for a while. That's *food for thought*. He's a *voracious* reader. We don't need to *spoon-feed* our students. He *devoured* the book. Let's let that idea *simmer on the back burner* for a while. This is the *meaty* part of the paper.

LOVE IS A JOURNEY

Look *how far we've come*. We're *at a crossroads*. We can't *turn back* now. I don't think this relationship is *going anywhere*. This relationship is *a dead-end street.* Our marriage is *on the rocks.* We've gotten *off the track. Where* are we? We're *stuck.* It's been a *long, bumpy road.*

SEEING IS UNDERSTANDING; IDEAS ARE LIGHT SOURCES; DISCOURSE IS A LIGHT MEDIUM

I *see* what you're saying. It *looks* different from my *point of view.* What is your *outlook* on that? I *view* it differently. Now I've got the *whole picture.* Let me *point something out* to you. That's an *insightful* idea. That was a *brilliant* remark. It really *shed light* on the subject. It was an *illuminating* remark. The argument is *clear.* It was a *murky* discussion. Could you *elucidate* your remarks? It's a *transparent* argument. The discussion was *opaque.*

LIFE IS A GAME OF CHANCE

I'll *take my chances. The odds are against us.* I've *got an ace up my sleeve.* He's *holding all the aces.* It's a *toss-up.* If you *play your cards right,* you can do it. He *won big.* He's *a real loser.* Where is he when *the chips are down?* That's my *ace in the hole.*

In the last example we have a collection of what are called "speech formulas," or "fixed-form expressions," or "phrasal lexical items." These function in many ways like single words, and the language has thousands of them. In the example given, a set of such prasal lexical items are coherently structured by a single metaphor. Although each of them is an instance of the LIFE IS A GAME OF CHANCE metaphor, they are typically used to speak of life, not of gambling situations. They are normal ways of talking about life situations, just as using the word 'construct' is a normal way to talk about theories. It is in this sense that we include them as what we have called "literal" or "conventional" metaphors. If you say "the odds are against us," or "we'll have to take our chances," you will not be viewed as speaking metaphorically, but rather as using the normal everyday language appropriate to the situation.

VIII. The Partial Nature of Metaphorical Structuring

So far we have described the systematic character of metaphorically defined concepts. Such concepts are understood in terms of a number of different metaphors (e.g., TIME IS MONEY, TIME IS A MOVING OBJECT, etc.). The metaphorical structuring of concepts is necessarily partial, and is reflected in the lexicon of the language—including the phrasal lexicon, which contains fixed-form expressions such as 'be without foundation'. Because concepts are metaphorically structured in a systematic way, e.g., THEORIES ARE BUILDINGS, it is possible for us to use expressions (*construct, foundation*) from one domain (BUILDINGS) to talk about corresponding concepts in the metaphorically defined domain (THEORIES). What *foundation*, for example, means in the metaphorically defined domain (THEORY) will depend on the details of how the metaphorical concept THEORIES ARE BUILDINGS are used to structure the concept of a THEORY.

The parts of the concept of a building which are used to structure the concept of a theory are the foundation and outer shell. The roof, internal rooms, staircases, and hallways are parts of a building not used as part of the concept of a theory. Thus the metaphorical concept THEORIES ARE BUILDINGS has a "used" part (foundation and outer shell) and an "unused" part (rooms, staircases, etc.). Expressions such as *construct* and *foundation* are instances of the used part of such a metaphorical concept and are part of our ordinary literal language about theories.

But what of the linguistic expressions that reflect the "unused" part of a metaphor like THEORIES ARE BUILDINGS? Here are four examples:

His theory has thousands of little rooms and long, winding corridors.
His theories are always baroque.
He prefers massive Gothic theories covered with gargoyles.
Complex theories usually have problems with the plumbing.

These sentences fall outside the domain of normal literal language and are part of what is usually called "figurative" or "imaginative" language. Thus literal expressions ("He has constructed a theory") and imaginative expressions ("His theory is covered with gargoyles") can be instances of the same general metaphor (THEORIES ARE BUILDINGS).

Here we can distinguish three different subspecies of imaginative (or nonliteral) metaphor:

(1) Extensions of the used part of the metaphor, e.g., "These facts are the bricks and mortar of my theory." Here the outer shell of the building is referred to, but the metaphor stops short of mentioning the materials used.

(2) Instances of the unused part of the literal metaphor, e.g., "His theory has thousands of little rooms and long, winding corridors."

(3) Instances of novel metaphor, that is, a metaphor not used to structure part of our normal conceptual system, but a new way of thinking about something, e.g., "Classical theories are patriarchs who father many children, most of whom fight incessantly." Each of these subspecies lies outside of the *used* part of a metaphorical concept that structures our normal conceptual system.

We note in passing that all the linguistic expressions that we have given to characterize general, metaphorical concepts are figurative. Examples are TIME IS MONEY, TIME IS A MOVING OBJECT, CONTROL IS UP, IDEAS ARE FOOD, THEORIES ARE BULDINGS, etc. None of these is literal. This is a consequence of the fact that they are only *partly* used to structure our normal concepts. Since they necessarily contain parts that are not used in our normal concepts, they go beyond the realm of the literal.

Each of the metaphorical expressions we have talked about so far (e.g., the *time* will *come, construct* a theory, *attack* a *position*) is used within a whole system of metaphorical concepts—concepts that we live and think in terms of. These expressions, like all other words and phrasal lexical items in the language, are fixed by convention. In addition to these cases, which are part of whole metaphorical systems, there are idiosyncratic metaphorical expressions that stand alone and are not systematically used in our language or thought. These are well-known expressions like the *foot* of the mountain, a *head* of cabbage, the *leg* of a table, etc. These expressions are isolated instances of metaphorical concepts, where there is only one instance of a used part (or maybe two or three). Thus the *foot* of the mountain is the only used part of the metaphorical concept A MOUNTAIN IS A PERSON. In normal discourse we do not speak of the *head, shoulders,* or *trunk* of a mountain, though in special contexts it is possible to construct novel metaphors about mountains based on these unused parts. In fact, there is an aspect of the metaphorical concept A MOUNTAIN IS A PERSON in which mountain climbers will speak of the *shoulder* of a mountain (namely, a ridge near the top) and of *conquering, fighting,* and even *being killed* by a mountain. And there are cartoon conventions where mountains become animate and their peaks become heads. The point here is that there are metaphorical concepts like A MOUNTAIN IS A PERSON which are marginal in our culture and our language, whose used part may consist of only one conventionally fixed expression of the language, and which do not systematically interact with other metaphorical concepts, because so little of them is used. This makes them relatively uninteresting for our purposes, but not completely uninteresting, since they can be extended to their unused part in framing novel metaphors, making jokes, etc. And our ability to extend them to unused parts indicates that, however marginal they are, they do exist.

Examples like the *foot* of the mountain are idiosyncratic, unsystematic, and isolated. They do not interact with other metaphors, play no particularly interesting role in our conceptual system, and hence are not metaphors that we live by. The only signs of life that they have is that they can be extended in subcultures, and that their unused portions can be the basis for (relatively uninteresting) novel metaphors. If any metaphorical expressions deserve to be called "dead," it is these, though they do have a bare spark of life, in that they are understood partly in terms of marginal metaphorical concepts like A MOUNTAIN IS A PERSON.

It is important to distinguish these isolated and unsystematic cases from the systematic metaphorical expressions we have been discussing. Expressions like 'wasting time', 'attacking positions', 'going our separate ways', etc., are reflections of systematic metaphorical concepts that structure our actions and thoughts. They are "alive" in the most fundamental sense—they are metaphors we live by. The fact that they are conventionally fixed within the lexicon of English makes them no less alive.

IX. Inadequacies of a Theory of Abstraction

On the basis of our previous analysis of the nature of literal metaphor we may now begin to draw out what we consider to be the more important implications for recent linguistic and philosophical treatments of language. We shall begin with the theory of abstraction, one strategy which linguists have occasionally tried for dealing with isolated cases of literal metaphor.[5] For example, consider 'construct' in "We constructed a theory" and "We constructed a building." According to the abstraction proposal, 'construct' has a very general, abstract meaning which is neutral between buildings and theories and can apply to both. Another example would be the 'in' of 'in the kitchen', 'in the ruling class', and 'in love'. The abstraction solution is that 'in' has an abstract meaning which is neutral among space, social groups, and love, and which can apply to all. This proposal has typically been suggested only for isolated lexical items rather than whole domains of literal metaphor, so it is not clear that there is any proposal for abstraction that is relevant. Still, the idea keeps popping up that it ought to be a viable program; so we shall indicate several shortcomings of this view relative to our account of literal metaphor.

(1) Under the abstraction view, there would be no conventional metaphors and, therefore, no partial metaphorical structuring such as we have proposed. But then how can one explain the apparent systematic grouping of expressions under single metaphors and the fact that different metaphors based on a single concept may have different partial structurings? Consider the metaphors LOVE IS WAR, RATIONAL DISCOURSE IS WAR, STOPPING INFLATION IS WAR, and CANCER IS WAR. ATTACK is in CANCER, INFLATION, and DISCOURSE. STRATEGY is in LOVE, DISCOURSE, and INFLATION. CONQUERING is in LOVE, INFLATION, and CANCER. VICTORIES and SETBACKS are in all of them. There is a FIRST LINE OF DEFENSE in INFLATION and CANCER. On our hypothesis, WAR is the basis for all four metaphors, each of which has a different partial structuring. On the abstraction hypothesis, there is no unity at all, but only a hodgepodge of different abstract concepts of different sorts.

(2) Since the abstraction proposal has no partial metaphorical structuring, it cannot account for metaphorical extensions into the unused part of the metaphor, as in "Your theory is constructed out of cheap stucco" and many others that fall within the unused portion of the THEORIES ARE BUILDINGS metaphor.

(3) The abstraction proposal does not seem to make any sense at all for UP-DOWN spatialization metaphors, such as HAPPY IS UP, CONTROL IS UP, MORE IS UP, VIRTUE IS UP, THE FUTURE IS

UP, REASON IS UP, NORTH IS UP, etc. It seems impossible to imagine a single general concept with any content at all that would be an abstraction of HEIGHT, HAPPINESS, CONTROL, MORE, VIRTUE, THE FUTURE, REASON, and NORTH and which would precisely fit them all. Moreover, it would seem that UP and DOWN could not be at the same level of abstraction, since UP applies to the FUTURE, while DOWN does not apply to the PAST. We account for this by partial metaphorical structuring, but under the abstraction proposal UP would have to be more abstract in some sense than DOWN, and that does not seem to make sense.

(4) The abstraction theory would not distinguish between metaphors of the form "*A is B*" and those of the form "*B is A*," since it would claim that there are neutral terms covering both domains. For example, English has the LOVE IS A JOURNEY metaphor, but no JOURNEYS ARE LOVE metaphor. The abstraction view would deny that love is understood in terms of journeys, and would be left with the counterintuitive claim that love and journeys are understood in terms of some abstract concept neutral between them.

(5) Different conventional metaphors can structure different aspects of a single concept. For example, LOVE IS A JOURNEY; LOVE IS WAR; LOVE IS AN ELECTROMAGNETIC PHENOMENON; LOVE IS MADNESS; LOVE IS A GAME. Each of these provides one perspective on the concept of love and structures one of many aspects of the concept. The abstraction hypothesis would seek a single general concept of love which is abstract enough to fit all of these. This would miss the point that these metaphors are not jointly characterizing a core concept of love, but are separately characterizing different aspects of the concept of love.

(6) Finally, the abstraction hypothesis assumes, in the case of LOVE IS A JOURNEY, for example, that there is a set of abstract concepts, neutral with respect to love and journeys, which can "fit" or "apply to" both of them. But in order for such abstract concepts to "fit" or "apply to" love, the concept of love must be independently structured, so that there can be such a "fit." As we will show, love is, on its own terms, not a concept that has a clearly delineated structure; it gets such structure only via conventional metaphors. But the abstraction view, which has no conventional metaphors to do the

structuring, must assume that a structure as clearly delineated as the relevant aspects of journeys exists independently for the concept of love. It's hard to imagine how.

X. How Is Our Conceptual System Grounded?

We claim that most of our normal conceptual system is metaphorically structured; that is, most concepts are partially understood in terms of other concepts. This raises an important question about the grounding of our conceptual system. Are there any concepts at all that are understood directly without metaphor? If not, how can we understand anything at all?

The prime candidates for concepts that are understood directly are the simple spatial concepts, such as UP. Our spatial concept UP arises out of our spatial experience. We have bodies and stand erect. Virtually every motor movement that we make involves a motor program that either changes our UP-DOWN orientation, maintains it, presupposes it, or takes it into account in some way. Our constant physical activity in the world, even when we sleep, makes UP-DOWN orientation not merely relevant to our physical activity, but centrally relevant. The centrality of UP-DOWN orientation in our motor programs and everyday functioning might make one think that there could be no alternative to such an orientational concept. Objectively speaking, however, there are many possible frameworks for spatial orientation, including Cartesian coordinates, which don't in themselves have UP-DOWN orientation. Human spatial concepts, however, include UP-DOWN, FRONT-BACK, IN-OUT, NEAR-FAR, etc. It is these that are relevant to our continual everyday bodily functioning, which gives them a relative priority over other possible structurings of space *for us.* In other words, the structure of our spatial concepts emerges from our constant spatial experience, that is, our interaction with our physical environment. Concepts that emerge in this way are concepts that we live by in the most fundamental way.

Thus, UP is *not* understood purely in its own terms, but emerges from the collection of constantly performed motor functions that have to do with our erect position relative to the gravitational field we live in. Imagine a spherical being living outside of any gravitational field, with no knowledge or imagination of any other kind of experience. What could UP possibly mean to such a being?

Some of the central concepts in terms of which our bodies function—UP-DOWN, IN-OUT, FRONT-BACK, LIGHT-DARK, WARM-COLD, MALE-FEMALE, etc.—are more sharply delineated than others. Our emotional experience is as basic as our spatial and perceptual experience, but our emotional experiences are much less sharply delineated in terms of what we do with our bodies. Although a sharply delineated conceptual structure for space emerges from our perceptual-motor functioning, no sharply defined conceptual structure for the emotions emerges from our emotional functioning alone. Since there are *systematic correlates* between our emotions (like happiness) and our sensory-motor experiences (like erect posture), these form the basis of orientational metaphorical concepts (such as HAPPY IS UP). Such metaphors allow us to conceptualize our emotions in more sharply defined terms and also to relate them to other concepts having to do with general well-being (e.g., HEALTH, LIFE, CONTROL, etc.). In this sense, we can speak of *emergent metaphors* as well as emergent concepts.

The concepts of OBJECT, SUBSTANCE, and CONTAINER also emerge directly. We experience ourselves as entities, separate from the rest of the world—CONTAINERS with an inside and an outside. We also experience things external to us as entities—often also CONTAINERS with insides and outsides. We experience ourselves as being made up of SUBSTANCES, e.g., flesh and bone, and external objects as being made up of various *kinds* of SUBSTANCES—wood, stone, metal, etc. We experience many things, through sight and touch, as having distinct boundaries. And when things have no distinct boundaries, we often project boundaries upon them—conceptualizing them as entities and often as containers (for example, forests, clearings, clouds, etc.).

Like orientational metaphors, basic physical metaphors are grounded by virtue of *systematic correlates within our experience.* For example, the metaphor THE VISUAL FIELD IS A CONTAINER is grounded in the correlation of what we see with a bounded physical space. The TIME IS A MOVING OBJECT metaphor is based on the correlation between an object moving toward us and the time it takes to get to us. The same correlation is a basis for the TIME IS A CONTAINER metaphor (as in "He did it *in* ten minutes"), with the *bounded* space traversed by the object correlated with the time the object takes to traverse it. EVENTS and ACTIONS are correlated with bounded time spans, which makes them CONTAINER-OBJECTS.

Perhaps the most important thing to stress about grounding is the distinction between an experience and the way we conceptualize it. We are *not* claiming that physical experience is in any way more basic than other kinds of experience, whether emotional, mental, cultural, or whatever. All these experiences may be just as basic as physical experiences. Rather, what we *are* claiming about grounding is that we typically *conceptualize* the nonphysical in terms of the physical—or the less clearly delineated in terms of the more clearly delineated. To see this more clearly, consider the following examples:

(1) Harry is *in* the kitchen.
(2) Harry is *in* the Elks Club.
(3) Harry is *in* love.

The sentences refer to three different domains of experience: spatial, social, and emotional. None of these has experiential priority over the others; they are all equally basic kinds of experience.

But with respect to conceptual structuring there is a difference. The concept IN expressed in (1) emerges *directly* from spatial experience in a clearly delineated fashion. It is not an instance of a metaphorical concept. The other two sentences *are* instances of metaphorical concepts. (2) is an instance of the SOCIAL GROUPS ARE CONTAINERS metaphor, in terms of which the concept of a social group is structured. This metaphor allows us to "get a handle on" the concept of a social group by means of spatialization. Both the word 'in' and the concept IN are the *same* in all three examples; we do not have three different concepts of IN or three homophonous words 'in'. We have one emergent concept IN, one word for it, and two metaphorical concepts which partially define social groups and emotional states. What these cases show is that it is possible to have equally basic kinds of experiences while having conceptualizations of them that are not equally basic.

Thus, (1) happens to be, according to our account, a nonmetaphoric literal sentence, containing a directly spatial nonmetaphoric instance of the spatial concept IN. But for most linguistic purposes this doesn't give it any particularly special status over (2) and (3).

However, sentences like (1) do seem to have special status in philosophical papers dealing with literal meaning. Sentences like (1) are much more likely to be used as clear examples of literal meaning than are sentences like (2) and (3), since philosophers seem instinctively to shy away from using sentences containing conventional metaphors as examples of literal meaning. That is the reason for the predominance of examples such as "The cat is on the mat," "Snow is white," "Brutus killed Caesar," etc.

XI. An Example of An Emergent Category

Our discussion in the two previous sections of the grounding of our conceptual system and the nature of nonmetaphoric literal meaning may seem to provide a framework for a "building-block" theory, in which all meaningful utterances either are or are constructed from certain unanalyzable semantic units. But we reject the notion of unanalyzable simples which might serve as the atoms for a linguistic or epistemological foundationalism. Instead, we wish to identify emergent categories and concepts that are best understood as experiential gestalts, which, though decomposable into other elements, are yet basic and irreducible in terms of grounding our conceptual system.

To explain this important notion, let us now move beyond our use of spatial examples of concepts that emerge from our successful functioning in our environment (e.g., UP-DOWN, IN-OUT, etc.) to a consideration of the concept of causation. Piaget has hypothesized that infants first learn about causation through the realization of their ability to manipulate directly objects around them—pulling off their blankets, throwing their bottles, dropping toys. There is, in fact, a stage in which infants seem to "practice" these manipulations, e.g., repeatedly dropping their spoons. As the child masters these more primitive manipulations of external objects, it moves on to other tasks which are to become part of its constant everyday functioning in its environment, for example, flipping lightswitches, opening doors, buttoning shirts, adjusting glasses. Though each of these actions is different, the overwhelming proportion of them share common features of what we may call a "prototypical" or "paradigmatic" case of direct causation. Among these shared features are included:

1. The agent has as a goal some change of state in the patient.
2. The change of state is physical.
3. The agent has a "plan" for carrying out this goal.
4. The plan requires the agent's use of a motor program.
5. The agent is in control of that motor program.
6. The agent is primarily responsible for carrying out the plan.
7. The agent is the energy source (i.e., the agent is directing his energies toward the patient) and the patient is the energy goal (i.e., the change in the patient is due to an external source of energy).
8. The agent touches the patient either with his body or with an instrument (i.e., the change in the patient is due to an external source of energy).
9. The agent successfully carries out the plan.
10. The change in the patient is perceptible.
11. The agent monitors the change in the patient through sensory perception.
12. There is a single specific agent and a single specific patient.

This set of properties characterizes "prototypical" direct manipulations, and these are cases of causation par excellence. We are using the word 'prototypical' in the sense used by Eleanor Rosch in her theory of human categorization.[6] Her experiments indicate that people categorize objects, not in set-theoretical terms, but in terms of prototypes and family resemblances. For example, small flying singing birds like sparrows, robins, etc., are prototypical birds. Chickens, ostriches, and penguins are birds, but not central members of the category—they are nonprototypical birds. But they are birds, nonetheless, because they bear sufficient family resemblances to the prototype; that is, they share enough of the relevant properties of the prototype to be classified by people as birds.

The twelve properties given above characterize a prototype of causation in the following sense. They recur together over and over in action after action as we go through our daily lives. We experience them as a gestalt, in which the complex of properties occurring together is more basic to our experience than their separate occurrences. Through their constant recurrence in our everyday functioning, the category of causation emerges with this complex of properties characterizing prototypical causations. Other kinds of causation, which are less prototypical, are actions or events that bear sufficient family resemblances to the prototype. These would include action at a distance, nonhuman agency, the use of an intermediate agent, the occurrence of two or more agents, involuntary or uncontrolled use of the motor program, etc. In physical causation the agent and patient are events, a physical law takes the place of plan, goal, and motor activity, and all the peculiarly human aspects are factored out. When there is not sufficient family resemblance to the prototype, we cease to characterize what happens as causation; for example, if there were multiple agents, if what the agents did was remote in space and time from the patient's change, and if there were neither desire nor plan nor control, then we probably wouldn't say that this was an instance of causation, or at least we would have questions about it.

Although the category of causation has fuzzy boundaries, it is clearly delineated in an enormous range of instances. Our successful functioning in the world involves the application of the concept of causation to ever new domains of activity — through intention, planning, drawing inferences, etc. The concept is stable, because we continue to function successfully in terms of it. Given a concept of causation that emerges from our experience, that concept can be applied to metaphorical concepts. In "Harry raised our morale by telling jokes," for example, we have an instance of causation where what Harry did made our morale go UP, as in the HAPPY IS UP metaphor.

Though the concept of causation as we have characterized it is basic to human activity, it is not a "primitive" in the usual building-block sense; that is, it is not unanalyzable and undecomposable. Since it is defined in terms of a prototype that is characterized by a recurrent complex of properties, our concept of causation is both analyzable into those properties and capable of a wide range of variation. The terms into which the causation prototype is analyzed (e.g., control, motor program, volition, etc.) are probably also characterized by prototype and capable of further analysis. This permits us to have concepts that are at once experientially basic and indefinitely analyzable.

XII. Novel Metaphor

We have already discussed some cases of novel metaphor as instances of the extensions of a conventional metaphor drawn from ordinary language. We gave examples of extensions of both the "used" and "unused" portion of the THEORIES ARE BUILDINGS metaphor and also of a truly novel metaphor not normally used to structure our conceptual system (for example, the CLASSICAL THEORIES ARE PATRIARCHS metaphor). We now want to explore more fully the workings of novel metaphor by focusing on two problems of special philosophical importance. First, what makes one metaphor more appropriate or fitting than another, and second, in what sense, if any, may we speak of the truth of a metaphor?

A. *What Makes a Novel Metaphor Appropriate?*

Consider the new metaphor: LOVE IS A COLLABORATIVE WORK OF ART. This is a metaphor that we personally find particularly forceful, insightful, and appropriate, given our experiences as members of our generation and our culture. The reason is that it makes our experiences coherent—it makes sense of them. But how can a mere metaphor make coherent a large and diverse range of experiences? The answer, we believe, comes out of the fact that metaphors have entailments. A novel metaphor may entail both other novel metaphors and literal statements. For example, the entailments of LOVE IS A COLLABORATIVE WORK OF ART arise from our knowledge and experience of what it means for something to be a collaborative work of art. Here are some of the entailments of this metaphor, based on our own experiences of what a collaborative work of art entails.

LOVE IS WORK.
LOVE IS ACTIVE.
LOVE REQUIRES HELPING.
LOVE REQUIRES COMPROMISE.
LOVE REQUIRES PATIENCE.
LOVE REQUIRES SHARED VALUES AND GOALS.
LOVE DEMANDS SACRIFICE.

LOVE IS AN AESTHETIC EXPERIENCE.
LOVE IS VALUABLE IN ITSELF.
LOVE IS AN EXPRESSION OF DEEPEST EMOTION.
LOVE IS CREATIVE.
LOVE INVOLVES BEAUTY.
LOVE REQUIRES HARMONY.

LOVE INVOLVES
FRUSTRATION.
LOVE REQUIRES
DISCIPLINE.
LOVE BRINGS JOY
AND PAIN.

LOVE CANNOT BE ACHIEVED
BY FORMULA.
LOVE IS UNIQUE IN EACH
INSTANCE.
LOVE IS UNPREDICTABLE IN
ITS OUTCOME.
LOVE IS AN ACT OF
COMMUNICATION.

Some of these entailments are literal (e.g., LOVE REQUIRES PA-TIENCE); others are themselves novel metaphors (e.g., LOVE IS AN AESTHETIC EXPERIENCE). Each of these entailments may itself have further entailments. The result is a large and coherent network of entailments which may, on the whole, either fit or not fit our experiences of love. When such a coherent network of entailments fits our experiences, those experiences form a coherent whole as instances of the metaphor. What we experience with such a metaphor is a kind of reverberation down through the network of entailments which awakens and connects our memories of our past love experiences and serves as a possible guide for future ones.

Let's get more specific about what we mean by "reverberations" in the metaphor LOVE IS A COLLABORATIVE WORK OF ART.

(1) The metaphor highlights certain features while suppressing others. For example, the ACTIVE side of love is brought into the foreground through the notion of WORK both in COLLABORATIVE WORK and in WORK OF ART. This requires the masking of certain aspects of love which are viewed passively. In fact, the emotional aspects of love are almost never viewed as being under active control in our literal language. Even in the LOVE IS A JOURNEY metaphor, the relationship is viewed as a vehicle that is not in the couple's active control, one that can be OFF THE TRACKS, or ON THE ROCKS, or NOT GOING ANYWHERE. In the LOVE IS MADNESS metaphor ("I'm crazy about her," "She's driving we wild"), there is the ultimate lack of control. In the LOVE IS HEALTH metaphor, where the relationship is a patient ("It's a healthy relationship," "It's a sick relationship," "Their relationship is reviving"), the passivity of health in this culture is transferred to love. Thus, in focusing on various aspects of activity (e.g., WORK, CREATION, PURSUING GOALS,

BUILDING, HELPING, etc.), the metaphor provides an organization of important love experiences that the literal language does not make available.

(2) The metaphor does not merely entail other concepts, like WORK or PURSUING SHARED GOALS, but it entails very specific *aspects* of these concepts. It is not just any work, like working on an automobile assembly line, for instance. It is work that requires special balance of power and letting go which is appropriate to artistic creation. It is not just any kind of goal that is pursued, but a joint aesthetic goal. And though the metaphor may suppress the out-of-control aspects of the LOVE IS MADNESS metaphor, it highlights another aspect, namely, the sense of almost demonic possession which lies behind our culture's connection between artistic genius and madness.

(3) Because the metaphor highlights important love experiences and makes them coherent, while it masks other love experiences, the metaphor gives love a new meaning. If those things entailed by the metaphor are for us the most important aspects of our love experiences, then the metaphor can acquire the status of a truth—for many people, love *is* a collaborative work of art. And because it is, the metaphor can have a feedback effect, guiding our future actions in accordance with the metaphor.

(4) Thus, metaphors can be appropriate because they sanction actions, justify inferences, and help us set goals. For example, certain actions, inferences, and goals are dictated by the LOVE IS A COLLABORATIVE WORK OF ART metaphor but not by the LOVE IS MADNESS metaphor. If love is MADNESS, I do not concentrate on what I have to do to maintain it. But if it is WORK, then it requires activity, and if it is a WORK OF ART, it requires a very special *kind* of activity, and if it is COLLABORATIVE, then it is even further restricted and specified.

(5) The meaning a metaphor will have for me will be partly culturally determined and partly tied to my past experiences. The cultural differences can be enormous because each of the concepts in the metaphor under discussion can vary widely from culture to culture—ART, WORK, COLLABORATION, and LOVE. Thus LOVE IS A COLLABORATIVE WORK OF ART would mean very different things to a nineteenth-century European romantic than to a Greenland

Eskimo of the same time period. There will also be differences within a culture based on the structure and significance of one's past experiences. LOVE IS A COLLABORATIVE WORK OF ART will mean something very different to two fourteen-year-olds on their first date than to a mature artist-couple. Only when the entailments of a metaphor fit our cultural and personal experience closely enough and when it seems reasonable to ignore what it hides, can we speak of it as being appropriate, and perhaps even true.

B. *Metaphor, Truth, and Action*

In the previous section we established the following:

(1) Metaphors have entailments through which they highlight and make coherent certain aspects of our experience.

(2) A given metaphor may be the only way to highlight or organize coherently exactly those aspects of our experiences.

(3) Through its entailments, a metaphor may be a guide for future action. Such actions will, of course, fit the metaphor. This will, in turn, reinforce the power of the metaphor to make experience coherent. Metaphors, therefore, can be like self-fulfilling prophecies.

For example, in the energy crisis President Carter declared "the moral equivalent of war." The WAR metaphor generated a network of entailments. There was an ENEMY, a THREAT TO NATIONAL SECURITY, which required SETTING TARGETS, REORGANIZING PRIORITIES, ESTABLISHING A NEW CHAIN OF COMMAND, PLOTTING NEW STRATEGY, GATHERING INTELLIGENCE, MARSHALLING FORCES, IMPOSING SANCTIONS, CALLING FOR SACRIFICES, and on and on. The WAR metaphor highlighted certain realities and hid others. The metaphor was not merely a way of viewing reality, but constituted a license for policy change and political and economic action. The very acceptance of the metaphor provided grounds for certain inferences: there was an external, foreign, hostile enemy (pictured by cartoonists in Arab headdress); energy needed to be given top priorities; the populace would have to make sacrifices; if we didn't meet the threat, we would not survive. It is important to realize that this was not the only metaphor available. Amory Lovins, for example, suggested the SOFT ENERGY PATH metaphor, which highlighted different facts and had entirely different inferences for action. But Jimmy Carter is more powerful than Amory Lovins. As Charlotte Linde (in conversation) has sadly observed, whether in national politics or in everyday interaction, people in power get to impose their metaphors.

Novel metaphors can have the power of defining reality. They do this through a coherent network of entailments that highlight some features of reality and hide others. The acceptance of the metaphor, which forces us to focus *only* on those aspects of reality which it highlights, leads us to view the entailments of the metaphor as being *true*. Such "truths" are true, of course, only relative to the reality defined by the metaphor. Suppose Carter announces that his administration has won a major energy battle. Is this claim true or false? Even to address oneself to the question requires accepting at least the central parts of the metaphor. If you do not accept the existence of an external enemy, if you think there is no external threat, if you recognize no field of battle, no targets, no clearly defined competing forces, then the issue of objective truth or falsity cannot arise. But if we see reality as defined by the metaphor, that is, if we do see the energy crisis as a war, then we can answer the question relative to whether the metaphorical entailments fit reality. If Carter, by means of strategically employed political and economic sanctions, forced the OPEC nations to cut the price of oil in half, then we would say he would indeed have won a major battle. If, on the other hand, his strategies had produced only a temporary price freeze, we couldn't be so sure and might be skeptical.

Though questions of truth do arise for novel metaphor, the more important questions are those of action. In most cases, what is at issue is not the truth or falsity of a metaphor, but the inferences that follow from it and the actions that are sanctioned by it. In all aspects of life, not just in politics or in love, we define our reality in terms of metaphor, and then proceed to act on the basis of the metaphor. We draw inferences, set goals, make commitments, and execute plans, all on the basis of how we structure our experience, consciously and unconsciously, by means of metaphor.

XIII. Implications for Theories of Meaning and Truth

It is common for contemporary philosophers and linguists to assume (1) that metaphor is a matter of language, not thought, (2) that our everyday conventional language is literal (not metaphorical), and (3) that the central task of a theory of meaning is to give an account of meaning for literal language. The task of a theory of meaning is typically thought to be a matter of supplying truth conditions for literal (that is, nonmetaphorical) utterances. There are, of course, various versions of how this fundamental task is to be carried out, but they all agree that what is needed is a theory of meaning and truth for *literal* sentences. Within this dominant school of thought some insist that the meaning of literal sentences is the only meaning there is. Others argue that the meaning of any nonliteral utterance is merely some function performed on the literal meaning of the sentence used in making the utterance. But, again, both groups focus on giving an account of meaning for literal sentences alone.

What we are suggesting, among other things, is that such a project is not workable when we are dealing with natural languages. We have tried to show that most of our everyday, ordinary conceptual system (and the literal language used to express it) is metaphorically structured. Not only are systems of concepts organized by basic orientational metaphors, but the very concepts themselves are *partially* defined in terms of multiple *physical* and *structural* metaphors. Concepts are not determinable in terms of necessary and sufficient conditions for their application; instead, we grasp them, always in a *partial* fashion, by means of various metaphorical concepts.

What this suggests to us is that no account of meaning and truth can be adequate unless it recognizes and deals with the way in which conventional metaphors structure our conceptual system. Of course, this is no modest claim, for, if we are correct, it calls into question the assumption of many that a complete account of literal meaning can be given without reference to metaphor. It also calls into question, we believe, certain traditional assumptions in the Western philosophical and linguistic traditions about the nature of meaning, truth, logic, rationality, and objectivity.

In a paper of this length, it is impossible even to begin to spell out and support these strong claims. We have recently completed a book-length treatment of the topic (*op. cit.*). Here are the major conclusions that we reach there:

Metaphorical concepts provide ways of understanding one kind of experience in terms of another kind of experience.

Typically this involves understanding less concrete experiences in terms of more concrete and more highly structured experiences.

Many concepts are defined metaphorically, in terms of concrete experiences that we can comprehend, rather than in terms of necessary and sufficient conditions.

This permits cross-cultural differences in conceptual systems: different cultures have different ways of comprehending experience via conceptual metaphor. Such differences will typically be reflected in linguistic differences.

We are thus led to a theory of truth that is dependent on understanding: a sentence is true in a situation when our understanding of the sentence fits our understanding of the situation.

An account of understanding is worked out in terms of a theory of experiential gestalts, that is, structurings of experience along certain natural dimensions: perceptual, functional, etc.

For the present, we hope to have shown only that metaphor is conceptual in nature, that it is pervasive in our everyday conventional language, and that no account of meaning and truth can pretend to be complete, or basically correct, or even on the right track if it cannot account for the kind of phenomena discussed above.

NOTES

1. For a more comprehensive and thorough working out of the implications for several areas, especially philosophy and linguistics, see our *Metaphors We Live By* (Chicago: University of Chicago Press, 1980).

2. The account of systematicity and coherence we are developing may seem similar to Nelson Goodman's claim that metaphor involves a transfer in which "(a) label along with others constituting a scheme is in effect detached from the home realm of that scheme and applied for the sorting and organizing of an alien realm. Partly by thus carrying with it a re-orientation of a whole network of labels does a metaphor give clues for its development and elaboration" [*Languages of Art* (Indianapolis: Bobbs-Merrill, 1968), p. 72]. Here Goodman comes down squarely on the side of those who view metaphor as a matter of language (that is, "labels") rather than as a matter of thought. We are at odds with Goodman on this, as well as other matters. For example, Goodman does not seem to regard most everyday conventional language as metaphorical. Nor, presumably, would he go along with our experientialist account of truth, in which truth is secondary to understanding (cf. our *Metaphors We Live By, op. cit.*).

3. "The Conduit Metaphor," in A. Ortony, ed., *Metaphor and Thought* (New York: Cambridge, 1979).

4. *Figurative Patterns and Redundancy in the Lexicon,* unpublished dissertation, University of California at San Diego, 1974.

5. A philosophical example of the abstractionist position is contained in L. Jonathan Cohen and Avishai Margalit, "The Role of Inductive Reasoning in the Interpretation of Metaphor," in D. Davidson and G. Harman, eds., *Semantics of Natural Language* (Boston: Reidel, 1972), pp. 722-740. "The metaphorical meanings of a word or phrase in a natural language are all contained, as it were, within its literal meaning or meanings. They are reached by removing any restrictions in relation to certain variables from the appropriate section or sections of its semantical hypothesis" (735). The result of merely removing restrictions would always result in a very general meaning in common between the metaphorical and literal meanings.

6. "Human Categorization," in N. Warren, ed., *Advances in Cross-cultural Psychology* (New York: Academic Press, 1977), vol. I.

Selected Annotated Bibliography of Key Sources

Selected Annotated Bibliography of Key Sources

This bibliography is offered as a tool for anyone who wants to determine quickly the relevance of a particular essay or book to a specific issue. Toward this end I have attempted to provide abstracts of each item to give a sense of the author's approach and main claims. Thus, the abstracts are descriptive rather than evaluative. I have also tried to include all the major perspectives on all the important philosophical problems. My primary constraints were to select essays chiefly, though not solely, by philosophers, and to focus primarily on work of the last two decades. There are, no doubt, interesting and important works that I have overlooked. If so, these will be discussed in works included here, and in this way one can become readily familiar with the key sources in the field of metaphor.

Aldrich, Virgil C. "Visual Metaphor." *The Journal of Aesthetic Education*, 2, no. 1 (1968): 73-86.

To express ourselves figuratively requires that we have figurative perceptions as well; if we do not see something figuratively, we cannot speak about it figuratively either. This applies to metaphor in the denial that metaphors can be reduced to literal language. Such a reduction might be possible if there were only two elements involved in the metaphor (the two subjects). But there are actually three elements—the material of the metaphor (the subsidiary subject), the subject matter of the metaphor (the primary subject), and a new element, the content of the metaphor. The subject matter is "bodied-forth" by the material; we grasp the subject matter by means of the material. This produces a new object, the "bodied-forth" subject, which is the real content of the metaphor. The subject matter remains as the meaning of the content, although the latter does not swallow up the former.

In a visual metaphor, one may see the subject matter in terms of the material, but one "prehends" the content. The content is the "expressive portrayal" of the other two elements, without which it would have neither form nor meaning. This means that the content functions much like a symbol—symbols and metaphors represent points on a single continuum—because it expresses the character of the blending of the other elements. There is, therefore, an irreducible element in all metaphors—namely, the symbolic content of the metaphor which we prehend—that stubbornly resists translation into literal language.

Alston, William P. *Philosophy of Language*. Englewood Cliffs, N.J.: Prentice-Hall, 1964. Chap. 5, pp. 96-106.

A metaphor is an extension of a term whose literal meaning we know. The extension enables us to elicit new meanings as we apply the term to new objects in different situations. But this suggests that words can be understood without being used in any established sense. This is possible because all meanings that are ordinarily assigned to words are literal meanings. There is no such thing as a strictly metaphorical meaning. Whatever meaning it is possible to detect in a metaphor is derived from the literal, established meaning; metaphors are parasites on literal meanings. A word used metaphorically extends the conventional meaning of the term into a new domain, and this novel extension accounts for the force of the metaphor. In addition, since the metaphor is just a term thrust into an alien semantic landscape, there is no justification for assuming that the expression is unverifiable.

Barfield, Owen. "The Meaning of the Word 'Literal'." In *Metaphor and Symbol*, edited by L. C. Knights and Basil Cottle, pp. 48-63. London: Butterworths Scientific Publications, 1960.

Barfield challenges the traditional view that words originally had literal meanings, from which metaphorical meanings evolved over a period of time. If there were only literal meanings at the beginning, how could figurative meanings ever arise? People would have needed to experience some figurative use of the language before they could see the possibilities of multiple, diverse meanings for the same word. Thus, words must have had that figurative potential from the very beginning, and ancient man did not fasten his words solely to material objects in a literal way. Barfield suspects that ancient languages must have been metaphoric, with a vehicle and tenor, a literal meaning and another figurative dimension. This view challenges the notion that there are, or ever have been, literal expressions designed to pick out a realm of fixed entities.

Barfield, Owen. "Poetic Diction and Legal Fiction." In *The Importance of Language*, edited by Max Black, pp. 57-71. Englewood Cliffs, N.J.: Prentice-Hall, 1962.

As a linguistic device, metaphor occupies a middle ground between symbols and similes. Similes invite us to compare two things, with the intent of picking out relevant similarities. Symbols, on the other hand, do not depend at all upon similarities being pointed out. Symbols serve as direct and obvious pointers to some other object distinct from the object serving as the symbol. What renders metaphor distinct from either similes or symbols is that in employing metaphors, we say one thing and mean another. An attempt to construe the way that metaphors can be meaningful will lead us to see how metaphors function as catalysts in the creative growth of a language.

This creative dimension of metaphorical usage discloses itself by analogy with the creative aspects of the evolution of legal codes within a society. It is the intent of a law to be fixed, treating impartially all persons and all situations that fall under the law. But no society is static enough to be served by a code of laws that is not flexible and open to change. And it is possible to trace the development of legal "fictions" as means whereby a set of laws is expanded, extended, and manipulated to permit it to cover the dynamic possibilities of a living culture. The same process can be detected in the growth of a language. Whereas legal "fictions" are the vehicles for the extension of law in a society, metaphors are the vehicles for the extension of meaning in a language. Metaphors therefore function as something more than merely linguistic devices: they allow that which is unconscious in a given language to become conscious. A society that seeks to express itself with ever-increasing accuracy and variety will have recourse to metaphor as the means for accomplishing this.

Beardsley, Monroe C. "Metaphorical Senses." *Nous* 12, no. 1 (1978): 3-16.

Theories about metaphor can be described in two ways. *Constancy* theories insist that expressions carry at least one of their standard meanings even when employed in a metaphorical utterance. *Conversion* theories hold that a new sense is acquired by the expression when it is used metaphorically. There are at least two reasons for questioning the adequacy of constancy theories, such as comparison theories. First, there is no way to determine with any consistency the specific standard meaning intended since a satisfactory translation of the metaphor is often not available. Second, it is unlikely that a speaker has in mind the alleged translation, assuming that one were available.

The development of a "metaphorical sense" follows a general pattern. Words possess certain intensional meanings and a constellation of "credence-properties" as well, a "credence-property" being an attribute believed by the community of speakers to be associated with the word. Eventually, through a process heavily dependent on the use of metaphor, the "credence-properties" as applied to the extensions of words become accepted as part of the intensional meaning of the words. Thus, there comes to be, in the standard uses of a word, a "literal" sense and a "metaphorical" sense. This entire process is rule-governed, but only in the most general way; each example of an emergent "metaphorical sense" would display a unique reflection of the rule.

Beardsley, Monroe C. "The Metaphorical Twist." *Philosophy and Phenomenological Research* 22, no. 3 (1962):293-307.

In answer to the question "What is metaphor?" we may distinguish a "thing approach" from a "word approach." One popular "thing" approach, the object-comparison theory, treats metaphor as an implicit comparison in which the focus or vehicle term retains its standard designation but is used to highlight similarities between its referent and that of the principal subject of the metaphor.

Against this object-comparison view, Beardsley argues that inherent tensions within the metaphor cause the metaphoric predicate to lose its ordinary extension and to obtain a new intension, namely, its previous connotation. According to this "word approach," a term will have a central meaning (its ordinary designation) and a marginal meaning (its connotation). In metaphor there occurs a "logical opposition" between the ordinary designated properties of the two things juxtaposed by the metaphor. This failure of primary reference or designation forces us to call up the associated connotations of the modifying term, which are then applied to the principal subject in their new senses. This verbal-opposition theory sees metaphor as inducing insight by calling up or actualizing connotations that were potentially available but not yet noticed. Metaphorical insight, therefore, depends on a "twist of meaning" forced by inherent tensions or oppositions within the metaphor.

Berggren, Douglas. "The Use and Abuse of Metaphor." *The Review of Metaphysics* 16, no. 2 (1962):237-258; and 16, no. 3 (1963):450-472.

If we adopt an interaction theory of metaphor, we must also recognize the tension that exists between the two referents in any metaphorical statement. The tension is the result of employing a "stereoscopic vision" such that the metaphorical statement and its two referents are seen together with the two referents and the new way they are presented to us. Metaphors thus "construe" reality for us, enabling us to know things by "feeling their textures." These "textures" emerge for us out of the tension between "poetic truth" and the world as presented to us. The abuse of metaphor results in taking the metaphor literally, thereby making it into a myth. Statements in which terms retain their initial identity, even while being assimilated, are in tension, and are thus metaphorical. But terms that are so completely assimilated that their initial identity is temporarily lost have also lost the metaphorical tension, and are reduced to myth.

The abuse of metaphor has occurred in the fields of literature, science, and metaphysics. In poetry, for instance, although it is sometimes claimed that there must be a cleavage between the intellect and the poetic imagination, such a separation destroys the value of metaphor and sabotages aesthetic experience as well. In science, the truth of scientific models will depend on their tensional representation of scientific theories; and these theories themselves will require a tension between the "is" (observation) and the "must" (prediction). In metaphysics, there is a temptation to express ontological categories and forms in language that is devoid of tension, which renders metaphysics static and uncreative.

Bickerton, Derek. "Prolegomena to a Linguistic Theory of Metaphor." *Foundations of Language* 5, no. 1 (1969):34-52.

A new theory of metaphor is needed, and it must be *linguistic*, recognizing that meaning exists only in the relationship between speaker, language, and hearer. Metaphor involves an interaction between marked signs. A marked sign is a lexeme to which an attribute has been assigned (e.g., 'hardness' is an attribute of the marked sign 'iron'). Signs become marked by convention, and this establishes a network of oppositions containing distinct categories. A marked sign can thus "stand as representative of the entire category," and this sets up the possibility of transgression of category boundaries. In metaphor the boundary is crossed by the use of a marked sign in such a way that the sign gets a new meaning without eliminating the tension created by the category crossing. The context validates the extension of the marked sign, distinguishing metaphorical assignment from meaninglessness.

Binkley, Timothy. "On the Truth and Probity of Metaphor." *Journal of Aesthetics and Art Criticism* 33, no. 2 (1974):171-180.

Contrary to certain received opinions, some metaphors (a) do not involve false or nonsensical uses of language, (b) can have truth values, and (c) are not essentially different from literal statements in the way we evaluate their truth or falsity. The first claim is argued by citing examples of expressions that are true (or false) for both their literal *and* metaphorical readings. The last two claims are argued by showing that in many cases a claim made by using metaphor "is amenable to argument, which has more or less determinate criteria of evaluation, which can be supported and weakened with evidence, and so on" (p. 174). It is chiefly because we tend to see metaphors as parasitic on literal language that we take them as inferior, substandard, and incapable of having truth values. Once we recognize that there is no pure core of precise literal meaning, we lose the inclination to set up the literal as an ideal standard against which figurative language is to be measured. This approach does not collapse the metaphorical into the literal, but it destroys the basis for the traditional devaluation of metaphor.

Black, Max. "Metaphor." *Proceedings of the Aristotelian Society* N.S. 55 (1954-55): 273-294.

This important essay is the basis for much recent discussion in the field. It identifies several key philosophical issues, surveys the main theories, and claims that certain kinds of metaphor are cognitively indispensable. Black stresses the chief inadequacies of the "substitution" and "comparison" views. Both views make metaphors unnecessary stylistic frills, and the latter is too vague to explain how metaphors work. Black argues the merits of the "interaction" view, which explains metaphorical meaning as the result of a complex interaction ("filtering" or "screening" process) between systems of implications associated with the principal and subsidiary terms of the metaphor. The emergent meaning often cannot be reduced to any literal statement of preexisting similarities; instead, it may actually *induce* similarities. This semantic operation involves a creative and irreducible cognitive act in which some part of our conceptual system is restructured.

Black, Max. "More about Metaphor." *Dialectica* 31, nos. 3-4 (1977): 431-457.

In his earlier article, "Metaphor," Black focused his concern on the conceptual analysis of metaphor. Now the concern shifts to a constellation of problems that require a functional analysis of metaphor: How do metaphors actually work? The central problems that attach to metaphor in this area can best be addressed by considering "strong metaphors," which are both unique and rich in implication. Neither the "substitution theory" nor the "comparison theory" can adequately explain the strong metaphor, and so they must be discarded. Black's "interaction theory" comes closer to accounting for the strong metaphor. It explains the force of those metaphors by pointing to the structural correspondences between the two subjects and by showing how the metaphor mediates the relationship. It is claimed that metaphors produce a shift of meaning, but only a shift in the speaker's and the hearer's meaning. Further, it is held that metaphors operate at a conceptual level, allowing the user to manipulate concepts to reveal insights not otherwise available. Even so, it cannot be said that metaphors have any truth value; to inquire whether a metaphor is true or false is simply inappropriate. Since the world always exists as "a world under a certain description," and not given in an uninterpreted way, verdicts as to truth and falsity regarding metaphorical statements will always fall short of the mark. Finally, it can be shown that there is no fallible test for detecting a metaphor and distinguishing it from literal statements.

Charlton, William. "Living and Dead Metaphors." *British Journal of Aesthetics* 15, no. 2 (1975):172-178.

Max Black's theory of metaphor rests on the erroneous assumption that the central problem of metaphor involves a shift of meaning, a movement from ordinary senses to metaphorical senses. Black's theory is erroneous because it can be shown that there is no shift in meaning that takes place in metaphorical statements. This can be seen by considering the two basic issues of metaphor: first, what a metaphor actually is, and then, how metaphors work. The first concern can be addressed by distinguishing living from dead metaphors. A dead metaphor is one which has passed so completely into common usage that we scarcely recognize it as a metaphor. In these cases, the meaning of the metaphor is evident to all; there is no shift of meaning, since the meaning is already generally understood. In a living metaphor, we have a word used normally, but in an inappropriate context; here the metaphor acquires its force because of its alien context. As soon as a living metaphor is accepted as semantically justified, it becomes a dead metaphor. Meanings remain fairly constant, although subject to extension through metaphorical use.

Black's notion of interaction between the terms of a metaphor may be applied to the second concern. Metaphors are successful if the juxtaposition of terms yields a sense of satisfaction that the terms have been used correctly; that is, if we detect good reasons for the speaker's use of the terms, we are justified in accepting the metaphor. Black's mistake was to claim that a new meaning arose from the interaction of the terms, when in fact the interaction breeds an aesthetic power.

Clark, Ann K. "Metaphor and Literal Language." *Thought* 52, no. 207 (1977): 366-380.

Traditional accounts of metaphor resulted in the claim that metaphors were either liable to a reduction to literal language, or meaningless. But this denies too much about the force and the scope of metaphors, since it assumes that literal meanings are fixed and final and that metaphorical meanings are merely parasitic on the literal. Even those contemporary philosophers who defend metaphor as irreducible ultimately rely on the literal meanings of words as the only legitimate means of grounding an understanding of metaphor. What is needed is a theory not merely of metaphor, but of literal language as well, which will do full justice to both forms of expression.

Literal language must be seen as transparent. This means that although there are general limits to the meaning of a term used literally, the meaning is in no way final or closed. Instead, the meaning of the term allows us to see through the term to the underlying reality beneath it. Since words do not have the power to depict reality absolutely, there must be several ways for an expression to point out the reality that a speaker intends to cover. Literal language, then, becomes one way of seeing a portion of reality, metaphor another. In fact, we see through the literal language to the metaphorical language; both seek to elicit meaning from reality. But this does not suggest that there are no limits to the range of meaning for a single utterance. Literal language has evolved its literal meaning simply because we do require limits to our language; the literal is the limit. But within that limit, the task is always to see more and more of the reality to which the literal and the metaphorical expressions point.

Cohen, Ted. "Figurative Speech and Figurative Acts." *Journal of Philosophy* 72, no.19 (1975):669-684.

Cohen explores the view that metaphors are illocutionary analogues of figurative speech acts, i.e., that they are special cases of the general phenomenon of successful aberration within a speech act. Based on Austin's distinction between acts done *in* saying something (illocutions) and acts done *by* saying something (perlocutions), it is argued that certain speech acts cannot be performed unless the appropriate perlocution associated with each act is possible in the given context. Thus I cannot perform the illocutionary act of promising, if the situation of my utterance is such that I cannot make the promise in question. I may utter the words "I promise to live past 1992," but since this is something I cannot promise, the normal illocution fails. However, I may still make a successful utterance, though it would be a sort of aberration—a figurative speech act. There may be an analogous process at work in cases of metaphor. Our identification of an utterance as metaphorical involves a strain between the normal sense of the utterance and the total speech situation in which it occurs. Seeing metaphor as analogous to a figurative speech act may eventually lead us to an understanding of how we are able to identify and comprehend metaphors.

Cohen, Ted. "Metaphor and the Cultivation of Intimacy." *Critical Inquiry* 5, no. 1 (1978):3-12.

Philosophical debates over the cognitive status of metaphor typically focus on whether metaphors can be bearers of knowledge. But perhaps knowledge is not the only, or even the most important, reason for using metaphors. In addition to their cognitive and aesthetic import, metaphors may play a role in the achievement of intimacy. In this respect metaphors are very much like jokes. In order to recognize a joke *as a joke* and get its point, the hearer must share certain beliefs, attitudes, experiences, etc., with the teller of the joke. Grasping the point of a joke draws one into the community of those who share the requisite background for appreciating the humor involved. Whereas some jokes require very little background knowledge, others can be understood by only a select group. Metaphors, too, depend upon shared knowledge, attitudes, intentions, etc., for their recognition and comprehension by the hearers, who are thus drawn into a community of those capable of appreciating particular metaphors. Good jokes.

Cohen, Ted. "Notes on Metaphor." *Journal of Aesthetics and Art Criticism* 34, no. 3 (1976):249-259.

The mistaken belief that the mechanism of metaphor is clear can be traced, in part, to two widely held theses: (1) In a metaphor the meaning of at least one term has changed, and (2) a metaphor taken literally is false. Concerning the first thesis, Cohen shows that, whatever the relation between the literal and metaphorical senses of a term is, it is a far more complex matter than has been supposed. For example, if I apprehend "X is F" as a metaphor, it does not follow, as most claim, that some of its normal implications must fail. This error is a companion to the second thesis, above—that a metaphor taken literally is false. Literal falsity cannot be a necessary condition of a metaphor, since there are indefinitely many "twice-true" metaphors, i.e., expressions that are true taken both literally and metaphorically.

In sum, contrary to the standard opinion, there do not seem to be any simple criteria for identifying metaphors, nor is there a rule-governed function for getting at the meaning of a metaphor. With respect to these problems, we are back where we started in our attempts to figure out how metaphor works.

Davidson, Donald. "What Metaphors Mean." *Critical Inquiry* 5, no. 1 (1978):31-47.

Nearly all the standard accounts of metaphor rest on a serious error: they assume that a metaphor has, in addition to its literal sense or meaning, some special "metaphorical meaning." The only meaning a metaphor has is its literal meaning—metaphor is a special *use* of this literal meaning to "intimate" or "suggest" what might not otherwise have been noticed. An attempt is made to explain why it has been so tempting to posit mysterious metaphorical senses. This leads to a critique of the view that a metaphor's meaning is identical with that of some corresponding simile. In short, the assumption of "metaphorical meaning" is neither necessary nor useful for explaining how metaphors work or what they can be used to do.

de Man, Paul. "The Epistemology of Metaphor." *Critical Inquiry* 5, no. 1 (1978): 13-30.

It has been traditionally assumed that, even if metaphors assist us in appreciating certain features of perceived objects and events, they play no epistemological role in the way we come to understand the world. This claim is challenged, and the challenge is substantiated by a survey of three philosophers who evidently believed they were laying down epistemological foundations. In the case of Locke, Condillac, and Kant, the ubiquity of the figurative language of rhetoric is acknowledged, and an attempt is made to diminish its importance for knowledge. In spite of the efforts of these thinkers, it turns out to be impossible to isolate rhetoric from language with fixed meanings and to banish the former to the fever-swamps of aesthetics, where meanings are supposed to be ambiguous: "the resulting undecidability is due to the asymmetry of the binary model that opposes the figural to the proper meaning of the figure" (p. 28). It is futile to seek to eliminate the rhetorical structure of texts in favor of some more "objective" structure. At this point aesthetic and epistemological distinctions collapse, and metaphor can be seen as operating creatively in the shaping and extending of our understanding.

Dickie, George. "Metaphor." In *Aesthetics: An Introduction*, pp. 131-140. Indiana-polis: Bobbs-Merrill, Pegasus, 1971.

It appears that in most metaphors the term that is being used metaphorically does not refer to any determinate thing. In "Richard is a lion," "Richard" designates a specific object, but "lion" suggests only a general class of things. When we inspect the metaphor-ical term in most metaphors, we discover that there is no specific meaning, only the most general meaning that can be provided by the dictionary. Thus, the "object-comparison" theory of metaphor cannot be correct, since this theory assumes that there are two objects being compared. On the contrary, there are not two distinct objects. There is only one object designated, and one general class of things suggested. The class referred to by the metaphorical term is grasped through the dictionary meaning, which records normal usage.

In addition to employing the meanings available in dictionaries, understanding a meta-phor will require us to pay attention to the context of the metaphor. Indeed, we cannot know whether we are to take a sentence metaphorically until we understand the entire sentence. Only by grasping the whole context of a metaphorical term can we even identify it as such. By forcing us back to the meanings that emerge in common usage and by making us note the context of metaphors, we can see that metaphors are very unlike similes: they are not to be understood as literal statements. Hence, the traditional view of metaphor as an elliptical simile is inadequate.

Dilworth, John B. "A Representational Approach to Metaphor." *Journal of Aesthetics and Art Criticism* 37, no. 4 (1979): 467-473.

The difficulty with many current theories of metaphor is that they focus on meaning. But semantic concerns frequently are plagued with a fundamental dependence on subjec-tive judgments as to what a word or expression means. What is called for is some general and public way of explaining metaphors, one that will treat metaphors as public objects. It is suggested that successful metaphorical phrases can represent what the words in the phrase might ordinarily describe literally, but because the words are combined in a new way, we understand the phrase in a different way. In this sense, one term in a metaphor represents an-other. "That dog is a dead sheep" can be understood as meaning, "That dog is intended to be a representation of a dead sheep." A distinction must be drawn between those acts of representation in which the representing object simply is asserted to be the representation of some object X, and those acts in which the representing object does in fact reveal some discernible features of X. In this way, the limits of a successful metaphor can be established.

Such a representational theory does away both with the necessity of searching out com-parisons between the objects suggested by the two terms, and with the need to look for similarities, since one thing may represent another regardless of any antecedent similarities. The test of the metaphor's success is whether or not it does tell us something reliable about the object being represented.

Edie, James M. "Expression and Metaphor." *Philosophy and Phenomenological Re-search* 23 (1962-63): 538-61.

When we examine language phenomenologically, we are able to situate it in the larger category of expression. Expression involves the total experience of humans; it describes the means by which we are able to organize and understand our experience as well as to communicate it. Metaphor plays an important role in this process, since it enables us to structure our experience by moving from those things we understand to those things we do not understand. A phenomenological account of metaphor will depend on making a distinction between words and meaning. Words may point to meanings, but they cannot encapsulate the complete meaning pointed to. This is because meanings are ambiguous and "open-textured." Meanings are multidimensional and constantly changing; even as a person is not to be identified by reference to some eternally fixed entity ("mind" or "reason"), so is it similarly impossible to cut meanings to fit the words that express them. Metaphors are particularly apt, then, as ways of interpreting our experience, since there is no assumption that words and meanings can be permanently fastened to one another. Metaphors are composed of words that have distinguished and named certain dimensions or aspects of our experience. These words are then available for new applications in the interpretation of our experience. This interpretive process begins anew by the deployment of words to cover new dimensions of meaning.

Gass, William H. "In Terms of the Toenail: Fiction and the Figures of Life." In *Fiction and the Figures of Life*, pp. 55-76. New York: Alfred A. Knopf, 1970.

Metaphors are models that bring together otherwise disparate elements in order to gain insight into our experience. The scientist has, on the one hand, a mass of observed data, but it has no obvious logical relations or causal connections. On the other hand, the scientist does have mathematical and logical structures, which yield no useful information about the world. But when the scientist puts these two domains together—when the scientist sees the data in terms of the structures—he or she has constructed a model that is, first, fundamentally metaphorical and, second, an aid in understanding our experience. It is claimed that metaphors "argue" a point of view and that they are a form of "presentation" or "display." This "presentational" aspect of metaphor means that we are asked to acquaint ourselves directly with the subject presented in the metaphor, rather than settle for a second-hand description of the subject. In this way, metaphors are like novels: they are invitations to enter into a different kind of reality and to engage the subject in a novel way.

Goodman, Nelson. *Languages of Art*. Indianapolis: Bobbs-Merrill, 1968. Chap. 2, secs. 5-8, pp. 68-95.

Goodman provides an extensional and nominalistic account of metaphor as a kind of "calculated category mistake." It involves projecting a label belonging to one realm of objects upon another realm to which that label does not normally apply. "In metaphor, . . . , a term with an extension established by habit is applied elsewhere under the influence of that habit" (p. 71). The result of this transfer is a sorting and organizing of the new realm onto which an entire set of labels is projected. Metaphor is pervasive in *all* language and can be used to make truth claims, although *how* metaphors are true or false is just as mystifying as how literal expressions can be true or false. In neither case do we have any explanation of why a certain predicate applies as it does.

Haynes, Felicity. "Metaphor as Interactive." *Educational Theory* 25, no. 3 (1975): 272-277.

Andrew Ortony, in his "Why Metaphors are Necessary and Not Just Nice," is unable to argue the indispensability of metaphor, because he still assumes that it is basically comparative in nature. There *is* a *comparative level* of metaphor where characteristics of Y are transferred to X in order to say something about X. At the comparison level we comprehend similarities between objects (X and Y) in a rule-governed systematic way. But there is also an *interactive level* where "placing known characteristics of Y against those of X may provide *new* insights, either about X or about a new third, Z, an irreducible synthesis by juxtaposition which it is difficult to reduce to simile or literal language" (p. 273). This second level is not a rule-governed comparison; rather, it involves an "intuitive grasping of a whole that is not reducible to any system" (p. 276).

Henle, Paul. "Metaphor." In *Language, Thought, and Culture,* edited by P. Henle, pp. 173-195. Ann Arbor: University of Michigan Press, 1958.

The way metaphors work can be explained in terms of Peirce's distinction between a *symbol,* i.e., a sign that signifies by convention, and an *icon,* which signifies by virtue of similarity with the thing signified. In metaphor there is an underlying analogy in which one component, the iconic, is used to present the other. This iconic element is never actually present; rather, it provides a rule for reflecting on the object or situation that it signifies. The richness of meaning of a given metaphor is a matter of how fully and extensively one can elaborate the similarities between the icon and what is iconized. However, a metaphor's meaning is not merely some literal statement of the initial similarities that make the metaphor possible; there may also be, in many cases, an additional (or induced) similarity caused by the metaphor.

Hesse, Mary B. "The Explanatory Function of Metaphor." In *Models and Analogies in Science*, pp. 157-177. Notre Dame: University of Notre Dame Press, 1966.

Scientific models are understood to be types of metaphor, whereby the domain of the explanandum is modified and redescribed by the application of the explanans. In adopting an interaction theory of metaphor, it is possible to show that a theoretical explanation operates as a subsidiary subject does in poetic metaphor: it enables us to "see" the principle subject (in the case of scientific models, this is the explanandum) in a new way. However, scientific models differ from poetic metaphors in that the former are more logically rigorous, and they are subject to more extensive empirical testing. Not all explanations are metaphorical, because not all explanations are intended to be theoretical. Theoretical explanations give rise to scientific models, which are then best understood as metaphors.

This account has two advantages over the traditional interpretation of scientific models. First, the deductive-nomological account assumed that there must be a deductive relation between the explanadum and the explanans, but such a relation could seldom be demonstrated. Relations of approximate fit between the two elements could be pointed out, however, and this is compatible with an interaction theory of metaphor. Second, there has always been a problem with accounting for the necessary correspondence rules that manage the relation between the explanandum and the explanans. But if we understand scientific models as metaphors, we do away with the need for correspondence rules.

Hester, Marcus B. "Metaphor and Aspect Seeing." *Journal of Aesthetics and Art Criticism* 25, no. 2 (1966):205-212.

Poetic metaphor can be understood as a version of what Wittgenstein called "seeing as" or "noticing an aspect." It is not, however, a *visual* seeing, but rather a "seeing as between the metaphorical subject and the metaphorical predicate, either one or both of which must be image-exciting." Whereas visual "seeing as" involves the discernment of different aspects of one given configuration (as in the duck-rabbit figure), the metaphorical counterpart moves in the opposite direction, requiring us to find the basis of the isomorphism that unites two separate things. Thus, comprehending a poetic metaphor requires an irreducible imaginative accomplishment on the part of the hearer, who must grasp the underlying unity of seemingly disparate things.

Horsburgh, H. J. N. "Philosophers against Metaphor." *Philosophical Quarterly* 8, no.32 (1958):231-245.

Horsburgh examines some of the stock criticisms levied against metaphor and suggests that the critics have perhaps gone overboard in their injunctions against the "misleading" nature of metaphorical expression. There are at least three criteria helpful in clarifying how metaphors function. The first is the Criterion of Standard Questions, in which the metaphorical statement suggests a series of questions that might be addressed to, and theoretically answered by, the speaker. If the questions cannot be answered in accordance with the evident meaning of literal language, we have the prospect of a metaphor. The second is the Criterion of Standard Echoes, wherein we come up against words, usually prepositions, that cannot be handled by the first Criterion. Here the suggestion is that such words bear implicit meanings that resonate with the meanings of other words in the metaphorical expression, creating new meanings in the process. Finally, Horsburgh takes on the complaint that metaphors are not a serious philosophical problem; they are "mere metaphors." He introduces the Criterion of Logical Dependence, in which he shows that metaphorical statements are extensions of literal language, so that the meaning of a metaphor will be logically dependent on some antecedent literal meaning.

Horsburgh believes his efforts at muting the criticisms of metaphor will assist in the effort to reveal metaphors as the clearest and most precise form of language in many instances, and in the task of redressing the superficiality of positivism in the treatment of language. Metaphorical language is frequently accused of being misleading because it leads to logical confusions. If metaphors are regarded as literal falsehoods, they must be anathema to clear thinking. What is needed, if metaphors are to be accepted as epistemologically respectable, are criteria that will indicate the limits within which metaphors can be understood and employed.

Isenberg, Arnold. "On Defining Metaphor." *The Journal of Philosophy* 60, no. 21 (1963):609-622.

There is a fundamental tension in the frequent attempts to define metaphor. On the one hand, it seems that we cannot escape the notion that metaphors involve "resemblance in difference." But on the other hand, we cannot embrace the idea of "resemblance in difference" as the foundation of a definition of metaphor, since this definition does not tell us nearly enough. We have no way of telling when we have satisfied such a requirement, no way of knowing when we have sufficient "resemblance" and sufficient "difference." It would seem that "resemblance in difference" is a particular instance of the traditional rubric invoked to designate a successful work of art: that it possesses "unity in variety." But this definition of "unity in variety" has the same problem as "resemblance in difference": namely, it does not tell us how we are to find the marks of unity or the marks of variety.

In order to arrive at an adequate definition of metaphor, then, we must acknowledge three things. First, that all metaphors are aesthetic objects; that is, that their force is directed toward the imagination. Second, that all metaphors are, if not fully works of art, at least strokes of art. Third, that metaphors will produce the judgment in the recipient as to the appositeness and truth of the metaphor.

Johnson, Mark. "A Philosophical Perspective on the Problems of Metaphor." In *Cognition and Figurative Language*, edited by Robert Hoffman and Richard Honeck, pp. 47-67. Hillsdale, N.J.: Lawrence Erlbaum, 1980.

Surveys recent work on the central philosophical issues raised by metaphor and concludes that the most pressing need is for a fuller account of how metaphors work. It is suggested that a workable model of metaphoric comprehension is provided in Kant's account of reflective judgment. Specifically, there are two levels of comprehension in metaphor, paralleling Kant's two kinds of reflective judgment: (1) There is a *canonical* (or comparative) level where we comprehend, in a systematic, rule-governed way, similarities between the referents of the terms of the metaphor. This is analogous to the mental act of *teleological* reflective judgment, in which I imaginatively reflect on various objects to find unifying concepts for them. (2) There is also a *noncanonical* (or interactive) level of comprehension, analogous to *aesthetical* reflective judgment, in which the play of imagination generated by the metaphor is *felt* as being adequate to the ideas it organizes. This level is not rule-governed and is, therefore, not reducible to literal (determinate) concepts or language. Seen in this way, metaphors are creative products of what Kant called genius.

Johnson, Mark, and Erickson, Glenn W. "Toward a New Theory of Metaphor." *The Southern Journal of Philosophy* 18, no. 3 (1980):289-299.

The debate over whether there are insights expressible metaphorically that cannot be reduced to literal language has become deadlocked. This is because both parties in the dispute (i.e., the empiricists [reductionists] and the intellectualists [antireductionists]) share common assumptions about objectivity. In particular, they share the view that beings are objects, and they assume that objective aspects of experience are knowable and may be expressed in terms of universally communicable concepts. What is needed to break this deadlock is a reformulation of the problem, such that metaphor is considered in the context, not primarily of a theory of knowledge, but rather of a theory of being. This new way of seeing the issue preserves the insights of both the traditional disputants, while showing that their disagreement rests on a mistaken view of the way we experience beings. Briefly, the third alternative denies that all being is objective. Metaphor is a basic process by which beings become objectified in various ways. The new formulation of the problem "involves asking how metaphors make beings meaningful in a manner that allows concepts to reflect this meaning. It is not the cognitive (conceptual), but the pre-cognitive, role of metaphor that becomes problematic" (p. 296). What must be explained is how metaphors restructure our experience and the concepts by which we understand it.

Khatchadourian, Haig. "Metaphor." *British Journal of Aesthetics* 8, no. 3 (1968): 227-243.

Khatchadourian argues (1) that metaphors involve a different kind of meaning and use from the meaning and use that is involved with literal language; (2) that there is no fixed way to tell when you have a metaphor and when you have some other kind of statement; (3) that the only hint that a metaphor is present is the tension between the literal "frame" of a metaphor and the metaphorical expression itself; (4) that all metaphors require interpretation on the part of the one using or receiving the metaphor; and (5) that a metaphor is coherent when it organizes the features of the two subjects adequately.

Two of the customary interpretations of metaphor—the resemblance theory and the analogical theory—are faulted for emphasizing too strongly the positive characters that mark the similarities of the two subjects. It is the differences that produce the tension between the subjects, and between the subjects and the literal "frame." Nonetheless, if a metaphor is to be successful, it must not be too overweight with differences, lest it become farfetched and artificial. But it must not be too fastidious either, with the similarities too obvious, lest it be flaccid and dull. The only way to tell when a metaphor has been sufficiently striking is to inspect the context. But inspecting the context will not help establish the existence of a metaphor. Metaphors are free and "open-textured," so that we cannot always tell whether an expression is literal or metaphorical in a given context. Perhaps the most important quality for a metaphor to possess is coherence. Coherence results from the organization of the metaphor, the way in which the two subjects of the metaphor integrate their features.

Khatchadourian, Haig. "Symbols and Metaphor." *Southern Journal of Philosophy* 6 (1968):181-190.

There are certain interesting and enlightening similarities and contrasts between metaphors and symbols, which cast light on why metaphors have sometimes been discussed as though they were some kind of symbol. First, we should not say that symbols and metaphors serve the same function. Metaphors are grounded in the notion of similarity; symbols are not. Metaphors enable us to see one thing in terms of another, whereas symbols point to some reality beyond themselves, regardless of whether there is some basis for resemblance between the two things. Furthermore, we can demonstrate that complex metaphors depend on the interaction of the principal subject and the subsidiary subject. But there is no interaction with symbols. Symbols and their objects need not cast light on each other. In this sense, metaphors must have some natural grounding, whereas a symbol may be conventionally determined.

Second, it is possible to show that both metaphors and symbols may communicate ideas, but they do so in quite different ways. Symbols are figures that stand for some other object, usually a complex of objects. Since they are conventionally designated, they will always communicate an idea. Sometimes an image will be associated with a symbol, but the emergence of an image in no way affects the way in which the symbol produces the idea. Metaphors, on the other hand, may produce ideas, or they may not. But when a metaphor communicates a vivid idea, which directs us to see something in terms of another thing, an image will always be created to correspond to the idea. Images provide metaphors that communicate ideas with an aesthetic force. This is why metaphors may not always be successful (as opposed to symbols), inasmuch as a metaphor that creates a weak image will also communicate a vague or inappropriate idea.

Lakoff, George, and Johnson, Mark. "Conceptual Metaphor in Everyday Language." *Journal of Philosophy* 77, no. 8 (1980):453-486.

It is commonly assumed by contemporary philosophers and linguists (1) that metaphor is a matter of mere language, not thought; (2) that our everyday conventional language is literal (not metaphorical); and (3) that the central task of a theory of meaning is to give an account of meaning for literal language. It is argued, on the contrary, that our ordinary thought, action, and language are all structured by metaphor. These "conventional" metaphors systematically organize our conceptual system and arise naturally within our mundane experience. Therefore, no acount of meaning and truth for natural languages can be adequate unless it recognizes and explains the way in which conventional metaphors coherently structure human experience.

Lakoff, George, and Johnson, Mark. *Metaphors We Live By*. Chicago: University of Chicago Press, 1980.

Metaphor is often thought of as a decorative or figurative use of language appropriate for poetry and rhetoric. Philosophers and linguists have therefore tended to treat it as a matter of peripheral interest. Actually, our ordinary, everyday language is metaphorical in ways we do not usually notice. These "conventional" metaphors in our *speech* are generated by more fundamental metaphorical structures in our *thought* and *experience*. Much of the coherence and order in our conceptualization and action is based on the way systems of conceptual metaphor coherently structure our experience.

Therefore, some of our most basic realities—our inner selves, institutions, personal relationships, work, social life, moral experience, etc.—are not objectively given, but are defined by the metaphors of our culture. And as experiential metaphors differ from culture to culture, so do the literal realities they define. While this view challenges absolutist or objectivist accounts, it does not lead to mere relativism or subjectivism. A detailed account of how these conventional metaphors emerge from our successful functioning in our environment and how they then influence future action provides the basis for an alternative "experientialist" account of meaning and truth. Truth is not absolute but is always based on human understanding, which is metaphorically structured. Such a view challenges certain dominant theories of language, meaning, and truth in Western philosophy and linguistics.

Lewis, C. S. "Bluspels and Flalansferes." In *Rehabilitations and Other Essays*, chap. 7, pp. 133-158. Oxford, 1939.

The most useful distinction to make in regard to metaphors is between the "Master's metaphor" and the "Pupil's metaphor." The Master's metaphor is one manufactured in order to explain something to someone. The Master knows what the subject in question is (we might say he knows it "literally"), but in order to instruct another, he describes what he knows in terms of some other subject with which the learner may be more familiar. But the Master can always have recourse to the original subject, quite apart from the metaphor that he has devised for the pupil. But let us put ourselves in the pupil's place. We only know what the Master knows through the device of the metaphor he has created for us. We do not know the subject as the Master knows it; we know it only as it comes to us embedded in the metaphor. But the Master, of course, came to understand the subject himself in the same way; he, too, grasped it by means of some prior metaphor. In this way, we can see that much of what we assume to have learned "literally" is in fact learned metaphorically. Dead metaphors are in fact the ground of our knowledge.

We can also see how metaphors do not haphazardly emerge within a language. Most metaphors are intentionally manufactured in order to advance the understanding. Badly or hastily made metaphors can direct the understanding to badly or hastily made judgments about reality. We need to be careful, then, in the metaphors that we create, and especially careful regarding the metaphors that pass into the language as dead metaphors.

Loewenberg, Ina. "Creativity and Correspondence in Fiction and in Metaphors." *Journal of Aesthetics and Art Criticism* 36, no. 3 (1978):341-350.

Like works of fiction, metaphors can be creative in changing our world. The writer of fiction exploits the normal creative aspects of perception and linguistic expression, but also, through the work as a whole, creates a "new possible world." This new world "intersects with" and thereby influences how we perceive, conceive, and act in our actual world. But whereas the novel works as a unified whole, metaphors function typically as single-sentence utterances. The creativity of a metaphor results from its novel combination of previously existing elements which have never before been related in just the way the metaphor specifies. "What the maker of a novel metaphor creates is a new view of a subject, existing in the world after, but not before, his metaphorical utterance" (p. 347). Good metaphors are not assertions; rather, they are directives, suggesting new perspectives to be "tried out" by the hearer.

Loewenberg, Ina. "Identifying Metaphors." *Foundations of Language* 12 (1975): 315-338.

Some metaphorical expressions are identifiable neither by syntactic nor by semantic deviance. Virtually any sentence "can be provided contexts . . . in which it can receive either literal or metaphorical interpretations" (p. 322). This shows that linguistic information (syntactic, semantic) is sometimes not sufficient for recognizing an utterance as metaphorical. Instead, we must have knowledge, not just of relations among linguistic symbols, but also of the speaker's intentions and of the truth or falsity of various statements. In short, we must treat metaphors not as *sentences* (linguistic entities) but as *utterances* whose meaning is highly context dependent.

What kind of utterance is a metaphor? It is not an assertion, and therefore it makes no truth claims. If taken literally as an assertion, metaphorical utterances are false. This falsity typically leads us to search for a more charitable interpretation, taking into account our knowledge of speaker and situation. We find that a metaphor is a speech act with a special illocutionary force, *viz.*, that of *making a proposal*. When one encounters a metaphorical utterance, one "judges that the speaker was not making a truth claim . . . but rather a *proposal* about a way to view, understand, etc., those referents" (p. 335).

Loewenberg, Ina. "Truth and Consequences of Metaphor." *Philosophy and Rhetoric* 6 (1973):30-45.

If metaphors are to be understood, identified and assessed, it is important to note that there are various kinds of metaphors and that it is frequently impossible to treat these separate types under a single interpretation. Three different types of metaphors can be identified: "dead" metaphors, which have passed into the language so completely that we now fail to recognize them as metaphors; "live-but-not-new" metaphors, to which the culture has become accustomed, but which retain their freshness owing to the vagaries of the language; and "novel" metaphors, which are expressions received for the first time by the hearer. Some metaphors can be adequately understood by reference to a "comparison" theory, or to a "filter" theory. But these are limited in their explanatory scope, and many metaphors are better understood when we turn to an "interaction" theory.

If we are to settle the question of how to recognize metaphors, we must look first to the context in which the metaphor is uttered. There are no rules for the recognition of metaphors that will hold in every case. We may conclude, in a general way, that whenever a literal rendering of an utterance seems implausible to a native speaker, the utterance is a possible metaphor. Finally, metaphors may be rightly judged true or false, but only on the assumption that we have abandoned a positivistic framework for the determination of the conditions of truth and falsity. Metaphors are said to be true in the sense that they enable us to expand our knowledge of the world, inasmuch as all knowledge consists in seeing old concepts in terms of new insights.

MacCormac, Earl. *Metaphor and Myth in Science and Religion.* Durham, N.C.: Duke University Press, 1976.

The basic strategy of the book is to argue that science, previously worshiped as *the* model of cognitive virtue, grounded solely on precise, theory-independent, and verifiable observation language (as opposed to religious discourse, alleged to be vague, nonrational, or even meaningless), is similar to religious language in its use of metaphor. Chapter one is a reliable brief history of recent debates in the philosophy of science over the nature of explanation, the verification controversy, the problem of meaning-variance in theory change, and so on. Chapter two traces several misguided attempts to reduce religious language to cognitive insignificance, and it argues that scientific and religious languages are fundamentally alike in their reliance upon metaphor.

The foundation of MacCormac's view (chapter three) is that metaphor consists of an *epiphoric* aspect, which *expresses* experience analogous to that of the hearer, and a *diaphoric* aspect which "suggests possible meanings rather than expresses meanings that are confirmed by hearers" (p. 85). A metaphor is thus an imaginative explanatory hypothesis, partly grounded in experience (epiphoric aspect) and yet also highly suggestive through projected new meaning that has no current confirmation. The hypothetical nature of all metaphor is emphasized: "Since taking metaphors literally produces absurdity and emotional shock, we must consider the metaphor 'as if' it were true" (p. 75).

MacCormac suggests that the failure to respect the hypothetical nature of any extended ("root") metaphor results in myth, defined as "the false attribution of reality to a theory by taking a root metaphor to be literal rather than suggestive" (p. 106). Chapter four develops the implications of this broadened conception of myth, which is shown to cover not only traditional religious myths but even explanations in the "rational" disciplines previously believed to be essentially different in nature from religious belief.

Manns, James. "Goodman on Metaphor." *The Personalist* (April 1977):173-178.

In *Languages of Art*, Nelson Goodman makes at least three claims about metaphor that do not appear to be justified. The claims have to do with the relation of metaphors to similes, the truth and verification of metaphors, and the importance of novelty in the definition of a metaphor. Goodman wants to give priority to metaphors over similes, saying that similes grow out of, and are dependent on, some antecedent process of metaphorical construction. In this sense, it is possible to say that metaphors "create" similarities. Some proponents of this view hold that a metaphor may actually create similarities that do not exist prior to the fashioning of the metaphor. But this *sui generis* manufacture of similarities would make metaphors both noncognitive and unverifiable. Others who accept the creative activity of metaphors soften the first argument by saying that metaphors create the similarities for those who are hearing the metaphor for the first time; the similarities exist independently of the metaphor, but only become alive to us when revealed by the metaphor. But this would make metaphor unremarkable, since this is what all language, literal or figurative, is intended to do. We must say, then, that metaphors grow out of similes, which in turn are dependent on literal language.

If Goodman would reduce a great deal of language to metaphor in order to understand the structure of language, he moves in the opposite direction when it comes to the verification of metaphorical utterances, reducing them to the status of literal utterances, and he then claims that there is not much difference between the two. The real question here is not how things must be for predicates to apply to them but rather about the nature of the 'bond' between objects and the predicates we apply to them. Literal language is based on conventional usage, and metaphors are based on a transgression of that literal usage; it is not possible to collapse one into the other. Finally, although Goodman would emphasize the importance of novelty in the identification of metaphors, he cannot thereby account for the existence of dead metaphors.

Manns, James. "Metaphor and Paraphrase." *British Journal of Aesthetics* 15, no. 4 (1975):358-366.

Manns examines Martin Warner's criticisms of Max Black's article "Metaphor." He finds that Warner has read an alien interpretation into Black's concern for "the loss of cognitive content" in the paraphrasing of a metaphor into its alleged literal equivalent. Warner defines "cognitive content" as capacity to be true or false. Warner has overlooked Black's suggestion that metaphor provides *insight* and that such insight may involve more than truth and falsity. There are at least three different ways in which metaphor functions cognitively without being subject to verifiability or falsifiability: first, by directing our attention to a feature or features of our perceived environment that we may have previously missed; second, by aiding us in cultivating a skill or in mastering a practical obstacle; third, by altering our way of categorizing the world. Finally Manns argues that the entire discussion of the extent to which metaphors can be reduced to literal paraphrases is misdirected. First, paraphrases are only guides that point us toward the metaphor and adumbrate the space that the metaphor occupies; literal paraphrases do not serve to unravel the metaphor and are never intended to. Second, Manns disputes the notion that the literal is clear and the metaphorical opaque. At times, the metaphorical is perfectly clear and the literal obscure. In any case, either literal or metaphorical statements ought to be governed by a concern for gleaning insight into the utterance or the cognitive situation—the pragmatic concern.

Matthews, Robert J. "Concerning a 'Linguistic Theory' of Metaphor." *Foundations of Language* 7 (1971):413-425.

Matthews distinguishes between a "competency" and a "performance" model as methodological vehicles for the assessment of what is going on when a speaker uses a metaphorical expression. The competency model evaluates metaphor strictly within the confines of rules of grammar of a given language; a metaphor acquires its force, in this view, from the creatively deviant way it manipulates the rules. A performance model would locate the unique qualities of a metaphor in usage, and Matthews feels that this approach will yield little that is helpful. Beginning with a critique of Derek Bickerton's analysis of metaphor, Matthews seeks to distinguish deviant sentences from nondeviant ones. This can be done entirely within the confines of the competency model, by observing sentences that violate selection restrictions. Bickerton sought to distinguish deviant sentences from metaphors by identifying certain "marks" that attached to metaphors that did not attach to other deviant sentences, but could not succeed in telling the one from the other. Bickerton eschewed any context within which to fit the metaphorical construction, and this robbed him of any ground for isolating metaphors from nonmetaphors. Matthews concludes that metaphors can be distinguished from nonmetaphors because metaphors will always reveal an underlying violation of selection restrictions. Metaphor is understood in the same fashion as its literal counterparts, but because of the selectional restriction violation, the features of the terms in question are diluted in their literal impact, thus suggesting the metaphorical meaning.

Mew, Peter. "Metaphor and Truth." *British Journal of Aesthetics* 11 (1971): 189-195.

R. K. Elliott claims that in order to establish the truth of any poetic statement, the "full meaning" of the words must be established first. This requires that an examination be made of the environment in which the subject of the poetic statement is located. By noting the features of this environment, it will be possible to move from a preliminary grasp of the meaning of the statement to a complete grasp of its "full meaning." It is out of such a move to the fuller meaning that the truth or falsity of the poetic statement can be assessed. This theory seems to be erroneous on at least three counts. First, it will suggest that such literary statements as are judged false will likewise be judged meaningless. Second, it raises a question as to how certain poetic statements that are judged to be false as descriptions of the world, are nonetheless perfectly plausible (i.e., meaningful) as utterances. Third, Elliott would have to deny that his theory applies to fictional metaphors, since there would be no occasion for the examination of an actual context.

Olscamp, Paul J. "How Some Metaphors May Be True or False. "*Journal of Aesthetics and Art Criticism* 29, no. 1 (1970):77-86.

The question of whether metaphors may be said to be true or false has been compounded with the question of what a metaphor means. This linking of meaning with the verification of a metaphorical statement makes it unreasonably difficult to address the problem of truth and falsity in metaphors. What needs to be acknowledged from the outset is that there is a difference between theories of meaning and theories of truth. For a statement to be true or false, it must be meaningful. But the converse is not true: a statement need not be true or false in order to be meaningful. In justifying this, we must recognize that epiphoric metaphors (those that involve a direct expression of similarity and comparison) are essentially elliptical similes. Thus, we can judge the comparison being made empirically, by noting the properties that are alleged to be similar in the two objects being compared. When this has been done, we can then judge the aptness of the metaphor and determine its truth and falsity.

Ortony, Andrew. "Why Metaphors are Necessary and Not Just Nice." *Educational Theory* 25, no. 1 (1975):45-53.

Because human experience is continuous, not discrete; dynamic, not static, the meanings of words must be supple and fluid, able to stretch to fit the variety of experiences that language is intended to express. But language is often unable to bend enough to be expressive of these aspects of human life, which causes gaps between our language and our experiences. Figurative language, particularly metaphor, fills the gaps and "fleshes out" our attempts to express the continuous and dynamic nature of our experiences.

Ortony offers three theses to explain the indispensability of metaphor. (1) *Compactness Thesis:* metaphors allow for a great deal of information to be compressed into a single utterance. Any given human experience is complex, and it would be possible to extend a string of predicates for every subject that I encounter; this is what Ortony calls "particularization." But the metaphor allows me to telescope the particulars into a single large chunk, which can then be transferred from one term of the metaphor to the other. (2) *Inexpressibility Thesis:* there are many aspects of experience that simply cannot be expressed in literal language. Literal, discrete language simply cannot cope with the dynamics of human experience, so it becomes more fruitful to hand over those dynamic elements to a more figurative language, a language that can keep up with human experience. (3) *Vividness Thesis:* because metaphors are more fluid and dynamic, they are closer to the rhythm of human life, and thus they have a force and vividness that literal language cannot match. The effect of such vividness is felt particularly in education, where metaphors can serve as models since they can lead us from that which is relatively well known to that which is relatively less well known.

Paul, Anthony M. "Metaphor and the Bounds of Expression." *Philosophy and Rhetoric* 5, no. 3 (1972):143-157.

Paul attacks the "indispensability theory," i.e., the view that metaphors cannot be translated or paraphrased without doing damage to the meaning of the metaphorical expression. His critique is based on a conviction that meaning is intended to be communicated and that communication requires that such meanings be public. Any meanings of words or sentences that are not available for public inspection are deemed "souvenir language," and of interest only to the individual. There is no way to determine whether a statement is meaningful or nonsense as long as it is not placed within the context of public discourse. And this is precisely the problem with the indispensability theory. If a metaphorical statement cannot be translated, there is no way to tell if it is meaningless or not. We would never know if the statement were consistently understood in varying contexts by different people—which is the manner in which meaning acquires its force.

The second prong of the indispensability theory is that metaphors invariably have some effect upon the individual who receives the metaphor. But this does nothing to guarantee the meaning of the statement. Further, if the claim is made that the metaphor provides a flash of insight for the person and produces a concomitant effect, this does not prove there is not some paraphrase available for the insight. Any insight that can be represented in a metaphor can be analyzed and translated into a literal counterpart. The meaning of a statement can only be determined by the way in which speakers use and understand it. And this can only take place within the public domain. Anything else is a souvenir language and is meaningless.

Price, J. T. "Linguistic Competence and Metaphorical Use." *Foundations of Language* 11 (1974):253-56.

Price examines Matthews's "Concerning a 'Linguistic Theory' of Metaphor" and concludes that Matthews cannot sustain his argument by reference to a competence method of approaching metaphor, apart from a consideration of performance. Price insists that some account needs to be taken of the role played by usage in the recognition and comprehension of metaphor. Matthews is able to distinguish metaphors from nondeviant expressions, but not from nonsense. In order to do this, and to complete the task that he has set for himself, Matthews would need to incorporate a performance model into his analysis. Further, Matthews may have collapsed the distinction pertinent to creativity in language formation between (1) creativity that takes place within the confines of grammatical rules, but which leaves the language essentially unchanged; and (2) creativity that radically changes the rules of grammar. Metaphors may be more adequately explained by pointing to their flaunting of the regulative restrictions within a given language. Metaphor may then be understood as a rule-changing activity.

Richards, I. A. *The Philosophy of Rhetoric*. Oxford: Oxford University Press, 1936.

Richards's two lectures on metaphor offer a rudimentary theory later developed by Black into the "interaction" view. The four other lectures in the volume seek to develop a new rhetoric, i.e., a "study of verbal understanding and misunderstanding," based on a general theory of meaning. Within this framework metaphor is seen, not as some deviance from ordinary discourse, but rather as a pervasive principle of language and thought. Our "projected world" is structured, in part, by fundamental metaphoric processes of experience. In particular, a metaphor involves "two thoughts of different things active together and supported by a single word, or phrase, whose meaning is a resultant of their interaction" (p. 93). Although this interaction may be based on similarities between things, it may be more the result of dissimilarities, so that the resultant meaning cannot be reduced to literal statements of similarity.

Ricoeur, Paul. "Creativity in Language." *Philosophy Today* 17 (1973):97-111.

Contrary to the traditional view, metaphor is not merely a trope based on analogy or resemblance, nor is it a mere stylistic decoration without cognitive value. Rather, as Richards saw, metaphor is a semantic innovation arising within a sentence from the tension between the tenor and vehicle. A metaphorical statement "proceeds from the violation of semantic rules which determine appropriateness in the application of predicates"(p. 106), and ends in the emergence of new meaning. Metaphor is a creative use of polysemy, "that remarkable feature of words in natural languages which is their ability to mean more than one thing" (p. 97). In the metaphorical twist of meaning (Beardsley) the old and new meanings are assimilated, though the semantic tension between them remains.

Thus, metaphor is able to redescribe reality through the tension existing between sameness and difference—the old remains, but is seen in a new light. We often describe the unknown in terms of something familiar, by virtue of projected similarity in structure. In this way, metaphor can restructure our experience by shattering established structures of language and instituting new ones. "But if we assume that metaphor redescribes reality, we must then assume that this reality as redescribed is itself novel reality" (p. 111). Metaphor's "strategy of discourse" is to enhance our sense of reality—"with metaphor we experience the metamorphosis of both our language and reality" (p. 111).

Ricoeur, Paul. "The Metaphorical Process as Cognition, Imagination, and Feeling." *Critical Inquiry* 5, no. 1 (1978):143-159.

An understanding of how metaphors work awaits a theory of the imagination in its productive or creative function. Such a study treads the boundary between a *psychological* theory and a *semantic* theory, i.e., "an inquiry into the capacity of metaphor to provide untranslatable information . . ." (p. 143). Ricoeur takes up this awesome task by offering the beginnings of an account of the mode of functioning of similarity in the predicative process of metaphor. There are three facets of this cognitive activity: (1) The metaphor schematizes (i.e., provides a procedure for) the synthetic operation in which disparate things are seen as similar. (2) Then there is a pictorial dimension in which images are provided to give content to the meaning. (3) There is also an *epoché* or suspension of ordinary reference, so that the emergent meaning can open up new ways of describing the world (or some aspect of it). Paralleling these three moments of imagination, there are three analogously structured moments of feeling, taken as part of, rather than extrinsic to, the cognitive operation of metaphor.

Ricoeur, Paul. *The Rule of Metaphor*, translated by Robert Czerny with Kathleen Mchaughlin and John Costello. Toronto: University of Toronto Press, 1977.

This is clearly the most significant study of metaphor to emerge in recent years. It is also the longest and most difficult to summarize. Roughly, the book consists of eight studies which trace significant historical developments in the theory of metaphor as treated in philosophy, linguistics, literary criticism, and other disciplines. In addition to examining the making of a traditional view, Ricoeur masterfully draws together more recent work in both the Continental and analytic traditions.

There are multiple levels of analysis which provide insight into the workings of metaphor, namely, the word, the sentence, and the text. Basically, metaphor is an innovative attribution, somehow deviant in its literal reading, which issues in new meaning by virtue of this semantic tension. In moving toward a fuller understanding of the nature and role of metaphor, we do not discard previous analyses (e.g., the classical focus on *words*); rather, we incorporate those insights into a larger picture. Thus, Ricoeur's detailed examination of how metaphors function at the level of sentences or utterances is followed by an account of metaphor in the broader realms of poetic or philosophical discourse. At this level, especially, we discover how metaphor retains its referential function and plays a central role in redefining our reality.

Searle, John R. "Metaphor." In *Expression and Meaning,* pp. 76-116. Cambridge:
Cambridge University Press, 1979.

Searle reformulates the question of how metaphors work in terms of the speech-act distinction between *word or sentence meaning* (i.e., what the word or sentence means literally) and *speaker's utterance meaning* (i.e., what the speaker means by uttering words or sentences). "Metaphorical meaning is always speaker's utterance meaning" (p. 77). Thus, the central problem of metaphor is to state the principles relating literal sentence meaning to metaphorical utterance meaning. That is, how can a speaker utter a sentence "S is P" (having a literal sentence meaning) and mean metaphorically "S is R"? The most popular statement of the relevant principles for metaphoric comprehension, namely, the comparison theory, is attacked on several points. The basis of Searle's objections is that "though similarity often plays a role in *comprehension* of metaphor, the metaphorical assertion is not necessarily an *assertion* of similarity" (p. 88). The comparison theorist assumes, perhaps correctly, that similarity plays a role in our grasping of the metaphor's meaning, but he or she erroneously concludes that the metaphor's meaning is some set of literal similarity statements.

An attempt to state *some* of the relevant principles of metaphoric comprehension is made. In particular Searle provides specific principles for the three basic steps in understanding a metaphor: (1) How does the hearer know to seek out a metaphorical interpretation? (2) What strategies allow the hearer to compute possible values of *R* (where "S is P" is uttered in order to mean metaphorically "S is R")? (3) What principles guide the restriction of the range of possible Rs to determine the precise meaning of the metaphor?

Shibles, Warren. *Metaphor: An Annotated Bibliography and History*. Whitewater,
Wisconsin: The Language Press, 1971.

This large bibliography includes sources from several different fields (e.g., philosophy, literary criticism, linguistics, psychology, etc.) in several languages. Many of the entries include short summaries of key ideas. A general index and a metaphor index accompany the alphabetically listed entries. This is a useful place to hunt down historical references. Its major limitation is that it covers material only through the late 1960s, just prior to the explosion of literature in all fields.

Shibles, Warren. "The Metaphorical Method." *Journal of Aesthetic Education* 7
(1974):25-36.

Not a methodological primer, but a survey of metaphorical types and metaphorical operation. Shibles is emphatic in denying the "metaphor to myth fallacy," the fallacy of believing that all metaphors can be reduced to literal statements. He detects the fallacy in conventional explanations of cognitive processes and details his conviction that all mental activities are metaphorical. There really are no such things as mental states, ideas, or thoughts; these are all metaphorical expressions. Even the notion of a metaphor is a metaphorical expression.

Metaphor is a deviation, of which there are seven different types, ranging from linguistic to behavioral to cultural deviation. Shibles goes on to note twenty-one different kinds of metaphor, including the customary types like anagogical and juxtapositional metaphors, and more extreme forms, such as visual and therapeutic (cathartic) metaphors. Shibles supports the notion that metaphors are active and indispensable agents in the tasks of observing, classifying, and reporting human experience. There appears to be little for literal language to do here; geometry and logic are metaphorical in their operations, and the framework within which metaphors reside is composed of other metaphors.

Srzednicki, J. "On Metaphor." *Philosophical Quarterly* 10 (1960):228-237.

Do metaphors produce an extension of meaning for the terms involved in the metaphor? It seems that this judgment, so frequently made, cannot be substantiated. We do not see evidence of an actual extension of meaning growing out of words that are used metaphorically; the words retain their original meaning but are used in such a way that they cover new areas of meaning previously uninhabited by other words. In fact, metaphors produce homonyms, or words that may look the same and are pronounced the same, but which have different meanings. Thus, instead of new meanings, we get new words. Through metaphorical usage, some word or phrase—like the infinitive, "to run"—with a fixed meaning is used in a different context. What results is not a new meaning for the same word, but a new word with a meaning all its own. It bears strong resemblances to the original word or phrase—all homonyms do—but we actually employ the word in such a way that it becomes a distinct entity with a particular meaning. The test for this theory is to ask two questions. Does the original meaning drop out when we use the word or phrase metaphorically? Since it does seem to do so, we cannot easily say that what we have is simply an extension of the original meaning. Does the new meaning include the original meaning? Again, this does not appear to be what takes place in a metaphor, such that the original meaning lurks under the metaphorical meaning. We can only conclude that metaphors do not extend the meaning of a word, but rather produce entirely new words that are types of homonyms.

Stewart, Donald. "Metaphor and Paraphrase." *Philosophy and Rhetoric* 4, no. 2 (1971):111-123.

The efforts expended in translating metaphorical statements are not destructive; they are merely useless. Both metaphors and literal statements can be paraphrased, but in very different ways. Literal statements have but a few alternatives from which to choose; the words must be synonymous, the meanings identical. But such is not the case with metaphors. They can be translated, but the possibilities from which the "correct" meaning may be chosen are indeterminate, perhaps endless in some cases. The important questions for getting at the meaning are: How do speakers actually intend the use of the metaphor? What are the accepted interpretations that have been put upon the metaphor within a public context?

Although it is useless to continue to seek literal translations for metaphors—the public context will provide for sufficient meaning—still the attempts persist. This is due to a widespread assumption, the "two-expression" view, according to which there are two levels in every metaphor: a literal and inconsistent level, and a figurative and consistent level. The force of the metaphor allegedly consists in moving from the inconsistency to the consistency. But this is not what happens at all. When we justify the use of a particular metaphor, we point out the literal and inconsistent meaning of the statement as the field from which we pull the metaphorical meaning; the other level of consistent and metaphorical meaning can hardly be specified at all.

Literal expressions are not given their meanings; they simply possess their meanings by virtue of being literal expressions. But metaphorical expressions need to have their meanings attributed to them, because the metaphorical expression is literally inconsistent. To paraphrase a literally inconsistent expression would mean either preserving the inconsistency, which would be awkward and redundant, or removing the inconsistency, and thus removing the metaphor. Hence it is useless to attempt a paraphrase of a metaphor. Stewart leans toward embracing a "one-expression" version of metaphor: that it contains only a literal and inconsistent meaning. Inconsistency, therefore, is the mark of a metaphor.

Stewart, Donald. "Metaphor, Truth, and Definition." *Journal of Aesthetics and Art Criticism* 32, no. 2 (1973):205-218.

If we are truly to understand the meaning of metaphors, we must have recourse to the basic task of all language: providing definitions. A definition is a description of reality, and a definition of the way things are generally is said to be a literal definition. All definitions, then, involve literal meanings. This has the consequence of denying metaphorical meanings. But we can temporarily define words in ways that go beyond their permanent definitions. Thus, metaphors are to be understood as expressions that provide for an extended meaning to an established definition for an immediate and subjective purpose. Words normally have multiple meanings, and such definitions are meant to represent the choices made in the language as to the literal meaning of the words. Metaphors offer alternatives—not new additions—to those choices. Metaphors, therefore, are a kind of definition, but they give us the meaning of things as they are now, as they appear to us in this instant. They are not part of the permanent meanings that we attach to the words. The definitions that a metaphor provides are transient; as they become more common they pass into the language as part of the process of making choices as to the literal meaning of words. Metaphors may be regarded, then, as the beginnings of a new language. They help create a new conception of the way things are, albeit in a subjective and impermanent fashion.

Turbayne, Colin. *The Myth of Metaphor.* Columbia, S.C.: University of South Carolina Press, 1970.

The model or metaphor has been one of the chief devices for communicating and explaining facts, inducing attitudes, and influencing behavior. Metaphor involves the pretense that something is the case when it is not—it is a kind of intentional category mistake or sort-crossing. Such pretense, i.e., representing the facts of one sort *as if* they belonged to another sort, is useful for inducing insight, only as long as we do not forget the *pretense*. Too often, in all disciplines, metaphors have been taken literally—the pretense is dropped and the model is mistaken for the thing modeled. Taking metaphors literally typically results in erroneous metaphysical assumptions being smuggled in, once the 'as if' character is forgotten. The mistake is not in using metaphors and models, for they can be profitably used to gain insight in all fields; rather, the error is in using them without awareness of their true nature.

This general thesis is then illustrated by numerous examples of those who have both used and been trapped by their metaphors. In particular, the metaphysics of mechanism is challenged, especially insofar as Descartes and Newton were victimized by their metaphors. An alternative metaphor (nature as universal language) is suggested, as a way of showing the dispensability of the mechanistic model. Berkeley's attempt to represent facts of vision in terms appropriate to language is used to develop the language metaphor.

Warner, Martin. "Black's Metaphors." *British Journal of Aesthetics* 13, no. 4 (1973): 367-372.

Black's claim, that a literal paraphrase cannot be given for a metaphor without a loss of cognitive content, is rejected as untenable. If an assertion's "cognitive content" is its truth claims, there is no good reason why we should not be able to specify the truth conditions of any metaphor. Black's mistake was to conflate the claim that a metaphor can provide distinctive insights with the claim that it can convey information that is unparaphrasable by any literal utterance.

Once we stop treating metaphors as assertions with special properties, we discover their function as a distinct class of speech acts having a certain "hortatory" or "suggestive" (as opposed to constative) force. Metaphors are useful, not as irreducible assertions, but as illocutionary acts that open up new ways of seeing or understanding ourselves and our world.

Wheelwright, Philip. *Metaphor and Reality*. Bloomington: Indiana University Press, 1962.

Language is indispensable in all inquiry and in all attempts to grasp What Is. We cannot separate out as independent the knowing subject, the subject's language, and the objects he or she seeks to know—they are three interdependent aspects or poles of an interaction that constitutes reality. And just as we experience a full range of reality from aspects that are fixed to those that are "alive" and changing, so language, too, moves from the conventional and precise to the fluid and open. On the conventional end of the scale there are "steno" or "block" meanings, i.e., meanings shared in exactly the same way by a large number of people. On the other end of the scale there is "fluid" language, which is full of tensional ambiguities and provides novel perspectives on reality.

Metaphor is a kind of tensive language involving two kinds of activity: *epiphor* applies a term with a standard meaning to some other object on the basis of, and in order to highlight, similarities between the two things—it typically involves the use of an image as the basis of comparison. *Diaphor* involves the juxtaposition of things to produce new insight, regardless of underlying similarity. Metaphor, varying from epiphor to diaphor, is thus the chief means for expressing a reality that is "tensive," "perspectival," "coalescent," and changing. Reality reveals itself "only partially, ambiguously, and through symbolic indirection" (p. 154).

Yoos, George. "A Phenomenological Look at Metaphor." *Philosophy and Phenomenological Research* 32, no. 1 (1971):78-88.

Much recent literature on metaphor has gone astray because of a failure to recognize that metaphors operate at the level of thought rather than at the level of words. Metaphors are themselves metaphorical descriptions of reality, through which we gain new ideas about things through the interaction of two ideas juxtaposed in a novel way. This can be seen when metaphors are approached as phenomenological objects. We must first be aware of a distinction between our awareness of a metaphor and our interpretation of a metaphor. When we initially come upon a metaphor, it strikes us at a level of aesthetic appreciation. We are aware of the thought that organizes the metaphor. It is only after this that we become aware of the words that are used in the construction of the metaphor. Thus, metaphors cannot be understood simply by inspecting their linguistic form or usage. Metaphor is a cognitive process; it involves thought and the shaping and directing of our thought; therefore, we need to locate an investigation of metaphor at the level of thought.

When we inspect metaphors at this level, we discover that they are in fact descriptions of a sort. They direct our attention to something that we had not previously been aware of—they point out a new state of affairs to us. But their pointing consists of describing the things set before us when we might otherwise not know what to say about those things. Where we could not offer literal descriptions of things we could not name, we can provide metaphorical descriptions.

Index

Index

Mark Johnson received his Ph.D. at the University of Chicago, and is assistant professor of philosophy at Southern Illinois University at Carbondale. He is co-author, with George Lakoff, of *Metaphors We Live By*.